Letters of the Catholic Poor

This innovative study of poverty in Independent Ireland between 1920 and 1940 is the first to place the poor at its core by exploring their own words and letters. Written to the Catholic Archbishop of Dublin, their correspondence represents one of the few traces in history of Irish experiences of poverty, and collectively they illuminate the lives of so many during the foundation decades of the Irish state. This book keeps the human element central, so often lost when the framework of history is policy, institutions and legislation. It explores how ideas of charity, faith, gender, character and social status were deployed in these poverty narratives and examines the impact of poverty on the lives of these writers and the survival strategies they employed. Finally, it considers the role of priests in vetting and vouching for the poor and, in so doing, perpetuating the discriminating culture of charity.

Dr Lindsey Earner-Byrne is a lecturer in modern Irish history in the School of History at University College Dublin. She has researched and published on sexuality, gender, health and welfare in modern Ireland with a focus on mothers, widows and children.

Letters of the Catholic Poor

Poverty in Independent Ireland, 1920–1940

Lindsey Earner-Byrne

University College Dublin

CAMBRIDGE
UNIVERSITY PRESS

CAMBRIDGE
UNIVERSITY PRESS

University Printing House, Cambridge CB2 8BS, United Kingdom

One Liberty Plaza, 20th Floor, New York, NY 10006, USA

477 Williamstown Road, Port Melbourne, VIC 3207, Australia

314-321, 3rd Floor, Plot 3, Splendor Forum, Jasola District Centre, New Delhi - 110025, India

79 Anson Road, #06-04/06, Singapore 079906

Cambridge University Press is part of the University of Cambridge.

It furthers the University's mission by disseminating knowledge in the pursuit of
education, learning and research at the highest international levels of excellence.

www.cambridge.org
Information on this title: www.cambridge.org/9781316631805

First published 2017
First paperback edition 2019

A catalogue record for this publication is available from the British Library

Library of Congress Cataloging in Publication data
Names: Earner-Byrne, Lindsey, author.
Title: Letters of the Catholic poor : poverty in independent Ireland,
1920–1940 / Lindsey Earner-Byrne (University College Dublin).
Description: Cambridge, United Kingdom ; New York, New York : Cambridge
University Press, 2016. | Includes bibliographical references and index.
Identifiers: LCCN 2016025906 | ISBN 9781107179912 (Hardback)
Subjects: LCSH: Poor–Ireland–History–20th century–Sources. |
Poor–Ireland–Dublin–History–20th century–Sources. |
Poverty–Ireland–History–20th century–Sources. |
Poor–Ireland–Correspondence. | Catholics–Ireland–Correspondence. |
Byrne, Edward J., 1872-1940–Correspondence. | Catholic
Church–Ireland–Dublin–Bishops–Correspondence. | Charity–Social
aspects–Ireland–History–20th century–Sources. |
Ireland–Social conditions–1922-1973–Sources.
Classification: LCC HV4088.A3 E27 2016 | DDC 305.5/690922417–dc23 LC
record available at https://lccn.loc.gov/2016025906

ISBN 978-1-107-17991-2 Hardback
ISBN 978-1-316-63180-5 Paperback

To Patrick St. John Byrne (1984-2003)
This book is written in memory of you.

Contents

Acknowledgements

Historians are always dependent upon and indebted to archivists and librarians and I have been particularly fortunate in that regard. It was in 1997 that David Sheehy, the then archivist of the Dublin Diocesan Archives (DDA), directed me to the charity cases upon which this book is based. I am deeply grateful to him not just for this, but also for his enlightened, gentle and erudite company on many a dull day.

Noelle Dowling has continued the tradition of openness and professionalism at the DDA. Anyone who has ever requested assistance from Noelle will know the lengths to which she goes to answer every query and accommodate researchers whenever possible. The DDA is overseen by the Archbishop of Dublin, Diarmuid Martin, who has ensured that the diocesan archives are an open resource at the disposal of all those interested in understanding the history of Dublin and Roman Catholicism in Ireland.

The path of research has also been made smoother by the staff at the National Archives of Ireland, in particular, Aideen Ireland, and also my colleagues in UCD Archives. I am particularly grateful to Gerry Kavanagh of the National Library of Ireland for his feedback on sections of this book and to him and the rest of the team for their constant assistance.

I am fortunate to work in UCD's School of History in which collegiality is the norm and upon which our research leave system depends; without it this book would never have been written. I owe a deep debt of gratitude to the many people who have offered particular advice and friendship over the years: Ciara Breathnach, Kate Breslin, Catherine Cox, Judith Devlin, Marnie Haye, Michael Laffan, Roy Foster, Senia Pašeta, Kathrine O'Donnell, Tadhg ÓhAnnracháin, Declan O'Keeffe and his mother Phil (whose memoir is cited in this book), Margaret MacCurtain, John McCafferty, Ivar McGrath, Susannah Riordan, Michael Staunton and Diane Urquhart. I am also indebted to Mary Daly, from whom I have learnt so much and who read sections of this book.

Thank you to everybody at Cambridge University Press, in particular, Michael Watson who believed in this book from the start. Also to John Bergin, for the index.

No words can express how grateful I am to my friends for their loyalty and love, in particular, Caragh McCloskey and Lisa Murphy. Proof that you are never too old to make new and deep friendships, Carole Holohan and Róisín Higgins have given me invaluable support – thank you for the many wonderful conversations about history and life. Similarly, Katie Holmes has been both a friend, mentor and trusted critic, her insights have changed my work and life in many ways.

My family have weathered many a storm and always made me feel safe and valued. To my fabulous extended family and my parents, John and Lesley, I owe a debt that can never be repaid, but I wish them to know how much I am aware of that and how much I love them. I need also to mention my mother's editing skills and the fact that she has read every-thing I have ever written including this book – several times – there is no greater love! To my brother Adam and those we have lost and continue to miss deeply: Paul, Patrick and Graham.

UCD has given me so much in my life thus far, but the greatest gift was my husband, whom I met there in 1997. Thank you Georg for your constant encouragement, patience and love, and for our two precious daughters Hannah Mae and Ellen Lee. And, of course, a special thank you to the girls themselves for keeping us on our toes and always laughing.

Abbreviations

AB	Archbishop Byrne
CBS	Christian Brothers' School
CC	Charity Cases
Clonliffe	Holy Cross College, Clonliffe
CSTI	Catholic Truth Society of Ireland
CUS	Catholic University School, Leeson St., Dublin
DDA	Dublin Diocesan Archives
DD	Doctor of Divinity/Theology
DV or *Deo Volente*	['God willing']
E. de M.	Enfant de Marie Immaculée i.e. a member of the Sodality of Our Lady
JSSISI	*Journal of the Statistical and Social Inquiry Society of Ireland*
Maynooth	St Patrick's College, Maynooth
Mgr	Monsignor
NAI	National Archives of Ireland
NLI	National Library of Ireland
PC	Parish Chaplain
PE	Pastor Emeritus
POS	Protestant Orphan Society
Pro-Cathedral	St Mary's Pro-Cathedral, Dublin
SVP	Society of Saint Vincent de Paul
UCDA	University College Dublin Archives

Editorial Rubric

This book was inspired and deeply influenced by the work of David Fitzpatrick and Thomas Sokoll.[1] I wish in particular to credit Sokoll's work for much of the editorial principles and transcription conventions that have been adopted in this study.

Transcription Guidelines

[ ] insertions of editorial text are placed in these
[ ] suggested readings of ambiguous, indecipherable or illegible parts, where it is not possible to guess, hyphens are provided i.e. *[-----]*
< > conjectured readings of physically destroyed and irrecoverable parts
/ indicates page breaks except where the pages were numbered by the authors; then this is indicated by the number and line space.

Editorial Principles

When letters are cited the original spelling, punctuation or lack thereof is retained. There is no editorial correction or standardization, for example, abbreviated words have not been extended, irregular capitalization or erratic spelling has been maintained. Editorial suggestions and/or additions have only been made when words were missing, illegible or could possibly cause confusion.

Topography: Errors and/or crossed out words have been retained in order to capture as much as is possible of the original 'look' of the texts.

---

[1] D. Fitzpatrick, *Oceans of Consolation: Personal Accounts of Irish Migration to Australia* (New York: Cornell University Press, 1994); T. Sokoll, *Essex Pauper Letters 1731–1837* (Oxford University Press, 2001), pp. 70–87.

Names and Addresses: While the first names of those who applied for charity have been fictionalised, the initials have been maintained and surnames have been reduced to initials. As this collection is uncatalogued, keeping the initials but fictionalising the names allows others to follow the archival trail while affording anonymity to the writers of the letters. Addresses have been retained but identifiable features such as the house/flat number or house name have been removed.

Priests' full names have been retained since they were public figures easily linked to their parish.

Introduction
A History of the Experience of Poverty
'It is hard to state my case in writing'

> I take the liberty to write & put my case before you, but am only doing so as a last resource. It is hard to state my case in writing but will do so as well as I can.[1]

This book owes its life and spirit to the thousands of people like Mrs H. who found themselves in a position where their only recourse was to write to the Roman Catholic Archbishop of Dublin, Dr Edward Byrne (1921–1940) to ask for help. In seven large archival boxes, tucked away in the abundant Dublin Diocesan Archives, lie over four thousand letters labelled 'Charity Cases' written by the Roman Catholic laity of Ireland between 1922 and 1940. On letter-paper, copybook page, the backs of envelopes, postcards, and bill paper; in ink, pencil and crayon, the unemployed, widowed, under-paid, in debt, temporarily 'embarrassed' and dispossessed composed their poverty. In immaculate script or poorly formed letters, in fluid prose or sub-literate stuttering, these people have left one of the few traces in history of the *experience* of poverty, and collectively they illuminate the lives of so many during the foundation decades of Irish independence. They offer insights into the reality of poverty and how it was perceived and negotiated by those who struggled permanently in its embrace or drifted in and out of its clutches. Their letters articulate the hard edge of rage, the debilitating reality of impotence, the humiliation of need, the sour taste of failure, the unflagging spirit of hope, the tenacious sense of fight, the stirrings of entitlement, along with love and a sense of responsibility. They are also acts of testimony describing in highly personal ways the realities of living in appalling conditions, of having to beg, of losing the chief breadwinner and of

---

[1] Mrs H., X Leinster Rd., Rathmines, Dublin, 15 July 1939. Dublin Diocesan Archives, Archbishop Byrne Papers, AB7, Charity Cases, Box 7 [hereafter DDA, AB 7 CC, Box 1 etc.]. Please note all letters in this collection were addressed to either Archbishop Byrne or his secretaries unless otherwise stated.

1

being exposed to physical and sexual exploitation.[2] By committing their reality to paper, these people carried from the private to the public domain, from the powerless to the powerful, a record of the hidden realities of poverty and in so doing complicated the boundaries between those domains.[3]

These Irish charity letters were created in the dynamic context of encounter, when the poor or those in need negotiated with those in control of the purse strings. Peter Mandler and other historians of poverty and charity have noted that it is particularly difficult for the historian to find sources that allow a penetrative analysis of this 'site of encounter'.[4] These letters, and the responses they elicited, provide an important and rare window into the cosmology of poverty in early independent Ireland. Hence, this is not an empirically based social history, but rather a history of the 'socio-cultural experiences of the poor' through the prism of their begging letters – their poverty stories.[5] A central focus of this research has been how, in these letters, the poor reworked their experiences of poverty, not only in terms of their own self-perception and sense of identity, but also in response to their understanding of the mentality and values of the universe they shared with their church and wider society.[6] It is this interplay between self and social knowledge that is the heart of the charity engagement; on occasion this was conscious, for example, when a threat of apostasy was made to extract assistance, but often it was unconscious, a social reflex that the historian must decode.

The story of poverty is all too often told solely from the perspective of those who encountered the poor through charity or social work. This book offers a history told from the perspective of those who lived as 'the poor'.

---

[2] For a discussion of this historiographical trend, see, S. Bhattacharya, 'History from below', *Social Scientist*, 11 (April 1983), 3–20, 24.

[3] Rebecca Earle has argued that to define letters as sources of the public or private domain is to impose an 'artificial clarity'. R. Earle, 'Introduction: letters, writers and the historian' in R. Earle (ed.), *Epistolary Selves: Letters and Letter-Writers, 1600-1945* (Ashgate: Aldershot, 1999), pp. 1–12, 3.

[4] P. Mandler, 'Poverty and charity in the nineteenth century metropolis: an introduction' in P. Mandler (ed.), *The Uses of Charity: The Poor on Relief in the Nineteenth-Century Metropolis* (Philadelphia: University of Pennsylvania Press, 1990), pp. 1–37, 23.

[5] S. King, 'Negotiating the law of poor relief in England, 1800–1840', *History*, 96 (2011), 410–35, 410; Bailey also describes her examination of English pauper letters as a cultural history rather than an empirically based social history. J. Bailey, '"Think wot a mother must feel": parenting in English pauper letters', *Family & Community History*, 13 (2010), 5–19, 5.

[6] On letter writing, identity and 'narrative impetus', see K. Holmes, *Between the Leaves: Stories of Australian Women, Writing and Gardens* (Crawley: The University of Western Australia, 2011), pp. 61–81.

Negotiating charity was an intrinsic part of the experience of poverty in modern Ireland; as Chapter 1 outlines, the limited state relief was inadequate to sustain the majority of recipients without supplementary assistance from charity. Thus having to 'compose' and tell a story that explained and justified poverty was an essential part of being poor. In his work on poverty, Mark Peel has explored the way the poor used the conventions of storytelling to explain their poverty; he noted that their 'autobiographies must be produced on demand' for the social worker or the police officer.[7] In many respects the letters written by the Irish poor in the 1920s and 30s fulfil the criteria of storytelling and autobiographical writing, confirming Toby Ditz's argument that the context of a letter could become a part of the experience.[8]

The driving force of this book is to explore both poverty as it was experienced, with a particular emphasis on individual strategies of survival, and how 'the poor' shaped and perceived their own identity when seeking charity. Mrs H. wrote to the archbishop in 1939: 'I could not explain how heart broken I am or even the extent of my troubles for I am honest & like to be able to pay my way.'[9] She characterised herself as honourable and someone for whom it was important to be financially independent. The identity she shaped in her letter was based on reinforcing these characteristics which had powerful social resonance in a society endlessly debating the boundaries of legitimate poverty. As Andreas Gestrich, Elizabeth Hurren and Steven King have noted, 'it is unthinkable that the conditions making for a re-evaluation of self – of a new interiority – did not also percolate down to the very poorest and shape both whether they wrote but also the standards by which they judged their conditions and thus how and about what they wrote.'[10] Nowhere more than in the letters of the poor is the quest for the individual voice so central, for this was a fundamental purpose of the letters. They wrote to differentiate themselves from the rest of the poor – they sought to say: I am genuine, I need help, I deserve help, I cannot be ignored. As Mrs H. explained to the archbishop: 'that is why I write to you, to see if you could help me over this trouble, I could not tell you what it has cost me to write this letter of appeal only that I am in such

---

[7] M. Peel, *The Lowest Rung: Voices of Australian Poverty* (Cambridge University Press, 2003), pp. 6, 12; Caroline Steedman refers to this as 'autobiographical narration'. C. Steedman, *Dust* (Manchester University Press, 2001), p. 48.

[8] T. Ditz, 'Formative ventures: eighteenth-century commercial letters and the articulation of experience' in Earle (ed.), *Epistolary Selves*, pp. 59–78, 62.

[9] Mrs H., X Leinster Rd., Rathmines, Dublin, 15 July 1939.

[10] A. Gestrich, E. Hurren and S. King (eds.), *Poverty and Sickness in Modern Europe: Narratives of the Sick Poor, 1780-1938* (London: Continuum, 2012), p. 14.

terrible trouble I would not do so.' Here I am, I place myself before you; it was both a challenge and a plea – hear *me*. Mrs H. could not afford her plea to fall on deaf ears, therefore she had to converse with a world her reader(s) knew. She was writing a letter seeking assistance, but she was also having a conversation with her society and constructing a relationship with her church, both of which involved a 'performance of self' that created an identity which would explain and elicit a favourable response.[11] Letters do not just 'record or describe', they 'inscribe' and 'rework'.[12] Mrs H. and all those who wrote to the archbishop recorded their poverty, but they also reworked it into a narrative that reinterpreted poverty as a personal experience and gave space for the individual.

The majority of authors in this collection were involved in a form of anti-correspondence; they were not beginning a writing relationship with the archbishop, and it was made clear that they could write only once. Therefore, they had one chance to get it right, to establish the *persona* and story that would gain them the help required. In the quest to read and hear these voices this book owes much to Peel's study of social work and the story of poverty, in which he argued: 'In a broad sense, the task of social and cultural history must always be to account for what people made of themselves, not just what others made of them.'[13] The majority of those who wrote to the archbishop were underemployed, unemployed, underpaid, widowed or generally those who were never asked about poverty and the many policies adopted to relieve it. In these letters the people who so rarely set the record in their own words, spell out word after word, page after page, what it meant *to them* to be poor.

Text and Context

In order to explore both this creation of self and the experience that led to writing in the first place, these Irish letters will be read both 'textually and contextually': examined both as texts constructing poverty *and* as texts embedded in a particular world and time that they explain and that helps to explain them.[14] The letters were subject to a complex set of cultural norms and by placing them in their social context it is possible to explore

---

[11] L. Stanley, 'The epistolarium: on theorizing letters and correspondences', *Auto/Biography*, 12 (2004), 201–235, 212.

[12] Ditz, 'Formative ventures', p. 61.

[13] M. Peel, *Miss Cutler and the Case of the Resurrected Horse: Social Work and the Story of Poverty in America, Australia, and Britain* (The University of Chicago Press, 2012), p. 18.

[14] L. Colley, *Captives: Britain, Empire and the World 1600-1850* (London: Jonathan Cape, 2002), p. 93; S. King, 'Pauper letters as a source', *Family & Community*, 10 (2007), 167–170.

their tremendous value to our understanding of how the normally silenced voiced their concerns and articulated their struggle for survival in a world so frequently hostile to the dependent. Therefore, the way in which these people sought to beg, bargain and sell their lives, reveals much about their room for manoeuvre and how they understood and negotiated the power structures that confined them. Their words, use of language, repetitions, and reference-points provide us with evidence of the contemporary understandings of class, family, gender and religion. Mrs H. was a convert to Catholicism writing at a time when that made her 'a case of concern', particularly as a mother of several children. She knew this and waited only until her second sentence to clarify her status: 'I am a convert to the Catholic Church married & have had 4 children.' Her text – how she arranged her story, what she told first and how she linked one facet of her life to the next – speaks to her context and her identity within that universe. In this book, the rhythm and details of the letters are considered inseparable in the quest to reach a better understanding of the history they convey. It is argued that how, for example, Mrs H. punctuated the details of her life – her dead and sick children, underpaid husband and bad tenants – with an image and sense of her 'self'– 'I was able to manage & was very happy, until last year' and a few lines later 'I am distracted & heart broken' – is an essential part of the truth she wished to communicate about her identity that legitimised her request. Thus, while these letters provide raw material for an analysis of the experience of poverty and the art of begging, they are also artefacts in their own right.[15]

In order to explore their textual and contextual potency large sections of the letters have been cited throughout this book. It is not possible to recreate the topography of the page – the readers of this book do not hold in their hands the yellowed page penned in fading pencil, or the beautiful joined script on family headed paper. The impact of a writer's desperate need to use every square inch of the page, writing up the sides, in the top and bottom margins or the stark three lines on torn paper – simple, nude, in its insistence – cannot be recreated. However, the texts have been respected insofar as is possible and thus mistakes have not been silently corrected, spellings and punctuation remain as they appear in the originals and any alterations are clearly indicated.[16] In fact, it is argued in Chapter 2 that the punctuation, erratic capitalisation and structure of these letters are intrinsic to our understanding of them as sources. In order to respect

---

[15] See Earle's discussion of letters as sources and artefacts. Earle, 'Introduction: letters, writers and the historian', pp. 1–12.
[16] See Editorial Rubric, p. 3.

the privacy of the individual authors, however, the first names have been changed and surnames have been initialised with the exception of priests or others who were writing in a professional capacity; house names or numbers have been removed.[17]

The collection is not catalogued; however, by the author's count there are 4,343 letters of which 1,747 (40.4 per cent) were written by women and 1,365 (31.5 per cent) by men and only 15 (0.3 per cent) were signed by a husband and wife, although in reality many were probably joint enterprises.[18] Almost a quarter of the collection was written by priests – 1,032 (23.8 per cent) – usually in relation to a parishoner's letter. While Dublin predominates in this collection, because the letters were written to the head of the Catholic diocese in Dublin and the city was the site of the greatest amount and degree of poverty, there are letters from most counties in Ireland and from as far afield as India and Australia. In total there were 698 (16.1 per cent) letters from outside Dublin and they allow an exploration of the commonalities in the experience of poverty and supplication, while pointing to some of the differences.

Stanley has astutely pointed out, the ethics of the selection process by its very nature involves the *de*selection of some letters.[19] This was an unavoidable dilemma faced in writing this book, as there were simply too many to include the entirety of the collection. It was not productive to adopt a structured selection process whereby every fifth or tenth letter was included as this would have resulted in divorcing a series of related correspondence and rendering only a partial telling of certain cases. The letters cited in this study are 'exemplar narratives' that reflect the most prominent styles and themes found throughout the collection.[20] While individual letters offer particularly vivid personal stories, taken together they represent a collective experience and shed light on the status and meaning of poverty in twentieth-century Ireland. Thus the book is organised thematically; a strictly chronological structure made little sense as it is argued that change during this period was less of a reality than the

---

[17] The collection is not catalogued and there are no clear reference codes identifying each letter, therefore, initials have been maintained to allow future researchers follow the archival trail.

[18] 103 (2.3 per cent) letters are deemed as 'other' either because the gender was unidentifiable or because they were written by an organisation, for example, the Vincent de Paul or Council of the Unemployed.

[19] See Stanley for an interesting discussion of this selection process. Stanley, 'The epistolarium', 201–235.

[20] I borrow this phrase from King, who also based his analysis of pauper letters on a large collection of 2,842 of which only a small sample could be cited or reproduced. See, King, 'Negotiating the law of poor relief', 414.

constancy of the experience of poverty lived in the light of shared values that changed little in real terms.

Irish History and Irish Poverty

While poverty is an undeniable constant in the story of Ireland, the pages of its history run relatively dry after political independence in 1922. Historians of modern Ireland have accepted poverty's ubiquitous shadow after independence, but there has been no detailed analysis of its history.[21] Undoubtedly, the history of poverty has suffered due to the strong emphasis on political history in Ireland, but also because of a general reluctance to offer a class analysis of Ireland's history since independence.[22] When poverty enters the historical narrative after 1922 it has tended to do so sideways, for example, in relation to how it impacted on the history of women and sexuality,[23] motherhood,[24] religion, social

---

[21] This is all the more curious since the history of poverty prior to independence is very well served. See, for example, J. Prunty, *Dublin Slums 1800-1925: A Study in Urban Geography* (Dublin: Irish Academic Press, 1998); M. E. Daly, *Dublin – The Deposed Capital, 1860–1914* (Cork University Press, 1984); M. H. Preston, *Charitable Words: Women, Philanthropy, and the Language of Charity in Nineteenth-Century Dublin* (London: Praeger, 2004); V. Crossman and P. Gray (eds.), *Poverty and Welfare in Ireland 1838–1948* (Dublin: Irish Academic Press, 2011). For studies with a particular focus on popular attitudes to poverty and the strategies of the poor themselves, see V. Crossman, *Poverty and the Poor Law in Ireland, 1850–1914* (Liverpool University Press, 2013); C. Breathnach, *The Congested Districts Board of Ireland, 1891–1923* (Dublin: Four Courts Press, 2005); N. Ó Ciosáin, 'Boccoughs and God's poor: deserving and undeserving poor in Irish popular culture' in T. Foley and S. Ryder (eds.), *Ideology and Ireland in the Nineteenth Century* (Dublin: Four Courts Press, 1996), pp. 93–99;

[22] There are a few exceptions: P. O'Dea (ed.), *A Class of Our Own: Conversations about Class in Ireland* (Dublin: New Island Books, 1994); F. Lane and D. Ó Drisceoil (eds.), *Politics of the Irish Working Class, 1830–1945* (New York: Palgrave Macmillan, 2005), pp. 1–5; F. Lane (ed.), *Politics, Society and the Middle Class in Modern Ireland* (New York: Palgrave Macmillan, 2010); M. Silverman, *An Irish Working Class: Explorations in Political Economy and Hegemony, 1800–1950* (University of Toronto Press, 2001). In his history of Fianna Fáil, Richard Dunphy incorporates a strong class analysis of the party's ideology and policies. R. Dunphy, *The Making of Fianna Fáil Power in Ireland, 1932–1948* (Oxford University Press, 1995). See, also, T. Garvin, *Preventing the Future: Why was Ireland so Poor for so Long?* (Dublin: Gill & Macmillan, 2004); Newell has a chapter considering poverty in Galway during the 1920s. U. Newell, *The West Must Wait: County Galway and the Irish Free State, 1922–32* (Manchester University Press, 2015).

[23] D. Ferriter, *Occasions of Sin: Sex and Society in Modern Ireland* (London: Profile Books, 2009); M. Luddy, *Prostitution and Irish Society, 1800–1940* (Cambridge University Press, 2007); J. M. Smith, *Ireland's Magdalen Laundries and the Nation's Architecture of Containment* (Manchester University Press, 2007).

[24] L. Earner-Byrne, *Mother and Child: Maternity and Child Welfare in Dublin, 1922–1960* (Manchester University Press, 2007); C. Rattigan, *'What Else Could I Do?' Single Mothers and Infanticide, 1900–1950* (Dublin: Irish Academic Press, 2012).

welfare,[25] housing,[26] or emigration and population decline.[27] These studies all provide insights into various aspects of poverty, policy and charity, but neither poverty nor its protagonists are the focus of attention in their own right. Collectively these works point to the fact that we cannot understand twentieth-century Ireland without considering the impact of economic power and class.[28] Virginia Crossman, in her work on poverty and the Poor Law in nineteenth-century Ireland, argues that 'the ideological roots of these debates lay as much in class and religion as in politics and ethnicity.'[29] Her study of the Poor Law in Ireland, while focused on 'the system', succeeds in providing a sense of how the poor interacted with and experienced statutory relief. She convincingly demonstrates that 'the concept of the deserving and undeserving poor became deeply rooted in Irish popular culture.'[30] While Finola Kennedy, in her work on the Irish family, argues that 'at the start of the twentieth century the factors that most differentiated families were economic and class factors.'[31] This book will go some way to establishing that these observations remain pertinent in relation to Irish society until at least 1940. It was not religion, or gender, but economics and class that most shaped each individual's life experience in modern Ireland.

It is oral history and autobiographies that have taken up the challenge of exploring the history of Irish poverty. In fact, autobiographies that seek to come to terms with the experience of poverty in modern Ireland, which include the many documenting abuse in the various orphanages and industrial schools of Ireland,[32] rival, in terms of quantity, any other

---

[25] Cousins and Kennedy offer particularly useful historical analyses of poverty in relation to the development of the welfare state and family policy. M. Cousins, *The Birth of Social Welfare in Ireland 1922–1952* (Dublin: Four Courts Press, 2003); F. Kennedy, *Cottage to Crèche: Family Change in Ireland* (Dublin: Institute of Public Administration, 2001); F. W. Powell, *The Politics of Irish Social Policy, 1600–1990* (Lampeter: The Edwin Mellen Press, 1992).

[26] MacManus points out that in 1911, 22.9 per cent of Dublin city's population lived in one-room tenements. R. McManus, *Dublin, 1910–1940: Shaping the City & Suburbs* (Dublin: Four Courts Press, 2002), p. 32 and p. 41; J. Brady, *Dublin, 1930–1950: The Emergence of the Modern City* (Dublin: Four Courts Press, 2014), pp. 46–51.

[27] M. E. Daly, *Slow Failure: Population Decline and Independent Ireland* (University of Wisconsin Press, 2006).

[28] For some interesting reflections on the relationship between class/status, gender and employment see, E. Kiely and M. Leane, *Irish Women at Work 1930–1960: An Oral History* (Dublin: Irish Academic Press, 2012).

[29] Crossman, *Poverty and the Poor Law in Ireland*, p. 3.

[30] Ibid; See also, Ó Ciosáin, 'Boccoughs and God's poor'.

[31] Kennedy, *Cottage to Crèche*, p. 57.

[32] I would include these in this category as almost all of them identify poverty as the main reason for their incarceration in one (or more) of these institutions. See, for example, D. Whelan, (ed.) Peter Tyrrell, *Founded on Fear* (Dublin: Irish Academic Press, 2006), which provides a harrowing account of poverty in 1920s Ireland.

form of Irish autobiography. This phenomenon indicates a burning desire to open this topic to analysis and an insistence that it finds its place in the historical record. This motivation is explicit, for example, in Máirín Johnston's *Around the Banks of Pimlico*. She begins her story with a detailed historical context, she refers constantly to historical sources, and embeds her knowledge of history in the personal narrative of her family: 'All during the recession of the late 1920s, when unemployment was very high and getting worse, we were almost destitute.'[33] For Johnston the rest of Irish society looked at her 'type' from behind 'protective wire' giving the 'impression that all the poor ... were there under false pretences'.[34] Other memoirs are less explicit, but equally insistent about the idea of literary inclusion to compensate for historical exclusion. The title of Angeline Kearns Blain's account of growing up in Irishtown in Dublin in the 1930s and 40s, *Stealing Sunlight*, hints at the complex motivations behind these autobiographies: she 'stole' her childhood by siphoning little bits of what was good (sunlight) in order to survive in a hostile society. Through her writing she reclaimed a place in the narrative of 'growing up' in Ireland for the poor and dispossessed.[35] She wanted her life and the story of poverty to see the light of history, to come out from the shadows of denial. She opens up her story with an image of dirty sheets, hinting at how the poor were consigned to the darkness yet they lived in plain view: 'We were born and raised, my three brothers and I, in a single room in one of the dilapidated whitewashed tenements which were strung along O'Brien's Place like dingy bedsheets.'[36] Elaine Crowley sought to resurrect a world where 'pawning was no disgrace' and the goal was to join the propertied side of life: 'My mother had two ambitions. To be on the pig's back and to have a private house.'[37] If you owned property you became one of those who *belonged* in Irish history; in the Irish project of self-determination, private property was king. In these stories the characters 'waged constant war' on their surroundings and on the limitations of their 'place' in society.[38] They may have been relatively powerless, but they were never portrayed as passive. These memoirs deserve our attention and they challenge us to

---

[33] M. Johnston, *Around the Banks of Pimlico* (Dublin: Attic Press, 1985), p. 54.

[34] Ibid., p. 58.

[35] A. Kearns Blain, *Stealing Sunlight: Growing up in Irishtown* (Dublin: A & A Farmar, 2000).

[36] Ibid., p. 3.

[37] E. Crowley, *Cowslips and Chainies: A Memoir of Dublin in the 1930s* (Dublin: Lilliput Press, 1996), p. 2;

[38] I borrow this image from Crowley who refers to her mother as 'waging constant war' on vermin, but it is representative of the portrayal of many of the families in these autobiography/memoirs, particularly the women. Ibid., p. 110.

find a way to include them and the story they tell in the history of modern Ireland.[39]

Projects such as the development of a women's oral history archive and the work of Mary Muldowney on women's experiences during the Second World War, reveal the potential of oral history to help flesh out and enrich the narrative of ordinary people's experiences in the past.[40] The recent oral history project by Elizabeth Kiely and Máire Leane explores aspects of how class distinctions were experienced and conveyed, revealing that notions of 'respectability' were profoundly important and often associated with one's employment.[41] The oral historian Kevin Kearns has produced several books using oral history to discover how the 'other half lived' in modern Ireland.[42] Kearns grounds his studies in historical research, but his ultimate achievement is in exploring how working-class Dubliners *recall* surviving poverty. While many of his subjects vividly recapture aspects of life in the poorest parts of Dublin, they also obscure or downplay more painful or complex aspects of 'being poor' filtering, as people inevitably do, life through the lens of time and contemporary sensibilities. However, Alistair Thomson has done some interesting work exploring the differing accounts that emerge from present centred letters during the migration process and oral history recollections of those letters. He has shown quite convincingly that both sources include and omit and that neither can be regarded as a 'superior source'.[43] Thus, in this study a rich array of official sources have been drawn upon that track contemporary attitudes

[39] Liam Harte makes a similar point. L. Harte (ed.), *Modern Irish Autobiography: Self, Nation and Society* (Basingstoke: Palgrave Macmillan, 2007). There are numerous childhood memoirs relevant to this period. The main ones drawn upon for this study are: P. Bracken, *Light of Other Days: A Dublin Childhood* (Cork: The Mercier Press, 1992); Crowley, *Cowslips and Chainies*; E. Newman Devlin, *Speaking Volumes: A Dublin Childhood* (Belfast: The Blackstaff, 2000); P. Galvin, *Song for a Poor Boy: A Cork Childhood* (Dublin: Raven Arts Press, 1990); Johnston, *Around the Banks of Pimlico*; Kearns Blain, *Stealing Sunlight*; C. Kenneally, *Maura's Boy* (Cork: Mercier Press, 1996); F. Kennedy, *Three Storeys up: Tale of Dublin Tenement Life* (Dublin: Marino Books, 1997); F. O'Connor, *An Only Child* (London: Macmillan, 1961); S. O'Connor, *Growing Up So High: A Liberties Boyhood* (Dublin: Hachette Books Ireland, 2013); P. O'Keeffe, *Down Cobbled Streets* (Dingle: Brandon Publishers, 1995).

[40] A Women's Oral History Archive is a Clare County oral history project directed by Jacquai Hayes. See, www.oralhistorynetworkIreland.ie; M. Muldowney, *The Second World War and Irish Women. An Oral History* (Dublin: Irish Academic Press, 2007).

[41] Kiely and Leane, *Irish Women at Work 1930-1960*.

[42] K. Kearns, *Dublin's Lost Heroines: Mammies and Grannies in a Vanished City* (Dublin: Gill & Macmillan, 2004), p. 16; See, also, K. Kearns, *Dublin Tenement Life: An Oral History* (Dublin: Gill & Macmillan, 1994).

[43] See, A. Thomson, *Moving Stories: An Intimate History of Four Women Across Two Countries* (Manchester University Press, 2011).

to poverty and the poor, from governmental reports to parliamentary debates, as well as charitable reports, various commissions and more general sources such as newspapers, periodicals and journals. However, the level of textual analysis in this book may make some historians uncomfortable as it pushes the boundaries of what constitutes historical methodological analysis by placing a close reading of these texts at the centre of the narrative.[44] This is also a conscious act of counterbalance; so much of Irish history is driven by the narratives of official voices and this book challenges the implicit hierarchy often afforded to certain source material. Like the poor themselves, the sources they created have been distrusted, or regarded as inherently unreliable. However, these letters were created in a particular context for a particular purpose – like all other sources – and once this is factored into any analysis they pose no greater challenge to our historical skills than a governmental report into the housing crisis of the 1930s.

A 'New' History from Below

In 2004, Tim Hitchcock wrote of the need to write a 'new history from below' that draws predominantly from the voices of those at the bottom of the social universe.[45] Martyn Lyons quite consciously responded to this idea in writing his history of the writing culture of ordinary people, explaining that this 'new history from below' is different for four reasons: it re-evaluates individual experience, it seeks out the 'personal and private voices of ordinary people', it explores how 'dominant discourses were actually consumed' by these people and finally, it regards these ordinary voices as active agents (however constricted) in 'shaping ... their own lives and cultures'. [46] Each of these four components is woven throughout this study of the voices of ordinary Irish Catholics in need in twentieth-century Ireland.

This book draws on the imaginative scholarship of historians like Thomas Sokoll, whose pioneering working on Essex Pauper letters of the late eighteenth and early nineteenth centuries has, in many senses, set

---

[44] For a beautiful example of this use of letters in relation to history see, Holmes, *Between the Leaves*.

[45] In Hitchcock's review of Sokoll's *Essex Pauper Letters* he argued that the 'old' history from below had generated a faceless collective approach to the history of those subordinate to the main power structures. T. Hitchcock, 'A new history from below', *History Workshop Journal*, 57 (2004), 294–298.

[46] M. Lyons, *The Writing Culture of Ordinary People in Europe, c. 1860–1920* (Cambridge University Press, 2012), pp. 252–255.

the gold standard for dealing with such vibrant and complex source material.[47] The English pauper letters were generated in the particular context of the English Poor Law, when the pauper needed to write (or have written) a letter to their parish of settlement seeking assistance.[48] However, Sokoll presents these pauper letters as first-hand accounts of living conditions during the period and as sources that provide accounts from 'below' of the Old Poor Law.[49] Steven King similarly argues that they offer 'a unique window on the lives, experiences and feelings of the poor'.[50] These historians have revealed the potential of historical textual analysis for examining the power of rhetoric, the process of self-definition, the contours of shared cultural understanding and negotiation.[51] Although the Irish charity letters were constructed in a very different context, they are nonetheless, like the English pauper letters, 'forms of written evidence created when the poor confronted, and were confronted by, the hierarchies and institutions of authority'[52] and thus afford similar potential for understanding the experience of seeking charity and living as 'the poor' in early twentieth-century Ireland. Hence, this study explores the writing skills of these Irish petitioners and the degree to which the letter liberated or constrained these authors. It is argued that the relatively safe confines of letter etiquette enabled power-less people to say powerful things. The writers drew on deep cultural understandings of honour, gender, charity and faith to extract a small space for their telling of poverty and, often, an insistence upon their innocence. As Rab Houston has argued, petitions allow us to see 'how cultural scripts were enacted or amended in everyday life'.[53]

The research and analysis of Sokoll, Joanne Bailey, Jeremy Boulton, Peter Jones, Steven King, Alison Stringer and others on English pauper letters, written over a hundred years before the Irish begging letters to

---

[47] T. Sokoll, *Essex Pauper Letters 1731–1837* (Oxford University Press, 2006); See also, T. Sokoll, 'Negotiating a living: Essex pauper letters from London, 1800–1834', *International Review of Social History*, 45, Supplement 8 (2000), 19–46; T. Sokoll, 'Writing for relief: rhetoric in English pauper letters, 1800–1834' in A. Gestrich, S. King and L. Raphael (eds.), *Being Poor in Modern Europe: Historical Perspectives 1800–1940* (Switzerland: Peter Lang, 2006), pp. 91–111.

[48] S. King, 'Pauper letters as a source', *Family & Community*, 10 (2007), 167–170, 167.

[49] Sokoll, *Essex Pauper Letters*, pp. 3–4.

[50] King, 'Pauper letters as a source', 170.

[51] David Fitzpatrick has done something similar for the history of emigration in his analysis of emigrant letters. See, D. Fitzpatrick, *Oceans of Consolation: Personal Accounts of Irish Migration to Australia* (New York: Cornell University Press, 1994).

[52] T. Hitchcock, P. King and P. Sharpe (eds.), *Chronicling Poverty: The Voices and Strategies of the English Poor, 1640–1840* (New York: Palgrave Macmillan, 1996), pp. 3–5.

[53] R. A. Houston, *Peasant Petitions: Social Relations and Economic Life on Landed Estates, 1600-1850* (Basingstoke: Palgrave Macmillan, 2014), p. 271.

Archbishop Byrne, raise many questions about the degree to which the essences of the poverty narrative crossed temporal and geographical boundaries.[54] This book will explore the ways in which this Irish collection conforms and/or differs from these earlier English letters and other European examples such as the more formal *Bittbriefe* (petition letters) written in Austria in the nineteenth and early twentieth centuries.[55] While accounting for the different time, location and context, there are remarkable similarities between these various collections of 'strategic writing' from below with regard to how their authors 'told' poverty and negotiated within the confines of their respective societies.[56] Chapter 2 places these Irish letters in this international context and provides a detailed analysis of the Irish letters' main historical and literary features from composition to writing, provenance and representativeness.

The second chapter concludes with a consideration of these letters as sources for the experience of poverty, and addresses questions regarding authenticity and 'truthfulness'. It argues that these letters are authentic insofar as they were almost certainly written by the hand of the sender and for various reasons can be considered representative of those living in poverty, even those that did not write seeking charity. However, with regard to the more controversial issue of truthfulness, the aim of this study is to examine not just what these authors wrote, but how and why they chose to do so, and therefore a distinction is made between notions of truth and fact. It is argued that these letters were attempts at 'self-representation', and for each author poverty had a personal meaning they needed to communicate, even if to do so they had to engage in common tropes, motifs, and possibly, untruths.

---

[54] J. Bailey, '"Think wot a mother must feel"'; J. Boulton, '"It is extreme necessity that makes me do this": some "survival strategies" of pauper households in London's West End during the early eighteenth century', *International Review of Social History*, 45, Supplement 8 (2000), 47–69; S. King, 'Regional patterns in the experiences and treatment of the sickpoor, 1800–1840: rights, obligations and duties in the rhetoric of paupers', *Family & Community History*, 10 (2007), 61–75; King, 'Friendship, kinship, and belonging in the letters of urban paupers 1800–1840', *Historical Social Research*, 33 (2008), 249–77; King, 'Negotiating the law of poor relief in England'; King, 'Welfare regimes and welfare regions in Britain and Europe, c. 1750–1860', *Journal of Modern European History*, 9 (2011), 44–67.

[55] See also, P. J. Jones, '"I cannot keep my place without being deascent": Pauper letters, parish clothing and pragmatism in the South of England, 1750–1830', *Rural History*, 20 (2009), 31–49; C. Hämmerle, 'Requests, complaints, demands. Preliminary thoughts on the petitioning letters of lower-class Austrian women, 1865–1918' in C. Bland and M. Cros (eds.), *Gender and Politics in the Age of Letter Writing, 1750–2000* (Aldershot: Ashgate, 2004), pp. 115–134.

[56] Sokoll, 'Negotiating a living', 29.

This study also enters the increasingly 'lively debate over the character, execution and limits' of the agency of the poor in Europe between the 1700s and the 1900s.[57] The idea that the poor had some room for negotiation is not new in either history or historiography.[58] However, recent scholarship based on sources constructed by the poor has added considerable nuance to our understanding of how that space for negotiation was created, mediated and controlled.[59] While it is essential to appreciate the limits of any agency the poor may have managed to extract, in examining the letters of the poor as places where power was contested we can gain a much deeper understanding of the reality and limitations of that power. Chapter 3, therefore, investigates the ingredients of the 'deserving case', how unemployed men wrote about their sense of failure, mothers bartered faith for food, and the raped, beaten and abused chose their words. It is important to hear as much as possible of what the letter writers were saying, in other words, to allow multiple readings to co-exist thus reflecting the real complexity of writing self and experience in these letters. For example, a letter-writer may have stressed their conversion to Catholicism, as Mrs H. did, as part of a rhetorical strategy because she knew how the hierarchy fretted over such mothers, but she may also have done so because the fact of her conversion made her more vulnerable both within her adopted church and to the manipulation of those outside it. Mrs H. expressed the co-existence of her vulnerability and power within this society of religious wrangling thus:

I have no parents & nobody to help me, owing to the changing of my religion, there is one who I put my trouble to & has offered to help me an Aunt who is a protestant, a sum of money has been offered but I would in return have to return to her faith & also to take what children I could with me, I am 8 years in the Catholic faith & was so happy for I love the only true religion. I am sorry to say that at times I have been tempted to accept this offer, but I pray hard for God to give me strength not to yield to this temptation & that is why I write to you, to see if you could help me over this trouble.[60]

---

[57] A. Gestrich, E. Hurren and S. King, 'Narratives of poverty and sickness in Europe 1780–1938: Sources, methods and experiences' in Gestrich, Hurren and King (eds.), *Poverty and Sickness in Modern Europe*, pp. 1–33, 2.

[58] See, for example, O. Hufton, *The Poor of Eighteenth-Century France, 1750–1789* (Oxford University Press, 1974); Digby noted that the stereotype of the female applicant as powerless and passive has obscured the potential for empowerment. See, A. Digby, 'Poverty, health, and the politics of gender in Britain, 1870–1948' in A. Digby, and J. Stewart (eds.), *Gender, Health and Welfare* (London and New York: Routledge, 1996), p. 69.

[59] David Gerber provides a very thought-provoking discussion about this 'space' in immigrant letters and how it can be explored. D. Gerber, 'The immigrant letter between positivism and populism: American historians' uses of personal correspondence' in Earle (ed.), *Epistolary Selves*, pp. 37–55.

[60] Mrs H., X Leinster Rd., Rathmines, Dublin, 15 July 1939.

Mrs H. portrayed herself as both a victim and someone who had the power to decide, however, she wrote to place the ultimate responsibility of her decision at the archbishop's feet. She also demonstrated that a threat of religious defection could, without any apparent contradiction, lie beside a declaration of loyalty. Particular attention is paid to exploring these letters as acts of individual protest embedded in a value-system that the poor actively engaged with allowing them to make calls upon it and their rights within it. These letters are littered with examples of constrained defiance, from argument to everyday resistance, whereby people refused to 'act poor' or threatened defection.[61]

This book examines not only how the poor made their case but also what they considered to be the cost of poverty. Chapter 5, in particular, analyses how those in need recorded the impact of want and dependence on their lives. In examining the ways the poor documented the impact of poverty on their lives, this chapter also investigates the various survival strategies employed by these writers beyond the letters, which often exacted their own toll of suffering. These ranged from the remarkable tenacity of the family economy, the pawning and bartering of goods, the ability to play a myriad of relief agencies off one another, to the daily reality of family break up and emigration. Crucially, these letters underscore how these strategies were understood as damaging and were (on these pages) eloquently resented.

It is important also to be attuned to the inherent silences in these sources. These may have been influenced by a multitude of factors: from reticence of the writer, to the cultural emphasis on 'discretion' with regard to certain topics, to the perception of the writer regarding the recipient's bias or priorities. As Peel advocates, this study seeks to read these letters 'against the grain, for their silences and their strategies, and for what lies half-spoken on their edges'.[62] An Irish Catholic mother writing to her archbishop was unlikely to lament her repeated pregnancies, for example, in the same way as the hundreds of British women in the 1930s who responded to a questionnaire about their lives organised by the Women's Health Enquiry Committee.[63] However, there were oblique ways of

---

[61] J. C. Scott, *Weapons of the Weak: Everyday Forms of Peasant Resistance* (Connecticut: Yale University Press, 1985), p. 233.

[62] M. Peel, *Miss Cutler*, p. 18.

[63] M. Spring Rice, *Working-Class Wives: Their Health and Conditions* (London: Virago, 1981 [1939]). There is no Irish example of the frankness displayed in the letters of French Catholics to Abbé Viollet of the Association du Mariage Chrétien [Christian Marriage Association] between 1924 and 1943. In that collection the strain of unlimited fertility is vividly recorded. See, M. Sevegrand, *L'Amour en Toute Lettres: Questions à l'Abbé Viollet sur la Sexualité (1924–1943)* (Paris: Albin Michel Histoire, 1996).

underscoring that burden. Many Catholic mothers expressed relief when God took their children and thus spared them further poverty, or they referred to being 'burdened with' a large family. The authors of these letters were seeking something and how they framed their narrative was ultimately shaped by that request. All historical sources are mediated by a variety of factors relating to their creation, environment and objective, and begging letters are no exception. The historical debate will lie in how we interpret the impact of these various mediating forces.[64]

This study also uses this specific collection of letters to explore how the Catholic clergy and hierarchy administered charitable relief. It was a requirement of the Archbishop of Dublin's charity that all applicants should have a priest's reference and, as already noted, the priests' letters constitute 23.8 per cent of this collection. Chapter 6 analyses what cases and categories of need were most successful and how the priests interpreted their role as advocate. Unfortunately, the archbishop's rationale is more difficult to discern; the only evidence of his thought process are the notes, often scribbled by his two secretaries, Fr. Patrick Dunne[65] and Fr. Thomas O'Donnell,[66] on the top left hand corner of the applicant's letter. However, even this rather rudimentary paper trail has afforded a fairly good map of where the money went revealing the power of the class rationale behind charity in action. While both distrust and compassion underlay the relationship between the Catholic Church and 'its poor', it is essential to understand the human element of both sides of the charity equation, in order to honour the responsibility we have as historians to all protagonists of the past. Some priests were empowered by the quest to hunt out the 'genuine case', others were stressed and demoralised by the process, and yet collectively they perpetuated the system that accepted and depended on the existence of poverty.

Who Were the Poor?

This book is concerned with knowing the poor and understanding their version of poverty, hence Richard Dyson's 'holistic definition of poverty' has been adopted, which includes those dependent on relief and/or charity constantly, intermittently and those who experienced once-off

---

[64] In fact, Peter Jones wonders if historians will in time be criticised for implying the poor dissembled and strategised to extract assistance. Jones, "'I cannot keep my place without being deascent'", 41.

[65] Patrick Dunne, born 1891, ordained 1913 and died 1988. J. A. Gaughan, *The Archbishops, Bishops and Priests who served in the Archdiocese of Dublin 1900–2011* (Dublin: Kingdom Books, 2012), p. 94.

[66] Thomas Harris O'Donnell, born 1893, ordained 1917 and died 1973. Gaughan, *The Archbishops, Bishops and Priests*, p. 219.

encounters with poverty.[67] This is effectively the approach advocated by Gestrich, King and Raphael who argue that there is no such thing as a 'clear cut poverty line in any given society, but that poverty takes place when a situation of penury combines with social practices of assistance and categorization'.[68] Thus, this book explores the letters written to the archbishop from the categorically impoverished, scraping together every source of income or relief and still failing to pay rent or secure adequate food, and letters from those who lived in 'nice homes' with good pensions, but through accepted social pressures required assistance to avoid losing their social status. These two criteria of need represent opposite ends of a broad spectrum of poverty; in the middle were the many, many families struggling with the daily hazards of life from bereavement to domestic violence, all requiring financial assistance of some kind.

Crudely, the hierarchy of those at risk of poverty ran something like: widows, mothers with large families with absent or unemployed fathers, children, the sick and single elderly women.[69] In fact, the Sick and Indigent Roomkeepers provided a revealing list of its main clients, in order of priority: widows with children, families in which the breadwinner is unemployed, invalids requiring extra nourishment, those in need of attire to seek employment and petty dealers in need of new stock.[70] While it was generally accepted that people were more susceptible to poverty at certain vulnerable phases of the life cycle, this too was highly gendered[71]: women were more exposed to such hardship by pregnancy, childbirth, while caring for young children, when faced with the loss of a spouse and in old age.[72] The idea that poverty's greatest victims were women and children was universally accepted and borne out by the figures on Home Assistance. In 1931 there were 77,474 people in receipt of Home Assistance; of these, 15,339 were men, 24,786 were women and 37,349 were children.[73] By the end of the decade (despite the

---

[67] R. Dyson, 'Who were the poor of Oxford of the late eighteenth and early nineteenth centuries?' in Gestrich, King and Raphael (eds.), *Being Poor in Modern Europe*, pp. 43–68.

[68] Gestrich, King and Raphael (eds.), *Being Poor in Modern Europe*, p. 31.

[69] The observation regarding widows' vulnerability to poverty is often made regarding other periods and places. See, for example, Boulton, 'It is extreme necessity that makes me do this', p. 53.

[70] D. Lindsay, *Dublin's Oldest Charity: The Sick and Indigent Roomkeepers Society, 1790–1990* (Dublin: The Anniversary Press, 1990), p. 81.

[71] S. Williams, *Poverty, Gender and Life-Cycle under the English Poor Law 1760–1834* (Woodbridge: Boydell Press, 2011).

[72] Dyson, 'Who were the poor of Oxford of the late eighteenth and early nineteenth centuries?' p. 50; S. Woolf, *The Poor in Western Europe in the Eighteenth and Nineteenth Centuries* (London and New York: Methuen, 1986), p. 3.

[73] *Department of Local Government and Public Health: First Report, 1930–31* (Dublin: The Stationary Office, 1932), p. 124.

introduction of more comprehensive Unemployment Assistance (1933) and a Widows' and Orphans' Pension (1935)), there were 89,511 on Home Assistance; of these, 19,791 were men, 29,120 women and 40,600 were children.[74] While men were by no means immune to poverty, they were less likely to be the primary carers of either children or elderly relatives and they had more social options at their disposal (like seasonal migration). Women with dependent children also constituted the majority of those who wrote to the Archbishop of Dublin seeking assistance, in fact, if you had no family it was often quite hard to be considered for charity or relief.[75] This is borne out by the profile of writers to the archbishop with one caveat: as the 1930s dawned the unemployed breadwinner began to feature more prominently in the charitable hierarchy of concern. This was both because of the introduction of the Widows' and Orphans' Pension in 1935 (in reality too small to stave off anything but the sharpest edge of need) and the deepening crisis of male unemployment. This shift is also reflected in applications to the Saint Vincent de Paul and the Sick and Indigent Roomkeepers.

The shame attached to the label 'poor' drove many people to hide their poverty and has resulted in a significant underestimation of those who were actually in need at any given time. Chapter 4 considers the correspondence of those who were in the process of 'becoming poor' or who had fallen temporarily from their relatively privileged perch in society. These people did not swell the statistical ranks of the poor. Instead, they struggled beneath the surface of Irish society, trapped by their own understandings of the stigma of being identified as poor. This tendency to hide their poverty has also skewed our historical understanding of poverty itself. It was often a much more transient experience than has been previously thought, touching people's lives temporarily or periodically.[76] Stuart Woolf noted in his study of the poor in Western Europe that sources imply a 'static state of being poor, which tends to ignore or mask the fluidity and gradualness of the process by which people decline,

---

[74] *Department of Local Government and Public Health: First Report, 1939–40* (Dublin: The Stationary Office, 1941), p. 72.

[75] This is a common finding across time and geography, for example, Boulton also found that the elderly and widows with children were most likely to receive assistance in eighteenth-century England. Boulton, '"It is extreme necessity that makes me do this"', 53; Dyson, 'Who were the poor of Oxford of the late Eighteenth and early Nineteenth Centuries?' p. 50; T. Sokoll, 'Old age in poverty: the record of Essex pauper letters, 1780–1834' in Hitchcock, King and Sharpe (eds.), *Chronicling Poverty*, pp. 127–154.

[76] Dyson raised these issues when arguing for a more holistic interpretation of poverty. See Dyson, 'Who were the poor of Oxford of the late eighteenth and early nineteenth centuries?' pp. 43–68.

sometimes more than once, into a condition of poverty.'[77] This idea of decline and the sense of the perpetual threat of poverty hanging over people's head permeated the letters written to the Archbishop of Dublin well into the twentieth century. While theirs was a relative poverty – relative to the profound and long-term deprivation of the slum dwellers – it was nonetheless real and altered, fundamentally, people's life choices resulting in considerable stress and mental anguish. This chapter considers the role ideas of character, charity, gender and social status played in the construction of these poverty stories. It also provides two detailed case studies – one of a solicitor's widow and the other of an erstwhile businessman struggling to regain his social and financial footing – in order to probe the construction of a middle-class narrative.

Conclusion

Olwen Hufton has argued that writing the history of the poor is 'predominantly a qualitative not a quantitative exercise'. She urged the social historian to consider evidence relating to how poverty was experienced, however 'fragmentary or impressionistic' it might be, and to make it the 'very heart of the matter'. If this was not done she warned that we could have no idea or understanding of 'the way the poor maintained their tenuous grip on life'.[78] In this study the letters and voices of the poor do not constitute the 'hidden underpinnings' of historical research, they are the focus of research.[79] By using the words of the poor to provide the narrative thrust, the book keeps the human element central, which is often lost when the framework of the history is policy and legislation. Thus this is in many senses a history of *mentalité* in which an understanding of behaviour, values and negotiation strategies of the poor take centre stage. While this study runs the risk of privileging 'the noisy poor' or those with the ability to write for charity,[80] it is a calculated risk and one based on a conviction that these letters, in their essence, represent many features of living in poverty in modern Ireland that were universal for much of the period. In many ways these letters allow us to create an alternative narrative of the history of Irish independence, one in which the lost and forgotten tell the story. This is a history of poverty written through the letters of the poor.

---

[77] Woolf, *The Poor in Western*, p. 4.
[78] Hufton, *The Poor of Eighteenth-Century France*, pp. 7–8.
[79] Earle, 'Introduction: letters, writers and the historian', p. 1.
[80] S. King, '"Stop this overwhelming torment of destiny": negotiating financial aid at times of sickness under the English Old Poor Law, 1800–1840', *Bulletin of the History of Medicine*, 79 (2005), 228–260, 239.

1 The Social Setting
'Is this a Civilized Country?'

Ireland endured a prolonged period of unrest from 1912 that involved a rising in 1916, a war of independence with Britain in 1919 and culminated in civil war between 1922 and 1923. Amid this chaos the Irish Free State was born in 1922 and began the task of asserting its legitimacy and reinstating law and order and rudimentary services of civil society and government.[1] The new Irish state was remarkably stable under the leadership of Cumann na nGaedheal until 1932 and then under Fianna Fáil until 1948.[2] Much hope and fear was vested in the birth of the state, however, the Professor of Philosophy at Maynooth College, Rev Peter Coffey, wasted his mental energy when he fretted that an independent Ireland would be guided by 'the voice of Irish Labour', which would result in the confiscation of the property of the bourgeoisie without due compensation: no such social reform occurred, quite the contrary.[3] The new Irish state, cheered on by the main churches, fortified the protection of private property for those who could afford it.[4] The interests of this class were protected (and furthered) while tight books were balanced, unforgiving ideology was cemented in legislation and limited welfare provision was pruned and depleted to survive the economic reality of political independence.

Mrs Paula C., X Talbot Place, Dublin, n.d. *c.* 1937. DDA, AB 7 CC, Box 7.

[1] The Irish Free State, established in 1922, equated to the same geographical area as the Republic of Ireland. The Free State existed until 1937, when the state became known as Éire and the Republic in 1949.

[2] Cumann na nGaedheal was founded in March 1923 and was made up of all those serving in the Provisional Government. Sinn Féin (the main political opposition, later to split resulting in the formation of Fianna Fáil in 1926) did not serve in either the Dáil or the Provisional Government after the Treaty vote of January 1922. Fianna Fáil, led by Eamon de Valera, entered the Dáil for the first time after the general election of 1927.

[3] Rev Peter Coffey, *The Social Question in Ireland* (Dublin: CTSI, 1919).

[4] R. Dunphy, *The Making of Fianna Fáil Power in Ireland, 1923–1948* (Oxford University Press, 1995).

'Apathy of citizens who lack confidence in the existing regime'

The highest price for the years of conflict and unrest was paid by the poorest in Irish society. The largest Catholic charity, the Society of the Saint Vincent de Paul's [hereafter Vincent de Paul] monthly bulletins recorded the deteriorating situation for certain vulnerable groups. In July 1918, its president noted that the increase in unemployment and prices throughout the country had brought many 'widowed charwomen' and large families 'below the poverty line'.[5] The early years of political independence only brought worse tidings. The closure of factories and companies that had catered for the demands of the British army had a significant impact on local areas.[6] In March 1922, for example, there was unrest in Wexford following the closure of Messrs Doyles' works and the Wexford Engineering Company and a massive reduction in staff at Messrs Pierces' works from 600 to 100.[7] The withdrawal of the British army from Buttevant Barracks in north county Cork had resulted in the need for emergency relief schemes to deal with the distress caused by the consequent unemployment.

On 6 March 1922, Rev John Godfrey c.c. wrote from Letterfrack in Galway to the Provisional Government: 'On behalf of the people of this parish of Ballinakill situate (sic) in Western Connemara on the shores of the Atlantic I wish to put before you a few painful facts so that you might put them before your Government.'[8] He spoke for a community that lived on dried fish and needed potato seed to plant their meagre bog land, but were told by those that administered poor relief 'there has been no grant so what can we do'. He lamented that many of the men in the area had had no work for the previous eighteen months and decried the paltry small-scale relief works as 'a poor joke'.[9] Godfrey also recorded a decline in the services available to help this community since independence. The Congested Districts Board had helped the fishing community to maintain their nets,[10] but it was no longer functioning and 'we think your Government which has acquired all the privileges of that old Board

---

[5] *Bulletin of the Society of St. Vincent De Paul*, 83 (July 1918), p. 207.

[6] 'Distress and unemployment in Saorstát generally', Department of an Taoiseach, S4278A, NAI. [hereafter S4278A].

[7] S4278A.

[8] Rev Godfrey, c.c., Letterfrack in Galway to the Secretary of the Provisional Government, City Hall, Dublin, 6 March 1922, S4278A.

[9] Ibid.

[10] Congested Districts Board was established in 1891 with the intention of improving agriculture and industry in areas of acute poverty, for example, along the west coast from Donegal to Cork. Eventually, the board operated in as much as one-third of the

should also take on some of its obligations & give to those poor fishermen a substantial help.' He was not just sketching a wretched situation; he was challenging a 'native' government to live up to the high expectations of many and not to 'treat these people as the alien Government which has gone, has done'.[11]

These accounts of the detrimental social impact of the revolutionary period and the realities of growing unemployment also reveal increased social tensions throughout the country as farmers, employers and the government pushed to reduce wages. In July 1923 the wages of Dublin dockers were cut by two shillings and the building workers, coalmen, carters, tradesmen, transport and manufacturing workers soon suffered the same fate.[12] On 27 October 1923, the fishermen and labourers of Tramore, County Waterford sent a petition: 'TO THE GOVERN-MENT OF THE IRISH FREE STATE seeking relief as a result of the distress caused by a lock-out initiated by the chief employer in the area.' They claimed the employer had tried to reduce wages although the cost of living in the district had greatly increased since the 'initiation of the Free State'.[13] Mr C. Ambrose, who wrote on behalf of the fishermen and boatmen as an honest broker, confirmed that there was a vicious dispute between agricultural labourers and the Farmers' Union: 'houses and haggards have been burnt where work was attempted – and as a retalia-tion...labourers' cottages have also been destroyed.' He believed the agricultural 'labourers [were] induced by the Transport Union to resist a reduction of wages', but he also pointed out that 'the farmers had organised things in such a way that v. few of the labourers will ever be taken back.' Tapping into pervasive social fears, Ambrose warned the Department of Fisheries that 'there will be, and are, many idle men, who are open to dangerous and evil courses that instigators around here are not slow to suggest.'[14] He urged the government to introduce relief work that would improve the harbour facilities for the fishermen and provide much needed employment and 'stop many from adopting the evil course

---

country. It was very popular with local people because of the amount of money it invested in local economies. The CDB wound up in 1923 following Irish independence. During its lifetime it invested considerable sums of money into the rural Irish economy. See, C. Breathnach, *The Congested Districts Board, 1891–1923* (Dublin: Four Courts Press, 2005), 73.

[11] Rev Godfrey to Secretary of the Provisional Government.
[12] Dunphy, *The Making of Fianna Fáil Power in Ireland*, p. 53.
[13] Petition from the Fishermen, Boatmen and Inhabitants of Tramore for a Grant in connection with the relief of unemployment to THE GOVERNMENT OF THE IRISH FREE STATE, 23 October 1923, S4278A.
[14] Mr C. Ambrose, Crobally, Tramore, [County Waterford] to the Minister for Fisheries, 27 October 1923, S4278A.

that outside influences are suggesting'.[15] Official discussions on the worsening situation generally accepted that unemployment and its bed-fellow poverty were on the increase, however, this was accompanied by an unwillingness to change policy and provide a 'dole'. This latter consideration was usually bolstered by oblique references to trouble-makers who were stoking the flames of discontent. Ambrose was raising a spectre of social unrest that was guaranteed to send a shiver down the official spine of government.

In November and December 1923, Charles Gordon Campbell,[16] sec-retary to the Department of Industry and Commerce, described the unemployment situation as 'rapidly becoming critical'.[17] He revealed that of the 39,000 workers in receipt of unemployment benefit, three-quarters would exhaust their entitlement by February 1924. The govern-ment was faced with a situation where 31,250 people would have neither work nor benefit. Nor did Campbell consider this figure an accurate reflection of the situation as it only included industrial workers. If demobilised men and agricultural workers were included, he calculated that 80,000 workers in the country would be without work or benefit 'and little or no prospect of any private employment'.[18] This he characterised in terms of its impact on national security rather than in terms of human distress – it was a 'serious, if not dangerous problem'. He was firmly against an extension of benefits and proffered relief works in the form of road and house building as the only option, but 'the main difficulty in each case is to ensure that the cost of the work to be carried out shall be reasonable and this primarily involves a considerable reduction in wages'.[19] He acknowledged that the 'cost of living has just risen ten points' and was 'higher than at any time since independent figures were published for the Free State'.[20] However, the only suggestion with regard to the anomalous situation of pushing for lower wages while acknowledg-ing the increasing cost of living was to recommend a bill to require

[15] Ibid.
[16] Gordon Campbell was the secretary to the Department of Industry and Commerce between 1922 and 1932. P. Dempsey, 'Charles Gorden Campbell' in J. McGuire and J. Quinn et al., The Dictionary of Irish Biography, Volume 2, (Cambridge University Press, 2009), pp. 281–282.
[17] 'Memo on the Unemployment position' resulting from a discussion with the Ministers of Finance and Agriculture to be placed on the Agenda of the Exe Council for consideration, signed Gordon Campbell, 10 December 1923, S4278A.
[18] Ibid.
[19] 'A memo prepared by Mr Gordon Campbell on the matter of unemployment during the coming winter', circulated by the secretary of the Minister of Industry and Commerce, 19 November 1923, S4278A.
[20] This admission appeared in the final draft of the very bleak and frank memo on unemployment for the winter of 1923/4, S4278A.

'retailers of the more important commodities of life to display their prices in their windows'.[21]

Nonetheless, Campbell had the malcontents in his sights: 'Disruptive elements profit by the situation in every way. When they are not given direct support, they gain by the apathy of citizens who lack confidence in the existing regime.'[22] All this despite the fact that he himself admitted that 'even if the road and housing schemes absorbed their max number of workers it would only be 20,000 combined.'[23] When ministers spoke of 'departure from normal policy' it was to consider stabilising building wages for twenty-four months.[24] Ultimately, they were forced to extend benefit in December 1923, to deal with the immediate need in the state. Nothing was certain – the state could still have failed, as Campbell recorded '[B]usiness is languishing; bank deposits are diminishing. The National trade balance is adverse. Taxation is high; public expenditure is necessarily heavy.'[25] Civil unrest coupled with widespread apathy with the new regime was a frightening prospect for these new ministers.

Úna Newell's study of 1920s Galway documents horrendous poverty along the western seaboard with famine-like conditions in parts of Connemara. These were exacerbated by particularly wet winters in 1923 and 1924, which reduced harvest and turf yields leading the medical health officer for the Clifden district to declare 'I have no hesitation in stating that at no time in my experience has poverty and unemployment been greater.'[26] By 1925 the government was called upon to deny reports in the American media of a famine in Connemara, this it had to do delicately not wishing to deter American donations.[27] It acknowledged that Cork, Kerry, Galway, Mayo, Donegal, Leitrim and Cavan were affected by a severe fuel shortage, but the government emphasised its relief measures. The *New York Evening World* was told that arrangements were 'nearly completed providing a daily meal for

---

[21] 'Memo on the Unemployment position', 10 December 1923.
[22] Final draft of Campbell memo 'Unemployment', December 1923, S4278A.   [23] Ibid.
[24] Memo of the Minister for Local Government concerning Roads and Housing, 26 November 1923, S4278A.
[25] Final draft of Campbell memo 'Unemployment', December 1923, S4278A.
[26] Ú. Newell, *The West Must Wait: County Galway and the Irish Free State, 1922–32* (Manchester University Press, 2015), p. 75; For contemporary accounts, see, for example, 'Numerous Black Spots – Chronic Poverty – Evils and Remedies for Them', *Irish Independent*, 2 February 1924; Pádraig Ua Dúbhthaigh, 'Immediate needs of the Gaeltacht – How the might be supplied', *Irish Independent*, 7 October 1924.
[27] Prof. Timothy A. Smiddy, Ireland's envoy to the United States, cabled the government on 30 January 1925: 'Papers here carry statement of famine in Connemara, Kerry and Fermanagh. Thousands imperilled. Crisis worse since 1847. Cable me promptly statement.' He was referring to *New York Evening World* and *Gaelic American*, S4278A.

18,000 children in Counties Galway, Donegal, and Kerry'.[28] Only four years later Peadar O'Donnell's book *Adrigoole*[29] dramatised the deaths in 1927 of a mother and two of her five children from fever and starvation in Adrigole in the Beara peninsula in Cork.[30] While not a famine, it was indicative of the private misery of thousands of impoverished families in the new state who lived on the verge of starvation and destitution. As Finola Kennedy noted: 'Absolute poverty persisted for decades after Independence' and semi-starvation remained commonly observed reality in Dublin city and elsewhere until at least the mid 1940s.[31]

In 1931 the Vincent de Paul characterised the previous ten years as a period during which 'the condition of those who are normally near the border-line of want had gradually become worse; unemployment insurance, which was intended to tide families over short spells of idleness, had in many cases lapsed altogether, and whole families were faced with practical starvation.'[32] Phil O'Keeffe, who grew up in the Liberties in Dublin, described the unemployment of the 1930s as a sudden event that caught her family off guard: 'Then without warning my father became unemployed due to economic recession. Unemployment was biting into every home, with sometimes fathers and sons in the same household losing their jobs.'[33] Her family had held its own until the recession, when it joined the ranks of the struggling poor. It is significant that O'Keeffe did not portray her family as part of the 'real poor', while the poor 'were part of everyday life...we edged away from their cold, raw figures as they stood beside us in the shops'.[34] While Seán O'Connor, who also grew up in inner city Dublin during the late 1930s and early 1940s, noted that his grandmother, who was a shopkeeper, did not

---

[28] The first report of the Department of Local Government and Public Health since independence (which covered the period 1922 to 1925) recorded the complete loss of the turf harvest of 1924 in these areas resulting in '[T]he conditions which prevailed towards the close of 1924 and the early months of 1925 were unparalleled for many years.' These areas were aided under the Fuel and School Meals Schemes. *Department of Local Government and Public Health: First Report, 1922–25* (Dublin: The Stationery Office, 1927), pp. 144–145.

[29] Peadar O'Donnell, *Adrigoole* (London: Jonathan Cape, 1929); A file prepared on this Sullivan tragedy for the Executive Council in April 1926 gives interesting insight into official anxiety to absolve the government of any blame. In this file everyone from the Sullivan family themselves to their neighbours are blamed. W. J. Gilligan, 'Statement on conditions in Adrigole' in UCDA: Fitzgerald Papers, P80/1081 DLG.

[30] For an eyewitness account see 'P. J. Doyle to the Editor', *Irish Examiner*, 1 April 1927.

[31] F. Kennedy, *Cottage to Crèche: Family Change in Ireland* (Dublin: Institute of Public Administration, 2001), p. 58.

[32] 'Supplement of Irish Conference, April 1931', *Bulletin of the Society of St. Vincent De Paul*, 96 (April 1931), p. 2.

[33] Phil O'Keeffe, *Down Cobbled Streets* (Dingle: Brandon Publishers, 1995), p. 28.

[34] Ibid., p. 119.

distinguish between the 'poor' and the working class: 'To her, the poor were the widowed, the unemployed and the sick, and the working classes were families where the man had employment but was always at risk of losing his job anyway. In that way the two categories were almost inter-changeable. The shopkeepers and the property owners were all well able to take care of themselves.'[35]

There was, however, considerable anecdotal evidence that those who could normally 'manage' were slipping into the unforgiving pit of pov-erty: the phrase 'people who had seen better days' began to emerge repeatedly in the charitable literature of the period as a growing new category of poverty. As Mrs Karen M., a widow from Cork wrote to Archbishop Byrne in the mid 1930s: 'I saw better days, its hard cruel world for some. better times may come soon please God.'[36] Of course, this form of poverty was not in fact new, but it was on the increase and served as a potent motif of the failing confidence in the possibilities of independence to improve the long-term (or even immediate) economic needs of the people of Ireland. By 1928, the Sick and Indigent Room-keepers' Society was reporting that 'the position was worse now than it was before the war. There was a wave of false economy in Dublin at present and people who were entitled to have assistance were not getting it.'[37] Throughout the country there were routine reports of starvation, for example, people existing in a state of 'protracted starvation' in Kerry,[38] or 'semi-starvation' in Leitrim[39] or generally living in a state of poverty incompatible with human dignity.[40] Not infrequently, this narrative was part of a story of failure since independence with one writer lamenting, for example, in 1938 that: 'Under the English regime everyone recog-nized that one of the greatest stigmas on its government was the wretched state of poverty ... and the passion to right this evil played no small part in inspiring the struggle which drove the English out. With fifteen years of native rule we still await the righting of this wrong.'[41] The ebb and flow of the begging letters to Archbishop Byrne certainly support the general lament among charities that poverty was increasing and the profile of those seeking charity was diversifying. In 1922, the first year of the

---

[35] Seán O'Connor, *Growing up so High: A Liberties Boyhood* (Dublin: Hachette Books Ireland, 2013), p. 92.
[36] Mrs Karen M., Convent Road, Doneraile, Co Cork, *c.* 1933. DDA, AB 7 CC, Box 4.
[37] 'Poverty in Dublin', *Irish Independent*, 2 May 1928.
[38] 'Poverty in Kerry – Protracted Starvation', *Irish Independent*, 13 November 1928.
[39] 'A Black Picture – Poverty in Leitrim', *Irish Independent*, 18 December 1929.
[40] 'Unholy Poverty', *Irish Press*, 16 December 1931.
[41] 'Poverty in Connemara', *Connacht Tribune*, 28 May 1938.

collection, a mere 46 letters were sent (or have survived); by the mid 1920s the annual number had risen to 160 letters and throughout the 1930s the figure never fell below 300.[42] In 1939, the final year of the collection, when the archbishop was dying and the world teetered on the precipice of war, 376 letters were saved, reflecting the deterioration in the barometers of wellbeing such as life expectancy, infant mortality and unemployment figures.[43]

'Our own poor'

Ironically, in view of the policy decisions taken in the first decade of independence, Irish officialdom engaged in a rhetorical appropriation of the country's poor: they became the symbol of an Irish determination to see the shadow of the coloniser banished. This is unsurprising in many ways, as Virginia Crossman has argued that from 1860s the poor relief system became a site of contestation. The Catholic Church used criticisms of the system to assert its claim over 'its poor', by arguing that the system did not cater for the needs of poor Catholics, often framing those objections in moral terms.[44] With the coming of Irish independence it was not the poor who had inherited the earth, but the Catholic middle class, which had been 'in waiting' for decades. In June 1923, the President of the Executive, William T. Cosgrave,[45] declared the treatment of the country's poor a benchmark of civilisation: 'It has been well and truly said that kindly care for the poor is the best sign of true civilization, and, again, that the condition of a nation's poor indicated the character of the national mind.' He proclaimed that 'With the coming of Freedom the people ... were quick to realise that at last it was in their power to end for ever the contemptuous treatment of the poor resulting from the workhouse system, and they set about inaugurating a new system with energy and zeal'. He hoped that through the 'Free State the new Schemes established for the better relief of the poor and the better care of the sick,

---

[42] 1934 was the only exception when the archbishop received 230 letters.
[43] M. E. Daly, 'Death and disease in independent Ireland, c. 1920–1970: A research agenda' in C. Cox and M. Luddy (eds.), *Cultures of Care in Irish Medical History, 1750–1970* (Basingstoke: Palgrave Macmillan, 2010), pp. 229 250.
[44] V. Crossman, '"Attending to the wants of poverty": Paul Cullen, the relief of poverty and the development of social welfare in Ireland' in D. Keogh and A. McDonnell (eds.), *Cardinal Paul Cullen and his World* (Dublin: Four Courts Press, 2012), pp. 146–165; V. Crossman, *Poverty and The Poor Law in Ireland, 1850–1914* (Liverpool University Press, 2013), pp. 168–197, p. 229.
[45] President of the Executive was the title for the Taoiseach (Prime Minister) of Ireland from 1922 until 1932. See, M. Laffan, *Judging W. T. Cosgrave: The Foundation of the Irish State* (Dublin: Royal Irish Academy, 2014).

will be administered prudently and humanely, and that these schemes will win for themselves the confidence of the people'.[46] The people whose confidence must be won were doubtless not the poor, but the ratepayers. In these pronouncements the integrity of Irish independence was expressed in simplistic terms that defined the old system of relief (that of the coloniser) as 'alien', 'unsympathetic' and 'wasteful'. In juxtaposition, the native system of relief would be 'humane', 'prudent' and 'discerning' to prevent 'fraud' and 'demoralizing' welfare.[47]

The first few reports emanating from the Department of Local Government and Public Health represent a self-conscious exercise in establishing the credentials and benefits of the new regime mingled with anxiety about the cost of its new ideology of compassion.[48] The old regime was characterised as indiscriminate by dumping all the poor in the workhouse and adding isolation and stigma to the burden of the 'respectable poor'. The first departmental report, which covered the 1922 to 1925 period, opened its section on 'poor relief' with the following explanation:

The Workhouse was the sole refuge of vagrants, and of the physical wreckage of the population, and being largely availed of by these classes came to be regarded with abhorrence by the respectable poor, amongst whom relief in a Workhouse carried with it an enduring stigma.[49]

However, the new regime introduced legislation in 1923 to remove restrictions on 'the respectable poor' who sought relief outside the workhouse and for this a new vocabulary was created: workhouses became much more benign sounding 'county homes' and 'outdoor relief' became 'home assistance'.[50] The report stressed the benefits of these changes was

---

[46] Cited in *Report of the Commission on the Relief of the Sick and Destitute Poor, including the Insane Poor* (Dublin, 1927), p. 18; Also cited in Joseph E. Canavan, S.J., 'The Poor Law Report', *Studies: An Irish Quarterly Review*, 16 (December 1927), p. 631.

[47] See the Department of Local Government and Public Health's description of the duties of the Superintendent Assistance Officers, who would adjudicate on home assistance cases, as someone 'experienced to give advice in doubtful or difficult cases, and while sympathetic in all cases of poverty and affliction, he must be capable of discerning easily the presence of fraud or deception, and where relief, if granted, would be unnecessary or demoralizing'; *Department of Local Government and Public Health: First Report, 1927–28* (Dublin: The Stationery Office, 1929), p. 87.

[48] D. Seán Lucey, '"These schemes will win for themselves the confidence of the people": Irish independence, Poor Law Reform and hospital provision', *Medical History*, 58 (January 2014), 44–64.

[49] *Department of Local Government and Public Health: First Report, 1922–25* (Dublin: The Stationery Office, 1927), p. 52.

[50] The Poor Law remained in operation in Dublin until 1929 with old outdoor relief and the workhouse. However, throughout the country, Cousins points out that significant reform of these county schemes was instituted by way of ministerial regulation in 1923; it

the facilitation of better discrimination: 'Respectable poor persons ... are not compelled as a condition of obtaining relief to separate themselves from friends and relatives and to associate with the objectionable types who frequented the workhouses.'[51] The implicit idea was that there was always a residue of people – 'the wreckage of the population' – but Irish authorities would endeavour not to confuse 'people in humble circumstances' with these 'wretches'.[52]

The poor were objectified into abstract categories of the 'worthy and unworthy', the 'deserving and undeserving',[53] 'the respectable and the incorrigibly idle', the 'shamefaced and the toucher'. These dichotomies of discrimination were not new, this 'vocabulary of poverty'[54] had a long international history,[55] but the new Irish state made the rigorous policing of these divisions a distinguishing characteristic of its more discriminating system. It argued that the old regime had offended the sensibilities of the 'genuine' Irish poor by failing to treat them differently to the 'unworthy', and worse, it had operated a system that 'demoralized' the poor. In 1924, during a debate about the cost of the old age pension, the Minister for Local Government, Séan Burke revealed how deep this view of 'false' charity ran:

the most serious defect of the Irish character is this tendency to dependence of one kind or another, and it is a very serious thing in the State at the present time. The number of people who lead a parasitic existence, more or less, is increasing in proportion to the number of people who are striving to make an honest living, and it is, therefore, not an easy thing to encourage thrift and providence. The country was brought to the verge of disaster by the famine in the 'forties of the last

---

defined eligibility for relief 'as any poor person who is unable by his own industry or other lawful means to provide for himself or his dependents the necessaries of life'. Local boards had considerable discretion and could, for example, insist that able-bodied recipients work for assistance. M. Cousins, *The Birth of Social Welfare in Ireland, 1922–1952* (Dublin: Four Courts Press, 2003), pp. 33–35.

[51] *Department of Local Government and Public Health: First Report, 1922–25* (Dublin: The Stationery Office, 1927), p. 64.

[52] Garraty has noted that the term 'residuum' emerged internationally in the 1890s to describe the long-term unemployed. J. A. Garraty, *Unemployment in History: Economic and Public Theory* (New York and London: Harper & Row, 1978), p. 128.

[53] Woolf noted that this categorisation emerged in the 15th century and 'was to condition all future attitudes to the poor'. S. Woolf, *The Poor in Western Europe in the Eighteenth and Nineteenth Centuries* (London and New York: Methuen, 1986), p. 18.

[54] O. Hufton, *The Poor of Eighteenth-Century France, 1750–1789* (Oxford University Press, 1974), p. 117.

[55] Peel argues that the old vocabulary of poverty, which was pervasive in Australia until the 1920s, took a considerable battering as a result of the large-scale poverty caused by the Great Depression. This new reality required different terminology to encapsulate its overwhelming pervasive quality. M. Peel, *Miss Cutler and the Case of the Resurrected Horse: Social Work and the Story of Poverty in America, Australia, and Britain* (The University of Chicago Press, 2012), p. 76.

century, and it was mainly as a result of charity continually distributed at the expense of the provident and thrifty, who continually decreased in proportion as the destitute and the dependent increased.[56]

The first minister responsible for the welfare of the Irish people after independence was willing to part with the deeply nursed conviction that the Great Famine (1845–50) had been caused by negligent British policy, to replace it with a narrative that blamed the Irish parasitic character as typified by the shiftless masses that lived on benefits and charity. While not everybody may have been willing to go this far, the view that generous welfare or charity was a fallacy was widely shared, as was the suspicion that the shiftless, thriftless poor existed and disguised themselves as the 'genuine' poor.[57] These 'parasitic people' were never identified in this discourse; they hid among the statistics (that were always growing) and justified a default policy of suspicion and miserly assistance. The fact that Burke felt comfortable and justified in casting aspirations over the integrity of all those living on state welfare, even old age pensioners, although all public officials and all governmental committees and commissions recorded that real unemployment was growing, is indicative of the depth of the cultural ambivalence towards the dependent. Of course, this rhetoric was very difficult to counteract – even if there had been the will to do so – because who was going to raise their voice in defence of people portrayed as existing at the expense of not just the state but also the truly vulnerable? This sort of talk helped to silence any alternative call for compassion; the only thing imaginative contemporaries could do was attempt to refocus the debate on the 'worthy' poor.

While the semantics of poverty remained so important to the spirit and intent of the welfare system after independence, it continued to be ill defined, deeply coded and shut off to those it named and described. The assumption throughout all the literature was that those who needed to, understood this terminology. Therein lay its brutal power; it was the vernacular of the privileged and it set the agenda of judgement its subjects could not control, often forcing them to accept its prejudices and adopt its values. Thus the poor engaged in the very semantic web

---

[56] Minister for Local Government, Mr Burke, 'The Adjournment – Old Age Pension Cases', *Dáil Debates*, 25 June 1924, vol. 7, col. 3054–3056. Cousins argues these kinds of comments were 'characteristic of their views and not unrepresentative comments'. Cousins, *The Birth of Social Welfare in Ireland*, p. 55.

[57] Sarah-Anne Buckley observed that in the pre-independence period, nationalist women were perceptive enough to associate poverty and poor housing and espoused a version of reform that would 'help the poor to help themselves', but still cautioned against the harm of 'indiscriminate charity'. S. Buckley, *The Cruelty Man: Child Welfare, the NSPCC and the State in Ireland, 1889–1956* (Manchester University Press, 2013), pp. 93–94.

that ensnared them describing themselves as thrifty, genuine and grateful, in order to be heard and found deserving. The lack of coherent definitions also allowed the skill of discernment (which was in fact *ad hoc* and subjective) control the destiny of each individual applicant seeking relief or charity. For the poor there was neither strength in numbers – one was always undistinguished in the generalisations about the 'feckless' – nor comfort in personal integrity – one had to constantly prove and remake oneself depending on who controlled the purse strings.

Irish independence did not change the language or spirit of welfare and charity, nor did it remove the deep contradictions in discussions about the poor and the nature and extent of relief measures.

In March 1925, the Commission on the Relief of the Sick and Destitute Poor, including the Insane Poor, was established with the 'object of devising permanent legislation for the effective and economical relief of the sick and destitute poor'. The final report displayed the profound ambivalence of the contemporary response to the poor. This is hardly surprising as the commission was made up of representatives from the main religions, charities and from the parliament and senate; furthermore it held thirty-two public sessions and heard testimony from 180 witnesses.[58] The report congratulated the government for dismantling the old workhouse system, while in fact revealing that most of the new county homes were the old workhouses (physically the same buildings) and were 'not fit and proper places for the reception of the various classes' found in them.[59] In the context of saving on Home Assistance, it recommended a work test, which could be as effective 'a test of their need as the workhouse was intended to be'.[60] Thus, while the stated intention of the new welfare system was to move away from the workhouse and its stigma, the main authorities of that new system rapidly sought to reincorporate the 'workhouse test' element, embedding its principle of distrust in the heart of the new system. It acknowledged (and accepted) the many complaints from witnesses that the new system had resulted in 'great extravagance and that the cost of Home Assistance was [now] altogether excessive'.[61] The report recommended rigorous investigation. Yet only three pages later it outlined the paltry sums paid to various groups on Home Assistance acknowledging that:

---

[58] The members were the Right Rev. Mon. Dune, P. P.; Sir Joseph Glynn, Dr Thomas Hennessy T.D.; Senator Sir John Keane, Bt.; Rev. M. E. Murphy, Major J. Myles T.D., Sen. Mrs Wyse-Power, Padraig Ó Siochfhradha.

[59] *Report of the Commission on the Relief of the Sick and Destitute Poor*, p. 124.

[60] Ibid., p. 54.   [61] Ibid., p. 53.

An analysis of the amounts allowed shows that the assistance granted can only be looked on as a supplement to other means or to what can be got by begging and from charitable sources, and we fear that in many cases it is altogether inadequate to provide the necessaries of life.[62]

While the Department of Local Government and Public Health claimed that the move from the workhouse to a system of providing outdoor assistance through the Home Assistance payment was a 'striking feature' of its new policy,[63] the origins of this shift lay in the previous 'alien regime'. Crossman notes that by 'the end of the nineteenth century outdoor relief had become a means of relieving poverty rather than destitution.'[64] Undoubtedly, the shift was finalised during the transition to independence as official figures clearly demonstrate: in 1913–14 14,663 people received outdoor relief while 26,791 were accommodated in the various institutional outlets (workhouses and hospitals); in 1924–25 21,650 people were in receipt of Home Assistance, while 18,113 people were in institutional care.[65] However, the new government did not hesitate long before fretting over the growing cost of Home Assistance, which had increased from £113,651 to £372,654.[66] In this regard the department noted that it was supported by the report of the Commission on the Relief of the Sick, which had noted that the payment was 'a form of relief which is peculiarly subject to abuse, [and] must give rise to misgiving'. However, it did not reiterate the commission's concerns that the amounts paid in Home Assistance were insufficient to live on and that the new boards of health, while 'perhaps acting with more liberality than their predecessors, still fall short of discharging their full obligations in regard to persons eligible for relief who cannot be sent to institutions'.[67]

'I am striving to live on the old age Pension'

As the new state wished to consciously mark itself as more compassionate than the 'old regime', it seems fair to ask what it did to other relief

---

[62] Ibid., p. 56.

[63] *Department of Local Government and Public Health: First Report, 1922–25* (Dublin: The Stationery Office, 1927), p. 69.

[64] Crossman noted that the numbers in receipt of outdoor relief in Ireland were low when compared to England: at the beginning of the 1870s, 24 per cent of those on relief received outdoor relief compared to 85 per cent in England. V. Crossman, 'The humanizing of the Irish Poor Laws: Reassessing developments in social welfare in post-Famine Ireland' in A. Gestrich, S. King and L. Raphael (eds.), *Being Poor in Modern Europe: Historical Perspectives 1800–1940* (Switzerland: Peter Lang, 2006), pp. 229–249, p. 231.

[65] *Department of Local Government and Public Health: First Report, 1922–25*, p. 69.

[66] Ibid.   [67] *Report of the Commission on the Relief of the Sick and Destitute Poor*, p. 59.

legacies it inherited. The Old Age Pension, introduced in Britain and Ireland in 1908, was particularly beneficial to Ireland: it was non-contributory, means tested and the rate payable was uniform across the United Kingdom. Hence, Ireland's lower cost of living and higher level of poverty meant more elderly Irish people qualified for a payment that went further in Ireland than in any other part of the Kingdom.[68] Furthermore, because of Ireland's high rate of emigration, the country had, proportionately speaking, a larger elderly population, which meant this cash injection into the Irish economy (particularly the family economy) had a much greater impact than elsewhere.[69] Perhaps in the long run the greatest importance of the Old Age Pension in Ireland was the principle of redistributing the risks of old age on to the whole community by a tax-funded benefit. It also disproportionately benefitted women, who tended to be poverty's greatest victims.[70] Finally, Timothy Guinnane has argued that as a result of the pension, fewer elderly people were reliant on the Poor Law and they were thus more likely to live with their extended family or indeed alone.[71] For many elderly people in Ireland, however, there was often a long decade to wait when age-related debility increased, before qualifying for the pension. In 1937, Mr Jake H. wrote to the archbishop from Bantry in Cork to explain he was 'very badly off and near 70 years'. He needed a few shillings towards a £12 debt and was fearful he faced prison: 'I am not out for any frauding but I am hard up through no fault of my own'.[72] Furthermore, with relatively uncontrolled fertility, many Irish parents in their late fifties and early sixties were still responsible for young children. Contemporary policy makers were aware of the correlation between a husband's occupation and his wife's fertility: the less a man earned the more children he sired. Furthermore, there was concrete evidence emerging that each child after the third increased the risk of poverty for these families.[73]

---

[68] Cousins, *The Birth of Welfare in Ireland*, p. 18–19.
[69] The proportion of pensions was 4.62 per cent compared to 1.85 per cent in England and Wales. Cousins, *The Birth of Welfare in Ireland*, pp. 18–19; C. Ó Gráda, '"The greatest blessing of all": The Old Age Pension in Ireland', *Past and Present*, 175 (2002), 124–161, 129.
[70] Cousins, *The Birth of Welfare in Ireland*, p. 28.
[71] T. Guinnane, 'The Poor Law and the Pension in Ireland', *Journal of Interdisciplinary History*, 24 (1993), 271–91. Ó Gráda concurs that the old age pension was 'of paramount importance' in reducing the number of elderly people entering the workhouse. Ó Gráda, '"The greatest blessing of all"', 147.
[72] Jake H., Adrigole, Bantry, Co. Cork, 31 July 1937. DDA, AB 7 CC, Box 6.
[73] M. E. Daly, 'Marriage, fertility and women's lives in the twentieth-century Ireland', *Women's History Review*, 15 (2006), 571–585; M. E. Daly, 'The Irish family since the Famine: continuity and change', *Irish Journal of Feminist Studies*, 3 (1999), 1–21.

The Old Age Pension was a costly inheritance for the new Irish government and when, in 1922, the Cumann na nGaedheal government began its course of retrenchment it was firmly in its sights. In 1924, the pension was cut by 1s. per week, reducing the pension from 10s. to 9s. per week, and the means test was altered resulting in reductions of up to 4s. a week in many cases. The impact of these measures was quite significant: spending on pensions fell from 3.2 million to 2.6 million between 1924 and 1926, the average pension dropped from 9s.8d. to 8s.7d. per week, and the proportion of those who qualified for the pension dropped from 76 per cent to 66 per cent of the population.[74] To place these weekly pensions in context: in 1930, a top civil servant earned £1,500 per annum, while the average civil service salary was £179 a year, the average industrial wage was £126 per annum, whereas a casual labourer could expect to get 6s. a day in urban areas and as little as 15s. a week in rural areas (and of course the work was not guaranteed or consistent).[75] Many pensioners were in a position familiar to Mrs E. C. of Dublin's slums, who wrote in the mid 1930s to Archbishop Byrne: 'I am striving to live on the old age Pension I would be very Thankful if you could assist me to buy some Tread so I might earn a few shillings making socks & sewing.'[76] Elderly people in debt or unable to make ends meet continued to feature prominently in charity narratives. However, despite the cost-of-living increasing by almost two-thirds between 1932 and 1942, the maximum pension remained 10s.[77] It was clear that the government had little interest in the principle of redistributing wealth via the tax system; during its tenure, the Cumann na nGaedheal government reduced income tax from 25 to 15 per cent.[78] By 1932, when many of Cumann na nGaedheal's policies had taken effect, *if* people in Ireland paid tax, they paid on average 6 per cent of their gross income.[79] Mel Cousins is damning about the treatment of Irish pensioners claiming that there 'can be little doubt that leading politicians attempted to "pauperise" pensioners – as they were clearly

---

[74] Cousins, *The Birth of Welfare in Ireland*, pp. 31–32.

[75] T. Farmar, *Privileged Lives: A Social History of Middle-Class Ireland, 1882–1989* (Dublin: A. & A. Farmar, 2010), p. 134; F. Kennedy, *Cottage to Crèche*, p. 60.

[76] Mrs E. C., X Foley St., Dublin City, 15 December 1935. DDA, AB 7 CC, Box 6.

[77] Cousins, *The Birth of Welfare in Ireland*, p. 97. In 1932, the Fianna Fáil government increased spending on the pension and extended entitlement to the pension. Ó Gráda, '"The greatest blessing of all"', 158, 161.

[78] Ibid. , 133; Powell points out that income tax was almost halved with a reduction from 5s. to 3s. and between 1923 and 1927 expenditure was cut from £28.7 million to £18.9 million. F. W. Powell, *The Politics of Irish Social Policy, 1600–1990* (Lampeter: The Edwin Mellen Press, 1992), p. 166.

[79] Farmar, *Privileged Lives*, p.124.

convinced that large numbers were 'undeserving'.[80] Similarly, J. J. Lee argues that Cumann na nGaedheal 'took the view that the poor were responsible for their poverty'.[81] It is hard to disagree with either; the President of the Executive's generous annual salary of £2,500 was not reduced until de Valera became Taoiseach, when it was cut to (a still handsome) £1,500.[82]

Widows: '[I]t is hard cruel world for those, whom God has bereft of their "Bread-winners"'

Next to the question of old age, widowhood was the biggest challenge to the *laissez faire* principles in vogue in the early twentieth century. Widows exposed the weaknesses of a system that was based on the ideal of the male breadwinner and stay-at-home mother because in her case fate, rather than what could be deemed as any personal failing, had broken the model arrangement. It was more straightforward for society to accept that the widow was blameless in her downfall. She was often favourably juxtaposed with the unmarried mother, who was regarded as guilty through moral failure for her poverty.[83] Thus there was a social sense that widows should engender the rightful protection of society and, ultimately, the state. Few would have disagreed with Mrs Lillie F., who had been left a widowed mother of three children, when she wrote to Archbishop Byrne in 1925 that '[I]t is hard cruel world for those, whom God has bereft of their "Bread-winners".' She, like so many other widows in and beyond Ireland,[84] was 'sorely depending on one lodger' and the hope that one of her daughters would secure a job, and she explained it was 'impossible for us to live, under these circumstances'.[85] However, as there was no widows' pension, Lillie F., like the thousands of other widows, simply had to 'parade their poverty'[86] every week in order to receive, frequently inadequate, Home Assistance. In June 1928, there

---

[80] Cousins, *The Birth of Welfare in Ireland*, p. 52.

[81] J. J. Lee, *Ireland, 1912–1985: Politics and Society* (Cambridge University Press, 1989), p. 124.

[82] T. Farmar, *Privileged Lives*, p. 172.

[83] L. Earner-Byrne, *Mother and Child: Maternity and child welfare in Dublin, 1922–60* (Manchester University Press, 2007), pp. 172–220.

[84] B. Stadum, *Poor Women and their Families: Hard Working Charity Cases, 1900–1930* (Albany: State University of New York Press, 1992), p. 55.

[85] Mrs Lillie F., X Booterstown Avenue, Blackrock, Co. Dublin, 2 February 1925. DDA, AB 7 CC, Box 1.

[86] *Report of the Commission on the Relief of the Sick and Destitute Poor*, p. 57.

were 6,973 widows in receipt of Home Assistance and of those 3,806 had dependent children.[87]

Since the earliest discussions on widows' pensions, the focus was on widowed mothers, there were no social qualms that widows without children should forgo their domestic calling and become self-supporting: patriarchy had its limits.[88] Patrick J. Dunne, the honorary secretary of the Irish Mothers' Pension Society, had quite consciously addressed the new 'Patriot Parliament' in 1922 regarding its responsibility for the 'deserving poor'. By the late 1920s his patience appeared to be fading and his pamphlet entitled *Waiting the Verdict: Pension or Pauperism: Necessitous Widows and Orphans in the Free State* implied that the new Irish government was in the dock and the verdict hinged on how widows would be treated. Dunne portrayed widowed mothers as a 'deserving' cohort for state assistance, arguing that in the absence of the father the state should become 'the custodian of necessitous women and children'.[89] In Ireland, the anxiety to provide some form of statutory welfare for widowed mothers was driven by a desire to protect the social ideal of stay-at-home mothers and to ensure that 'fatherless children' did not end up in institutional care. As Dunne pointed out 'humanity and economy…point to the moral': it was cheaper to keep these children in their mother's care than pay for them in state care. According to the 1926 census report 48,181 or 5.6 per cent of children were dependent on widows.[90]

It was Fianna Fáil that introduced the Widows' and Orphans' Pensions Act in 1935, ten years after the British equivalent; it was informed by the moral and patriarchal concerns that had driven the debate about widows' welfare for a hundred years as the act only dealt with widows deemed deserving in moral and social terms.[91] There were two schemes: a contributory pension and a non-contributory pension. Irish widows qualified for this pension on the basis of either their husband's contributions or their motherhood and poverty. Ironically, the goal of the

---

[87] *Department of Local Government and Public Health, 1928–29* (Dublin: The Stationery Office, 1930), p. 111.

[88] This argument is fully developed in L. Earner-Byrne, '"Parading their poverty": Widows in twentieth-century Ireland' in B. Faragó and M. Sullivan (eds.), *Facing the Other: Interdisciplinary Studies on Race, Gender and Social Justice in Ireland* (Cambridge Scholars Publishing, 2008), pp. 32–46.

[89] P. Dunne, *Waiting the Verdict: Pension or Pauperism: Necessitous Widows and Orphans in the Free State* (Dublin, n.d. *c.* 1930), p. 195.

[90] Chapter 10, Dependency, *Census of Population, General Report, 1926, Vol. X* (Dublin: Stationery Office, 1934), p. 146.

[91] N. W. Hancock, 'On the importance of substituting the family system or rearing orphan children for the system now pursued in our workhouses', *Dublin Statistical Society*, 8 (January 1859), 16.

campaigners was not achieved with this legislation because the amount paid was so small that the numbers of widows on Home Assistance continued to increase. Máirín Johnston, whose mother was a widow, summed up the impact of the widows' pension thus: 'It was no bonanza, but it was a step in the right direction. The pension was means-tested and every so often an inspector would call to question my mother on any other income. One of the questions which always amused us was "Have you any land?" which seemed superfluous and we living in a dog-box.'[92] Johnston's mother, who dreaded the invasion that the visits and questions of the various agents of charity and welfare represented, was still subjected to the process after the widows' pension was introduced. While her mother found the question about land somewhat ridiculous when posed to a Dublin tenement dweller, it was a reference to the fact that widows living on holdings worth more than £8 were ineligible for the pension, meaning many of them lived in poverty.[93] Hence the widow and her cow was a common rural story found in this letter collection. Either a widow feared having to sell the only cow to make ends meet, thus losing a vital source of milk and revenue, or her cow had died and she needed funds to procure another one.[94] Ultimately, she represented the rural poverty trap – she did not qualify for assistance because of her field and her cow, but neither supplied her or her children with all the necessaries of survival.

Housing: '[T]he kernel of the great nut that has to be split'

Since the nineteenth century, contemporaries had accepted that poverty and poor housing were synonymous and many were relatively comfortable professing on the resultant evils to moral and physical health.[95] However, a solution was more difficult to settle on as long as the cherished ideology of self-sufficiency was maintained.[96] From the

[92] M. Johnston, *Around the Banks of Pimlico* (Dublin: Attic Press, 1985), p. 62.
[93] See, *Seanad Éireann*, vol. 22, col. 1119, 8 March 1939. [Debates in the second house of the Irish parliament.]
[94] See, 'Poverty in Erris – A Diet of Potatoes and Sweetened Water', *Irish Independent*, 21 October 1927.
[95] See, for example, S. Shannon Millin, Esq., 'Slums: A sociological retrospect of the city of Dublin', *Journal of the Statistical and Social Inquiry Society of Ireland* [hereafter *JSSISI*], 13 (December 1914), 130–159; D. S. Doyle, Esq., LL.B., [Assistant Registrar-General], 'Housing' *JSSISI*, (December 1915), 255–268; J. E. Canavan, 'Slum clearance in Dublin', *JSSISI*, 16 (1937), 21–32; C. O'Connell, *The State and Housing in Ireland: Ideology, Policy and Practice* (New York: Nova Science Publishers, 2007), pp. 17–27.
[96] C. P. Cowen's piece on the housing situation written in 1918 provides a classic example of this contemporary anxiety. He was quite compassionate regarding the negative impact of poor housing, though he blamed a portion of the poor for this due to 'bad habits',

1914 housing enquiry to the first census of the Free State in 1926, the poor state of housing, particularly in Dublin's inner city slums, was accepted, lamented and largely left to fester. The early stages of independence induced fervent optimism, of which J. Maguire's call to arms was typical: 'Let Irishmen and Irishwomen therefore, in God's Name, concentrate on this question of Housing, which will require for its proper solution all the good sense, ability, intelligence and patriotism this little island can command.'[97] However, when he referred to what a 'working man' could afford in rent, he estimated his salary to be £3 a week, but there were few city or rural labourers on as much and those who were under or unemployed stood no chance of paying rent.[98] Kennedy has noted that the average industrial wage was £126 per annum, in other words, less than £3 a week. Furthermore, from the mid 1920s to the mid 1940s real wages scarcely rose at all.[99] While, the Dublin Housing Survey of 1939 revealed that 20 per cent of families in Dublin and 22 per cent in Cork survived on incomes of less than 20/- per week. For most people who depended on charity and welfare the sums did not add up to a viable existence. This was the essential nub of the problem: those living in the worst housing conditions could simply not afford to pay the rent of newer builds (however meagre) and contemporaries could not contemplate a system that would fund their housing in any other way. Throughout the 1920s working-class wages were falling and between 1931 and 1935 the average weekly wage for agricultural labourers, over the age of twenty-one with no rent allowance, was only 21 shillings and 3 pence.[100] Richard Dunphy cites a report submitted to the Minister for Local Government for the period 1920–25 that revealed that 20 per cent of all rents due in the state were in arrears.[101]

The 1926 census clearly outlined the social background to the housing issue:

---

he was still drawn to the example of Liverpool where the slum dwellers had been rehoused despite the 'great burden on the rate payers'. C. P. Cowan, *The Difficulties of the Housing Problem and Some Attempts to Solve it* (Dublin: n.d. c. 1916).

[97] J. Maguire, B.L., 'The housing problem in Ireland and Great Britain and the essentials of its solution', *JSSISI*, 14 (1925), 47–60, 49.

[98] Prunty also argued that the problem of the 'grossly inadequate and insecure incomes, at the heart of the grinding slum problem' confounded contemporaries. J. Prunty, *Dublin Slums 1800–1925: A Study in Urban Geography* (Dublin: Irish Academic Press, 1998), p. 149, p. 337. O'Connell, *The State and Housing in Ireland*, p. 36.

[99] Kennedy, *Cottage to Crèche*, p. 53; C. Ó Gráda, 'The rise in living standards' in K. A. Kennedy (ed.), *From Famine to Feast: Economic and Social Change in Ireland 1847–1997* (Dublin: Institute of Public Administration, 1998), pp. 12–22.

[100] Dunphy, *The Making of Fianna Fáil Power in Ireland*, p. 99.   [101] Ibid., p. 58.

most of the population live in three-room dwellings. This is true of each size of family, from those with only two persons to those with 11 persons. The size of the dwelling is, of course, mainly determined by social status, and not by the numbers in the family. More than a quarter of the population live in three-room dwellings, two-thirds live in two, three or four-room dwellings.[102]

Accepting the international measurement of overcrowding as more than two persons per room, the report noted that 75.2 per cent of those in one-room dwellings existed in overcrowded circumstances, as did 59.3 per cent of those in two room dwellings. There were 22,915 families in the state living in one-room dwellings.[103] According to the census, Drogheda, a town of moderate size and comparatively bad housing, had 32.7 per cent of its population in overcrowded dwellings, whereas in Dublin city the percentage was 45.3. There was some consolation to be found in the fact that Scotland remained more overcrowded than Ireland, however nothing but shame when the same inquiry was made of England or Northern Ireland: 27.7 per cent of the population of the Free State lived in overcrowded conditions; in Scotland the percentage was 43.3; whereas in Northern Ireland, Wales and England the percentages dropped to 18.1, 7.2 and 9.8 respectively.[104] Furthermore, when the figures were examined according to family size Ireland slipped further in the rankings; the larger the family in Dublin city the more overcrowded they were even compared to Glasgow.[105]

Dublin, the acknowledged heart of deprivation, remained the Cinderella of official concern, in a similar way that so many of those in need were judged responsible for their own plight Dublin was somehow guilty and rarely prioritised for relief funds.[106] As Cathal O'Connell has argued, 'building the national home would remain a decidedly rural affair and housing policies pursued throughout the subsequent decade [1920] explicitly avoided addressing the housing needs of the urban poor...on the grounds that the new state could not afford to build for the very

---

[102] Chapter 5: 'Housing', *Census of Population, General Reports, 1926, Vol. X* (Dublin: Stationery Office, 1934), p. 58.
[103] Ibid., p. 59.   [104] Ibid., p. 61.
[105] In Dublin city 23.4 per cent of people lived four per room, whereas in Glasgow the rate was 19.6 per cent. Ibid., p. 61.
[106] M. Daly, *Slow Failure: Population Decline and Independent Ireland* (University of Wisconsin Press, 2006), pp. 47–50; Daly has noted that this bias continued into the 1950s. M. Daly, *The Buffer State: The Historical Roots of the Department of the Environment* (Dublin: Institute of Public Administration, 1997), pp. 336–337. Dickson notes this attitude to Dublin was based on a sense of it being 'really a foreign town'. D. Dickson, *Dublin: The Making of a Capital City* (London: Profile Books, 2014), p. 479.

poor'.[107] Within Dublin city overcrowding was commonplace, but the worst and most dangerous tenements were concentrated in the north of the city in Dominick Street, Summerhill, Mountjoy, Sean MacDermott Street and the southside, around Aungier Street and in the Liberties.[108] In its final report, published in 1927, the Committee on the Relief of Unemployment observed that more people lived in Dublin's slums than in 1913.[109] The committee was under no illusions about the consequences of these housing conditions, but it was dubious about the moral sensibilities of the Irish public, or rather, the taxpayer:

We think that the taxpayer and the ratepayer have so far failed to realise that they are paying a great deal more in respect of sickness and disease arising from defective waterworks or sewerage systems in their immediate neighbourhood than would be the case if the much needed improvements were carried out.[110]

However, of 2,090 houses built with government funding between 1922 and 1926, only 947 had been constructed in Dublin city.[111] Furthermore, Ruth McManus argues that Dublin Corporation effectively turned its 'back on the most needy members of society', by concentrating on subsidising houses built for tenant purchase.[112] Significantly, for a society that valorised the large family and prohibited birth control unequivocally since 1935, the worst housed were young families.[113] Even in newer developments like Cabra in Dublin, one-third of the people lived in overcrowded conditions[114] – a clear indicator of the connection between poverty, high fertility rates and poor housing. The 1926 census report openly acknowledged that the negligence with regard to Dublin's housing crisis had deadly consequences[115]: in north Dublin city, where

---

[107] O'Connell puts numbers on this discrimination noting that of 60,000 houses built between 1880 and 1932 with state aid, only 17,000 were in urban areas and an even smaller number of these were directed towards the poorest working class households. O'Connell, *The State and Housing in Ireland*, p. 19, p. 24.

[108] J. Brady, *Dublin, 1930–1950: The Emergence of the Modern City* (Dublin: Four Courts Press, 2014), p. 48.

[109] In 1913 there had been 73,973, while in 1926 there were 78,934. *Committee on the Relief of Unemployment, 1927: Final Report* (Dublin, 1928), p. 6.

[110] *Committee on the Relief of Unemployment*, p. 10.   [111] Ibid., p. 5.

[112] R. McManus, *Dublin, 1910–1940: Shaping the City & Suburbs* (Dublin: Four Courts, 2002), p. 126.

[113] Chapter 5: 'Housing', *Census of Population, General Report, Volume X, 1926*, p. 69. For a good discussion see, S. McAvoy, '"Perpetual nightmare": Women, fertility control, the Irish state, and the 1935 ban on contraceptives' in M. H. Preston and M. Ó hÓgartaigh (eds.), *Gender and Medicine in Ireland, 1700–1950* (New York: Syracuse University Press, 2012), pp. 189–202.

[114] Brady, *Dublin, 1930–1950*, p. 51.

[115] O'Connell points out that the association between poor housing and increased mortality was consistently made in all official inquiries since the *Royal Commission of*

the percentage of two or more people living per room was 63.4 per cent, the infant mortality rate was 170 per 1,000 births; in Blackrock, where the proportion of the population living in one room was 16 per cent or Clontarf and Howth, where it was 9.6 per cent, the corresponding infant death rates fell to 84 per 1,000 and to 79 per 1,000, respectively.[116] This negative death differential continued at all ages: the badly housed – the poor – had higher mortality rates in all age cohorts.[117] Úna Newell confirms that primitive housing in the west of Ireland also often impaired the health of inhabitants noting housing 'was inferior except in the case of a few newly built cottages, the priest's house, the doctor's house and the teacher's house'.[118] In Connemara, on the west coast, witnesses testified to the fact that large families frequently shared small mud cabins with their sick relatives and fowl. The shortage of decent housing was equally a problem in Galway city, where many rural dwellers migrated through-out the 1920s and 1930s in search of work. In 1930 the inhabitants of the tenements of Middle Street in the city centre were removed on the basis that the buildings were dangerous.[119]

It was during the Fianna Fáil government that the idea of slum clear-ance was re-energised to some degree with the introduction of the Housing (Financial and Miscellaneous Provisions) Act, 1932.[120] Under this act Dublin Corporation began slum clearance that led to vast working-class housing estates in the southern suburban district of Crumlin. However, these housing estates contained the seeds of new problems: many of the tenants could not afford the high rents charged or the increased costs of transport and suffered from a new isolation away from the familiar slum networks of the city. In the 1930s, Elaine Crowley's family was given a corporation house because of her father's health, she recalled:

Living in the new house became expensive compared to living in the street. Everything bought in the local shops cost more. The loan for the removal van was being paid back. The minimum furnishing of four rooms, then lighting and heating them swallowed up my father's wages. In bad weather there were bus-fares as well. And in emergencies no-one to borrow a loan from until the weekend.[121]

Inquiry into the System of Sewerage and Drainage in the City of Dublin (1880). O'Connell, *The State and Housing in Ireland*, pp. 8–11.

[116] Chapter 5: 'Housing', *Census of Population, General Report, Volume X, 1926*, p.70.

[117] Ibid.   [118] Newell, *The West Must Wait*, p. 82.   [119] Ibid., p. 83.

[120] Daly has noted that Fianna Fáil increased housing subsidies from 40 to 66.6 per cent for slum clearance housing and 15 to 33.3 per cent for other Local Authority housing. Daly, *The Buffer State*, p. 220.

[121] E. Crowley, *Cowslips and Chainies: A Memoir of Dublin in the 1930s* (Dublin: Lilliput Press, 1996), p. 119.

The Vincent de Paul also noted the added challenges of assisting its 'adopted families' who were relocated out to these new suburbs.[122] While McManus argues that much of the criticism of the lack of facilities in these estates was unjustified, she points out that the 'Corporation's policy of placing the lowest rent paying poor in central flats increased social segregation'.[123]

Although in 1935, the Dublin city manager seemed confident that he was 'shortly about to attack the kernel of the great nut that has to be split and that is how you are going to house the man who has no money at all',[124] it appears that circle was not squared or the nut cracked.[125] While the housing programme of the thirties was an achievement in comparison to what had gone before, it barely scratched the surface; and of the 99,000 houses built under the act, 56,000 were constructed for private ownership.[126] Furthermore, the act did not overcome the central problem of affordability. In February 1935, Mr James E. wrote to the archbishop to ask him to send a letter on his behalf to the 'Housing Department in City Hall to see if he can give a house any where? I am in a very bad way with 5 girls in one small room 11 x 10'. Although James E. was 'working constant discharging coal boats. . .earning from £3-10 to 4£ per week also British Navy pension' and had his daughter's weekly wage of 12/6, he was unable to afford better accommodation. His wife was so ill she could not return to these unsuitable lodgings: 'People are crying shame on a good living Catholic family living like this. My little children are losing their faith through having no mother to look after them.'[127] Many of the people who wrote to the archbishop seeking assistance, however, were out of work and in arrears facing eviction. Mrs Leah H. was a classic example, her twenty-six year old husband was unemployed and in receipt of 24/- a week from the 'Labor Exchange on which I have to Keep him and fore children ... I have done the best I could, but this is not enough to Keep six With rent and insurance to be paid ... I am three pounds behind with the rent & have a notice to quit by the 18th of the month'.[128]

---

[122] Gallagher, 'Charity, Poverty and Change', p. 39.

[123] R. McManus, *Dublin, 1910–1940*, p. 225.

[124] *Report of the Local Government Tribunal, 1938*, p. 18 cited in J. V. O'Brien, *"Dear, Dirty Dublin": A City in Distress, 1899–1916* (Berkeley: University of California Press, 1982), p. 158.

[125] W. F. Brown, 'The housing problem', *The Dublin Review*, 196 (1935), 10–21.

[126] O'Connell, *The State and Housing in Ireland*, p. 29.

[127] Mr James E., X Thorncastle St., Ringsend, Dublin, 27 February 1935. DDA, AB 7 CC, Box 4; Fr Fahy (Presbytery, Ringsend, Dublin) wrote a supportive reference DDA, AB 7 CC, Box 4.

[128] Mrs Leah H., X Lr Kevin St., Dublin, n.d. *c.* 1935. DDA, AB 7 CC, Box 4.

The Citizens' Housing Council, made up of voluntary workers, doctors, labour activists and religious leaders,[129] reported in 1937 and identified those who could not pay rent as the casual labourer and the unemployed noting that they were 'the heart of the problem'. The council did not blame 'this class', but rather unemployment and insufficient wages, and called for the courage required to change ideology and policy:

If employment cannot be found by or for those poor people, for which they will receive a wage that will enable them to live decently in suitable dwellings, then the State should bear the expense of rent and necessary transport. We can never hope to solve the Housing problem ... until we have the courage to add rent to subsistence allowance and to make special arrangements for transport.[130]

Led very much by the voices of those in charitable organisations and active members of the various religions, the tone of the public debate had perceptibly changed with more focus on policy and how it failed those most in need. In October 1934, the *Irish Press*, criticising the concentration of resources on housing the better off, declared 'no housing policy is worth its salt which fails the poor' and characterised the 'unnecessary continuance of slums' as a 'challenge to the claim of any Government to have a Christian social policy'.[131] The Citizens' Housing Council, reflecting the increased social focus on unemployment, pushed for housing to be considered as a form of social subvention: 'The principle must be to house the people correctly, even though this entails uneconomic rents.'[132] It was not until the housing committee of 1939–43 that the issue of subsidised rent was seriously considered as a matter of policy, when it was suggested that 'those who cannot afford the economic rent should be charged only a reduced rent consistent with their means and needs.'[133] However, in a damning appraisal of the official response to the findings of this inquiry, O'Connell concluded that 'the housing deficit was to persist right through the decade of the 1940s'.[134] It is telling that in 1945 the Jesuit periodical *Studies* could still feature an article on the

---

[129] For example, Rev J. E. Canavan, who had written much on the issue was a member, as was the President of the Saint Vincent de Paul, Sir Joseph Glynn and the labour activist Louie Bennett, the doctor Kathleen Lynn and the Church of Ireland Archbishop of Dublin, Dr Gregg.

[130] Citizens' Housing Council, *Interim Report on Slum Clearance in Dublin 1937* (Dublin: Cahill & Co., 1937), p. 11.

[131] 'Slums', *Irish Press*, 12 October 1934.

[132] Citizens' Housing Council, *Interim Report on Slum Clearance in Dublin 1937*, p. 12.

[133] *City Manager's Observations, Submitted in Pursuance of Request by Housing Committee on Report of Inquiry into the Housing of the Working Classes of the City of Dublin 1939/43* (Dublin: Sealy, Bryers & Walker, n.d.1944), p. 4.

[134] O'Connell, *The State and Housing in Ireland*, p. 38.

slums in which the author T. W. T. Dillon described conditions reminiscent of the 1913 inquiry:

The filthy yard with the unspeakable closet often choked, always foul-smelling, serving the needs of all the families in the house; the single tap, often situated in the basement or even in this foul-smelling yard; the cracked and crumbling walls and ceiling covered with scabrous peeling paper or blistered paint; the leaking roofs and rat-infested floors.[135]

He also pointed out that the numbers living in these conditions had increased since 1913 from 25,822 to 28,210 in 1939.[136] Highlighting the connection between bad housing and unemployment, Dillon argued that the inhabitants of these hovels were always the last to be employed when work was scarce.

'Workless army still growing'

In the wake of World War I, unemployment emerged as the biggest economic challenge for almost all European states; by the end of the 1920s, it was internationally regarded as a 'human tragedy' that was reshaping the world.[137] The international bulletins of the Vincent de Paul bristled with anxiety regarding the 'tragedy of unemployment'; phrases such as 'the menace of unemployment', the 'unemployment peril' and the 'grave evil of unemployment' reappeared in all the international reports as the charity grappled with the large-scale fall-out of the international depression.[138] The unemployed 'able-bodied man' emerged from the crowd of poverty as a leading *persona* and one that needed separate treatment and different solutions.[139]

Historians agree (as did contemporaries) that assessing the real level of Irish unemployment for the 1920s and 1930s is very difficult, as the recording of figures was more influenced by changes in legislation than

---

[135] T. W. T. Dillon, 'Slum clearance: past and future', *Studies*, 43 (March 1945), 13–20, 13.

[136] J. P. Haughton, 'The social geography of Dublin', *Geographical Review*, 39 (1949), 257–277; Canavan, 'Slum clearance in Dublin', 21–32.

[137] If one considers the shift in emphasis between the two Catholic papal encyclicals *Rerum Novarum* (1891) and *Quadragesimo Anno* (1931), it is possible to see the debates regarding unemployment and the right to certain benefits was crystallizing worldwide.

[138] *Bulletin of the Society of St. Vincent De Paul*, 96 (February 1931), p. 57.

[139] Reiss has pointed out that before 'the last third of the nineteenth century, the unemployed were not recognised as a separate group, but lumped together with the poor, old, infirm or the distressed.' M. Reiss, 'The image of the poor and the unemployed: The example of *Punch*, 1841–1939' in Gestrich, King and Raphael (eds.), *Being Poor in Modern Europe*, pp. 389–415, p. 389.

actual unemployment.[140] However, there is general agreement that the period witnessed an increase in unemployment, particularly long-term unemployment.[141] As previously outlined, this was a period of extreme uncertainty compounded by the Irish revolution, significant demobilisation of soldiers following World War I and the Irish civil war. While the government acknowledged that the most important factors in the Irish unemployment situation were the numbers of casual workers and the consequent high level of chronic under-employment, there were few ideas about how to alter this landscape.[142]

From the 1920s Ireland limped into the international depression of the 1930s, and during the final years of the Cumann na nGaedheal government the economic situation deteriorated markedly. Exports of meat and dairy produce dropped sharply, factories closed and growing unemployment led to increased emigration.[143] The situation was not helped by the fact that, as Cormac Ó Gráda put it, Cumann na nGaedheal 'set little store by industrial development, and employment and output in manufacturing may well have fallen during their years in power'.[144] Equally devastating for the unemployed, the government had no employment policy and a fatalistic conviction that the problem could not be solved in the short term, but would only be solved by job creation in the private sector.

Government policy regarding unemployment assistance was hampered by the same lack of imagination and unforgiving ideology that had constricted all other welfare considerations: how to ensure the 'undeserving' – in this case those deemed unwilling to work – were not assisted and how to prevent the 'demoralisation' of those that deserved help. These concerns limited the government to three alternatives, which were endlessly debated during the period: unemployment insurance, relief works and financial support through the poor relief system.[145] Thomas Adams notes that the harsh measures used to 'instil "regular" work habits' in the working class 'has been a sinister thread in social

---

[140] For example, the numbers claiming unemployment insurance dropped from over 30,000 in 1924 to 28,000 in 1925 and, sharply, to 17,000 in 1926, however, while these claims dropped, Home Assistance claims increased dramatically from 1927 on with over 6,000 able-bodied men on Home Assistance in March 1931. Cousins, *The Birth of Irish Social Welfare in Ireland*, p. 41.

[141] C. Ó Gráda, *Ireland: A New Economic History 1780–1939* (Oxford: Clarendon Press, 1994), p. 437; Cousins, *The Birth of Irish Social Welfare in Ireland*, p. 41.

[142] Daly, *Dublin*, p. 71.

[143] M. Curtis, *A Challenge to Democracy: Militant Catholicism in Modern Ireland* (Dublin: The History Press Ireland, 2010), p. 112.

[144] Ó Gráda, *Ireland: A New Economic History*, p. 396.

[145] Cousins, *The Birth of Irish Social Welfare in Ireland*, p. 35.

history'.[146] John A. Garraty confirms that these ideological impulses were not unique to Ireland, noting that despite increased understanding of the structural causes of unemployment by the turn of twentieth century, the 'work-relief idea ... remained appealing'. He argues, however, that it was the work schemes that demoralised rather than the relief.[147] In Ireland, despite the fact that the long-term unemployed were often too weak to work on relief schemes, such schemes remained the preferred option. The word officialdom dreaded above all was 'dole'; a system that doled out assistance without a strategy to discriminate and encourage was considered socially and economically disastrous. The principal problem was that unemployment had become persistent, in many cases long term and chronic, thus those that were insured, and many were not, were running out of benefits and there were no policy initiatives aimed at the long-term unemployed.

As with all other welfare issues, the Free State worked with what it had inherited from the British regime: the unemployment insurance introduced in 1911 remained central to the government's response to unemployment. This insurance scheme operated on the basis of contributions paid, could only be received for fifteen weeks in any year and only if the claimant had worked for twenty-six weeks in that year. In response to rising unemployment, the scheme was restructured in 1920 and extended to all manual workers and to non-manual workers earning less than £250 a year, but it still excluded large groups of workers in Ireland, for example, agricultural workers and domestic servants.[148] In 1925, Cumann na nGaedheal established a committee to explore the 'immediate relief of unemployment'. The committee reported in 1927 and was scathing of one of the government's preferred policies: 'The evidence which we have taken from various witnesses goes to show that Relief Works are generally demoralising and excessively costly.'[149] It also undermined the cherished idea that this method of 'relief' weeded out the 'workshy':

---

[146] T. M. Adams, 'The mixed economy of welfare: European perspectives' in B. Harris and P. Bridgen (eds.), *Charity and Mutual Aid in Europe and North America Since 1800* (New York, London: Routledge, 2007), pp. 43–66, p. 50.

[147] Garraty, *Unemployment in History*, p. 119.

[148] According to the 1926 census 60 per cent of Irish women were engaged in domestic service. M. E. Daly, *Women and Work in Ireland* (Louth: Dundalgan Press, 1997), p. 41. The same census also records 53 per cent of the population was engaged in agriculture. Chapter 3, Industries and Occupations, *Census of Population, General Report, 1926, Vol. X*, p. 24.

[149] *Committee on the Relief of Unemployment, 1927: Final Report* (Dublin, 1928), p. 2; Committee on Relief of Unemployment: Minutes of Evidence and Relevant Documents, S5553/D.

When it is borne in mind that a great number of the men employed on Relief Works are persons who have been idle for a considerable time, many of them in a state of semi-starvation or otherwise in poor physical condition, it will, we think, be agreed that employment for short terms on relief works can have nothing but unsatisfactory results.[150]

The report recommended a holistic approach to the problem and made various suggestions in relation to improving housing, education (regarding it as a long-term investment), public health and the development of various industries. The report was met with a 'stony reception' before its effective burial.[151] The problem of expiring benefits, identified as early as 1924, persisted, and in 1930 the Vincent de Paul recorded: 'The Unemployment benefit, designed to tide the individual over short periods of slackness, has in most cases been completely exhausted, and still the workers are faced with the problem of keeping themselves and their families from actual starvation.'[152]

In power from 1932, Fianna Fáil also grappled with the idea of relief works versus unemployment maintenance. In April 1934 the Unemployment Assistance Act (1933) came into effect, which allowed for the payment of unemployment benefit to all those who could prove that they could not get work, except women, who had to be single and have a previous record of insurable employment. Significantly, this act included farm workers, and Cousins has argued that Fianna Fáil used Unemployment Assistance 'to subsidise an agricultural population hard hit by the Economic War',[153] a war it had instigated by refusing to pay the full land annuities owed to the British government under the terms of the Anglo–Irish Treaty of 1921. During this war the British retaliated by imposing tariffs on Irish imports which devastated the agricultural community leading to what Ó Gráda described as the 'nadir of farmer welfare in the South' in the twentieth century.[154] Furthermore, as Dunphy argues, while Fianna Fáil's welfare initiatives should not be dismissed, 'they were in no way fundamental structural changes which offered any prospect of a disruption of the balance of power in Irish society'.[155]

The government had predicted only 40,000 would be eligible under the Unemployment Assistance Act, but by the end of the first year the figure was 100,000, consequently Fianna Fáil introduced changes to the

---

[150] Ibid.   [151] Dunphy, *The Making of Fianna Fáil Power in Ireland*, p. 115.

[152] 'Dublin Quarterly Meeting', 'Supplement for Irish Conferences' in *Bulletin of the Society of St. Vincent De Paul*, 95 (January 1930), p. 3.

[153] Cousins, *The Birth of Irish Social Welfare in Ireland*, p. 84.

[154] Ó Gráda, *Ireland: A New Economic History*, p. 413.

[155] Dunphy, *The Making of Fianna Fáil Power in Ireland*, p. 24.

means test to restrict benefit and reduce costs.[156] Fred Powell points out that the means test seriously limited the impact of the act, because any income in excess of 2s. per week resulted in a reduction of the benefit and, as the maximum benefit was £1 a week, in reality even those who qualified received very basic assistance.[157] Nonetheless, as the act introduced the principle of a right to assistance as a result of unemployment, rather than insurance, it was criticised by the members of the opposition; for example, Cumann na nGaedheal lamented that it was a 'dole policy' focusing on maintenance rather than employment.[158]

'The true concept of charity'

Central to the debates about poverty, unemployment and welfare provision was the balance between the role of the state and voluntary agencies.[159] The new state was anxious to use charities to supplement – and in some cases cater for – the relief of certain groups; charities, often driven by religious agendas, were both fearful of the state monopolising all forms of relief and anxious that their spiritual work would become swamped by basic material demands.[160] Most charities, irrespective of denomination, shared the conviction that their work was intrinsically different to that of the state, as the Catholic Archbishop of Tuam, Dr Gilmartin, explained in a sermon in 1920: 'In modern times States have levied taxes to support various forms of distress. But all these means of alleviating distress, good in themselves, may not include the true concept

---

[156] Cousins, *The Birth of Irish Social Welfare in Ireland*, p. 66.

[157] He calculated that a married man with three children living in an urban centre was entitled to 17s.6d. per week. F. W. Powell, *The Politics of Irish Social Policy*, p. 201.

[158] This was Patrick McGilligan's comment. *Dáil Éireann Debates*, 27 September 1933, vol. 49, col. 1670. Patrick McGilligan, Minister for Industry and Commerce (1924–32), and Ernest Blythe, Minister for Local Government (1922–23) and Minister for Finance (1923–32).

[159] This was an international conversation. P. Mandler, 'Poverty and charity in the nineteenth century metropolis: an introduction' in P. Mandler (ed.), *The Uses of Charity: The Poor on Relief in the Nineteenth-Century Metropolis* (Philadelphia: University of Pennsylvania Press, 1990), pp. 1–37: J. Lewis, 'Gender, the family and women's agency in the building of "welfare states": the British case', *Social History*, 19 (1994), 37–55; J. Weiss, 'Origins of the French Welfare State: poor relief in the Third Republic, 1871–1914', *French Historical Studies*, 13 (1983–4), 47–77; D. Crew, 'The ambiguities of modernity: welfare and the German State from Wilhelm to Hitler' in J. Eley (ed.), *Society, Culture, and the State in Germany, 1870–1930* (Michigan, 1996), pp. 319–344.

[160] For an interesting discussion of how religion has influenced the development of welfare in several European countries, see, S. Kahl, 'The religious roots of modern poverty policy: Catholic, Lutheran, and Reformed Protestant traditions compared', *European Journal of Sociology*, 46 (2005), 91–126.

of charity.'[161] For many, charity was first and foremost about the religious and moral 'uplifting' of its recipients, if this spiritual aspect was divorced from its material role it ceased to have any meaning and became harmful. The Protestant Aid Society, for example, only assisted Protestants that were church going and 'of strictly moral character'.[162] While a member of Vincent de Paul explained to the Commission on the Relief of the Sick in 1927:

the Society is not, as the public too often assume, a purely relieving society . . . The primary object of the Society was the moral uplifting of the members as well as the poor they visited, and to bring about friendly relations and associations between two bodies – those that had means and those that were without means . . . I should like to stress the fact that in its essence ours is a religious society rather than a purely relieving one.[163]

However, even non-denominational charities like the Dublin-based Sick and Indigent Roomkeepers' Society, increasingly expressed the concern that the charitable mission was being frustrated by having to step into the breach of statutory services. In 1926, the society told the commission that the 'deserving poor' were unable 'to properly clothe or feed their children on the present rates of outdoor relief'. The society estimated that these cases made up 40 per cent of its caseload and as a result its funds were diverted from intended recipients – 'the temporarily embarrassed'.[164]

As the enormity of the unemployment crisis began to dawn, charities increasingly believed that the state should be providing a basic cushion for able-bodied men unable to find work. However, it was argued that this should be 'a temporary expedient until conditions change' and the true role of the state should be to 'bring about such changes as will remove the need of public assistance'.[165] Catholic anxiety regarding the increasing role of the state was heightened by the economic crash of 1929, sparking widespread fears of the rise of Communism.[166] Catholics were not alone in this fear as echoes were heard within the Protestant churches also, however, it was the Catholic Church and its active laity that worked most successfully to shape the emergent state to

[161] Extract from sermon 'I have compassion on the multitude' delivered by Archbishop of Tuam, Dr Gilmartin on 4 July 1920 in *Bulletin of the Society of St. Vincent De Paul*, 85 (July 1920), p. 281.

[162] K. Milne, *Protestant Aid 1836–1986: A History of the Association for the Relief of Distressed Protestants* (Dublin: Protestant Aid, 1989), p. 5.

[163] *Report of the Commission on the Relief of the Sick and Destitute Poor*, p. 59.

[164] Cited in D. Lindsay, *Dublin's Oldest Charity: The Sick and Indigent Roomkeepers' Society, 1790–1990* (Dublin: The Anniversary Press, 1990), p. 81.

[165] J. E. Canavan, S.J., 'The Poor Law Report', *Studies: An Irish Quarterly Review*, 16 (December 1927), 631–640.

[166] M. Curtis, *A Challenge to Democracy*, pp. 103–105.

complement its wider agenda.[167] As Rev Coffey explained in 1931: 'the State has its authority from God... in securing [citizens'] temporal wellbeing the State is subordinate to the Church in the way in which man's temporal wellbeing is subordinate to his eternal welfare.'[168]

Charity played a crucial role in justifying the argument for state subordination: charity, it was claimed, could truly discriminate and offer its recipients a 'cure' beyond mere material assistance. It offered a level of inquiry into each case that was tantamount to a form of 'soul-searching'.[169] The 'deserving' were not just those who were blameless for their poverty, but also those who were 'genuine' in their faith, or could be rendered thus. Crucially, however, charity was also proffered as a means of compensating for inequality – accepted as inevitable by most commentators – and as a means to 'break down the barrier between the rich and the poor'.[170] This acceptance of inequality, yet simultaneous abhorrence of any sense of 'class war', was fundamental to the Roman Catholic Church's approach to the poor. As Powell has argued: 'Inequalities of class and gender have not simply been enforced by state power in Ireland: they have also been legitimated by the potent influence religion has exercised over Irish society.'[171] In 1929, reflecting on a 'Catholic Nation's' duty to its poor, Rev J. Kelleher argued that this acceptance of the unequal social order was necessary if Catholic's wished to 'help' their less fortunate brethren:

When one reflects on the glaring contrast between the excessive wealth and luxury on the one hand and the extreme poverty and destitution on the other which is to be found in every civilised country to-day, one experiences an almost irresistible temptation to denounce as un-Christian and inhuman the entire social and economic system in which those things are calmly accepted as part of the established order ... Such temptation, however, must be steadfastly resisted if we hope to make even the most modest contribution towards the practical amelioration of the condition of the poor and destitute ... directing men's thoughts towards the transformation or impracticable reformation of society, and making them impatient and contemptuous of the necessarily imperfect

---

[167] Maurice Curtis has argued that the real achievement of Irish Catholic Action was 'in helping to shape and consolidate public opinion, in copper-fastening the Catholic-Irish identity, and in helping to enshrine the moral code in Irish law. Curtis, *A Challenge to Democracy*, p. 9.

[168] Rev Peter Coffey, *The Christian Family and the Higher Ideal* (Dublin: CTSI, 1931), p. 4.

[169] J. Murphy, 'Suffering, vice and justice: religious imaginaries and welfare agencies in postwar Melbourne', *Journal of Religious History*, 31 (2007), 287–304, 290. Cited in Peel, *Miss Cutler and the Case of the Resurrected Horse*, p. 47.

[170] Rev P. Coffey, *The Church and the Working Classes* (Dublin: CTSI, n.d. *c.* 1906), p. 7.

[171] Powell, *The Politics of Irish Social Policy*, p. xi.

measures by which alone it is practically possible to come to the relief of those glaring social maladies.[172]

Aspirations to 'ascend the social ladder' were deplored, education was not a means to a better life – it was a means to spiritual enrichment and social stability.[173] In this respect what the givers of charity gained was also crucial; they fulfilled their spiritual and civic duty to society's weaker members.[174] This was true far beyond the island of Ireland, as Peter Mandler has argued in relation to the role of charity in the nineteenth-century metropolis, 'charitable assistance from the rich to the poor was seen by both parties as an essential part of the social order.'[175] Charity was to help people accept their position and to defuse class resentment, not to bring about economic or social equality. This intention – this hope – was expressed repeatedly by the charity most involved in 'visiting' the poor in Ireland, the Vincent de Paul. As the Very Rev A. MacArdle explained to the Dublin quarterly general meeting in March 1920:

The interchange of civilities and acts of courtesy between those in a higher social grade and the submerged classes of the slums make it impossible that the latter should continue to entertain the same feelings of hatred towards those who have sought them out in their wretchedness and endeavoured to comfort them.[176]

This class agenda was, of course, fraught with the risk of achieving the opposite of its intention: how could the relationship be an easy one, when the power imbalance inherent in that class difference was at the heart of the giving relationship? This tension is reflected in almost all the auto-biographical representations of this charity encounter, from Angeline Kearns Blain's subtle highlighting of the class differences in her reference to the Ladies of the Vincent de Paul 'attired in flounced, well-made dresses with cardigans tossed casually over their delicate shoulders',[177] to Elaine Crowley's more pointed recollection that while her mother

---

[172] Rev J. Kelleher, S.T.L., *A Catholic Nation: Its Destitute, Dependent and Helpless Classes* (n.d. *c.* 1929) (pamphlet no. 1001), p. 1.

[173] Rev P. Coffey, *The Church and the Working Classes*, p. 10.

[174] V. Crossman, '"Attending to the wants of poverty": Paul Cullen, the relief of poverty and the development of social welfare in Ireland' in D. Keogh and A. McDonnell (eds.), *Cardinal Paul Cullen and his World* (Dublin: Four Courts Press, 2012), pp. 146–165.

[175] Mandler, 'Poverty and charity in the nineteenth century metropolis', p. 3; See also, Woolf, *The Poor in Western Europe*, p. 27.

[176] 'Reprint of address by Very Rev. A MacArdle in Ireland: Quarterly General Meeting in Dublin', *Bulletin of the Society of St. Vincent De Paul*, 85 (March 1920), p. 91.

[177] A. Kearns Blain, *Stealing Sunlight: Growing up in Irishtown* (Dublin: A & A Farmar, 2000), p. 176.

'balked at the idea' of the humiliating means test involved in state relief, she would rather 'starve' than let 'the St. Vincent de Paul cross her door'.[178] In Crowley's retelling of poverty, the Vincent de Paul's association with religion and an invasion of the home was worse than the suspicious state: 'There was also the Society of St. Vincent de Paul, which gave food dockets to those they considered worthy – practising Catholics with their homes stripped of all but the bare necessities.'[179] Similarly, Máirín Johnston recalls in her memoir, '[E]very Friday night the Vincent's men came around to dole out the few ha'pence or the clothes dockets'. The children of her neighbourhood were given the job of alerting the mothers when 'Vincent's men' were coming: 'This was the signal that anything in the line of food, clothes or ornaments was to be hidden. As we were children we thought this was very funny, but in actual fact it was a terrible indictment of the charitable society's view of us.'[180] The society's own reports carry many hints of this class tension:

We do not patronise the poor, or give them to understand that we are superior people. We call and sit amongst them, and make ourselves at home with them. We talk of the crops, the weather, the absent friends, the local gossip, what the sermon at Mass to-day was about, and a hundred and one other topics that interest them, and in many cases are useful to us. Imperceptibly, we ascertain their conditions and needs, whether they are attending Mass and the Sacraments, and how the children are faring. We enter their houses with a "God save you," and leave with their blessing. Can anyone say that this has a demoralising tendency or effect?[181]

This was surely inevitable in view of the profile of the society's membership, which was made up predominately of middle-class middle-aged male civil servants, solicitors, doctors and university students.[182]

The Vincent de Paul has become almost synonymous with Irish poverty, and it features repeatedly in the letters of the poor, a family was either helped in the past, was currently on the 'books' or had had their case 'rested'. In February 1938, Mrs M. informed the archbishop that 'all through the unemployment we had a terrible time – we had to apply to Vincent de Paul for food'.[183] Others wrote to complain of a lack of

---

[178] E. Crowley, *Cowslips and Chainies*, p. 138.   [179] Ibid.

[180] Johnston, *Around the Banks of Pimlico*, p. 62.

[181] A paper on 'Our Work' read at the Quarterly meeting of the Conference of St Nathy, Ballaghadereen, 19 April 1931, in 'Supplement for Irish Conferences, July 1931', *Bulletin of the Society of St. Vincent De Paul*, 96 (April 1931), p. 19.

[182] Women could not become full members until 1962. See C. T. Gallagher, *Charity, Poverty and Change: The Society of Saint Vincent de Paul in Dublin, 1939–54* (University College Dublin MA Thesis, 1988), p. 4, p. 24.

[183] Mrs M., X Eustace St., Dublin, 20 February 1938. DDA, AB 7 CC, Box 7.

assistance from the society, such as Mr W. P., who 'had applied to St Vincent Depauls Society for some help as I not entitled to outdoor relief. they gave me no help and within that week my wif she got phenomunia *[pneumonia]* and now she is in Cork street Hospital very bad.'[184] In fact, sometimes the poor approached the Vincent de Paul for a reference to give to the archbishop, like Mr James L. in March 1932, who came to the archbishop's palace bearing a reference from the St. Laurence O'Toole's Conference, which helped to secure him £1 in assistance.[185] On several occasions the society petitioned persuasively on behalf of an applicant as in 1936, when Mr Gilligan of the Conference of the Holy Family, wrote on behalf of a Mrs H. who lived with her family of thirteen in 'one room at X North Brunswick Street, Dublin'. Prior to writing to the archbishop, the society had tried 'repeatedly to get the Corporation to provide them with adequate accommodation – so far without success'. The Vincent de Paul representative assured the archbishop that 'any sum would not be expended unwisely by these poor people whose total income is less than 30/- per week from all sources.'[186] In 1937, Harry M. who was sick with bronchitis, believed '[O]nly for the Gentlemen of St Vincent de Paul Society we would be starving, they give us a food order each week for 5/-. May God Bless them.'[187] However much the Vincent de Paul helped people – and the society helped thousands of desperate families through-out this period – its resources were finite and it was constantly trying to balance the overwhelming need it encountered with a strong sense that charity should not facilitate dependence. This last conviction did fade as the 1930s wore on, but the limited funds meant many families were cut off while still in real need. Mrs May F.'s letter to the archbishop in September 1936 was far from unusual. She was the mother of four children with an unemployed husband in receipt of 17/6 a week of which 7/5 went on rent and 1/- on burial insurance, this left them 'Completely starving for the want of proper meals':

And the Gentlemen of St Colombus Branch St Vincent De Paul are aware of our plight for they have been attending us up to three weeks ago and given us a ticket for 2/6 worth of Groceries and that unfortunatly they were unable to continue owing to the lack of funds.[188]

---

[184] Mr. W. P., X, Dolphin's Barn, (Dublin), n.d. *c.* 1933. DDA, AB 7 CC, Box 5.
[185] Richard Walker, Vincent de Paul Society, St Laurence O'Toole's Conference, Seville Place, Dublin, 3 March 1932. DDA, AB 7 CC, Box 5.
[186] Walter J. Gilligan, Vincent de Paul Society, Conference of the Holy Family, 117 North Circular Road, Dublin, 19 November 1936. DDA, AB 7 CC, Box 6.
[187] Mr Harry M., X Amiens St., Dublin, 1 February 1937. DDA, AB 7 CC, Box 6.
[188] Mrs May F., X Ravensdale Rd., Church Rd., Dublin, 21 September 1936. DDA, AB 7 CC, Box 6.

In 1924, the society's 4,368 members visited 20,197 families to assess their needs and spent £49,732 on various forms of assistance and a further £6,145 in the form of direct financial aid.[189] A decade later in 1935, the number of families assisted had increased to 33,100 and the cost of that aid had risen to £81,794.[190] If the society could not help, it often enlisted the services of other charities or the parish priest. It is safe to say that the attitude of the society and its evolution during the 1920s and 1930s had a significant impact on the lives of many of the poor. What is also evident from examining its reports through the period is that the poor had a significant impact on the society. Its greatest fear in the early 1920s appeared to be that it would 'degenerate into a mere relieving society', because poverty was so pervasive and state assistance so limited. However, by the close of that decade the society had effectively become a mediator between the poor and the state, offering advice on various issues relating to statutory relief through its Secretariat for the Poor, and articulating the ways in which new pieces of legislation fell short and failed their intended beneficiaries. In 1931, for example, the Vincent de Paul reported that several conferences were 'successful in establishing claims for their clients to Health Insurance, Military Service Pensions, Old Age Pensions'.[191]

As the Vincent de Paul documented rising unemployment, near starvation and horrendous living conditions affecting hundreds of new families, there was a perceptible shift in its tone that amounted to an attempt to 'voice' the meaning of this hardship and render the poor less 'abstract'. In March 1931, for example, the chairman at the Dublin Quarterly meeting observed:

The visitor from the local branch of the Society of St. Vincent de Paul knows what unemployment is, but he can do something more than define it. He can tell you what it means to the poor, he can actually see dejection in the faces of the unemployed, he knows what the hopes and what the disappointments of the unemployed are, he can do more than look upon these things in the abstract or as mere ideas.[192]

---

[189] 'Ireland, Annual report, 1924', *Bulletin of the Society of St. Vincent De Paul*, 90 (August 1925), p. 248.
[190] 'Annual Report of the Council of Ireland, 1934', *Bulletin of the Society of St. Vincent De Paul*, 100 (September 1935), p. 273.
[191] 'Supplement of Irish Conference, April 1931', in *Bulletin of the Society of St. Vincent De Paul*, 96 (April 1931), p. 6. Buckley also points out that the 1940s the Society 'was being utilised as an informal probationary service'. Buckley, *Cruelty Men*, p. 100.
[192] 'Dublin Quarterly meeting', in 'Supplement for Irish Conferences', March 1931, *Bulletin of the Society of St. Vincent De Paul*, 96 (March 1931), p. 10.

By the early 1930s some fairly radical things were being said about poverty within the confines of the society. In December 1931, the vice-president challenged many of the contemporary shibboleths about poverty.[193] The first error he believed the society should work to amend was fatalism, which accepted poverty as inevitable. The second 'wrong view' was that 'the poor must somehow be themselves responsible for their condition'. He declared that while some poverty could be laid at the door 'of intemperance, or lack of energy ... for many years past, the great bulk of the poverty we have been called up to relieve has been due to causes other than moral causes in the poor themselves':

It is not laziness that leaves so many men, physically strong and otherwise fit for employment, queued up at the Relief Office or Employment Exchange, or seated hopelessly in their cold and cheerless rooms; or so many youths, the product of our Catholic schools, without a chance of even starting on a life of industry.[194]

In some respects women, widows and children were the accepted victims of the patriarchal social structure and represented relatively uncomplicated cases for charity: the unemployed married man represented the potential collapse of that very social structure. While charity remained rooted in its spiritual mission, the leading Catholic charity was beginning to articulate a view of poverty closer to that which the poor themselves espoused.[195]

As Michael B. Katz has argued, 'sources of relief were landmarks on a complex topographical map that the poor had to learn to read in order to survive'.[196] The letters of the poor are replete with evidence of the busy schedule of survival with references to various efforts to sustain a minimum quality of life. The Vincent de Paul is almost omnipresent in these letters, but there are also references to other charities such as the Sick and Indigent Roomkeepers' Society, the Mendicity Institution, priests and nuns. However, attempts to track the correspondents in the files of other

---

[193] Increasingly, the idea that poverty was a natural state was being rejected and replaced with a demand for the redistribution of resources to respond to systemic poverty. See, for example, 'Unholy poverty', *Irish Press*, 16 December 1931. These views did not mean a rejection of the religious principles of charity. See, 'Pagan view of poverty: The social system', *Irish Independent*, 21 July 1931.

[194] Paper read by the Vice-President of the Council to Dublin Quarterly meeting on 13 Dec, 1931 entitled: 'The Society and Catholic Action' in 'Supplement of Irish Conferences', *Bulletin of the Society of St. Vincent De Paul*, 97 (1932), pp. 9–10.

[195] Despite this important shift in outlook, Gallagher has argued that the society did not seek fundamental reform of society and thus the ultimate eradication of poverty, it accepted that the poor would always be there. Gallagher, *Charity, Poverty and Change*, p. 6.

[196] M. B. Katz, 'The history of an impudent poor woman in New York city from 1918 to 1923' in Mandler (ed.), *The Uses of Charity*, pp. 227–246, p. 228.

charities have been frustrated largely by the lack of application records or access to those records.[197] Nonetheless, it is apparent from these letters that being poor required patience, strategy, negotiation skills and knowledge of the various welfare and charitable options. One had to be prepared and able to fill in forms, dodge the gaps in the system, accommodate the 'waiting periods', ensure that charity was not counted against your relief entitlements and convince the charity people that you had received your due from the state. Mrs Katherine L. wrote to explain to the archbishop how she was mired in the complex bureaucracy of the state relief system:

waiting for Widows Pension I was 9 weeks signing forms & getting certificates 3 weeks all sent to ... Head Office not having any Results so far also 4 months without 5/- outdoor relief I am sick for the past 3 weeks ... & more trouble my sister ... has being Dismissed from Work owing to no Business until xmas trade she will receive no employment money untill next week as they have to give a few days notice next week she will Receive 12/ per week and if I get Pension we will try & manage were worried about Rent.[198]

For the poor the acceptance of a loss of privacy was a reality of receiving assistance from any source – the state and the various charities made 'inquiry' a central part of the giving process. While the criteria for being found 'deserving' may vary, the 'system' was in essence the same for those on the receiving end. In 1936, Mrs May F. concluded her letter of appeal to the archbishop with the reassurance that investigation posed no threat to her: 'N.B. If its necessary to investigate our case through the St Vincent De Paul or our Local Clergyman we would gladly welcome it.'[199] It is no accident that both in memoirs and in contemporary accounts, the poor often discussed state relief and charity side-by-side. Crowley's mother considered both and eventually opted for the 'poor relief'. In fact, charity and welfare were often intertwined and certainly a reliance on both forms of support was integral to many people's budgets, a reality referred to by historians as 'a mixed economy of welfare'.[200] In 1937, Charles F. conflated both church and state, when he wrote to

---

[197] A written trail of applications to the Saint Vincent de Paul, for example, are not accessible or do not survive. There is no evidence of these letter writers in the records of the Protestant Orphans' Society and, at the point of writing this book, the Sick and Indigent Roomkeepers' Society records are not accessible.

[198] Katherine L., X St Joseph's Ave., Off Ann's Rd. Drumcondra, Dublin to Archbishop Byrne, n.d. c. 1937. DDA, AB 7 CC, Box 7.

[199] Mrs May F., X Ravensdale Rd., Church Rd., Dublin, 21 September 1936.

[200] For a discussion of this see, Adams, 'The mixed economy of welfare European perspectives', pp. 43–66.

Archbishop Byrne that he would be 'almost naked' by Christmas assuring the prelate that 'any member of the Church or State which your Grace may think fit to hear our statements' was welcome to inspect his home.[201] Charles F.'s confusion was symptomatic of the experience of poverty: church and state shared similar values, both objectified the poor, both fundamentally distrusted the poor and both demanded something in return for assistance.

Conclusion

During the first ten years of political independence Cumann na nGaedheal offered few crumbs of comfort to the poor and struggling classes. Cousins described the key players in the Cumann na nGaedheal government of 1922 to 1932 as '"souls without remorse", at least insofar as remorse implied public policy measures to improve the position of the poor'.[202] While Fianna Fáil introduced some of the most significant welfare measures of the twentieth century during the 1930s,[203] allowing for redistribution of resources to the most vulnerable in society, this period coincided with a severe international economic depression and the economic war with Britain. Cousins notes that the introduction of the widows' pension, the extension of the Old Age Pension and improved Unemployment Assistance had a real and beneficial impact on many vulnerable people's lives, he cautions, correctly, that 'the extent of social solidarity was limited'.[204] Ireland remained a deeply divided society in which there was little radicalism in the face of social inequality. The poor had a lower life expectancy at all ages and lived with higher degrees of morbidity; their children had a significantly higher chance of living in an institution and of losing one of their parents to premature death.

The poor as a class 'apart' permeates all discourse – the Irish Free State articulated a sense of ownership over the poor, but rarely a true sense of civic empathy. Contemporaries in Ireland, and elsewhere, regarded poverty along social and moral lines: in terms of social issues unemployment and housing were agreed upon as the main issues

---

[201] Mr Charles F., X Corporation Place, Dublin, 4 December 1936. DDA, AB 7 CC, Box 6.

[202] He was referring in particular to Patrick McGilligan. Cousins, *The Birth of Social Welfare in Ireland*, p. 55.

[203] Perhaps the most significant was Children's Allowances, also introduced by Fianna Fáil, but not until 1944. Cousins argues that the Fianna Fáil period in government between 1932 and 1938 'raised the building skyward' in relation to the creation of an Irish welfare state. Cousins, *The Birth of Social Welfare in Ireland*, p. 83.

[204] Ibid., p. 85.

requiring attention; in moral terms the big concern was appropriate discrimination between the 'deserving' and 'undeserving poor'. Allied to these issues were anxieties regarding prudence or extravagance and the meaning of true charity and the role of the state. The general attitude to the poor in Ireland, including the main churches, was at best equivocal and at worst cynical. Even the writings of the most compassionate chroniclers of poverty reflected a deep ambivalence and contradiction. This was mirrored in the wider society: while many wished to see the end of extreme want, in general society remained suspicious and resentful of the remedies supplied, particularly the 'dole' and 'indiscriminate charity'. However, throughout all the many writings and discussions about poverty and the poor, very little thought was given to the reality of living life in the Irish poverty trap, and virtually no attempt was made to ask those who did so their view on the possible solutions. Poverty was rarely personalised – it is always easier to deal cheaply with the lives of those lived in the abstract. However, the poor did leave a record; they did write their version of poverty. The letters in the collection explored in this book affirm that continuity rather than change was the hallmark of the experience of poverty in Ireland throughout the 1920s and 1930s. New welfare initiatives merely added to the medley of resources the poor had to negotiate, they were never enough (nor were they intended to be) to make charity irrelevant and resulted in no real change in the life strategies employed by the poor. The thousands of begging letters amount to a good deal more than a mere litany of requests; embedded and explicit in many of the writings of the poor is a deep social critique of the universe they inhabited. In 1937, in a purple crayon and a childlike script, Mrs Paula C. asked a question that hung over many other letters to the archbishop: 'Is this a Civilized Country'?[205]

---

[205] Mrs Paula C., X Talbot Pace, Dublin, *c.* 1937.

2   Artefacts of Poverty
'I Crave your Holy Pardon for Writing'

The collection of Irish letters explored here have their origins not only in the surge in ordinary people's writing in Europe that took place between the 1860s and 1920s,[1] but also in a much longer tradition of ordinary pauper petitions that can be traced back to at least the eleventh century.[2] Mark Cohen has explored pauper letters from between the eleventh and thirteenth centuries which emerged from the Cairo Geniza – a Jewish cache of buried sacred documents, which contained some documents of 'everyday life'.[3] Cohen reveals that these ancient sources 'contain remarkable parallels' to Thomas Sokoll's Essex pauper letters from the eighteenth and nineteenth centuries.[4] If the Cairo Geniza sources root the tradition of poverty letters back to pre-modern times, then the Irish charity letters establish its continuation well into the twentieth century.[5] Despite the differing contexts of their creation, it is argued here that these Irish begging letters also bear striking resemblance to the English pauper letters of the nineteenth century in terms of their narrative structure and cultural resonances. They allow us to consider historical and cultural processes by which meaning is given, in this case, to poverty, entitlement and charity. When regarded as cultural texts of poverty and as acts of social practice, these Irish letters offer a similar window into how the poor interpreted and translated their experiences and needs when seeking assistance.

---

[1] M. Lyons, *The Writing Culture of Ordinary People in Europe, c. 1860–1920* (Cambridge University Press, 2012) p. 8.

[2] M. R. Cohen, *The Voice of the Poor in the Middle Ages: An Anthology of Documents from the Cairo Geniza (Jews, Christian, and Muslim from the Ancient to the Modern World)* (New Jersey: Princeton University Press, 2005)

[3] Ibid., p. 4.   [4] Ibid., p. 8.

[5] Maarten Van Ginderachter has also examined supplication letters written to the Belgian Royal family, which continued throughout the twentieth century. M. Van Ginderachter, '"If your Majesty would only send me a little money to help buy an elephant": Letters to the Belgian Royal family (1880–1940)' in M. Lyons (ed.), *Ordinary Writings, Personal Narratives: Writing Practices in 19th and early 20th-Century Europe* (New York: Peter Lang, 2007), pp. 69–84.

For various socio-economic and cultural reasons the poverty letters examined in this book are very rare artefacts in the Irish context as few other examples exist in such quantities for the nineteenth or twentieth century. As Gestrich, Hurren and King have pointed out, certain welfare regimes were more likely to result in written documents originating from its claimants than others.[6] For example, residence-based systems – increasingly adopted throughout Europe by the mid-nineteenth century – generated considerable correspondence from the poor regarding settlement issues.[7] However, in Ireland, where there were no rules regarding the entitlement of migrants, there were relatively few 'pauper narratives' in relation to the Poor Law.[8] This did not change after the formation of the Irish Free State in 1922, when assistance was increasingly secured through Home Assistance, which demanded the physical appearance of the applicant at the local relief office.[9] Thus the Irish welfare system, certainly before the 1940s, simply did not provide the context for people to write about their own condition and needs.[10]

International research on poverty has revealed that where the balance of a relief system was towards philanthropy, as was the case in Ireland, there were fewer chances of narratives written by the poor because 'applying for and obtaining charity generated more narrative material *about* the poor than *by* them'.[11] While narratives written by the poor to charities, rather than individuals, do exist for urban areas of the Netherlands and Belgium, they are totally absent for England and Wales. Furthermore, it has been argued that where these letters exist, they are so shaped by the act of application that they take on 'the form of a petition rather than a plea, request or demand'.[12] However, these

---

[6] A. Gestrich, E. Hurren and S. King, 'Narratives of poverty and sickness in Europe 1780–1938: Sources, methods and experiences' in A. Gestrich, E. Hurren and S. King (eds.), *Poverty and Sickness in Modern Europe: Narratives of the Sick Poor, 1780–1938* (London: Continuum, 2012), p. 10.

[7] See T. Sokoll, *Essex Pauper Letters 1731–1837* (Oxford University Press, 2006).

[8] Gestrich, Hurren and King, 'Narratives of poverty and sickness in Europe 1780–1938', p. 11.

[9] People queued at their local office and were often assisted 'in kind'. S. Ó Cinnéide, 'The development of the Home Assistance service', *Administration*, 17 (1969), 284–308, 307.

[10] There are some letters written by the poor to poor law officials, but they survive in isolation and were usually connected to a particular dispute or grievance. See, I. Brandes, 'Odious, degrading and foreign' institutions? Analysing Irish workhouses in the nineteenth and twentieth centuries' in A. Gestrich, S. King and L. Raphael (eds.), *Being Poor in Modern Europe: Historical Perspectives 1800–1940* (Switzerland: Peter Lang, 2006) p. 220.

[11] Gestrich, Hurren and King, 'Narratives of poverty and sickness in Europe 1780–1938', p. 11.

[12] Ibid.

Irish charity letters are a clear exception to both arguments. While they were written to an individual – the Catholic Archbishop of Dublin – they are nonetheless charity letters, as they seek assistance from him as the representative of the Catholic Church and the overseer of all Catholic charities. In fact, his very status was often evoked in the letters as the moral basis for writing. Many of the letters implicitly or explicitly asked how the church he represented could allow such poverty and suffering to exist. Nevertheless, while these are charity letters, they were not so hidebound by the act of requesting assistance that they lost their individuality and vibrancy. They are not like formal petitions; on the contrary, they read very much like Sokoll's Essex pauper letters, as 'first-hand record[s] of the living conditions and experiences of ordinary people'.[13] However, these letters are relatively unusual because their context facilitated a broader reflection on poverty than the usual 'pauper letters'. Their authors were writing after or while they negotiated all other forms of relief on offer – that was the condition under which the archbishop considered requests – therefore, they frequently made reference to, or were obviously influenced by, that experience. Thus these letters offer an extraordinary insight into ordinary people's view of the entirety of the system they had to negotiate and this led, often, to wider reflections on the experience of poverty, begging, relief and/or charity. This tendency was perhaps exacerbated by the religious context: because they were writing to the Catholic archbishop, the letters offered more scope to reflect on the nature of life and the position they found themselves in, than those addressed to a public, ostensibly secular, official. These reflections frequently touched on the religious dynamics of the Irish charity market.

Another feature of this collection is that it contains a greater diversity of personal histories because the letters were not directed to a charity with a particular agenda (other than the obvious religious one) for example, a rescue agency or a charity that targeted only widows or the very poor.[14] This allowed people who either would have been ineligible under such circumstances or would not have been willing to apply for such charity to write to the archbishop. While the majority of the letter-writers had known poverty in childhood and wrote from a community where hardship and deprivation were the norm – a significant number of people had come

13 Sokoll, *Essex Pauper Letters 1731–1837*, p. 4.
14 For example, the Protestant Orphan Society (1828) and the Clergy Widows' and Orphans' Society (1863). O. Walsh, *Anglican Women in Dublin: Philanthropy, Politics and Education in the Early Twentieth Century* (University College Dublin Press, 2005) pp. 151–197.

upon 'hard times'. The latter comforted themselves that the archbishop's charity was somehow less degrading as it allowed them to address one person – a very senior person – and request compassion for their *particular* plight, rather than a charity committee that would conduct a more public examination of their case. Those who wrote as the 'temporarily embarrassed' did so consciously and were careful to stress that they did not belong in the usual charity category – rather they were normally the charity givers. These authors provide different perspectives on poverty and its social and cultural meanings; they offer personalised evidence of the fragility of financial security in a system with no statutory safety net and they testify to the social dread of 'becoming poor'. Many framed their letters around the idea of being 'saved' from such a fate, as though financial ruin would mean entering a new social category from which it would be impossible to re-emerge. While their letters share many of the characteristics of the letters from the poorest of society they also display different features, serve different functions and allow a more diverse exploration of a wide range of ordinary people's writing.

No other charity letter collection of this significance has been unearthed in Ireland to date.[15] There are random begging letters in the diocesan archives throughout the country, but many have been destroyed or simply not preserved.[16] This 'charity cases' collection continued under the subsequent Catholic Archbishop of Dublin, John Charles McQuaid, between 1941 and 1972, but as of yet these have not been thoroughly explored.[17] Oonagh Walsh makes excellent use of the applications written by widows to the Clergy Widows' and Orphans' Society and the Protestant Orphans' Society in the late nineteenth and early twentieth centuries.[18] However, these applications tend to give more information about the widow and her

---

[15] There are some interesting letters from Belfast, in particular, those written by the unemployed in 1930s Belfast to the Lord Mayor of Belfast, Sir Crawford McCullough. The PRONI ref is LA/7/3A/6.O. Purdue, '"Please pardon the liberty": voices of the unemployed from 1930s Belfast', unpublished paper presented at *The Meaning of Poverty Workshop*, UCD, 5 September 2014.

[16] For example, Delay has used letters from parishioners (not necessarily begging, in fact often letters of complaint) from Bishop William Keane's papers in the Cloyne Diocesan Archives, Cobh. C. Delay, 'Confidantes or competitors ? women, priests, and conflict in post-famine Ireland', *Eire-Ireland*, 40 (Spring/Summer 2005), 107–25. The Diocese of Galway, Kilmacdusgh and Kilfenora there is no collection of charity letters for the 1920s and 30s. The current policy is to keep such letters for a six-year period for audit purposes and thereafter to destroy them. This is possibly what occurred previously also. I am grateful to the archivist Tom Kilgarriff for this information.

[17] As part of an Irish Research Council post-doctoral project Carole Holohan has worked on this collection. See C. Holohan, 'Conceptualising and responding to poverty in the Republic of Ireland in the 1960s: a case study of Dublin', *Social History*, 41 (January 2016), 34–53.

[18] Walsh, *Anglican women in Dublin*, pp. 151–197.

children from the perspective of the local clergyman and the POS inspector. The letters from the widows are generally formulaic. For example, Mrs Lucy H., writing in July 1935 for a clothes grant for her son, wrote a brief statement–like letter requesting the grant with no other details or embellishments. The inspector's report and the clergyman's reference provide the details of the case.[19] We know from references in charity reports and papers that the poor did write to charity organisations. The Saint Patrick's Guild and Rescue Society, for example, referred annually to as many as two thousand such letters.[20] In his 1902 guide to Dublin charities, George Williams refers to a large number of 'professional begging–letter writer(s)' in disparaging terms lamenting that Dublin had many such 'clever schemers'.[21] So, the tradition of applying for charity in writing was relatively widespread, however many were simply not saved or have not survived. It is noteworthy that the letters of the poor were archived in the Catholic diocese of Dublin by both Archbishop Byrne and his successor. They record, of course, the expenditure of significant amounts of money, but they also record the mission of the church. Thus even if the words of the poor were not kept for their own sake, it is likely they were saved because of their place in the Catholic Church's work. They represent important artefacts of a long tradition of writing by the poor and marginalised, with textual features that speak particularly of their Irish religious context.

'Your saintly face ... told me to write to you'

The very act of picking up the pen was an act of agency on the part of the authors; in writing such a letter of appeal they *initiated* a process of negotiation that would – they hoped – lead to assistance of some kind. There is evidence that the tradition of writing to the archbishop for assistance predated Byrne's time. In 1922, for example, Mrs Elaine B. from County Kildare informed the archbishop that she had received '5 pounds' from Archbishop Walsh the previous year.[22] Similarly, in November 1924, Mrs Angela D. noted that 'the Secretary gave me a card to bring to the parish priest to explain all about my circumstances but I did not bring it as I got the same Card in Archbishop Walsh*['s]*

---

[19] File H.1 (7/12/23), NAI, Protestant Orphan Society, 1045/5/5.
[20] For example, its 1922–23 report in which it recorded receipt of 2,009 letters. *Annual Report of the Saint Patrick's Guild, 1923–24*, p. 8.
[21] G. D. Williams, *Dublin Charities, being a Handbook of Dublin Philanthropic Organisations and Charities* (Dublin: John Falconer, 1902), p. 13.
[22] Mrs Elaine B., Ballytore (Athy, Co. Kildare), 15 February 1922. DDA, AB 7 CC, Box 1.

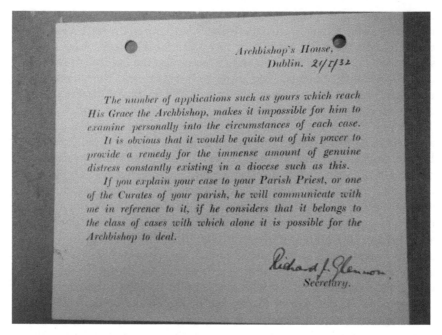

Figure 2.1 The card sent by the Archbishop of Dublin to all charity applicants.

time'.[23] The premise of the archbishop's 'charity cases' was that those who wrote had tried all other avenues of relief before writing, for example, relatives, state relief, Saint Vincent de Paul, etc. All those who wrote requesting assistance without a priest's reference were sent the following card (see Figure 2.1):

Archbishop's House
  Dublin

Dear Sir/Madam
The number of applications such as yours which reach His Grace the Archbishop, makes it impossible for him to examine personally into the circumstances of each case.
It is obvious that it would be quite out of his power to provide a remedy for the immense amount of genuine distress constantly existing in a diocese such as this.

[23] Mrs Angela D., Beaumount Convalescent Home, Drumcondra, Dublin, 23 November. 1924. DDA, AB 7 CC, Box 1. Archbishop William Walsh (1885–1921) was Byrne's immediate predecessor. While there were begging letters sent to him and previous archbishops, they were not systematically archived; some can be found scattered throughout the papers of each archbishop.

If you explain your case to your Parish Priest, or one of the Curates in your parish, he will communicate with me in reference to it, if he considers that it belongs to the class of cases with which alone it is possible for the Archbishop to deal.

Secretary[24]

This indicates that the impetus for the letters came at least partly from the writers themselves and in response to unprecedented need. Archbishop Byrne was already well known for his advocacy of the poor and his insistence on the pastoral role of the priests in his diocese. In February 1936, Mr Vincent A., a father of four with a sick wife and daughter, who could not make ends meet despite receiving Unemployment Assistance and limited help from the Vincent de Paul, wrote to the archbishop 'as the charitable feelings Your Grace has for the poor is so well known'.[25] Byrne's biographer Thomas J. Morrissey, noted that he supplied each priest with a *Liber Familiarum* (a book with the names and addresses of the members of the parish), to enable the clergy to make contact with their people, and also to provide continuity when parish priests moved on to other areas. He urged priests to visit homes: 'Where he found these being neglected he could be firm. It is believed that three men were assured of not being appointed parish priests during Dr Byrne's lifetime because of such pastoral neglect.'[26] As a result, priests may have been more diligent about their visiting under Archbishop Byrne and may have been given instructions – along with their *Liber Familiarum* – to refer certain cases of want to the archbishop. The archbishop made his interest in the poor widely known and he was also spurred by his abhorrence of, and obsession with, proselytism. The fact that he and his many priests also used charity to control the poor was an acknowledged part of the contract.

Those who wrote to the Archbishop of Dublin offered a variety of explanations for why they chose to write and they reveal how the poor discussed the options for assistance amongst themselves, offering each other strategic advice. In 1924 Mr James M. wrote from the heart of one of Dublin's poorest districts in Coombe Street that he had 'heard of [the archbishop's] charitable kindness from a friend'. This friend had told him 'if I wrote to you that I would be assisted as it is my first time'.[27] His friend had made him

[24] Archbishop's Card. See Figure 2.1.
[25] Mr Vincent A., X North Circular Rd., Dublin, 16 February 1936. DDA, AB 7 CC, Box 6.
[26] T. J. Morrissey, *Edward J. Byrne 1872–1941: The Forgotten Archbishop of Dublin* (Dublin: The Columba Press, 2010), p. 127.
[27] James M., Coombe St. to Archbishop Byrne, 27 April 1924. DDA, AB 7 CC, Box 1.

aware that the archbishop received such letters and also that people were expected to write only once seeking the archbishop's assistance. In 1925 Mrs Ann D., a widow with four children, explained: 'It has come to my hearing that there is under your charge a fund for the purpose of helping the poor + I wish to make an application for help.'[28]

It is clear that others were advised to apply to the archbishop by their parish priests or by charitable workers. In 1923 Mrs Margaret B. wrote from Enniscorthy in County Wexford because 'a leady that is good to the poor told me to send a few lines to you that it was on the paper that you would be geting peple in distress sum help'.[29] The Irish newspapers regularly reported on the archbishop's kindness to the poor, and his biographer notes that while he 'shunned the spotlight', he was 'known mainly for the quality of his sermons and for devotion to and empathy with the poor of Dublin'.[30] Indeed, upon his appointment the *Freeman's Journal* observed that his time as parish priest in Marlborough Street, which served some of the poorest tenement areas of Dublin, had provided him with 'no better training ground' as the future Archbishop of Dublin.[31] It is evident that some of the poor were reading the newspapers and were particularly motivated by reports of bequests to the archbishop for the poor.[32] The importance of newspapers as a source of information in working-class households is reflected in many memoirs. Frank O'Connor, who was born in Cork in 1903, recalled how, after work each day, his father 'sat at the head of the table by the window and read the evening *Echo* aloud to Mother, with comments that went on longer than the news'.[33] Similarly, Phil O'Keeffe, who grew up in inner-city Dublin in the 1920s, noted how her parents encouraged her to read the newspapers and her 'father would scan the *Evening Mail* or the *Herald* for an appropriate piece'.[34] Miss Agnes M. explained that it was the reports in the newspaper that had encouraged her to consider writing: 'I am reading in the papers every day about your grace's goodness in giving to every charity that is the reason I have written to you.'[35] Similarly, Miss Kathy D., from County Laois, wrote 'Having Seen our Late Bishop will on this weeks paper and His Kind Generosity to Poor of Ireland.'[36]

---

[28] Mrs Ann D., Upr Dominick St, Dublin, 17 January. 1925. Ibid.
[29] Mrs Margaret B., Scoby, Enniscorthy, Co. Wexford, 16 December. 1923. Ibid.
[30] Morrissey, *Edward J. Byrne 1872–1941* p. 9.   [31] Ibid., p. 14.
[32] Steven King has noted the importance of newspapers in nineteenth-century England in the transmission of information to paupers regarding legal rights to relief. S. King, 'Negotiating the law of poor relief in England, 1800–1840', *History*, 96 (2011), 410–435, 427.
[33] Frank O'Connor, *An Only Child* (London: Macmillan, 1961), p. 25.
[34] Phil O'Keeffe, *Down Cobbled Streets* (Dingle: Brandon Publishers, 1995), p. 208.
[35] Agnes M., Lucan, Dublin, n.d. *c.* 1924. DDA, AB 7 CC, Box 1.
[36] Mrs Kathy D., Portarlington, Queen's County (Co. Laois) 6 February 1922. Ibid.

It appears reports of bequests or funds received by the archbishop in the newspaper irritated him somewhat, or at least he did not like any hint of being told how to spend such funds. Mrs Margaret M., writing from County Mayo in the West of Ireland, asked the archbishop to 'extend [his] charity to the West', as she had read in the newspaper of a bequest to the archbishop by a man, she wrote, that had wanted all of Ireland to benefit from his estate.[37] She actually included a copy of the newspaper announcement, dated November 1936, with an asterisk to mark the passage that read: 'The testator left the residue of his property to be applied by the Archbishop of Dublin to such charitable purposes in Ireland as he shall deem fit.'[38] Although she followed instructions sent to her and enlisted a reference from her local priest, she was denied charity.[39] Similarly, both Mrs Margaret B. and Miss Kathy D. were given short shrift. The note on the left-hand corner of Miss Kathy D.'s letter curtly explained: 'I had funds all exhausted. No funds available.' The response to Mrs Margaret B. was even more pointed and not strictly true: the archbishop denied knowing anything about funds 'alluded to in newspapers', and rejected her request on the basis that 'Sorry no funds for any one outside diocese.'[40] In fact, the archbishop helped many people outside his diocese and, although the majority of people who wrote seeking his assistance were resident in Dublin, he rarely told anyone that he only assisted Dubliners. Only a few months prior to this letter he had assisted Mrs Annemarie N., a widowed mother of nine children from County Carlow, who had 'read a notice in the paper about a week ago where a Mr Seymour had willed some money to your Grace for such charitable purposes as your Grace in your discreesion thought fit'.[41] There were no quibbles about her address and she was sent £1 via her parish priest.[42] We are not privy to the reasons for these differing responses, but it is a reminder of the discretionary nature of the archbishop's benevolence.

---

[37] Mrs Margaret M., X Cappagh, Ballycastle, Co. Mayo, 30 July 1937. DDA, AB 7 CC, Box 7.

[38] 'Recent Irish Wills', 14 November 1936. Ibid.

[39] A simple 'No' is marked on Mrs M.'s second letter. Margaret M., X, Cappagh, Ballycastle, Co. Mayo, 15 January 1938. Her case cannot have been helped by an equivocal reference from her priest. See, Fr. J. Murphy, X, Ballycastle, Co. Mayo, 24 January 1938.

[40] This is the note written on the top left-hand corner of Mrs B.'s letter. Margaret B., Scoby, Enniscorthy, Co. Wexford, 16 December 1923. DDA, AB 7 CC, Box 1.

[41] Mrs Annemarie N., X, Ballykeenan, Myskall, Co. Carlow, 1 June 1923. Ibid.

[42] It was noted on the top-left hand corner of her letter that £1 had been sent to her parish priest.

Not surprisingly, many people claimed to have received inspiration from God or their religion to write and seek help. Mr Henry O'N., ex-national soldier and father of three 'very small Children', explained 'Dr A man might do anything to get an honest living', but he had tried everything and everywhere in vain. He had fallen back on his faith and was offering up novenas, as his heart was 'broke looking for something to do in regards to work'. It was during his novena that 'the thought has come into my head. If I wrote a letter to Your Most Rev'.[43] Of course, evoking such religious inspiration established the religious credentials of these writers and put God in their corner. Miss Tina McG. also wrote that she 'knelt down in my room in front of Sacred Heart picture to ask God to direct me where to turn my thoughts turned to your holy house'.[44] By drawing on such imagery they conjured biblical promises of God's protection of the poor and the sinner. Paul H., who wrote seeking help to clear his £30 gambling debt, enveloped his entire letter in religious imagery:

It goes very hard with me to have to write you this letter as i am in Great Trouble and on the verge of Dispair. I am here in Balbriggan 13 years and am Married and have Six Children The Eldest you Confirmed yesterday ... i Did not sleep this Past week But your Saintly Face gave me strength today and told me to write to you I will start a new life over and never again do what i have done ... i releize i could Pay it Back by the month and no one would never know as its a terrible way to be also if you could send me some little Medal to keep me from Timtation And our houshold will always remember you in our Prayers of how you saved us But you do not Need prayers as you are a Saint.
    Knowing you will love me and and i will Plege myself to led a good God fearing life from now and Repay.[45]

Paul H.'s pitch was effective and he received the significant sum of £30. We cannot know to what degree he believed in religious inspiration and the power of medals to ward off temptation – many people certainly did – however, it is clear from his letter that these ideas had a powerful social resonance and helped him to frame his failings in a culture of religious redemption.

'I take the liberty of writing'

Both David Fitzpatrick and Thomas Sokoll have established that to really appreciate letter collections as artefacts and sources it is essential to

---

[43] Mr Henry O'N., X Werburgh St, Dublin, 19 May 1924. DDA, AB 7 CC, Box 1.
[44] Miss Tina McG., X Eastmoreland place, off Upper Baggot St, Dublin, n.d. c. 1933. DDA, AB 7 CC, Box 5.
[45] Mr Paul H., X Hill St, Balbriggan, Co. Dublin, n.d. c. 1936. DDA, AB 7 CC, Box 6.

explore their physical and formal features. This involves considering every aspect of the composition process from the choice of greetings or valedictions, to the spacing, handwriting and phraseology, because all these represent choices made by each individual writer and reveal a host of other influences at work. What is remarkable about letters separated by so much time and history is the degree to which they largely conform to the rhetorical principles of the nineteenth-century writing manuals. According to these manuals every petition letter must have five parts: 1. the formal terms of address and greetings; 2. homage to the addressee; 3. the narrative explanation of the petitioning letter; 4. the actual request; 5. concluding remarks and signature.[46] While individual authors altered or omitted some of these steps, they all employed a majority of them to construct, at least in a structural sense, a conventional petitioning letter. However, the nature of the narrative explanation was very informal and often involved a personalising of poverty in order to justify the request. Steven King and Alison Stringer have observed something similar in relation to letters of the sick poor in England, Wales and Scotland between the 1780s and 1830s. They have argued that the classic type of letter combined formulaic expression with 'submissive posturing', and the description of the individual case, often accompanied by an implied or direct threat. King and Stringer's observation that this combination of 'rhetoric, fact, aspiration and despair' makes pauper letters less formal narratives of poverty than the petitioning letters of Germany and Austria is also applicable to the Irish letters written some hundred years later.[47]

These charity petitioners of the twentieth century drew from the same epistolary tradition as Irish emigrants writing personal letters home in the nineteenth century[48] and English paupers writing to the Poor Law authorities in the eighteenth and early nineteenth centuries.[49] Fitzpatrick's correspondents began their letters explaining that they were 'writing a few lines', 'a few words', or were taking, embracing or availing of 'this opportunity' or 'liberty', to write.[50] Sokoll's Essex paupers often

---

[46] Hämmerle notes that theoretical manuals on 'correct' letter writing date from the eleventh century. C. Hämmerle, 'Requests, complaints, demands. Preliminary thoughts on the petitioning letters of lower-class Austrian women, 1865–1918' in C. Bland, and M. Cros (eds.), *Gender and Politics in the Age of Letter Writing, 1750–2000* (Aldershot: Ashgate, 2004), p. 129, n. 6.

[47] S. King and A. Stringer, 'I have once more taken the Leberty to say as you well know': The development of rhetoric in the letters of the English, Welsh and Scottish sick and poor 1780s–1830s' in Gestrich, Hurren and King (eds.), *Poverty and Sickness in Modern Europe*, pp. 69–91.

[48] D. Fitzpatrick, *Oceans of Consolation: Personal Accounts of Irish Migration to Australia* (Cork University Press, 1994), p. 487.

[49] Sokoll, *Essex Pauper Letters.*   [50] Fitzpatrick, *Oceans of Consolation*, p. 487.

used apologetic openings, such as, 'I am Sorry to troble you' or 'i hope
you will excuse the Liberty i have taken in troubling of you.'[51] Those who
sat down to write to the Archbishop of Dublin also tended to open their
letters with a version of apology that underscored their regret at *having* to
write a begging letter at all. Mr H. C., who had written previously
without success, stressed: 'I am really sorry for being so troublesome'
concluding 'Hoping your Lordships will excuse *[me]* for being so
troublesome. I remain with very great respect your Lordships humble
servant.'[52] Mrs Anna L. expressed concern regarding how to address the
archbishop: 'Dear Archbishop, I humbly ask pardon for the liberty I take
of writing to you + also hope you will excuse me as I don't know how to
address you.'[53]

Sokoll noted the tendency among the Essex paupers to conclude their
letters with formulaic reverential valedictions, for example, 'Your
humble/obedient servant', with individual writers offering their own
variants such as Your trobbsom' or 'unfortunate Humble Serv'.[54] The
letters from the Irish poor reflect the same style, while including a
reference to the archbishop; for example, a common valediction was, 'I
remain My Lord Archbishop,/Your humble and devoted Servant/', with
some correspondents working into these formal endings their own
emphasis or message: 'Believe me/ My Dear Lord Archbishop/Yours
Most Obediently.'[55] By far the most common ending adopted in this
collection was a variation of 'Your obedient servant' and this, Fitzpatrick
has noted, was the ending Irish teachers were advised to teach their
pupils.[56]

Others stressed their lack of familiarity with the conventions of writing a
begging letter as proof that they were not habitual beggars. In the early
1920s Mrs E. D., a young mother, worried: 'Your Grace, I do not know if
that is the proper way to begin a letter to you, as I've never written a letter
like this before, but any mistakes I make I hope you will in your kindness
over look them' (see Figure 2.2).[57] In July 1938, Mrs May M. also
expressed concern about how to compose such a letter, 'I may not have
address[ed] you right', and she concluded with the hope 'Dear Lord you
not be annoyed *[with me]* for writing I pray for you always for a long life

[51] Sokoll, *Essex Pauper Letters*, pp. 444, 332.
[52] Harry C., Ballaghadereen, Co. Roscommon, 28 February 1924. DDA, AB 7 CC, Box 1.
[53] Mrs Anna L., X Desmond Avenue, Dún Laoghaire, Co. Dublin, 4 March 1922. Ibid.
[54] Sokoll, *Essex Pauper Letters*, p. 45,55.
[55] Marion G., X Foxrock, Co. Dublin, 28 November 1924. DDA, AB 7 CC, Box 1.
[56] See P. W. Joyce, *A Handbook of School Management and Methods of Teaching* (Dublin,
     15th edn. 1892), pp. 242–6. Cited in Fitzpatrick, *Oceans of Consolation*, p. 500.
[57] Mrs E. D., no address, n.d. *c.* 1924. DDA, AB 7 CC, Box 1.

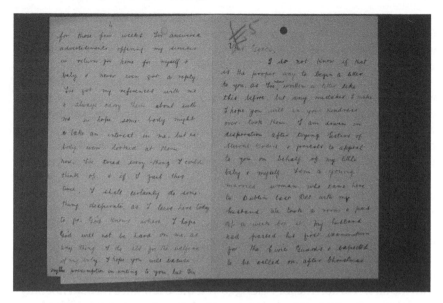

Figure 2.2 A section of the letter written by Mrs E. D., (no adress available) to the Archbishop of Dublin, c. 1924.

and God strinten *[strenghten]* you.'[58] Mrs L., who wrote in the late 1920s from inner city Dublin, omitted virtually all formalities, apart from the spartan 'Sir', and simply laid her case before the archbishop:

Sir
   I was speaking to Canon Magill he advised me to send this letter and His Lordship should give me some help. Father I have four small children and not a cut of bread to give them. My Husband lost his employment in Mr Guinness Brewery owing to the strike. I am in very poor circumstances and no help coming from anywhere. hoping dear Father you in your kindness will help me I am Rev Father your[s] humbly
   Mrs L.[59]

Her letter has a bleak sense of urgency about it although her valediction, however truncated, reveals that she had at least a basic familiarity with what was expected in a formal letter. She may not have fully engaged with the process because she could not or because she was simply too worn

---

[58] Mrs May M., X Middle Gardiner St, Dublin (city), 3 July 1938. DDA, AB 7 CC, Box 7.
[59] Mrs L., X James Street, Dublin (city), n.d. *c.* 1927. DDA, AB 7 CC, Box 2. She received a £1. Guinness Brewery was considered one of the best employers in Dublin as it offered high wages and permanent employment.

down by her situation. Her letter was unusual in its absence of letter–like features both in terms of terminology and physical structure: her brief valediction was not separated by spacing from the body of her appeal, for example, which was the case in most letters, however simple and short.

In a similar fashion to the Essex pauper writers, the Irish writers often wove the pretext for their writing into their opening as this helped to stress the legitimacy and necessity of writing. In Sokoll's collection James Smith wrote in September 1832 to the overseers of the Poor Law: 'I must be so troublesome to the Parish for A little asistance for I have been Laid up.'[60] In May 1826 David and Sarah Rivenall wrote: 'Gentlemen pardon the Liberty we take in Writing to you so Often but Necessity obliges US to do So.'[61] In Dublin in 1924 Mr James McN. wrote because 'Circumstances compel me to appeal',[62] and Joseph C. asked that he be excused 'in taking the liberty of writing those few lines to you as poverty permits me to do so'.[63] Similarly, Mrs Karen M., a widowed mother of eleven, claimed 'its the direct poverty make[s] me appeal to your Lordship'.[64] Mrs J. B., a mother of seven children framed her letter as part of her 'fight' opening with the line: 'Pardon me for writing to you these few lines I would not only for fighting for an honest living for my little hungry family.'[65] Others dispensed with any formal lamenting and opened immediately with the dramatic picture of their despair. For example, in 1939 a woman, describing herself as a 'brokenhearted mother', began her letter almost mid-flow:

Dear Father
    I am in great distress I have 10 children My Eldest is 23 Years old and has infantile Parlysis from birth he has to be washed fed and dressed just like a baby and he has been in bed all his life and <u>never</u> speakes only we understand him[66]

Thus the choice of greetings and valedictions were not merely part of the paraphernalia of letter writing, they were often stitched into a wider mission on the part of the letter writer and used as a launching pad for

---

[60] Letter from James Smith in Woolwich, Kent, to the overseers of Aveley, 6 September 1832 cited in Sokoll, *Essex Pauper Letters*, pp. 93–94.

[61] Letter from David and Sarah Rivenall in [St George in the East] London to the churchwardens or vestry clerk of Chelmsford, 10 May 1826 cited in Sokoll, *Essex Pauper Letters*, p. 231.

[62] Mr James McN., X Bushfield Terrace, Donnybrook, Dublin, 10 December 1924. DDA, AB 7 CC, Box 1.

[63] Mr Joseph C. & Wife, X Shamrock Cottages, North Strand, Dublin 14 December 1938. DDA, AB 7 CC, Box 7.

[64] Mrs Karen M., X Convent Road, Doneraile, Co. Cork, n.d. *c.* 1933. DDA, AB 7 CC, Box 5.

[65] Mrs J. B., X Lr. St Kevin's Street, Dublin City, 28 March 1932. DDA, AB 7 CC, Box 4.

[66] Mrs H., X Clonard Road, Crumlin, Dublin, n.d. *c.* July 1938. DDA, AB 7 CC, Box 7.

a petition, to stress the moral legitimacy of the request, or to reassert loyalty after an implicitly or explicitly critical letter. The etiquette of letter writing was indicative of a shared universe between writer and reader, one which both parties recognised. As Fitzpatrick has argued, these salutations are part of the 'poetic beauty' of these letters, but they also help us to see the ways in which individual writers chose to subvert these conventions, often to put moral pressure on the intended recipient.[67] Hence, after the humble beginning a writer may threaten to 'go to the Protestants', but would still sign off as an 'obedient servant' – the aim, after all, was a positive response not religious defection.[68] The writers made such threats within certain clearly understood parameters, which the formalities of letter writing helped to underscore. They were engaged in a dance – a spiritual jig – writer and reader understood.

Sub-Literacy and Oral Writing

By 1911, Ireland had attained almost complete adult literacy and in 1926 the Irish Free State made primary education between the ages of six and fourteen obligatory.[69] While it is important not to underestimate how many children still did not attend primary school regularly, this collection indicates that by the 1920s and 30s even those with only a rudimentary grasp of the written word, had learnt *how* to compose a letter.[70] Irish women were more likely to be literate than their male counterparts, marking them out from their western European peers.[71] Interestingly, and a testament to at least one aspect of the Irish education system, many of the writers, even the most illiterate, had beautiful joined handwriting. The high standard of handwriting displayed in the majority of these Irish letters often stands in sharp contrast to weaknesses in other aspects of their literacy. Thus many of the barriers that Lyons identified in the path of ordinary people's writing – gender, inexperience in mastering writing utensils or a lack of familiarity with the 'protocols' of writing – did not pose insurmountable obstacles to letter writers

---

[67] Fitzpatrick, *Oceans of Consolation*, p. 21.

[68] It is significant that Walsh has noted that Protestant widows made similar threats when applying to Protestant charities. See, Walsh, *Anglican Women in Dublin*, pp. 166–167.

[69] M. E. Daly, '"The primary and natural educator ?":The role of parents in the education of their children in independent Ireland', *Eire-Ireland*, 44 (Spring/Summer, 2009), 194–217, 197.

[70] In 1872 the composition of letters became part of the standard national curriculum in Ireland. Fitzpatrick, *Oceans of Consolation*, p. 500.

[71] Lyons has noted that Italian and Spanish female literacy rates, particularly writing skills, lagged considerably behind men's. Lyons, *The Writing Culture of Ordinary People in Europe*, p. 11.

motivated by poverty in Ireland.[72] In the Irish case it was a combination of instinctive articulacy, a desire and need to write, and the gift of a basic education for boys and girls (which obviously focused on penmanship), that allowed such a wide range of ordinary people to compose their poverty on paper.[73]

There are many letters in this collection written by those operating at a 'sub-literate' level[74]; these authors employed largely phonetic spelling, little punctuation, and often did not order their writing in paragraphs. Such letters invariably came from the most impoverished areas of Ireland, in particular the Dublin tenements or poorer rural areas. In 1929 David N. wrote one of the clearest examples of a sub-literate letter (see Figure 2.3):

David N.
2*1*2*

The very reverend,
Sebteng [sending] just a line to you hoping to find you in good helth as this leafs us the same thank god and his holy Blesset mother for it is so I ame gone to ask you if it lis in your pour for to help my poor wife to get hur boots and mine out of the pon and we promis you that we wont ever throble you any more we promis god and his holy mother that we wont ever throBle you any more in Clous the too tickets of the Boots to you as our feet are wet every day when it rains so for the s < sacred> Hart of Jesus get them for us and god Bless you and/ you see that we wont ever go near you any more so my poor wife is the worst off as she is expetin hur throBle soon and wet feet feet wood not soot hur you can see hur when she goes up to you. You can see hur feet the way the[y] are and you see i ame not telling any lis to you and my feet is the same so for the love of god and his holy mother Do your Best and get them and your Cant do any more than your Best and we wont ever throBl you any more so for god sake and his holy mother do it for us and it is the last think i or my wife will ask you to do for us may the satret hart of jesus Bless you night and Day and every where you go Call in the morn for the anser[75]

David N. barely provided a letter structure – there is no valediction or signature at the end of the letter. It contains the fixed formulas, redundancies and repetitions that Lyons identified as core characteristics of oral writing.[76] He repeatedly used the phrase 'for the Sacred Heart of Jesus' or

[72] Lyons, *The Writing Culture of Ordinary People in Europe*, pp. 1–3.
[73] D. Fitzpatrick, '"A share of the honeycomb": education, emigration and Irishwomen', *Continuity and Change*, 2 (1986), 217–234.
[74] Fitzpatrick, *Oceans of Consolation*, p. 35.
[75] David. N., no address, n.d. *c.* 1929. DDA, AB 7 CC, Box 2.
[76] Lyons, *The Writing Culture of Ordinary People in Europe*, p. 142.

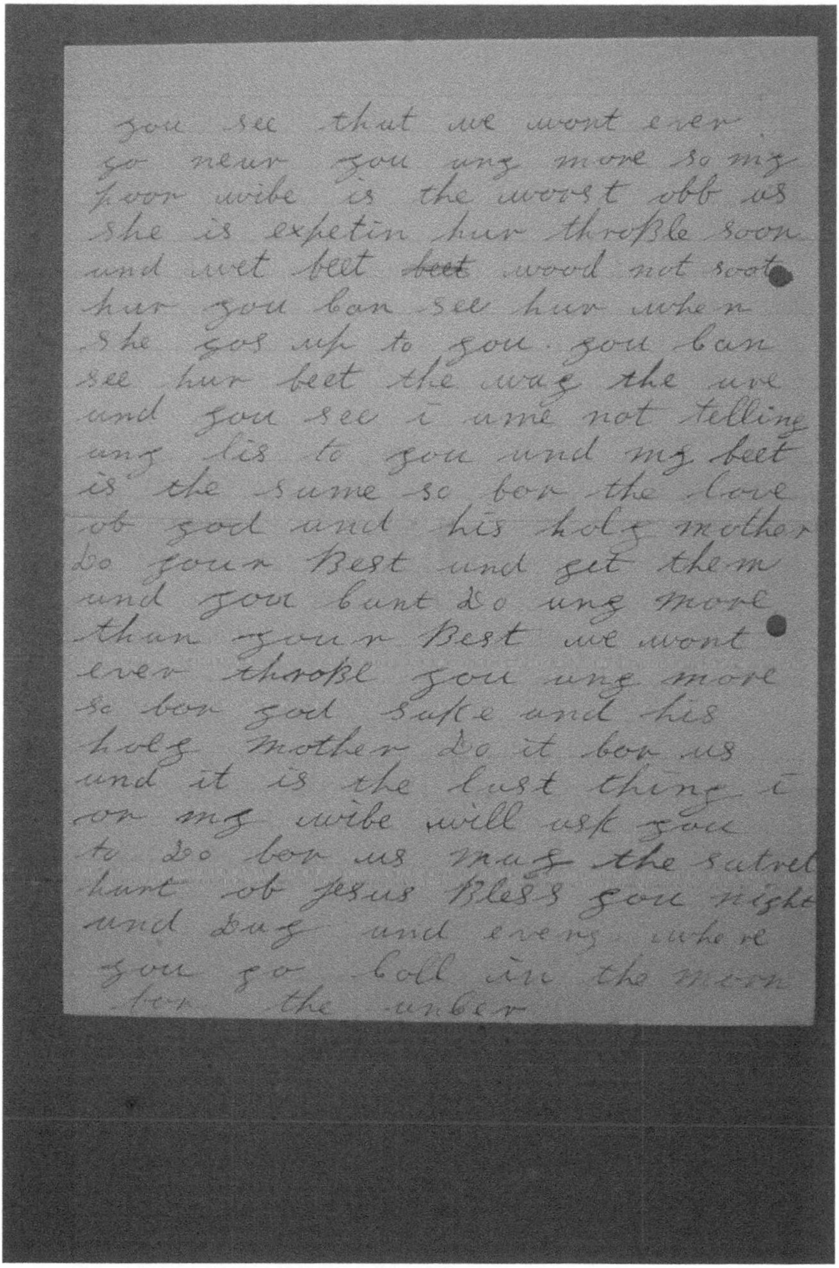
you see that we wont ever
go neur you uny more so my
poor wibe is the worst obb us
she is expetin hur throble soon
und wet beet ~~beet~~ wood not soot
hur you ban see hur when
she gos up to you. you ban
see hur beet the way the ure
und you see i ume not telling
uny lis to you und my beet
is the sume so bor the love
ob god und his holy mother
do your Best und get them
und you bunt do uny more
thun your Best we wont
ever throble you uny more
so bor god sake und his
holy mother do it bor us
und it is the lust thing i
or my wibe will usk you
to do bor us muy the sutred
hurt ob jesus Bless you night
und day und every where
you go boll in the morn
bor the unber

Figure 2.3 A section of the letter written by David N., (no address available) to the Archbishop of Dublin, c. 1929.

'Jesus/God Bless you', and he reassured the archbishop several times that he 'wont ever throBl you any more'. His letter did not create a coherent narrative structure, instead it circled around the issue of his and his wife's boots in the pawn, there is no obvious beginning, middle or end. Despite being one of the least literate of the archbishop's correspondents, David N. still engaged with basic epistolary rhetoric – 'hoping to find you in good helth as this leafs us the same thank god and his holy Blesset mother' – incorporating piety and poverty in a neat, if crude, appeal.

The fact that most of those writers that displayed strong oral aspects in their writing tended not to use paragraphs, or employ punctuation, impacted on the rhythm of their letter, making them appear more fluid.[77] In this way the original sentiment is captured and the 'orality' of the conversation these reluctant writers wished to have is retained, something which is so often lost when ordinary people's words were translated in formal settings such as courts.[78] A central feature of these oral writings is the different sense of order they construct; points are not sequenced in the same way as letters structured using the tools of written expression. However, it may be less that 'order and disorder in writing co-exist',[79] and more that the oral mind sees order differently. This lack of paragraphs, punctuation and other tools used to order writing means that repetition becomes an intrinsic part of the structure in these letters. A phrase repeated is often used to punctuate as well as reiterate and stress importance or significance: for David N. the central issues were his religious character and his wet feet and despite his lack of coherent structure his objective (of transmitting these two points) is achieved.[80] In 1937 Mrs Margaret McD. wrote in quite a childlike script a letter that displays many of the traits of oral writing: her letter has no paragraph breaks, virtually no punctuation and the space on the page is poorly used (she had to cram in her last few words into the bottom of the page), there is significant repetition and the way she ordered her narrative is reminiscent of the oral tradition. She told the archbishop that she and her husband were delighted to see he was at home and that she had buried her five-month-old daughter in the same literary breath.

---

[77] Lyons observed that these ordinary people's texts were 'close to oral speech and dialect, and their authors have some difficulty in maintaining a straight line and in observing the rules of syntax and correct spelling'. M. Lyons, '"Ordinary writings" or how the "illiterate" speak to historians' in M. Lyons (ed.), *Ordinary Writings, Personal Narratives*, pp. 13–32, 13.

[78] L. Abrams, *Oral History Theory* (London and New York: Routledge, 2010), pp. 19–20.

[79] Lyons, *The Writing Culture of Ordinary People in Europe*, p. 224.

[80] There is no record if David N. received any assistance as a result of this letter.

Margaret McD.
X North Great Georges Street – Dublin

His Grace the Lord Archbishop
May God Bless you And spared your health For A very Long time yet, I am Always[s] Praying for you A I know you 30 years when you were Curat in the Pro-Catheral Malborough St I used to go to confession I am 30 year in the one sodaltiy *[sodality]* I am Always at the Mission every year I do walk to see your home to the Palace when is over Myself and my husband we do Be delighted to see you home, The Most Rev, E, J. Byrned & Last week I Buried my Baby Girl 5 Months old from the children hospital we got no society money because she was Not 13 weeks in Benefit So my Husband Pledge his Clothes and Boots to help to Buried it So I just wrote this Letter to know could you Give some help to Get his Clothes and Boot out of the Pawn as he is going to work Next Monday Please God Please do your Best to help me for God sake Dont let me down For he is a Bad way For his Clothes and Boots all I am getting is 16/6 per week Labour exchange to keep 3 in family Please do your Best to help me and may god bless you I will always pray for you also our Pope.
Margaret McD..
X North Great
Georges Street
Dublin[81]

Margaret McD.'s order may not be incidental but central to her plea, she may very well have judged this structure to be the most effective way of appealing: first establishing a personal connection and deep loyalty to the archbishop and then explaining the cause of her distress. As in Sokoll's pauper letters, the focus was not on the emotional impact of the death of a child, but on the cost of burial. Margaret McD.'s reference to 'no society money' refers to burial insurance; she was not eligible for a payout because the baby died within thirteen weeks. While the purpose of this letter was not to elicit sympathy for her bereavement, the idea that a family had no pause for grief because of greater financial pressures was a powerful reminder of the depth and cost of poverty. Margaret McD.'s structure graphically highlights this fact for the modern reader: she did not open her letter with the death of her child because of itself this was a relatively common occurrence. In Mrs McD.'s part of Dublin infant mortality rates were the highest in the country at 109 per 1,000 registered births in 1937.[82] The importance of burial insurance was reiterated in letter after letter; the burying of one's dead has deep symbolic

---

[81] Mrs Margaret McD., X North Great George's Street, Dublin, n.d. *c.* 1937. DDA, AB 7 CC, Box 7.

[82] The national rural infant mortality rate was 61 per 1,000, whereas the urban rate was 91 per 1,000. L. Earner-Byrne, *Mother and Child: Maternity and Child Welfare in Dublin, 1922–60* (Manchester University Press, 2007), pp. 48–49.

significance in most cultures and the poor were no less immune to these sensibilities.[83] As Elaine Crowley notes in her memoir of growing up in poverty in 1930s Dublin: 'Like the rent-man, the society-man called every week ... It was as important to pay the insurance as it was to pay the rent. Eviction was dreaded and so was a pauper's funeral. The dead must be given a good send-off.'[84] In 1943, *The Bell* observed in relation to a Mrs K. from Dublin's tenements: 'To accept free food is one thing, but a charity burial for any of the family would be the ultimate and unbearable humiliation.'[85]

We can compare Margaret McD.'s appeal to a similar one written in 1931 by Mrs Eileen D.

X Foley St
Dublin

14/11/31

Your Grace
I Crave your holy Pardon for writing you those few lines I am a Poor woman with a man out of work and five young Children whos[e] ages are from 3 years to 12 yrs we are living on the Relief Ticket to the value of 17/-6 for food only /

No Rent fire and the Children are in a very bad way they are in their Bare feet and Very little Clothing on them my self and Husband have to go to 7. oc mass on Sunday morning we are in such a way.

I my self is only after getting out of a very sick bed after child berth which I am glad to say is Gone to God above./

Your Grace it is three years ago since you were so Good to assist me which I was very thankful for.

hoping your Grace will Give my case your Kind Consideration in Gods Name I am
Your Graces
Most Humble Servant
in God
Eileen D.[86]

Eileen D.'s letter has a more developed structure, she used paragraphs to order its contents – the death of her child, while not given first place in her letter, was given its own paragraph – and yet her spelling was phonetic, her use of capitals *ad hoc* and her punctuation virtually non-existent. Notwithstanding these technical shortcomings, her letter reveals experience of another kind: the experience of begging and of her religious

---

[83] E. Hurren, 'The business of anatomy and being poor: Why have we failed to learn the medical and poverty lessons of the past?' in Gestrich, King and Raphael (eds.), *Being Poor in Modern Europe*, pp. 135–155, 137.

[84] E. Crowley, *Cowslips and Chainies: A Memoir of Dublin in the 1930s* (Dublin: Lilliput Press, 1996), p. 7.

[85] Compiled, 'Other people's incomes - 3', *The Bell*, 7 (October 1943), 61.

[86] Mrs Eileen D., X Foley Street, Dublin (City), 14 November 1931. DDA, AB 7 CC, Box 4.

universe. By marrying her family's nakedness with a restriction on her religious observance (she had to go to early mass to hide her poor clothing) she shifted the moral weight of her appeal on to her church's shoulders, while displaying a deep understanding of its priorities. Duty, despair and a hint of where the latter might lead are all skillfully rendered in this relatively simple epistle. She had done her duty by Catholicism (five children and one sent 'gladly' to God), despite extreme poverty and its incumbent shame, she still attended mass, but in 'God's name' she needed to keep the roof over her family's head. In Mrs Eileen D.'s letter her child's death forms part of the grind of survival – she 'is only after getting out of a very sick bed after child berth' – but it is there, in its own paragraph, because it is important to that very picture. The only emotion she expressed was the relief that the child had 'Gone to God above', thus this letter tells us little about her feelings, instead it reveals how she characterised her child's death as part of the relentlessness of the life of a 'Poor woman' – it too had to be paid for.

While David N., Margaret McD. and Eileen D. wrote relatively long letters, other sub-literate letters were much more laconic. In late 1939 Mrs M. D., wrote a letter to the archbishop which represents the other classic type of semi-literate letter and yet she included all she needed in her brief missive to get her message across.

~~Dear~~   14.11.39
Mrs M. D.
X. House,
off Nth Cumberland St.,
Dublin

Dear Arthibish
I am verry sorry to have to trople you as I am getting put out of my home for Rent and my husbant is gone to Birmingham to Look for worke and is walking the Streets he is a member of the Tird Order and I went to the councle in adam ~~as~~ eve and they could do noting as there is Noting in the fun[d]s I will ~~But~~ pray for you and the six children will pray to as I have to be in court on Monday next hoping you will see your way an Do some thing I will now come to a close hoping you will give us your kind considerrating yours Ever Mrs M D.
in closing the summins to Let you see[87]

Sokoll recommends reading these sources aloud so we can hear the voices of the past.[88] Mrs M. D. wrote her short letter as she would have spoken it; we can hear her inner city Dublin accent – her 'husbant' who

[87] Mrs M. D. X House, off Nth. Cumberland St., Dublin (City), 14 November. 1939. DDA, AB 7 CC, Box 7.
[88] T. Sokoll, 'Old age in poverty: The record of Essex pauper letters, 1780–1834' in T. Hitchcock, P. King and P. Sharpe (eds.), *Chronicling Poverty: The Voices and Strategies of the English Poor, 1640–1840* (London: Palgrave, 1996) p. 130.

was a member of the Tird – rather than the Third – Order. Towards the end she attempted to adopt a more formal tone – 'I will now come to a close' hoping that her letter would receive 'kind consideratting' – presumably imitating what she knew of other letters, possibly from the classroom. The topography of her letter also indicates a basic familiarity with the format required: despite an abortive beginning (note the crossed out 'Dear' at the top of the page), she placed her address in the right-hand corner and spaced it line by line. The 'Dear Arthibish' was also designated its own line, but this structure breaks down somewhat towards the end, there is no valediction or name, and her note about the enclosure of her court summons was not formally denoted as a *post scriptum*. However, regardless of the limited grammar and punctuation, she included how many children she had, why her breadwinner was not fulfilling his role (emigration and unemployment), what her immediate problem was (eviction) and proof of it (court summons) and her religious *bona fides* (her husband was a member of the Third Order of Saint Francis – a Catholic sodality – and she and her children prayed).[89]

Sokoll has argued that in these pieces of oral writing people 'were quite obviously acting along the boundaries between the spoken and the written word'.[90] Perhaps what their letters reveal is that the boundary between the spoken and written word was highly porous. As Lyons has observed, there was a 'dynamic interplay' between the oral and the written world in the writings of ordinary people well into the twentieth century.[91] Indeed, precisely because this was so, people with such poor technical literacy skills felt they could write as the boundary did not seem impregnable. Often these writers used what little they knew of the epistolary form as a key to unlock the mystique of *writing* an appeal; they employed aspects of the formal structure to either bookend their appeal or, more often, to blend it with their oral style. While these Irish letters needed to make space for religious references and declarations, in view of their intended recipient, they are remarkably similar to Sokoll's pauper oral writings. In the early 1930s, Clara W. sent this short missive to the archbishop's palace:

X Wellington St. n.d.
    Your most Gracious may i beg leave to appeal to you for a little assistance as i am expecting to become a mother very soon and i am in need of help very badly and i am in need of nourishment my husband is unemployed and i have two

---

[89] P. Conlan, 'The secular Franciscans' in E. Bhreathnach, J. MacMahon and J. McCafferty (eds.), *The Irish Franciscans 1534–1990* (Dublin: Four Courts Press, 2009), pp. 260–70.
[90] Sokoll, *Essex Pauper Letters*, p. 7.
[91] Lyons, *The Writing Culture of Ordinary People in Europe*, p. 247.

young children attending school i will be very grateful for any little help to help
me over my confinement

I am your most
Obedient servant
Clara W.[92]

Clara W. appropriates the formal echoes of a letter 'i beg leave to
appeal' into her oral style. She does little scene setting, but rather relies
on the banal truth of her poverty. There is simply no more to say – for it is
more like a spoken than a written document. Read aloud her letter
contains the cadences of vernacular speech, one can almost hear her
hurry to have it said, to have the plea made. In a similar fashion Joseph
D.'s 1928 letter merely nods at the conventions of letter writing and its
narrative thrust is driven by the urgency of poverty.

14.1.28

Joseph D.
X upper Dominick
Street Dublin

Your grace
i Should Be Very thankfull to you if you would help me in Some little way as i
have a Family of 6 Children which are not able to look after them selves there are
Very Small and i am living up to my Religon as best i can their ages are from 11,
7, 7, 4, 2, 1 [above each age years is written]. And & never had to trubble any one
before hoping you Will See what little help you can give me and oblige, J D
    i have been told by the Boy on your Door to Send my litter Forward to you By
Post all my Children are nearly Bear Footed and Poor Close as my self[93]

Clearly Joseph D. would never have written a letter had he not been
instructed to do so by whoever answered the door at the archbishop's
palace. While his letter is succinct it still displays an oral structure, thus
his plea for his children is interrupted by a reassurance of his religious
fidelity: 'there are Very small and i am living up to my Religon as best i
can their ages are from 11, 7, 7, 4, 2, 1'. The listing of children's ages was
quite common in even the least literate letters, indicating how important
children (the more the merrier in this case) were to the chances of
success. However, this was not a mere act of cataloguing, but also a
graphic way of illustrating both the task of feeding such a crew and that
each child was an individual – a life.

[92] Mrs Clara W., X Wellington St., (Dublin city), n.d. c. 1932. DDA, AB 7 CC, Box 4.
[93] Joseph D., X Upper Dominick St, Dublin (city), 14 January 1928. DDA, AB 7 CC,
    Box 2.

'Excuse writing and spilling'

While composing one's poverty in a letter offered obvious advantages – the time and space to construct things as you saw them, possibly even to explain them to yourself – they also presented formidable challenges to many writers. Writing a letter required a certain level of literacy and the ability to articulate and explain one's self and situation. Many letter writers commented on their discomfort with the act of writing by apologising for their writing or spelling. This was not unique to Irish ordinary writers; Lyons observed the same phenomenon in letters from France, Italy and Spain.[94] However, it did not merely highlight an awareness of literary weaknesses, it also revealed the strain induced by the act of composition. Susan Whyman has defined what she called 'epistolary literacy', which involves the quality of handwriting, how the writer uses blank spaces on the page, capitalisation, paragraph breaks and punctuation.[95] The more educated and confident an author was the more highly developed their writing tended to be, the more inclined they were to use the space on the page evenly while ordering their story into coherent paragraphs and punctuating the narrative with a range of commas, question marks and other syntax tools. While many writers seemed unperturbed by their weakness in these areas, for others it was obviously a strain and on occasion some letters are quite difficult to follow or understand as a result.

Mrs May M., writing in July 1938, concluded by asking the archbishop to 'Excuse writing and spilling'; her narrative was complicated and she lacked the skills to make it comprehensible:

X Middle Gardiner St

3 July 1938

    To his Grace

The Archbishop I take the libarty of addressing you as a servant of God. minding my duty reciving holy cummunion at Holiday [holy day?] and on the first Friday to say I am in such trouble I got in to money lenders and cannot out of it god may forgive me my son got married 3 years ago a good boy he was my first husband son I am married second time since 1918 to 1938 I got nothing but worry from my second husband he is good I do my best to keep everything together but I cannot/ get out of bebt [debt] my husband is not aware of it I cannot sleep only pray that god and blesset Mother may risk a friend to take me out of all my bother confessor says I bare with patienes you will excuse me his

[94] Lyons, *The Writing Culture of Ordinary People in Europe*, pp. 34–52.
[95] S. E. Whyman, *The Pen and the People: English Letter Writers, 1660–1800* (Oxford University Press, 2009), pp. 9–11.

Grace Dear Archbishop for writing I may not have address your right I ask you to remember me in your prayers and that I may get some conclusion I pray to our Lady of Lourdes little Chaple each day I she help me over each day. My husband suffer from epelipsy fits he was a ex soldir he is ill and a scandle tongue to me the priest told me I own nothing my /—/on earth/ hoping Dear Lord you not be annoyed for writing I pray for your always for a long life for your always for a long life and God to strinten you

I now conclude
I Remain his Grace
The Rev. Dr byrne
Your obedient
servant
Your In Christ
May M.
Excuse writing and spilling.[96]

She could not spell 'receiving' or 'scandal' and she spelt many other words according to how she would have pronounced them – 'blesset' 'soldir' and 'Chaple' and 'strinten' *[strengthen]*. Yet she was familiar with medical terminology, her husband's diagnosis of 'epelipsy', and she also drew on conventional religious terminology, for example, the idea that she bore her circumstances with patience. However, her poor grammar and punctuation and the ordering of her narrative makes it difficult to follow what story she was trying to tell about her second husband. He had caused her nothing but worry, but was good and a 'scandle tongue' to her; perhaps this confusion emerges from the fact that his illness was responsible for his troubling behaviour, but she believed him to be essentially good. It is simply not clear. Other aspects of her story are there only by inference, for example, the mention of her son who had married. This was relevant presumably because he was a source of financial support to her prior to his marriage, however, she did not make this explicit. Nevertheless, the most important aspect of her story is clear: she was in the grip of moneylenders and the only thing worry had left her was her faith. She relied on her church to rescue her. In fact, it is not May M.'s 'spilling' that renders her letter difficult to follow, but by apologising for it she drew attention to the fact that she was aware her writing skills were poor and that she was afraid they might weaken her case.

Another common feature of these sub-literate letters was the pronounced use of capital letters; often this usage was *ad hoc*, for example, Joseph D. and Clara W. cited earlier. However, some authors appeared

[96] Mrs May M., X Middle Gardiner St, Dublin (city), 3 July 1938. DDA, AB 7 CC, Box 7.

to use capitals for emphasis, for example, Mrs Edith O'B., who had quite a good level of vocabulary, seemed to employ capitalisation in this way:

30 March   St X Lr Gardiner
1924   City

May it Please Your Grace I as a humble Catholic worker wife would respectfully beg that you would be Kind enough to Grant me some little Assistance. My husband has been idle for a long Period and as I have four Children to strive to support. My Case is very hard one i am/ living in this Parish since Childhood and my Father and Mother before me in making this appeal I Pray Your Grace may see Your way to Give it Your Consideration. I would Gladly answer any questions as to my need for relief.
  I Beg to Remain
  Your Graces Obedient
  Servant
  Mrs Edith O'B.[97]

Capitalisation is used to highlight status, thus his 'Grace' received capitals, but also what the author most valued and needed received this distinction.

Interestingly, while many of these letter writers did not refrain from asking questions – in fact the level of questioning is a feature of these letters – virtually none used a question mark. It appears the use of exclamation marks, question marks and inverted commas was the preserve of the very educated and even they used them sparingly, when compared to the over-usage in the twenty-first century. However, like many a modern writer, these writers often used abbreviations, for example, instead of 'and' many wrote +, others reduced 'Christmas' to 'xmas', 'servant' to 'Servt.' or 'reverend' to 'Revd'. One other feature is the lack of individualised signatures, most people signed their names in exactly the same hand as the rest of the letter, occasionally underlining it. While Sokoll notes that the individualised signature began in the twentieth century, it had not established itself in Ireland by the 1940s, except among the most highly educated.[98] Some of the least literate did not even sign their letters – their names appeared in the top right-hand corner only.

Often precisely because of their conventional limitations, these letters offer disarmingly poignant accounts of life in the margins. Dead babies, ill children and court summons were all recorded with little literary

---

[97] Mrs Edith O'B., X Lr Gardiner St. (Dublin city), 30 March 1924. DDA, AB 7 CC, Box 1.
[98] Sokoll, *Essex Pauper Letters*, p. 56.

embellishment, but the very starkness of the telling can be poetically powerful. As Fitzpatrick remarked about emigrant letters of the nineteenth century, the contrast between literacy levels and articulacy is often remarkable. David Gerber has also observed 'the force of an extraordinary creativity that strains against its technical deficiencies' in the letters of barely literate immigrants.[99] There are many letters in this collection that defy the normal conventions of the letter in their raw simplicity, but are nonetheless remarkable for their stark impact.

Begging Letters as Sources

James Stephen Taylor has identified four distinctive voices in the English poverty letters of the early nineteenth century: 'the formal, stylised petition, usually commissioned by the applicant; the informational voice, telling of life and reminding of needs to be met; the insistent voice, where the need is too compelling for anything other than the expression thereof; and the desperate, even threatening voice'.[100] Only the first of these voices is silent in the Irish poverty letters, there are no examples of commissioned letters. The Irish poverty letters are authentic not just in their accounts of poverty, but also in the very hand of composition.[101] King and Stringer have noted historians' concerns regarding provenance, for example, the issue of whether the person who signed the letter actually wrote it, or whether a scribe or group was involved in a letter's composition.[102] These Irish letters written between 1921 and 1940 were almost universally written by the sender. This can be established by reviewing a series of letters from the same applicant, as it is clear they were always written in the same hand.[103] However, of much more relevance is the fact that in the letters written on behalf of someone it is clearly stated by the author. For example, Gordon O'B.'s letter began 'I recommend The bearer To your Kind Considderation & have known him and his wife a number of years.' While the letter is signed 'I remain

---

[99] D. Gerber, 'The immigrant letter between positivism and populism: American historians' uses of personal correspondence' in R. Earle (ed.), *Epistolary Selves: Letters and Letter-Writers, 1600–1945* (Aldershot: Ashgate, 1999), pp. 37–55, 48.

[100] J. S. Taylor, 'Voices in the crowd: The Kirkby Lonsdale township letters, 1809–36' in Hitchcock, King and Sharpe (eds.), *Chronicling Poverty*, p. 111.

[101] T. Sokoll, 'Writing for relief: Rhetoric in English pauper letters, 1800–1834' in Gestrich, King and Raphael (eds.), *Being Poor in Modern Europe*, p. 91.

[102] King and Stringer, '"I have once more taken the Leberty to say as you well know"', p. 71.

[103] The exceptions to this are isolated and almost always in the case of husbands and wives, when a series of letters is sent and alternately signed as by the wife or husband, but clearly in the same handwriting on all occasions.

yours Gordon O'B.' there is a note 'writer of letter Derek K.'[104] On other occasions it appears that the petitioner had approached either the parish priest and/or the Vincent de Paul and the recommendation letter was presented in lieu of a personal letter, hence those priests' letters often began: 'I know the bearer of this letter.'[105] Furthermore, the frequency with which authors comment on either the circumstances of their writing (fading light, before going to bed, after praying, etc.) and the challenges of the act of writing (poor spelling, weakened eyesight, shaking/frail hands, etc.) all point to the fact that the applicant was the writer. The idiosyncrasies of handwriting and spelling (particularly of the least literate, therefore those most likely to seek assistance in writing) are so individualised that they all point to self-authorship. Finally, the signatures in all these letters are in the same hand as the body of the text. Of course, these letters were not necessarily solo acts of composition in terms of their content; it is highly likely that writers received advice on approach, strategy or content from family members, neighbours or priests.[106] However, that they were written by the person seeking assistance seems relatively certain.

As to the associated issue of representativeness, it is reasonable to argue that those that wrote to the Archbishop of Dublin were largely representative of the Catholic urban poor, huddled in the cities and towns throughout Ireland living in appalling conditions on low and inconsistent wages. While the rural poor are underrepresented in this collection, their letters point to the commonalities between their experiences and their urban counterparts and some important differences. For example, the rural poor were also compelled to scrape a living together by negotiation, barter, charity and relief. They too were frequently constrained by various dictates associated with poverty; they had to appear poor, be grateful and prove their worthiness. They also expressed hopelessness, fear, anxiety and anger. However, there is evidence that they found it even more difficult to reveal their need; this was partly due

---

[104] Gordon O'B., X Summerhill, Dublin, n.d. c. 1936. DDA, AB 7 CC, Box 3. See also, Mr John N., Fairview Strand, Dublin, 5 April 1924 and Mrs Penny M. wrote and received £10 on behalf of Beth L. Mrs Penny M., 35 Fitzwilliam Place, Dublin, June 1924. DDA, AB 7 CC, Box 1.

[105] Fr O'Riordan, The Presbytery, Seville Place, Dublin, 10 May 1932. Thomas O'Riordan, born 1879, ordained 1905 and died 1949. J. A. Gaughan, *The Archbishops, Bishops and Priests who served in the Archdiocese of Dublin between 1900–2011*, (Dublin: Kingdom Books, 2012), p. 232.

   Whereas, James J. L. of Common's Street, Dublin, submitted a recommendation note from the Vincent de Paul upon which the parish priest had also scribbled his two-line reference. DDA, AB 7 CC, Box 4.

[106] 0.3 per cent of letters are signed from the husband and wife.

to physical isolation – they were literally further away from sources of assistance – but it was also because of the high value placed on the family name in rural Ireland. For example, Fr Henry Talbot of Kilcullen in County Kildare, noted that his parishioner Mrs M. was 'greatly agitated at the thoughts of her having written the letter being found out … and wanted to bind me over to secrecy'. The priest himself was reluctant to make the 'rigid inquiries' necessary as he explained: 'You will readily understand that in a small remote place like this secrecy is impossible.'[107] While the issues in the rural letters were often about the lack of sureties regarding land tenure, uneconomic holdings, dying or unproductive animals, the consequences and needs were precisely the same as their urban equivalents: survival by a multiple of means, which almost always fell short of a decent standard of life.[108]

The middle-class writers also reflected the particular dangers to which their class was susceptible, and they were representative of a broad sector of that class from widows of solicitors to salesmen, civil servants and large farmers. However, one can ask whether these writers were only representative of Roman Catholics in need. The letters in this book emerge from a society in which religious faith and the identification with a religious denomination was crucially important to one's social (and arguably private) identity. The population of the new state was 2,971,992, out of which 92.6 per cent were Roman Catholics, while Protestant Episcopalians, Presbyterians, Methodists, Jews and Baptists accounted for the remaining 7.4 per cent.[109] Thus in a broad sense these writers were representative of the majority faith, but it is also likely that they were representative of others in Ireland who, while they might have identified with another faith, would still have regarded belonging to a religion as central to their lives. It was, for example, very rare for people to identify with no religion when filling out the census returns. Thus the idea of constructing one's identity through faith and association with a particular persuasion was not unique to Catholics, nor was the idea that one's religion was crucial to being considered worthy, deserving or eligible for charity.[110]

---

[107] Fr. Henry Talbot, Parochial House, Kilcullen, 23 August 1935. DDA, AB 7 CC, Box 6.

[108] The rural letters reveal a depth of poverty that requires further research, which would consider various occupational classes, for example, smallholding tenants, agricultural labourers and rural but non-agricultural households. I am very grateful to Dr Ciara Breathnach for advice on this issue. See, also, C. Breathnach, *The Congested Districts Board of Ireland, 1891–1923* (Dublin: Four Courts Press, 2005).

[109] *Census of Population, General Report, 1926, Volume X* (Dublin: Stationary Office, 1934) pp. 7, 45.

[110] Again, if one considers the letters by Protestant widows used in Walsh's study religious identification is central. Walsh, *Anglican Women in Dublin*, pp. 151–197.

However, one can still ask whether the people who wrote were representative of others in the same situation that did not write. Many other sources at our disposal from charitable to governmental reports indicate that they were and that the poverty or hardship they experienced was not particularly unusual. There are certain issues that surface repeatedly in these letters that are reflected in other accounts of poverty: the juggling of resources, the importance of faith and displays of loyalty, the issue of clothing, unemployment and high rent, the strategies of pawning, begging, and relying on family members. Furthermore, these writers often recorded their experiences with other major forms of relief or charity such as 'poor relief' (Home Assistance, although virtually no writer referred to it by its new name), unemployment benefit, old age pension and Saint Vincent de Paul. These letters offer rich individual accounts, but they nonetheless conform largely to our knowledge of the main difficulties and challenges poverty presented people in the early twentieth century.

Historians have been particularly concerned about the 'truthfulness' of such sources, but relatively happy with the fact that the regimes of investigation in operation in most areas made it very difficult for the writers to tell 'untruths or radical embellishments'.[111] As Ellen Ross observed, charity fraudsters were 'the bête noire of the whole charity world', but were in fact rare and their operations small-scale.[112] These letters, similar to all sources, are shaped by the circumstances of their creation, therefore, they inevitably conceal as well as reveal. However, as we know much about the universe that generated these letters, we can be fairly sure that they represent realistic accounts of poverty and need. Nonetheless, we have to ask ourselves what we are engaged in: are we involved in a 'truth' gathering exercise or, are we, in fact, concerned with understanding what the poor wanted to establish as true?[113] Is it vital to this enquiry to know if Doreen Q. actually had no bed or bedlinen and only had two protestant relatives who did 'not touch papists'?[114] The point is that she articulated a sense of being trapped

---

[111] Gestrich, Hurren and King (eds.), *Poverty and Sickness in Modern Europe*, p. 19; T. Sokoll, 'Negotiating a living: Essex pauper letters from London, 1800–1834', *International Review of Social History*, 45 (2000), 19–46, 29.

[112] E. Ross, 'Hungry children: housewives and London charity, 1870–1918' in P. Mandler (ed.), *The Uses of Charity: The Poor on Relief in the Nineteenth-Century Metropolis* (Philadelphia: University of Pennsylvania Press, 1990), pp. 161–196, p. 173.

[113] M. Peel, *Miss Cutler and the Case of the Resurrected Horse: Social Work and the Story of Poverty in America, Australia, and Britain* (The University of Chicago Press, 2012), p. 15.

[114] Doreen Q., X Upper Gardiner St, Dublin, Ascension Thursday (29 May) 1924. DDA, AB 7 CC, Box 1.

in a world that condemned her to articulate and justify her poverty and prove the conviction of her faith. The fact is that she was more than likely actually sleeping on the floor – she would have been given short shrift were she lying – but her faith lies in the realm of what we cannot know, but only appreciate in terms of its importance to her understanding of her position. As Sokoll's work has demonstrated, the wealth of these sources can only be realised if we focus not just on '*what* they tell us, but also on *how* they convey their message'.[115] These sources are the 'most authentic record of popular voices' because they were written by the hand and in the words of the poor themselves.[116] While these letters are not 'free-form ego documents' like, for example, diaries, they do possess many of the essential qualities of such sources as the creation of a 'self' and the recording/constructing of personal experience are essential to them.[117] The term that best captures these sources is 'life testimonies'[118] because the many authors seek to testify, usually in their defence, how life has brought them to the point of need. As with conventional ego-documents, our historical understanding of 'subjective experiences' of poverty and specific historical events and processes can be enriched by a careful reading of such documents; however, as a result of their sheer volume they also contribute to an understanding of the collective experience of poverty and begging.[119]

Conclusion

Peter Jones convincingly argues that poverty letters reveal that 'negotiation was never *simply* a matter of economic or practical need', but that 'the observation of behavioural and linguistic protocols' and the cultural context in which aid or relief is provided were all as important as actual level of need.[120] The language, form and metaphors used were intrinsic parts of the purpose and context of these letters and cannot be divorced from the process of begging and the realities of 'being poor'. In their style, vibrancy and testimony, these Irish poverty letters are

[115] Sokoll, 'Writing for relief: rhetoric in English pauper letters, 1800–1834', p. 91.
[116] Ibid.
[117] Gestrich, Hurren and King (eds.), *Poverty and Sickness in Modern Europe*, p.16.
[118] A. Gestrich and S. A. King, 'Pauper letters and petitions for poor relief in Germany and Great Britain, 1770–1914', *Bulletin: German Historical Institute London,* 35 (November 2013), 12–25, 12.
[119] M. Fulbrook and U. Rublack, 'In relation: The "social self" and ego-documents', *German History,* 28 (2010), 263–272, 264.
[120] P. J. Jones, '"I cannot keep my place without being deascent": Pauper letters, parish clothing and pragmatism in the South of England, 1750–1830', *Rural History,* 20 (2009), 31–49, 32.

connected to a long international history of ordinary letter writing in general and begging letters in particular. This very large collection of begging letters contains remarkable international hallmarks and idiosyncratic Irish ones. The conversational tone, Irish Catholic rhetoric and particular features of Hiberno-English found in these letters give them their own Irish characteristics and make them closer to a blend of the informal letter and formal petition letter models.[121] The essential narrative of poverty, the act of writing for relief and the various rhetorical strategies employed root them firmly in the international history of poverty or pauper letters. In a similar way to all other writings 'from below', these Irish writers engaged with the world they lived in and used what was at their disposal to improve their position in that world. Sokoll's argument is particularly important here: while these letters display clear rhetorical elements, these do not necessarily call into question the integrity of these sources or the legitimacy of what they were trying to say – on the contrary: 'they need to be seen as an integral and inseparable part of the narrative'.[122] In the following chapter this process of negotiation and its relationship to rhetorical strategies will be thoroughly explored.

---

[121] Sokoll notes that the Essex pauper letters of the eighteenth century also display this blend. He points out that the writers themselves may not have been aware of these models or that they had blended them to form their own unique records. Sokoll, *Essex Pauper Letters*, p. 57.

[122] Sokoll, 'Writing for relief: rhetoric in English pauper letters, 1800–1834', p. 81.

3   The 'Poor' Make Their Case
'Surely they are worth helping'

Charity letters offer the historian much more than a mere account of the 'give and take' of charity. To beg successfully the writer had to employ all the social skills of a negotiator, all the cultural savvy of a poet and the creative stamina of a storyteller. What the letter writers wanted, how they asked for it, their many asides and rhetorical flourishes, offer rich ground for historical interpretation. Individual letters provide particularly vivid personal stories, which still pulsate with emotional undercurrents, and taken together they represent a broader experience, shedding light on the status and meaning of poverty in twentieth-century Ireland. In his study of Australian poverty, Mark Peel noted that the poor were constantly compelled to 'perform' their poverty, to explain why they were poor and how their behaviour had either contributed to their position or would contribute to their 'rehabilitation'.[1] While the letters from the Irish poor provide rare examples of 'poverty stories' as told by the poor,[2] this does not mean that it is not challenging to read between the lines of these stories, or that they were stories written exactly as the poor would have liked. The pressure to explain one's poverty produced its 'own convincing stories'[3] inclining the poor to narrate their experience along expected lines, highlighting suffering, blamelessness, sobriety and a willingness to remedy their situation either through work or some other plan.[4] However, as Thomas Sokoll has ably demonstrated, poverty letters, while 'strategic pieces of writing . . . written for a specific purpose', also have a life beyond the intention of their author. In the act of writing their case, the poor entered into the 'territory of narrative imagination', which affords us a much deeper glimpse of the world they inhabited.[5]

---

[1] M. Peel, *The Lowest Rung: Voices of Australian Poverty* (Cambridge University Press), p. 25.

[2] M. Peel, *Miss Cutler and the Case of the Resurrected Horse: Social Work and the Story of Poverty in America, Australia, and Britain* (The University of Chicago Press, 2012), p. 9.

[3] Peel, *The Lowest Rung*, p. 73.   [4] Ibid., p. 74.

[5] T. Sokoll, 'Negotiating a living: Essex pauper letters from London, 1800–1834', *International Review of Social History*, 45, Supplement 8 (2000), 19–46, 29.

In these letters we can read *into* the very process of construction and learn what the poor felt must be included either because it was their version of the truth, perhaps the only part of the truth they could bear to part with, or because it was what they knew the recipient needed to hear or a combination of these and other factors. Often it is in the telling that we learn most about the stories themselves. In examining how the letter writers constructed a 'deserving case' we can discover much about the values and realities of their contemporary society and their experience of living under the burden of those values.

'One of Almighty Gods destitute deserving poor'

While the vast majority of those who wrote looking for help had a clear idea of what 'deserving' meant in early twentieth-century Ireland, not all engaged as directly with the rhetoric as Mrs Karen M. from Cork, who begged the archbishop to 'think kindly on one of Almighty Gods destitute deserving poor'.[6] Nonetheless, most writers were quick to establish their level of need, fidelity to the Roman Catholic Church, sobriety and willingness to work and, crucially, to offer reassurances that they would not become a 'burden'. This corresponds with what the various charitable organisations looked for, or valued, in the 'deserving poor': they must be sober, devout, willing to work and capable of independence. Few charities offered long-term support,[7] believing that charity should be an investment in 'getting people back up on their feet'.[8] In reality, the idea that most of those that applied for charity had *ever* been stable on their own financial feet was an illusion: how could they have been in a labour market that relied on casual labour and cast workers aside at a moment's notice? Nevertheless, the poor knew that they could very easily be tagged a 'nuisance' and that the line between proving you were in need and convincing those in authority that you were not fatally so, was fine indeed. Thus Mrs K. L.'s promise was one often given to the archbishop: 'Dr Father if you consider our case I promise you it will be the last time I will ever trouble you again thanking you for your kind Consideration.'[9]

---

[6] Mrs Karen M., Convent Road, Doneraile, Cork, n.d. *c.* 1933. DDA, AB 7 CC, Box 5.

[7] An obvious exception are those that catered for widows, for example, Clergy Widows' and Orphans' Society and the Protestant Orphans' Society, which provided long-term financial assistance. See, O. Walsh, *Anglican Women in Dublin: Philanthropy, Politics and Education in the early Twentieth Century* (University College Dublin Press, 2005), pp. 151–197.

[8] See, for example, 'Supplement of Irish Conference, April 1931', *Bulletin of the Society of St. Vincent De Paul*, 96 (1931), 6.

[9] Mrs Katherine L., Joseph's Ave., Off Ann's Rd., Drumcondra, Dublin, n.d. *c.* 1937. DDA, AB 7 CC, Box 7.

While most of those who wrote to the Archbishop of Dublin did so only once or twice, many of the letters show the hallmarks of a familiarity with the charity system, particularly the least literate from the poorest parts of the country. These correspondents were adept at pre-empting questions and familiar with what information would be required before charity would be forthcoming. These letters offer a chance to explore the 'social knowledge' of the poor and how they deployed it to access the assistance they required.[10] Mr Joseph C., from the North Strand in Dublin, was used to setting out his stall: 'It is like this I am in very poor circumstances living on £1.2.6 every week, I get £1.0.0 unemployment assistance & the 2/6 I get outdoor relief.' Out of this budget, he explained he had to 'pay 10/- a week rent 1/6 society get a bit a coal & other little things including a bit to eat, it is easy to talk to £1.2.6'. There was simply not enough to keep himself, his expectant wife and three children fed and clothed: 'Many a day passed and we had not a bite to eat or a fire to sit at.' To survive on this meagre income, Joseph C. relied on pawning which was threatening his religious life, as he explained: 'Being a Roman Catholic I must confess to you that I cannot go to mass on a Sunday owning to having no clothes the same applies to my wife, our only rags we have are in the pawn.'[11] He and his wife had braved public shame and gone to mass in order to

receive the Blessed Sacrement which we done a couple of weeks ago with the expectation of getting a bit of luck I need not tell you I felt much ashamed going to the alter of God to receive in my rags, but anyhow my soul felt proud and that is the mean [main] thing.[12]

Joseph C.'s letter demonstrates many of the most common attributes of the consciously deserving letter. These authors were familiar with poverty's indignities, they had survived in and out of charity for years thus they set out their budget quickly and clearly. They knew this information would be requested and was verifiable which would substantiate their need and honesty. Despite his formal opening and closing, Joseph C. adopted a familiar tone throughout his letter: he confided, 'I need not tell you I felt very much ashamed.' Later he attempted to make a personal connection with the archbishop telling him that, 'My wife tells me that her mother had the privilege of been [being] a maid of yours the time you

---

[10] P. Mandler, 'Poverty and charity in the nineteenth century metropolis: an introduction' in P. Mandler (ed.), *The Uses of Charity: The Poor on Relief in the Nineteenth-Century Metropolis* (Philadelphia: University of Pennsylvania Press, 1990), pp. 1–37, 1.

[11] Mr Joseph C. and wife, X Shamrock Cottages, Nth. Strand, Dublin, 14 December 1938. n.d. *c.* 1937. DDA, AB 7 CC, Box 7.

[12] Ibid.

were P.P. [parish priest] of Rush her name was Beth W. you may remember her.' Joseph C. humanised and personalised his case by effectively narrowing the distance between himself and his archbishop. He was no longer an abstract member of the poor masses but a parishioner, who felt the sort of shame the archbishop could relate to and who had a wife the archbishop could remember. He concluded his letter with the final ingredients of 'worthiness': 'I do not smoke or drink as regards to work I do not care what kind of work hard or soft.' He then resurrected the more formal tone of a petition letter signing off: 'Hope this my letter will meet with your kindest and fervent consideration. I have the Honour to be your Most Obedient & Humble Servant Joseph C & Wife.'

The most important motif of Joseph C.'s letter was his religious piety; he was loyal to Catholicism and observant of his duty *in spite* of his poverty. The normal shame of appearing in public in rags was overcome by the more important imperative to attend mass. The assurance of religious duty was almost *de rigueur* in these letters: letter after letter records daily mass attendance and membership of at least one sodality or confraternity. This pattern crossed the class divide; an 'embarrassed' public servant was just as likely as a tenement dweller to stress this aspect of their case. Maurice Hartigan argues that the 'religious zeal' of the Catholic laity of Dublin city was at its height in the 1920s and 1930s 'when the impact of the so-called "devotional revolution" of the nineteenth century and the augmented pastoral capacity of the Church were at their height'.[13] Sodalities and confraternities were not just sites of prayer and expressions of faith, they were markers of belonging and allegiance and weekly attendance was deemed obligatory for practising Catholics.[14] The Archbishop of Dublin set great store by the public nature of this culture and was convinced of the fundamental role that the various devotional societies played in building the faith. There were forty-five Catholic committees, guilds and associations in the Dublin diocese alone.[15] Hartigan's research reveals that the most active sodalities and confraternities in Dublin were in the poorest parishes.[16]

---

[13] M. Hartigan, 'The religious life of the Catholic laity in Dublin, 1920–1940' in J. Kelly and D. Keogh (eds.), *History of the Catholic Diocese of Dublin* (Dublin: Four Courts, 2000), pp. 331–48, p. 331.

[14] M. Curtis, *A Challenge to Democracy: Militant Catholicism in Modern Ireland* (Dublin: The History Press Ireland, 2010), p. 45.

[15] Morrissey, *Edward J. Byrne 1872–1941: The Forgotten Archbishop of Dublin* (Dublin: The Columba Press, 2010), p. 235.

[16] On the north side, the Jesuits at St Francis Xavier's, Lower Gardiner St., the Dominicans at St Saviour's, Dominic Street, and the Vincentians at St Peter's, Phibsborough. On the south side of the city, the Franciscans at Merchant's Quay, the Augustinians of John's Lane and the Carmelites of Whitefriar Street had the most

For example, the Franciscan Third Order at Merchant's Quay, which had brother and sister branches made up chiefly of working-class men and women, has good records for the 1920s and 30s which reveal a membership running to just under two thousand in the 1930s, and in 1937, 3,000 attended monthly devotions there.[17]

In 1924, Mr James M., a father of three small children regarded himself as 'in pretty bad Poverty', he had pawned everything, but assured the archbishop that 'the last things that left my Room was the Figure of the Holy Family and the picture of the Immaculate Mother', stressing that he belonged 'to the Holy Family Confraternity' and was 'also a weekly Communicant belonging to the Knights of the Blessed Sacrament'.[18] For a Catholic being visible in the church was vital to *proving* worthiness – religious observance was an investment in one's spiritual life, it provided succour and support to many, but it was also credit in the proverbial bank if one ever needed Catholic charity. In January 1936 Mrs K. D., the wife of an 'Ex British soldier', wrote of her inability to raise six children on her husband's £1 a week disability pension. She provided her budget, an explanation of why she was entitled to no other 'class off Relief' (her husband's pension disqualified them). Her husband could not find work and her daughter suffered from a 'leaking valv off the Heart'. However, she did not mention their religious credentials, which she must have noticed upon re-reading her letter, because after her valediction and signature she inserted: 'Your Grace i would like to add that my Husband is a Member off the Sacred Heart Sodality He is also a Brother Off the third order.'[19]

Mrs Margot F.'s short letter of barely 150 words contained her reluctance, her budget, her Catholic credentials and her own priorities,

> I would not dream of writing only I am desperate ... I [am] a good catholic as is my husband and 2 of my children are attending William street school for boys. I recieve Holy Commnunion once a week and my husband belongs to the Sodality in Gardiner St.[20]

She had established that she was desperate, a practising Catholic, her children attended a Catholic school – a marker of a good Catholic mother – and her husband was also observant. The archbishop was so concerned

---

devotionally active laity. Hartigan, 'The religious life of the Catholic laity in Dublin, 1920–1940', p. 332.

[17] Ibid., p. 334.

[18] James M., X Coombe St. (Dublin city), 27 April 1924. n.d. *c.* 1937. DDA, AB 7 CC, Box 1.

[19] Mrs K. D., Waterford St., Dublin, 8 January 1936. DDA, AB 7 CC, Box 6.

[20] Mrs Margot F., X Dunne St, off Portland Row, Dublin, 30 January 1938. Ibid.

about Catholic parents sending their children to 'non-Catholic' schools he issued a warning in his Lenten Pastoral of February 1927. Deriding 'a vague idea prevalent that the Church has modified her attitude in this matter', he warned those 'who send their children to non-Catholic schools should understand that in so doing they are acting directly in opposition to the laws of the Church and fail to perform their duty as Catholic parents'.[21] He declared himself confident that once parents realised that there was no change in the church's law 'this abuse, which has recently been on the increase, will die out'.[22]

Writing in 1924 Mrs Edith O'B. was able to encapsulate her need, willingness to work, number of children and religious devotion in her opening line:

May it Please Your Grace I as a humble Catholic worker wife would respectfully beg that you would be Kind enough to Grant me some little Assistance my husband has been idle for a long Period and as I have four Children to strive to support.[23]

In fact, the combination of these four points in a short letter was the most common form of impoverished appeal found in this collection, it was almost formulaic and certainly reflected a pervasive understanding on the part of the writers of the priorities of Catholic charity. Providing one's budget did not just prove need, it implied thrift and awareness of the need for a budget and a plan. Family size was obviously a factor in moving a case up the priority list – many single or childless people expressed the conviction that the lack of children diminished their chances of charity. Furthermore, in a culture that disapproved of birth control of any kind, a state that prohibited the promotion, sale and use of contraceptives, and a religion that valued large families, listing one's children proved that you respected that conviction in practice.[24]

Many other authors called God as their witness to highlight their honesty and the genuine nature of their particular case. In 1926 Mrs Maureen Q., in a very shaky and uneven pen – which marked her out from the vast majority of correspondents – asked twice in a short letter 'for God Sake give me a little help':

---

[21] *The Irish Catholic Directory, 1928* (Dublin, 1928), p. 570.   [22] Ibid.
[23] Mrs E. O'B., X Lr Gardiner St., (Dublin city), 30 March 1924. DDA, AB 7 CC, Box 1.
[24] C. Hug, *The Politics of Sexual Morality in Ireland* (London: MacMillan Press, 1999), pp. 76–84; S. McAvoy, '"Perpetual nightmare": Women, fertility control, the Irish state, and the 1935 ban on contraceptives' in M. H. Preston and M. Ó hÓgartaigh (eds.), *Gender and Medicine in Ireland, 1700–1950* (New York: Syracuse University Press, 2012), pp. 189–202.

Dear Father,

I write these few lines to Ask you if you can for God Sake give me a little help as I have 4 young children Starving with the hunger my husband is out of work for the Past 5 months and I am expecting to be confined on my fifth Baby anyday this week so I appeal to you Father for God Sake for a little help and I Shall pray for your intentions if you can Grant me this little favour trusting you will do Something in your Power for me.

I am
Your humble
Servant Mrs Maureen Q.[25]

Mrs Maeve M.'s appeal written ten years after Maureen Q.'s was almost identical: 'in the name of god and his Blessed Mother i wright this letter to you', she too was 'expcting a baby anney day this week' and all her 'baby colus' were in the pawn. She concluded by reiterating her request in God's name 'i can promas you that i will never ask you again, for it is only god that knows how much i am in need of help'.[26] God is my witness, I need help, but I will not ask you again – how impossible was this balance to strike convincingly? Mrs Maeve M. had very little chance of keeping her promise because her little family economy – made up of two small children and another in the wings – depended on her sick husband and his cart. However, to convince the archbishop that her ship stood a chance of staying afloat she did not ask for money without a purpose, she asked for it to help her husband 'start again'.

In asking for assistance to run, supply, or start a business the poor were tapping into the ideology of 'self-support', they were also proving a pro-active desire to work and be independent. While this was undoubtedly a good strategy, it is also painfully obvious that these writers fervently wished to be successful in this endeavour. In 1925 Mrs Ellen L. wrote looking for the means to supply her business: 'May it Please your Grace To pardon the liberty I take in writing to you. My reasons far doing so is to most Respectfully ask your Grace for little Financial help to enable me to buy a little Material to make up so as I can earn a little Money.' She repeatedly highlighted the temporary nature of her predicament 'I am very poor at the present Moment My Husband is out of employment far the past twelve months/ and also my little girl who is a Dress Maker.' She was 'a Good hand at sewing' all she required was the capital to buy material. She concluded that she was 'Hoping and praying that Your

---

[25] Mrs Maureen Q., X Upr Dorest St, Dublin, n.d. c. 1926. DDA, AB 7 CC, Box 2.

[26] Mrs M., X Little Denmark Street, Dublin, 3 March 1937. She received £3 thanks to her priest's letter. See, Fr. Fr Thomas Farrell, 83 Marlborough St., Dublin, 6 March 1937. DDA, AB 7 CC, Box 6.

Grace will accede to this My Most earnest appeal for help to enable me to earn my living.'[27] Martha Kanya-Forstner has observed that poor Catholic women in Liverpool also frequently asked the Vincent de Paul to help them to start a business thus seeking to 'buy the prospect of independence',[28] These requests were often successful, despite the fact that assisting women to work outside the home – many of these women requested money to stock stalls – cut across the ideology of domesticity so central to Catholic discourse on motherhood.[29] It appears that the financial independence of a family was more important than idealised notions of femininity. One could view this as a practical or hypocritical response to the reality of poverty; often, such assistance resulted in the breakup of the family as children (due to the lack of child care) were sent to relatives, orphanages, or industrial schools.

'My husband was 10 months from mass for want of clothes'

The poor had few cards to play, if they were not willing to threaten religious defection, they often engaged in 'a dialogue of moral persuasion'.[30] In 1929 Mr Joe R. introduced himself as 'one of Gods afflicted poor'. His letter displayed a keen sense of the symbolic place of the poor in Roman Catholic discourse:

I am appealing to you, on Behalf of my son who is making his First Holy Communion. Owning to being out of Employment for the past two years and with an Wife and six Children depending on me. I am unable to provide clothes for my son to go and recive the Holy Blessed Sacrement.[31]

While he may have been deterred from attending Mass because of the poor state of his clothing, he was also clearly aware that this idea went to

---

[27] Mrs Ellen L., Lr. Buckingham St., Dublin, 10 February 1925. DDA, AB 7 CC, Box 1. She received £5.

[28] M. Kanya-Forstner, 'Defining womanhood: Irish women and the Catholic Church in Victorian Liverpool', *Immigrants & Minorities*, 18 (1999), 178–184, 184.

[29] See, for example, Rev. C. Lucey, 'The problem of the woman worker', *The Irish Ecclesiastical Record*, 47 (July-December, 1936), 449–467; M. E. Daly, *Women and Work in Ireland* (Dundalgan Press, 1997), pp. 49–51. F. Kennedy, *Cottage to Crèche: Family Change in Ireland* (Dublin: Institute of Public Administration, 2001), pp. 81–102.

[30] This phrased is borrowed from Fitzpatrick who used it in relation to the negotiations involved in Irish emigrant letters to and from Australia. D. Fitzpatrick, *Oceans of Consolation: Personal Accounts of Irish Migration to Australia* (New York: Cornell University Press, 1994), p. 503.

[31] Mr Joe R., X Lr. Gardiner St., Dublin, 4 June 1929. DDA, AB 7 CC, Box 2. He was sent the Archbishop's Card.

the heart of the ideology of Catholic charity, which was to spiritually uplift the poor. Interestingly, Joe R.'s reason for writing to the archbishop was that the Vincent de Paul had refused his request, perhaps because they had become inured to such a strategy. The Vincent de Paul noted critically: 'We have to deal with the father who pleads that shabbiness of clothes prevents him from attending Mass ... and then, we have the good, God-fearing man.'[32] While the society resented being held over a religious barrel, it was realistic about the impact of deep poverty and testified repeatedly 'that hunger and privation tend to beget a frame of mind impervious to the consolations of religion'.[33]

Peter Jones has argued that nakedness was used in English pauper letters of the nineteenth century as a 'cipher of extreme distress', and that in doing so the poor were engaging with a wider cultural concern about clothing and poverty rooted in religious scripture.[34] The idea of nakedness also featured in Irish charity letters as shorthand for extreme poverty because it was both a powerful symbol and a verifiable marker of poverty. This had a long history, as Virginia Crossman observes of the Poor Law in nineteenth-century Ireland: 'clothing was a critical indicator...and played a vital role in determining entitlement to relief'.[35] Indeed, within working-class communities clothing and footwear were crucial in assessing the gradations of need. Phil O'Keeffe, for example, who grew up in the working-class Liberties of Dublin, remarked that '[P]oor children were part of everyday life ... [J]ust as we expected to have shoes on our feet, so they expected to have none.'[36]

Nakedness symbolised what poverty denuded people of, the loss of self-respect and dignity, but it could also be *seen* – the naked or ill-clad family *looked* poor and looking poor was important in the bid to prove need. The Irish poor loaded the image with religious significance: they could not attend to their religious duties, although they were loyal to a church that allowed such poverty to persist. In June 1932 Mrs Jane R. from County Waterford provided a good example of the complex deployment of the image *and* truth of nakedness. She had written twice previously and received no reply; she wondered if all her prayers and her

---

[32] 'Supplement for Irish Conferences', *Bulletin of the Society of St. Vincent De Paul*, 71 (May 1926), 13.

[33] *Bulletin of the Society of St. Vincent De Paul*, 83 (February 1918), 57.

[34] P. J. Jones, '"I cannot keep my place without being deascent": Pauper letters, parish clothing and pragmatism in the South of England, 1750–1830', *Rural History*, 20 (2009), 31–49, 33.

[35] V. Crossman, *Poverty and The Poor Law in Ireland, 1850–1914* (Liverpool University Press, 2013), p. 31.

[36] P. O'Keeffe, *Down Cobbled Streets* (Dingle: Brandon Publishers, 1995), p. 119.

children's Holy Communions had served any purpose, as they had experienced 'nothing but trial and trouble one after another'. She linked her family's nakedness with the poor fortunes of her family farm and her frustration with her religion:

the sow with her <sucklings> which we meant to sell to carry on lay dead on Christmas morning and my husband & four children going out to Holy Communion my husband was 10 months from mass for want of clothes only on a wet Sunday when he could cover the rags with a Shabby overcoat now the childrens clothes are beyond repair they also will be away and the ground is now ready for turnip crop and cannot get manure for it the few fowl are starving with hunger[37]

The way she ran these various things together was a feature of her lack of punctuation, but also, arguably, an indication of how she regarded all these aspects of her impoverished existence as intrinsic to the incoherence of suffering. Life could seem thin and as threadbare as poverty's worn clothing: it is hard not to visualise Jane standing in her fallow field amid her dead sow, starving fowl and naked family.

'I think I've told you every-thing there is to tell now'

People who wrote seeking charity were keenly aware of the imperative to explain themselves and their situation, a letter provided them with the space in which to strike a balance between how they saw their poverty and how it was perceived by those in control of the resources they so desperately needed. Thus they often wrote in story mode, for example, Mrs Karen M. from Cork opened her letter with herself as the main protagonist: 'As a widow who spent many happy days when young in Dublin and have my people still some where there I write your Lordship to forgive me and to listen to a tale of woe.' She asked to be *listened* to – she was preparing to *tell* a story – the emphasis was not on the written word but on the woven tale. She cast herself as 'the widow' and provided a narrative explanation of how a once happy girl from Dublin had ended up a widowed 'wreck' in Cork with 'No one now to help the widow.'[38] This distancing of herself from the voice of the storyteller

---

[37] Mrs Jane R., Island Tarsney, Fenor, Co Waterford, 9 June 1932. DDA, AB 7 CC, Box 3.

[38] Daniela Heinisch noted that German widows in the early nineteenth century were also conscious of casting themselves as 'the widow' because it implied an innocence and a 'God-given' right to assistance. D. Heinisch 'Petitions of the Council of the Free Imperial City of Frankfurt am Main', *Bulletin: German Historical Institute London*, 35 (November 2013), 26–42, 38–39.

helped to create the sense of an objective true story. She wrote about, and on behalf of, 'the widow' that no one else would help.[39]

Mr and Mrs Anthony M. constructed their narrative of heroism over three letters between 1933 and 1935. Mrs Anthony M., who never gave her own first name, began the story in September 1933 by telling the archbishop that she was married to 'a English man', a Protestant who had converted to Catholicism before their marriage, thereby placing her story in the context of religious vulnerability, clearly aware of the Church's sensitivity to the issue of converts and religiously mixed marriages.[40] She went on to explain that he had been working in a 'Protestant Place', but as there was a 'church service there' he left this employment. She cast herself in the role of defender of the faith: 'I used to work there too and I left to show him a good example.'[41] Leaving his employment had left her husband without resources, as he was not long enough in Ireland to qualify for statutory relief [two years was the required period]. Mrs M. explained that since having a baby she was no longer strong enough to work and, ominously, 'my husbands [health] is failing too Your Grace it has been terrible time trying to make ends meet many a time my husband and I fought against temptation'. She noted 'of course we are getting the food ticket of the St Vincent De Paul but we are unable to pay the rent'. Mrs M. showed all the signs of knowing the charity 'system': she explained her husband's loss of his job on religious grounds, she pre-empted the question about other forms of relief by explaining why they were not receiving out-door relief or employment assistance and clarified that, as any *bona fide* deserving poor family would be, they were in receipt of a Vincent de Paul ticket, but that this was not sufficient. The archbishop responded requesting a priest's reference, it is likely that this was not forthcoming as the next letter was written two years later.

When Mrs Anthony M. wrote again in February 1935, it was from a different address but in the same immediate area of inner city Dublin. The subtle differences between her first and second letter are interesting and reflect, perhaps, a longer acquaintance with poverty and the dictates of the charity machine. She reiterated the story of her husband's conversion to Catholicism and how this had cost him his job. However, now there were two small children and two more years of job-hunting behind them. Mrs M. noted that her husband had received only ten

[39] Mrs Karen M., Convent Road, Doneraile, Co Cork, *c.* 1933. DDA, AB 7 CC, Box 4.

[40] 'Mixed marriages' were a shared preoccupation, the Church of Ireland was equally eager to discourage such unions. D. Harman Akenson, *Small Differences: Irish Catholics and Irish Protestants, 1815–1922* (Montreal: McGill Queen's University, 1988), pp. 108–126.

[41] Mrs Anthony M., X Hardwicke St., Dublin, 2 September 1933. DDA, AB 7 CC, Box 4.

weeks work in the previous two years, the fact that she referred to the exact number of weeks reflects the language of statutory relief; qualification for Unemployment Assistance was calculated on the basis of the number of weeks worked and the number of weeks on benefit. Anthony M. was at this point in receipt of 15/– a week, but again indicative of her experience of explaining her poverty, Mrs M. clarified,

by the time I pay 4/6 rent and 3/6 for coal and oil and I also have to keep the gas light going all day as I am living in a every *[very]* dark back Kitchen and it costs me 2/6 a week so that hardly leaves me anything to live on.

Her need to explain why the gaslight remained on all day implies that she had become accustomed to justifying her behaviour. Thriftiness was a virtue prized by those in control of the charitable purse strings and the poor were frequently questioned about how they deployed their meagre resources. Despite Mrs M.'s lack of punctuation, or perhaps because of it, she made a poignant observation about male unemployment when reflecting on the condition of her husband's shoes: 'he has only got 10 weeks work for the past 2 years his shoes too are in a bad state'. For Mrs M. her husband's worn shoes flow seamlessly from his lack of work; the image of men walking their shoes into the ground in search of work was a common metaphor employed in these letters. In Mrs M.'s hands it also became a symbol for everything else that had become worn by poverty: 'his shoes *too* are in a bad state'.

By now she also had an explanation for why a reference from her parish priest was not forthcoming: 'it is almost impossible to see the parish priest I have been down to the house several times but the maid tells me that he is out'. For whatever reason, it is likely that she was denied access to the parish priest because she asked the archbishop to intervene 'could you send me a letter to take to the Rev. Father Condon of Marlborough Street'.[42]

When Mrs Anthony M.'s subtle approach elicited no response, her husband took pen to paper on 28 February. He provided a third version of the story, but with a different voice came a different emphasis: returning to the motif of heroism in the face of temptation, which his wife had foreshadowed in 1933, Anthony was much more direct. He provided the same basic facts as his wife and, revealingly, also explained their use of energy resources, 'We have to keep a fairly big fire as the kitchen we live in is very draughty.' So Anthony, his wife and two young children sat in a draughty kitchen with worn out shoes, insufficient clothing, and no relatives to turn to because 'they are against me for

---

[42] Mrs Anthony M., X Hardwick St, Dublin, 13 February 1935. DDA, AB 7 CC, Box 4.

turning from my religion'. If the archbishop was not aware of what this sacrifice had cost Mr M.'s little family, he spelled it out: 'Several times I was offered help from Protestants here; but they would expect me to send the children to Protestant schools when they are old enough.' This was an offer refused not without hesitation because '[W]hen one is living in poverty it certainly is a big temptation but I believe the Catholic faith to be the right faith, although sometimes in a temper I say things I ought not to say.'[43] Mr M. constructed a much more deliberate narrative of struggle, a fight against sectarianism and poverty in the name of the 'right faith'. However, his story was also haunted by distrust: he said things in a temper, possibly to the parish priest or a Vincent de Paul representative, about abandoning Catholicism if help was not forthcoming, something he feared may have reached the archbishop's ears.

In the early 1920s, at the end of her six-page letter Mrs E. D. concluded: 'I think I've told you every-thing there is to tell now. I thought it better to write it on paper + let you know exactly how I was situated.' She had sat down to tell her story of a journey into poverty. She framed her entire narrative around her motherhood making it clear that she appealed on behalf of her 'little baby', and punctuating her story repeatedly with the reality of her baby's needs: 'any-thing you do its for the baby, not for me' and later when she declared she 'shall certainly do some-thing desperate . . . for the welfare of my baby'.[44] The vast majority of Irish mothers who wrote to the archbishop were keenly aware that motherhood was their strongest asset. In her study of the poor of eighteenth-century France, Olwen Hufton noted the relative importance of the mother to the begging economy.[45] Ironically, Mrs E. D.'s letter highlighted that motherhood was also often the reason begging became necessary: the arrival of children frequently meant disaster for such finely balanced households.[46]

Mrs E. D. had come to Dublin with her husband who had 'passed his first examination for the Civic Guards + expected to be called on after Christmas'. Shortly after arriving in Dublin her baby was born and 'time went on + he [her husband] was not called', by mid February their 'little

[43] Mr Anthony M., X Hardwicke St., Dublin to Archbishop Byrne, 28 February 1935. DDA, AB 7 CC, Box 4.

[44] Mrs E. D., no address, n.d. c. 1924. DDA, AB 7 CC, Box 1.

[45] O. Hufton, *The Poor of Eighteenth-Century France, 1750–1789* (Oxford University Press, 1974), p. 114.

[46] Daly notes that the government was aware of this reality. M. E. Daly, 'Marriage, fertility and women's lives in the twentieth-century Ireland', *Women's History Review*, 15 (2006), 571–585; M. E. Daly, The Irish family since the Famine: continuity and change', *The Irish Journal of Feminist Studies*, 3 (1999), 1–21.

savings had all gone'. Revealing the very narrow margins that so many lived within, she explained that, although her husband had finally started work it was too late. Their landlady insisted on reclaiming her room and they could not pay for another one. Hence, she had embarked upon an odyssey of desperation, begging nuns and priests to secure accommodation for herself and her child: 'But every-where I go fate seems dead against me.' It was not for herself she begged 'I shouldn't mind myself being knocked about, as I've hardened now, but I cannot bear the thought of the wee baby being left homeless.' She had advertised her services in exchange for accommodation, but had received no replies. She painted a picture of utter exclusion – only months away from subsistence she could not find a room for herself and her child. The biblical significance of a mother and child seeking a room can surely not have escaped His Grace. She mentioned no family apart from her husband and no support network, her letter records the potential reality for a young couple from the country, if a move to the city was not properly calculated. She also documented how few options were open to women with small children even when, in theory, they had a male breadwinner. Employers were simply not interested in taking on a woman with a child and she was loathe to give him to 'strangers' and was willing to do 'any-thing as long as I would have him near me'. As Peel has argued, '[P]oor women were often confronted – and affronted – by a contradictory demand that they give their children to full-time care while doing whatever they could to earn an income.'[47] A woman with a child and no means, who was 'weary of begging', was potentially dangerous: she did not spell out what she meant by 'desperate' measures, but it was tantamount to an unspoken threat and the archbishop responded by sending her £5. Her story had portrayed her as deserving and desperate in equal and urgent measure. She would also have been regarded as a good investment as her husband was in the police force and he had a better chance than most of earning a sufficient amount to support his family into the future.

To some degree all of the more detailed stories told in these letters involved a level of intimacy, which was perhaps inevitable when people embarked on documenting the history of their personal lives. However, quite a few made intimacy a central thrust of their story seeking to draw the archbishop into their lives as a confidante and, hopefully, an ally. In 1922 Mrs Anna L., the mother of seven from Dun Laoghaire, a seaside suburb on Dublin's south side, made her case by telling her secrets and

[47] Peel, *Miss Cutler*, p. 158.

fears. The wife of a plasterer, she explained that her husband was driven out of Dublin as a result of a strike in the building trade, which 'forced him to go to England to get Bread for his children leaving me heartbroken as I was so ill'. It is likely that she was referring to the bricklayers' strike in Dublin, which lasted between October 1920 and June 1921, as she noted that the strike began 'last october twelve months' and ended 'last summer'. The bricklayers had been seeking 2s.6½ d. per hour, but the employers offered only 2s.2d. The strike cost many families dearly; as Padraig Yeates observed, it secured the workers only a temporary increase of 1d. per hour, while 'keeping the city's modest slum clearance programme on hold'.[48]

Anna's husband, like hundreds of others, secured work in England during the long strike, and in her letter she managed to keep the focus of her story on his religious safety: 'I heard from him that the people go nowhere no church no mass I am praying to the Sacred Heart for him we want him here.' While disclosing her husband's errant ways, she simultaneously bolstered her own religious (and sexual) fidelity: her husband not only belonged with her, but his religious safety depended on it. Her letter depicted the hardship migration caused families. Her husband's departure had rendered her 'heartbroken' but also unsure of his loyalty: 'I was unhappy all the time being separated from my husband while he was also in the beginning, but later he seemed not to mind while my children + myself were praying hard for God to send him home.'

In her story Anna's persona was built on loyalty to her faith and her narrative relied on the drama of her fear for her husband's religious faith and sexual fidelity. She felt guilty but driven to write 'I feel I am doing a terrible thing in writing to Your Grace.' She explained that the Union had imposed a fine of £5 on all workers who had not returned from England immediately after the strike was settled. Her husband had stayed in England until the job he was working on was completed and upon his return the Union had deducted 10/– a week towards the £5 fine from his salary: 'my husband is the only support of 7 young children leaving 9 in all depending on him, while they are taking his 10/- my children are in want they are taking the Bread from my children'. However, if this was not sufficient to engender the archbishop's protective instincts, she followed it with a confession: 'I will tell you a secret my husband has not been to the sacraments for 2 years being away when we had our last retreat.' In true story mode, Anna gave voice to her main character by quoting her disillusioned husband:

---

[48] P. Yeates, *A City in Turmoil: Dublin 1919–1921* (Dublin: Gill & Macmillan, 2012), p. 222.

my husband keeps saying this is free Ireland the Englishman can give the Irishman liberty to earn Bread for his family for 8d. per week while the Irishman who is supposed to be good roman catholic christians demand £5 to get the liberty to work in their own country

Many other men expressed a similar sense of anger at how the 'working man' was treated in a newly independent Ireland. For example, in her childhood memoir Angeline Kearns Blain characterised her father's loss of faith in the new Ireland very similarly: 'Da remarked that the poor, whether alive or dead, are sent to oblivion. "We're not within an ass's roar of being the country I pledged to die for".'[49] Thus Anna's rendition of her husband's set piece had a real ring of authenticity. Throughout her letter she maintained a sense of suspense and kept her reader travelling with her through the events. She explained that after her husband left Ireland in disgust to work again in England, she became desperate and enlisted the prayers of the Poor Clare nuns:

The poor Clares my children + myself kept praying + trusting in the Sacred Heart that he might come Back + this is what happened. I got seriously ill so ill that Dr Murphy 81 Upper George St Dun Laoghaire said I had better send for my husband my little girl wrote to her father + told him. So he came home[50]

It is unclear what Anna L. wished of the archbishop; she told him that her husband felt 'victimised' and 'a marked man' by the Union and that all she wanted was him at home. She ended by reiterating that he was unaware of 'me writing'. By juxtaposing her belief in prayer and the power of divine intervention with her anxiety to have her husband home and a sense of natural justice denied, she made a strong case for the intervention of her church to save her family. While there was a note on the corner of her letter, penned by the archbishop's secretary, indicating that she had received a reply on 4 March 1922; unfortunately there is no record of its contents.

The stories told about poverty incorporated various themes such as heroism, self-sacrifice, exclusion and victimhood. They were spoken in a multitude of voices from intimate to angry, but they all stressed a sense of impotence. Collectively, these letters demonstrate what Rebecca Earle has referred to as 'epistolary self-creation', in which the authors are required to 'enfold complex narratives about identity and

---

[49] A. Kearns Blain, *Stealing Sunlight: Growing up in Irishtown* (Dublin: A & A Farmar, 2000), p. 99.

[50] Mrs Anna L., Desmond Avenue, Dún Laoghaire, Co. Dublin, 4 March 1922. DDA, AB 7 CC, Box 1.

trustworthiness'.[51] In constructing narratives around poverty, the poor tapped into prominent cultural anxieties and stressed whatever attributes were valued or feared by society. Thus Anthony M. and his wife used his status as a convert to Catholicism to drive their narrative, obviously aware of the almost obsessive fear of the main Catholic charities regarding the faith of the children of such marriages. Mrs E. D. focused on her motherhood, the safety of her child, and the widespread fear that desperate mothers could be driven to the Protestants or prostitution. While Anna L.'s intimate letter touched on pervasive fears regarding the impact of emigration on religious observance, marital fidelity, and the idea that honest Irish workers were being denied justice in the new Catholic Ireland.

'The Convert Stunt'

It is hardly surprising when writing to the Roman Catholic Archbishop of Dublin one of the more common negotiation strategies the poor used centred on their religious loyalty, however, the fact that they deployed this tactic so often in an aggressive and threatening way complicates the picture of Irish Catholics as passively deferential.[52] Almost all charities operated on a strictly denominational basis, and since the nineteenth century the charity market was riven by deep religious rivalry and distrust. There was a large corpus of literature deriding what Rev John Keating referred to as, 'the nefarious traffic in souls which certain Protestant agencies carry on in Ireland, and which goes by the unlovely name of "Souperism"'.[53] 'Souperism' referred to the soup given in return for religious conversion during the Great Famine of 1845–50, by the Irish Church Missions. The poor who converted were known as 'Jumpers' or soupers, in fact, there was an entire vocabulary created to describe these Catholics from the rather innocuous term 'weak Catholics', to 'black in their faith', 'leakage' and 'backsliders'.[54] As Keating underlined, the real

---

[51] R. Earle, 'Introduction: letters, writers and the historian' in R. Earle (ed.), *Epistolary Selves: Letters and Letter-Writers, 1600–1945* (Aldershot: Ashgate, 1999), p. 2.

[52] F. O'Toole, 'A culture that failed to see evil', *Irish Times*, 1 November 2005.

[53] Rev J. Keating, S.J., *"Souperism"* (CTSI: Dublin, 1914), p. 3; Keating's pamphlet was just one of many produced by the Catholic Truth Society of Ireland on the issue. For the context to these, see, Curtis, *A Challenge to Democracy*, p. 38. There were also numerous articles in the Catholic press and periodicals; see, for example, Eithne, 'Unwanted Ones – VI', *The Irish Monthly*, (June, 1927), 289–294; Delia Gleeson, 'Our Schools and Catholic Action VIII: A Lesson of Work in Dublin Slums', *The Irish Monthly*, (July 1931), 403–408.

[54] The historical context of these terms see, M. Moffitt, *Soupers and Jumpers: The Protestant Missions in Connemara 1848–1937* (Dublin: The History Press, 2008); I. Whelan, 'The stigma of Souperism' in C. Póirtéir (ed.), *The Great Irish Famine: The Thomas Davis Lecture Series* (Cork: Mercier Press, 1995), pp. 135–154.

fear was 'the Catholic poor', who were 'exposed in their weakness and indigence to non-Catholic officialdom or moneyed fanaticism', would be susceptible to such inducements.[55]

The ghost of proselytism continued to haunt the Free State and the same language abounded: an article on 'Souperism' in 1922 in the *Irish Ecclesiastical Record* received such a response that the author published a fourteen page postscript on the subject a month later.[56] All Synods of Irish Catholic Bishops up to 1928 referred to proselytism as a real and current danger faced by the Catholic poor.[57] In 1929, the Bishop of Galway was relatively confident that while 'souperism' had been eliminated from Galway, the slums of Dublin continued to provide rich pickings for 'soul snatchers who descend upon the homes of poverty'.[58] Jacinta Prunty points out that this religious rivalry was also a motivating factor in the creation of new charities and increased assistance for the poor.[59] Rescue agencies such as the Saint Patrick's Guild (1910) and the Catholic Protection and Rescue Society (1913) had been formed to 'rescue' these Catholics, particularly their children, but all religions regarded it as their duty to 'rescue' while, and by, giving. The Vincent de Paul, not itself a 'rescue' society, often relayed stories of the 'evil of mixed marriage'[60] or of 'reforming backsliding parents' and the 'rescue of children from proselytising institutions'.[61] 'Mixed marriages' – marriages between Catholics and Protestants – provided a particular focus for this anxiety and both religions shared a horror of such unions. The papal decree *Ne Temere* issued in 1908, merely heightened inter-denominational tensions on the issue, particularly in relation to the children of such marriages, as it specified that the partners had to agree in writing that their future offspring would be raised in the Catholic faith.[62] In her memoir, Edith Newman Devlin,

---

[55] J. Keating, S.J., *"Souperism"*, p. 4.

[56] See also, Rev. M. H. MacInerny, 'The Souper problem', *Irish Ecclesiastical Record*, 18 (1921), 140–156; Rev. M. H. MacInerny, 'A postscript on the Souper problem', *Irish Ecclesiastical Record*, 19 (1922), 246–260.

[57] Curtis, *A Challenge to Democracy*, p. 37.

[58] Catholic Protection and Rescue Society, *16th Report of the Catholic Protection and Rescue Society 1929* (Dublin, n.d.), p. 3.

[59] J. Prunty, *Dublin Slums, 1800–1925: A Study in Urban Geography* (Dublin: Irish Academic Press, 1998), p. 273.

[60] 'Conference of St Michan, Dublin, Supplementary report', *Bulletin of the Society of St. Vincent De Paul*, 88 (August 1923), p. 238.

[61] 'Supplement of Irish Conferences', *Bulletin of the Society of St. Vincent De Paul*, 96 (April 1931), p. 5.

[62] For a discussion of the damage it caused to ecumenical relations in Ireland, see R. Roulston, 'The Church of Ireland and the Irish state, 1950–1972: education, healthcare and moral welfare' (unpublished PhD thesis: UCD, 2013); D. Ó Corráin, *Rendering to God and Caesar: The Irish Churches and the Two States in Ireland, 1949–73* (Manchester University Press, 2007), pp. 184–191.

born in 1926 of a Church of Ireland mother and a Presbyterian father, relates how mixed marriages altered the religious flow of her family tree on three occasions:

the catholic church was intent on bringing the protestants, whom it viewed as heretics, over to its faith so that they, too, would become supine. Look at its policy on mixed marriages: the non-catholic partner had to bring up the children as catholics, and the catholic partner had to try to bring the members of the other family over to the faith. This in fact happened three times in our family.[63]

While the religions feared each other they also distrusted the poor, as George Williams put it in 1902, in the divided charitable landscape the 'scheming hypocrite can reap a rich harvest':[64] where there was religious poaching there was scope for bargaining. The letters written by Catholics to Archbishop Byrne are replete with examples of this form of 'religious bargaining', but they also reveal that it was often borne of profound desperation and an understanding of how the charity system manipulated in its turn.

The Irish who wrote looking for assistance from their church used similar tactics to the working-class Austrians, who petitioned the civil authorities in nineteenth-century Austria, and the paupers who appealed to the Poor Law authorities in eighteenth- and nineteenth-century England: when they felt desperate they used threats. Sokoll noted that English paupers tended 'to combine defensive with offensive gestures'.[65] It is easy to see why – any other approach would have been self-defeating. Neither Hämmerle's Austrians, nor Sokoll's Essex paupers really wanted to carry out their threats, rather, they formed part of a design to get help. The Irish in a corner were no different; their threats merely reflected their context. Where Sokoll's paupers threatened to return home to their district (and thus increase the costs for the Poor Law),[66] Hämmerle's petitioners claimed they would turn their children over to the poorhouse,[67] and the Irish Catholic poor swore they would 'go to the Protestants'. Interestingly, Protestant charity applicants employed similar tactics

[63] E. Newman Devlin, *Speaking Volumes: A Dublin Childhood* (Belfast: The Blackstaff, 2000), p. 117.

[64] G. D. Williams, *Dublin Charities, Being a Handbook of Dublin Philanthropic Organisations and Charities* (Dublin: John Falconer, 1902), p. 2.

[65] Sokoll, *Essex Pauper Letters*, p. 68.

[66] Sokoll argues 'their knowledge of the disadvantages of their removal to their home parish was the poor's best card, and it is precisely their letters which reveal how effectively they played this card'. Sokoll, 'Negotiating a living', 28.

[67] C. Hämmerle, 'Requests, complaints, demands. Preliminary thoughts on the petitioning letters of lower-class Austrian women, 1865–1918' in C. Bland and M. Cros (eds.), *Gender and Politics in the Age of Letter Writing, 1750–2000* (Aldershot: Ashgate, 2004), pp. 115–134, 127.

when applying to, for example, the Clergy Widows' and Orphans' Society and the Protestant Orphans' Society [hereafter POS]. Oonagh Walsh cites one female applicant who reportedly threatened the POS inspector that 'if there was any more trouble in the matter she would hand the children over to the Roman Catholics'.[68] Indeed, the strategies employed by many of these letter writers conform to J. C. Scott's theory of 'cautious resistance and calculated conformity',[69] whereby people engaged in anything from subtle threats to abandon their faith, usually involving explanations of how their faith was being threatened by their poverty and often wrapped in a wider narrative that underscored loyalty and innocence, to outright declarations of reluctant defection driven by desperation. If charity could demand certain behaviour from the poor, refusal to conform or a threat to do so could prove very effective in shifting the balance of the relationship between the giver and the receiver.

These threatening letters often represented acts of conformance and resistance; in fact, the tension between the two was at the heart of the strategy. In the same letter, a writer might reaffirm membership of their community by expressing loyalty to either Ireland or Catholicism and implicitly or explicitly threaten defection or betrayal. As one letter writer put it: 'Wee are trying to bring up our children in the best way wee can in the Catholic religion, as I don't wish to rely on any other religion, like others for help.'[70] If, as Fitzpatrick has convincingly argued, 'religious affirmation was perhaps the most powerful symbol of community',[71] then implying one's religion had failed you when in need, or that you would leave it because it had effectively abandoned you, went right to the heart of the sense of community in Ireland. It was, therefore, an incredibly powerful tool and an implicit criticism of the meaning of community in the new state.

Threats were made in a range of ways from the unabashed threat to defect to another religion to the subtler request for guidance in the face of willing Protestants and tight-fisted Catholics. Although Hämmerle's petition letters were very formal in structure, she provides an example of a woman threatening the authorities that was very similar to the ways in which many Irish women threatened to hand their children to the opposite religion. In Austria in 1914, Mrs Maria Ana Grabher wrote:

[68] Walsh, *Anglican Women in Dublin*, pp. 166–167.
[69] J. C. Scott, *Weapons of the Weak: Everyday Forms of Peasant Resistance* (Connecticut: Yale University Press, 1985), p. 241.
[70] Mr A. R., the Basement, X Mountjoy Sq., (Dublin city), n.d. *c.* November 1936. He received £1. See his priest's reference, Fr P. O'Flynn, 83 Marlborough St., Dublin, 17 November 1936. DDA, AB 7 CC, Box 6.
[71] Fitzpatrick, *Oceans of Consolation*, p. 601.

I am therefore requesting relief again this week and if it is refused I shall have to send my children, at least 4 or 6 if not all of them, to the poorhouse for their dinner and supper. To be sure it's a sorry state of things to be in such a miserable state through no fault of your own and to find so little understanding[72]

Compare this to a short note from 'a sorrowful mother' written in the late 1930s to Archbishop Byrne:

Me and my six children are in a desperate state of distress and noticed to quit our home. We are to be summoned to court for non payment of rent. This is not great fault of myself or my husband. If something is not done for us I will have to seek help from some other Religion.[73]

A common tactic was to attempt to shame the archbishop and, implicitly, his Church. In a similar fashion to Maria Ana Grabher, who was so hurt to 'find so little understanding', many Irish Catholics cast their plea in terms of their disappointment with their religion. For example, Mrs M. C.'s barely veiled rebuke: 'I have often met Canon Downing PP and he asked me how I was getting on but did not say here is a shilling for you.'[74] In 1937 Joseph B., the father of two young children and a 'delicate wife', asked for help before 'I am forced to seek aid from people outside my own religious denominations.'[75] Mrs May J., a widow of a Church of England Naval man, asked: 'Your Grace help me to go the wright [right] Road dont drive me to the church of England with my 3 orphans.'[76] Joseph B. would be 'forced' and Mrs May J. feared being 'driven', the emphasis was on the fact that they were reluctant, but believed they had been left with little choice but to leave a church that failed to help them – a sense of blame drove the ink on these pages.

In 1935 Mrs B., from Kimmage on Dublin's west side, wrote as a 'Catholic mother with an Unemployed Husband with 9 children', who was and to/ know that in such unable to secure clothes for her children from any Catholic charities: 'my Children are like little Pagans dont know what school or Chapel is owing to their been barefooted and naked in Clothes'. Evoking the pathos of motherhood, Mrs B. blatantly attempted to implicate her Church as the bystander to her poverty:

---

[72] Mrs Maria Ana Grabher, Augarten, 1914, cited in Hämmerle, 'Requests, complaints, demands', p. 127
[73] Mrs C., X Kilfenora Rd. Off Stanway Rd., Kimmage, Co. Dublin, n.d. c. 1938. DDA, AB 7 CC, Box 7.
[74] Mrs Marie C., St Joseph's place, Off Dorset St., (Dublin city), 12 February 1924. DDA, AB 7 CC, Box 1.
[75] Mr Joseph B., 4 Upr Mercier Street, Dublin, c. September 1937. DDA, AB 7 CC, Box 6.
[76] Mrs May J., Forest Road, Swords, Co Dublin, 7 February 1936. Ibid.

It is very hard to look at your own Children Half starved and naked and to/ know that in such a distress Case that your own Religion could help. Well Rev. Fr what am I to do put them into schools for the sake of trying to pleas the people who by the word of God is placed in a position to help their Flock.

Should I take myself and Family to another Religion and they to know the distress plight I was in I wonder what the Catholics would say.

If she took her children to another religion she would shame *and* embarrass her church, but if those ordained by God failed to keep their end of the religious bargain, she asked why should a mother comply with its demands. She reminded the archbishop 'there are many Temptations where there is such Poverty My letter can bear any investigation'.[77] She remained 'yours Obediently': she did not want to carry out her threat, she was honest and could withstand investigation, but the temptation was real. This reassurance that a letter would bear investigation was a common rhetorical device also observed by scholars who have examined pauper letters of nineteenth-century Britain.[78] The suggestion that the reader could 'check' the facts in the letter, or consult a 'respectable person' about its claims, remained pertinent because of the cultural tendency to distrust the dependent remained pervasive.

Contemporaries interpreted Mrs B.'s claim that she would take her children to another religion as a tactical threat, as a member of the Vincent de Paul explained in 1936:

And even when they vehemently express the impossibility of "carrying on" without our help, and possibly threaten to go "where they will get relief," meaning thereby a proselytising institution, they in their heart of hearts have not the slightest intention of carrying out their threats. I have been so threatened by a client of ours on a Monday night and found her at evening devotions on the following night.[79]

However, the society's bulletins reveal an anxiety that this threat could be, and was, acted upon by the desperate poor. That the Catholic Church shared this anxiety was evidenced by the fact that many of these letters

---

[77] Mrs B., X Ferns Road, Kimmage, Dublin, 6 December 1935. Ibid. She had written previously from a different address, see Mrs B., X Lr Kevin St., Dublin, 28 March 1932. DDA, AB 7 CC, Box 4.

[78] S. King and A. Stringer '"I have once more taken the Leberty to say as you well know": The development of rhetoric in the letters of the English, Welsh and Scottish sick and poor 1870s-1830s' in A. Gestrich, E. Hurren and S. King (eds.), *Poverty and Sickness in Modern Europe: Narratives of the Sick Poor, 1780–1938* (London: Continuum, 2012), pp. 69–91, 72.

[79] These comments were made in a paper entitled 'The Spiritual Aspect of Our Society', read by one of the presidents of a Dublin council of the Saint Vincent de Paul. 'Supplement for Irish Conferences, June 1936', *Bulletin of the Society of St. Vincent De Paul*, 101 (July 1936), p. 2.

were assisted precisely because of the threat. For example, Mrs May
D. wrote in November 1931 to complain about the treatment she had
received at the hands of a Brother Smyth. She had been looking for boots
for her children:

I then went up on Friday night and Brother Smyth told me I could take them
to they <u>Souper</u>. So it speaks very Bad for a gentleman who is suppose to be
doing good work for the Catholic faith. God knows I am affected enough
without being degraded by Brother Smyth.[80]

Presumably, she was referring to an exchange between herself and
Br. Smyth in which she may have remarked that she would have to take
her children to the Protestants. May's husband had been in Grangegorman District Mental hospital, in Dublin's north inner city, and she had
eight children to support on out-door relief of £1, out of which she paid
5/– rent, 2/5 for coal and 1/– 'Society' or burial insurance. Her parish
priest wrote a supporting letter referring to her as a 'thoroughly decent
woman' and her case as 'a deserving one'.[81] In spite of her frankness she
received £5 from the archbishop.

However, those that did not withstand investigation or played their
card too forcefully were not so lucky. Paul B., who wrote that he was in
'an unhappy position concerning my Religion', had been turned down by
the Vincent de Paul, which had 'hardened' him and

it is turning me from my duties which I feel very sorry for doing. But Rev.
archBishop I cant do any thing else But turn to the opposite Reliegon for I am
not going to see my wife & children hungry when Father Barrett & the gentlemen
of St Vincents De Paul gentlemans wont give me some little assistance. I have
got an offer from a lady belong to the prosantant [Protestant] Reliegon Rev
Archbishop I would be most grateful & thankful to you if you could do something
for me as my wife is very determined also myself & the four children.[82]

There is one word written in the top left hand corner of Paul's letter:
'Rascal.' This appears to be in the archbishop's, at this point, shaky hand
(as a result of prolonged ill-health),[83] and it implies several things. That
he had followed up on Paul B.'s letter with the 'gentlemans' in the
Vincent de Paul, and had been convinced that the 'prosantant lady'
was a ploy. Also, it hints at a certain level of understanding – 'rascals'
chance their arms, they are not malevolent – while it was patronising, it

---

[80] Mrs May D., Upper Gloucester St., Dublin, 22 November 1931. DDA, AB 7 CC,
Box 4.
[81] Fr P. J. Dunlea, Pro-Cathedral, n.d. c. November 1931. Ibid.
[82] Mr Paul B., X St Eithnel Road, Cabra, Dublin, n.d. c. 1934. Ibid.
[83] Morrissey, *Edward J. Byrne 1872–1941*, p. 160, 241.

was without a trace of anger and with just a hint of condescending amusement.

Mrs Agnes F., who lived in the 'Parlour' in a house in Dublin's inner city, wrote on a Thursday in November 1935 seeking advice:

I am in very poor circumstances at present & only God & myself know how I am trying to manage I am writing this letter to you to try and ease my mind no one knows I am sending this to you to ask your advice a couple of persons called on me & of course I had no fire & told them my husband had a small pension & we were not able to exist & they said if I joined some mission it was not a catholic place they would not see me short they would provide food & clothes & get me work but not until I would promise to join them so I said to myself I would write to you & let you give me your advice God knows I am very poor tonight but I did & will not do their way I kept this 2d for a stamp to tell you hoping you will not think me very impertinent for writing. God Bless you & community[84]

She laid her dilemma at her church's door by asking the archbishop for advice in the daily struggle between remaining true to one's religion (which allowed such poverty to persist) or taking the sustenance offered from other non-Catholic sources. Throughout she kept her poverty centre stage: her very address underscored it – the 'Parlour' – in which 'of course I had no fire' and the letter itself had to be budgeted for, 'I kept this 2d for a stamp.' Mrs F. was as good as any storyteller in setting the scene of a dark, cold, one-room home in which the inhabitants are 'not able to exist', into which a visitor comes offering a way out.

In view of the deep fear regarding the spiritual welfare of impoverished children it is little wonder that unmarried mothers often resorted to the threat of religious defection. These women were in a very vulnerable position in Irish society; they were socially shunned and the state offered them few other options than institutionalisation in a home.[85] Death also had the upper hand with their children, who were up to five times more likely to die in infancy than their counterparts born within the relatively protective confines of marriage.[86] In July 1924 Mary M. wrote a detailed account of her rape during the Irish civil war (1922–1923) at the hands of 'a party of men armed to the teeth & calling

---

[84] Mrs Agnes F., Parlour, X Demark Place, off Little Denmark Street, Dublin, 7 November 1935. DDA, AB 7 CC, Box 6.

[85] For a detailed discussion of the position of unmarried mothers and their children in Irish society see, L. Earner-Byrne, *Mother and Child: Maternity and Child Welfare in Dublin, 1922–60* (Manchester University Press, 2007), pp. 152–172; J. M. Smith, *Ireland's Magdalen Laundries and the Nation's Architecture of Containment* (Manchester University Press, 2007).

[86] L. Earner-Byrne, 'The boat to England': An analysis of the official reactions to the emigration of single expectant Irishwomen to Britain, 1922–1972' *Irish Economic and Social History*, 30 (2003), 52–70.

themselves Republicans',[87] which had resulted in the birth of a son. She had managed, by stealing her blind Aunt's pension, to pay for her son's maintenance in the Saint Patrick's Guild – a Catholic rescue society based in Dublin[88] – but she was unable to keep up the repayments and requested £20 to have the baby 'taken completely off my hands' – this was the fee for private adoption.[89] While Mary M. was careful to reassure the archbishop of her strong Catholic pedigree – 'I have been brought up well and came of decent parents R.I.P. I was a child of Mary a member of St Francis 3rd Order besides been a weekly Communicant', she also offered him a stronger incentive to help her:

Oh My Lord for the love of the Holy Face of Jesus and the Sorrows of His Holy Mother help me do something for me to save this Angel's soul and keep it in the Catholic Faith I can't pay another month I'll have to ask some Protestant Lady to take it. I have not the money to save its dear soul And to be forced to part with it under those conditions my Lord would drive me insane but I see no way out of the difficulty[90]

Furthermore, the priest who acted as her referee testified to the veracity of her account, but also attempted to secure her assistance because: 'I do furthermore think that there is this chance – that the child might pass from Catholic hands to Protestant control –.'[91] Mary M. was sent the £20 she requested; there is little doubt that it was the anxiety regarding the faith of her child that prompted such speedy generosity.[92]

In 1933, one priest, weary of what he dubbed the 'convert stunt', described it as too well known to be heeded.[93] This conviction was clearly not borne out by the archbishop's response to many of those that

---

[87] Miss Mary M., Moate, Co. Westmeath, 3 July 1924. DDA, AB 7 CC, Box 1.

[88] Josephine Mary Cruice established the Saint Patrick's Guild in 1910 to assist mothers of the 'better classes' and to cater for their illegitimate infants either in the home or via fostering or private adoption. Memo by Cruice on 'Origins of St Patrick's Guild' c. 1932. Dublin Diocesan Archives, Byrne papers: Lay Organisations (2).

[89] There was no provision for statutory adoption in Ireland until 1952, thus some women paid high fees to have their children privately adopted. See, P. Conroy, 'Motherhood interrupted: adoption in Ireland' in P. Kennedy (ed.), *Motherhood in Ireland: Creation and Context* (Cork: Mercier Press, 2003), pp. 181–93.

[90] Miss Mary M., Moate, Co. Westmeath, 3 July 1924.

[91] Fr Cyprian, the Abbey, Galway, to Fr Dunne, 8 July 1924. Ibid. Cyprian is a pseudonym to protect the identity of Mary M.'s infant son, whom she called after the priest who assisted her.

[92] For a detailed consideration of this letter see, L. Earner-Byrne, 'The rape of Miss Mary M: A mircrohistory of sexual violence and moral redemption in 1920s Ireland', *Journal of the History of Sexuality*, 24 (January, 2015), 75–98.

[93] Fr Ferdinand, Capuchin Friary, Kilkenny to Fr Dunne, 25 November. 1931. DDA, AB 7 CC, Box 4. Interestingly, Delay's research into the role of priests in post-famine Ireland reveals that priests were capable of inverting the threat by telling unhappy parishioners to go to the Protestants. C. Delay, 'Confidantes or competitors? Women,

threatened to leave Catholicism or to take their children to Protestant schools. This threat *was* heeded. Clearly, it had considerable cultural resonance and reflected the reality of what Prunty referred to as the virtual 'spiritual warfare' in the charity market.[94] To the poor, who had so little else to bargain with, so few other cards to play, the threat of defection must have seemed irresistible – what was more valuable to their church than the souls of their children? As Peel has argued, impoverished people frequently managed to 'maintain a kind of moral independence from the system by revealing their knowledge of how it really works'.[95] Writers like Mrs Paula C., who wrote in 1937, furious that her husband's requests for charity had been refused, compensated for their limited literacy by exposing contemporary hypocrisy. In a few words Mrs C. reduced the complex world of religious manipulation she was trapped in to its bare essentials: 'Well Father my Husband was brought up in Miss Cars Protestant Home[96] and turned a Catholic with me I wont Trouble you as my Husband/ has got an offer of my 6 Children to be Educated and Clothed I can see now that Religion is only a Cloke what matter which side your on onse you have enough to eat.'[97]

In 1933 Mr Timothy B. wrote to complain of his treatment at the hands of various charities. Although he was clearly engaging in religious politics, he was also reflecting a charity market that thrived on religious manipulation:

I supose you come to the same conclusion as the st. Vincent de Paul who do Picket out side the medical mission that there must be something wrong but I can assure you that if my case is Proply looked into I have reson for complaint at the way I have been treated it is not very nice to be told by a Priest that you can turn Protestant but if I had not been taken from the Birds Nest Kingstown and Put into Denmark st orphanage I would never had reason to beg of anyone hoping that by this letter you will be able to understand the way the poor of this city is being Treated.[98]

By linking the picket carried out by the Vincent de Paul against the proselytising activities of the Dublin Medical Mission with his removal from a Protestant orphanage (Birds' Nest in Kingstown/Dun Laoghaire)

---

priests, and conflict in post-famine Ireland', *Eire-Ireland*, 40 (Spring/Summer 2005), 107–25, 116.

[94] Prunty, *Dublin Slums, 1800–1925*, p. 238.   [95] M. Peel, *The Lowest Rung*, p. 76.

[96] Elizabeth Hawthorn Carr established Miss Carr's Home for Destitute Children in Dublin in 1887 for Protestant children. There were soon a number of homes around Dublin. See, *Annual Report of Miss Carr's Home for Destitute Children for the Year 1887* (Dublin, 1888).

[97] Paula C., X Talbot Pace, Dublin, n.d. *c.* 1937. DDA, AB 7 CC, Box 7.

[98] Mr Timothy B., X Meath St., Dublin to Archbishop Byrne, n.d. c. 1933. DDA, AB 7 CC, Box 5.

to a Catholic orphanage (Saint Saviour's Orphanage in Denmark Street), Timothy was making a wider comment about religious hypocrisy: the souls of infants were saved, but little thought was given to their physical survival.[99] Those that threatened religious defection were often highlighting the injustice of a system that made this sort of religious bartering a consequence of poverty.

'My husband is a Protestant by birth'

Converts to Catholicism, or those married to one, were of particular concern to the Catholic Church. If 'marriages across the religious divide' could cause 'chilliness' in families,[100] they had the potential to cause virtual panic amid the hierarchy of the various denominations. Neither Catholic nor Protestant clergy were happy with their flock 'marrying out'; there was a long history on both sides of discouraging the practice, which Prunty referred to as a 'minefield' that charities were frequently drawn into.[101] Those writing to the archbishop were keenly aware of these concerns and often attempted to stoke those fears, particularly in relation to the children of mixed marriages. In 1935 Mrs Hannah R., whose husband was ill, explained: 'My husband is a Protestant by birth, but has never interfered in any way with the training of the children as they have been brought up in our faith.' However, she had Protestant relatives waiting in the wings should Catholicism fail her:

My husband's relatives especially his eldest brother who is a Protestant
clergyman would very willingly help with the charge of the younger children,
but we would not think of allowing their religious training to be tampered with
although such compliance would bring us substantial monetary relief. Our
declining to adopt this course has left us without any assistance from that source[102]

Despite her parish priest's conviction that the true reason for her husband's unemployment was his drinking, he still recommended her as a 'very deserving woman', who had reared her children well. She received £5 of the archbishop's charity.[103]

The spectre of Protestant relatives anxious to 'rob' Catholic children was a constant theme in the letters of those who had either converted to

[99] F. Kennedy, *Frank Duff: A Life Story* (London: Burns & Oates, 2011), p. 51.
[100] Fitzpatrick, *Oceans of Consolation*, p. 550.
[101] J. Prunty, 'Margaret Louisa Aylward (1810–1889)' in M. Cullen and M. Luddy (eds.), *Women, Power and Consciousness in Nineteenth Century Ireland* (Dublin: Attic Press, 1995), pp. 55–88, 70.
[102] Mrs Hannah R., Clonliffe Road, Drumcondra, Dublin, 10 November 1923. DDA, AB 7 CC, Box 1.
[103] Fr A. Moriarty, 595 North Circular Road, Dublin, 3 December 1923. Ibid.

Catholicism or married Protestants. In May 1931, Mr James B., a father of 'seven young children' wrote to put his 'sad case' to the archbishop:

I am unemployed since 28th sept 1929 continuously, I have a wife and seven children the eldest is 16 years of age and the youngest or baby of 3 months. Nine of us are Packed here in a small tenement back room, but I am in arrears of rent and threatened with eviction I became a convert into the Roman Catholic Church on my marriage, and since then my people, who are pretty well off disown me.

Mr B. was anxious to establish himself as a successful and true convert explaining:

I send my children regularly to school and to children's mass every Sunday morning. I go to Confession and Holy Communion once a month, so also does my wife. I do pray morning and night that God may send me some work to feed my children and bring them up in the fear and love of God.[104]

In 1922, Mr Frank B. sent a relatively simple and short missive requesting capital to continue manufacturing the 'first + only Band Drum every made in Ireland', in order to provide for his wife and four children. His valediction hinted at the currency of conversion and the fears regarding its manipulation: 'I remain/ One of your true Converts', the implication was that there were many untrue ones.[105] The note on Mr B.'s letter indicated that he was to be visited and if found to be 'true' awarded £5.

Walsh has argued that while Protestant charity workers were equally concerned about Protestant children raised by converts, the anxiety that these children might be lost to the faith tended to result in a refusal of assistance.[106] By contrast, there are plenty of letters in the archbishop's collection that testify to the success of this strategy for Catholic or convert parents. Mrs H., who featured in the introduction, was supported by her parish priest on the basis that '[A]s she is a convert, I am afraid she would easily be bought & the money in her circumstances would attract all the more. Any help given, with an assurance of no other appeal, will give her courage to carry on.'[107] This rather qualified endorsement of her loyalty earned her a generous £20.

Mrs Frances R., who wrote in December 1928 from the 'Top Front Room' of a tenement building in Dublin, revealed her status as a 'convert to the Catholic Religion' in her opening gambit. She then outlined her reasons for writing – due to her husband's unemployment her family

---

[104] Mr James B., X Upper Stephen's St., Dublin, 27 May 1931. DDA, AB 7 CC, Box 4.
[105] Mr Frank B., X Lr Gardiner St., Dublin, 3 April 1922. DDA, AB 7 CC, Box 1.
[106] Walsh, *Anglican Women in Dublin*, pp. 180–1.
[107] This was written on a piece of paper attached to Mrs H.'s letter, see letter. Mrs H., X Leinster Rd., Rathmines, Dublin, 15 July 1939. DDA, AB 7 CC, Box 7.

were in dire need of clothing – but it was in her concluding paragraphs that she combined her vulnerability and loyalty:

It is very hard to see ones little children running around almost barefoot and shivering with cold, in fact I have been sorely tempted to try to obtain these things from other sources, but have refrained from doing so with the strong intent to keep faithful to the religion.

Trusting His Grace may again pardon my liberty for writing this, and be kind enough to do something for myself + my little children and my husband and pray for us.[108]

Her parish priest confirmed that she was a convert who 'attends regularly to her sodality', however, due to a visit that discovered the family 'partaking of a substantial dinner of bacon' he did not regard them as being in 'extreme need', but as 'honest people' they were worthy of 10/– shillings.[109] The archbishop was minded to considerably greater generosity and the family received £2.[110]

Mr Peter McK. wrote in May 1927 'to make a general Complaint about the Carlesness of they [the] Clergy in the Parish', He and his wife had moved to the parish and in the first month had received no visit from the local clergy 'to find out whether we were Protestants or Catholics'. His real frustrations seemed to have been that he was receiving no assistance from the church or Vincent de Paul, and he was about to be cut off from the Labour Exchange and would thus be unable to pay for rent or food. His despair at trying to prise open the doors of charity are still palpable in his letters 'I am still waisting [wasting] my time every night stopping in house expecting to be visited or even a reply by letter'.[111] Although he had 'firstclass references for Sobriety, Honesty + Steadfastness attentive to business duties', he believed it was his wife's status as a convert that should have secured them assistance: 'My Wife being a convert to the Faith that is the reason all of them should take a special interest in the matter.'[112] He wrote a month later in one final attempt to shame his church into action: 'I know from my own experience of they [the] Belfast Priests visit the Slums of the city looking after the Poor but evidently Fairview Parish hasnt time from this work especially if you look to be in Poor Circumstances.' There is no evidence that he received the awaited 'esteemed reply'.[113] However, his second letter

---

[108] Mrs Frances R., Top Front Room, X Summer Hill, Dublin City, 11 December 1928. £2 is written on her letter. DDA, AB 7 CC, Box 2.
[109] Fr Charles F. Hurley, 25 Killarney St., Dublin, 16 December 1928. Ibid.
[110] This amount is noted in the top left-hand corner of the parish priest's letter.
[111] Mr Peter McK., X Carleton Road, Marino, Dublin, 9 May 1927. DDA, AB 7 CC, Box 2.
[112] Ibid.   [113] Mr Peter McK., X Carleton Road, Marino, Dublin, 1 June 1927.

revealed that he had also written to the parish priests to tell them that they were careless in their duties and the priests felt insulted. Above all else Mr McK.'s letters testify to the hopelessness felt by unemployed men in a world with thousands of other such men and ever diminishing resources.

'Is there no reciprocal duty?'

In her study of the Irish working class, Marilyn Silverman reflects on the social response to the new Unemployment Assistance introduced in 1933, when, for example, the *Kilkenny Journal* complained that the new weekly allowances was a 'tawdry sum' and lamented that

the worst system of red tape ... invoked under the British regime pales into insignificance in comparison ... can anyone say that it is just – that in the case of an unemployed father, a portion of the earnings of his son shall be regarded as an income and the amount of unemployment assistance to which the father is entitled, calculated accordingly?[114]

She argues that new discursive categories of 'degradation', 'insult', and 'self-respect' emerged in the 1920s and 30s and 'signalled new ideas about personal and political entitlements which were actualized not via good behaviour and generosity but through Free State citizenship'.[115] However, this also had a lot to do with the everyday reality of unemployment which, in its pervasiveness, upset comfortable judgments about the causes of poverty and hence the basis of entitlement. Mr Peter McK., who had been so incensed by his local clergy's lack of interest, also articulated a sense of himself as part of the 'new unemployed', when he wrote that he had been a member of Vincent de Paul for twenty-six years but 'men like myself now out of work' meant the world of clear distinctions was blurring.[116] Mr McK.'s anger came partly from his conviction that the church had a role to play in combating unemployment, as he explained: 'His Eminence Cardinal O'Donnell made some reference to unemployment at the meeting of your Lordships at Maynooth College said that Employers should try and help this matter as best they could and our Clergy also.'[117] Mr McK. and others like him were listening to the pronouncements of senior members of the church on the responsibilities of employers

---

[114] *Kilkenny Journal*, 18 August 1934 cited in M. Silverman, *An Irish Working Class: Explorations in Political Economy and Hegemony, 1800–1950* (University of Toronto Press, 2001), pp. 328–9.
[115] Ibid.　　[116] Mr Peter McK., X Carleton Road, Marino, Dublin, 1 June 1927.
[117] Ibid.

towards the unemployed and were demanding a practical response from the church.[118]

The anger expressed in such correspondence indicated a sense of entitlement, the sort of fury that comes from a deeper sense of justice denied. In the context of these letters anger was deployed as 'righteous' in response to injustice, it formed part of what Linda Pollack describes as 'dynamic negotiation', when writers sought to use anger to 'impose an interpretation on a situation' and assert that they deserved respect.[119] Similarly, Crossman notes that among those applying for poor relief in the early twentieth century 'there appears to have been a strong sense of entitlement amongst claimants. People became more assertive when applying for relief, and were more likely to complain if they were refused or did not receive what had been granted'.[120] Often these feelings of entitlement manifested themselves in a sense of being betrayed by the new state and/or the Roman Catholic Church. While the gender aspect should not be overplayed, it was more often male writers that conceptualised their story as one of betrayal. Men were also more likely to root their predicament in wider political realities, for example, the impact of the War of Independence (1919–1921) shaped Martin G.'s understanding of everything that had happened since then. His anger was not merely directed at the soldiers who had assaulted his wife and family, but more pointedly, at the new state that had forgotten them. In January 1924 he wrote from Crossmalena in County Mayo, along Ireland's west coast, to explain that:

I was left Pennyless and wricked by the Black and tans my Wife is in bad health sence through the raids my house was raided 14 times the[y] pulled my wife out of bead before her Confinement and abused her and treathened her life and my 6 Children and nearly Killed my oldest Child

His nerves had been shattered as a result of a beating received from the Black and Tans – the auxiliary forces deployed by the British during the war – and thus, through no fault of his own, he had been unable to work.[121] Although he was pursing a claim for compensation he had been unable to pay his rent: 'I appealed several times to the Government but the[y] forget the xxxx Poor and the Distress I hope Father you wont

---

[118] *Pastoral Address issued by the Archbishops and Bishops of Ireland to their Flocks on the Occasion of the Plenary Synod held in Maynooth 1927* (Dublin: Browne and Nolan, 1927).

[119] L. A. Pollock, 'Anger and negotiation of relationships in early Modern England', *The Historical Journal*, 47 (2004), 567–590.

[120] Crossman, *Poverty and The Poor Law in Ireland*, p. 89.

[121] D. M. Leeson, *The Black and Tans: British Police and Auxiliaries in the Irish War of Independence* (Oxford University Press, 2011), p. ix; D. Price, *The Flame and the Candle: War in Mayo 1919–1924* (Cork: Collins, 2012), pp. 66–85.

forget my Distress and Godwill reward you I can sertify this my Bishop.'[122] In his eyes the reward for loyalty had been slim and the new regime had easily forgotten the poor and distressed.

In the same year Mr J. K. wrote from Dublin's Lower Mount Street to complain of his treatment at the hands of the new state. A waiter by training, he had joined the Free State Army during the Irish civil war and after 'two years faithful service to the State' was 'dismissed without compensation'. The government acknowledged privately that these men were often reduced to desperate conditions.[123] Mr J. K. wrote of his 'ruined ... nerves' for which he was 'Still under treatment in Patrick Dunn Hospital', Grand Canal Street in Dublin. In mentioning his treatment at a specific institution Mr J. K. provided factual detail that could be verified. However, his letter was about a sense of betrayal:

I am left on the streets to Starve I done work day and night during the troublesome times and that was all my thanks for trying to educate some of them to be Gentlemen and I had hard dask [task] I was also in danger of my own life

He had pawned his dress clothes, which he needed to retrieve if he was to have any chance of resuming his career as a waiter. He asked for a 'little loan' and received £1 from the archbishop.[124] His second letter, nine days later, which reiterated the same story, was greeted with silence.

A very similar pattern emerged in the case of Patrick H. who wrote some four years later. While he apologised for not being a 'very good scollor', he was still able to communicate his story of unrewarded sacrifice:

I am a married man with a wife and 5 young Children. I am out of Empailment [employment] for Past 18 months now, I am Expecting to get a notice to leave my Home any time ... I have Served in grate War and all so in Free state army as you can sea by my Paper. I have good Papers. Dear Father I am stating the true facts of the case to you, my wife and children are at home Hungery now/ We havent as much as a slice of Bread or a bit to Eat in House I never was as Badely of[f] as I am now. I have Every thing sold in House to By food to keep us from starving ... god naws [knows] I am nearly out of my mind going abaught.

---

[122] Mr Martin G., Ballyduffy, Jahardane, Crossmalena, Co Mayo, 28 January 1924. DDA, AB 7 CC, Box 1.

[123] 'Memo on the Unemployment position', signed Gordon Campbell, 10 December 1923. 'Distress and unemployment in Saorstát generally', S4278A, NAI.

[124] Mr J. K., X Lower Mount Street, 20 October 1924. He wrote on three other occasions and received £1. DDA, AB 7 CC, Box 1.

Dear Father I wood be gratefull to you if you Could get me work of any sort/
I have suffored my share since I have Been idel. Poverty and Hunger day after
day.[125]

Demobilised and excluded, he received £1 for his letter, but he wrote
several more times in vain, with each account his sense of impotency
and injustice became more insistent.[126] There is a note written on the
top left-hand corner of his third letter, which reads simply 'No'.[127]
Evidently, these cases – and there were many letters from demobilised
soldiers and/or their wives – were supposed to find their feet relatively
quickly.[128] Patrick H. was one of many men who served in the 'grate
War' and then the Irish Free State Army: half the recruits to the Free
State Army during the civil war were ex-servicemen.[129] Irish soldiers
who had served in the British Army during the First World War experienced a much higher rate of unemployment in Ireland than their
counterparts in Britain.[130] There is also evidence that those who
secured government employment were discriminated against and made
redundant upon the change of government in 1922.[131] Once their
donation money ran out, many ex-servicemen availed of subsidised
settlement schemes in the colonies from late 1920, rather than tolerate
hostility and meagre charity at home.[132]

While writers might touch on political or religious issues their perspective was invariably personal and domestic. In 1934 Proinsias Ó C., a
widower with four young children, wrote in anger that his children were
condemned to live in intolerably cramped conditions 'with 2 daughters –
2 sons – my mother – and married brother & wife & 4 children 4 married
people (3 families) – 12 Persons man + wife + 4 children live in front
room. The house is only fit for one family'. He had been waiting for over
four years and reminded the archbishop that 'According to the Catholic
Church teaching – this is not modest my eldest daughter is 17 years.' He

---

[125] Patrick H., X Mary's Terrace, off Mountjoy St., Dublin, 4 June 1928. DDA, AB 7 CC,
Box 2.

[126] Patrick H. wrote two other letters see, dated 25 and 26 June 1928. Ibid.

[127] See Patrick H.'s, X Mary's Terrace, off Mountjoy St., Dublin, 26 June 1928. Ibid.

[128] Returning war veterans from the Great War were allowed to claim twenty-six weeks
'war donations', whereas civilians were only entitled to claim thirteen weeks. Yeates,
A City in Turmoil, p. 12.

[129] Yeates, *A City in Turmoil*, p. 58; Jane Leonard also noted this tendency of Irish veterans
to re-enlist in other armies after the Great War. J. Leonard, 'Survivors' in J. Horne
(ed.), *Our War: Ireland and the Great War* (Dublin: Royal Irish Academy, 2009),
pp. 209–223, 211.

[130] By autumn 1919, 10 per cent of veterans were unemployed in Britain, compared to
46 per cent in Ireland. One in two Irish veterans remained unemployed by the end of
1920. Leonard, 'Survivors', p. 212.

[131] Yeates, *A City in Turmoil*, p. 57.   [132] Leonard, 'Survivors', p. 216.

wanted the archbishop to intervene and recommend his family for one of
the new houses being built by Dublin Corporation in the south eastern
suburbs of Crumlin in the 1930s. He explained his sense of entitlement
in terms of his fight for Irish freedom:

I am an old I.R.A. man 1916–1923 + I fought for clean houses and clean living.
I have heard many sermons on Purity, etc. - so you understand 12 people = 8
children 4 married people – in a 5 room house is as bad as the slums.[133]

He was also tapping into an anxiety regarding the sleeping habits of
tenement dwellers, in which various charitable organisations (across the
religious divide) and social reformers fretted that such conditions bred
immorality.[134] In fact, this discourse had become so widespread that it
was recorded in many reports on housing as one of the reasons that the
drive for reform had become so important. In 1937 the Citizens Housing
Council, in its interim report of slum clearance in Dublin:

Many influences conspired during the 19th and 20th centuries to awaken the sense
of social responsibility ... many social reformers turned their energies towards
improving houses in which the poor were to live, because they saw that the slum
was the cause of much evil, physical and moral.[135]

While some historians have accepted this moral reading of tenement
living,[136] it should be regarded as part of reform rhetoric that sought to
render the poor subjects of 'salvation', a discourse that rested on deep
assumptions of inherent inferiority.[137] There is, in fact, no evidence that

---

[133] Mr Proinsias Ó C., X Alexander Terrace, Terenure, Co. Dublin, 3 August 1934. DDA,
AB 7 CC, Box 4.
[134] S. Buckley, 'The NSPCC in Ireland, 1889–1939 – a case study', *Saothar*, 33 (2008),
59–70.
[135] Citizens Housing Council, *Interim Report on Slum Clearance in Dublin 1937* (Dublin:
Cahill & Co., 1937), p. 3. Similar sentiments are to be found in P. Cowan, *The
Difficulties of the Housing Problem and Some Attempts to Solve it* (Dublin: n.d. *c.*1918),
p. 8; D. A. Chart, 'Unskilled labour in Dublin: Its housing and living conditions',
Journal of the Statistical and Social Inquiry Society of Ireland, 13 (December 1914),
160–175, 162; S. Millin, 'Child life as a national asset', *Journal of the Statistical and
Social Inquiry Society of Ireland*, 13 (September 1917), 301–316; M. Ó Buachalla, 'The
housing problem', *The Irish Monthly*, (June 1935), 341–360, 344; *Appendix to the Report
of the Departmental Committee Appointed by the Local Government Board for Ireland To
Inquiry into the Housing Conditions of the Working Classes in the City of Dublin (Minutes and
Evidence, with Appendices)* [Cd. 7317] (London, 1914).
[136] For example, Diarmaid Ferriter repeatedly observes that overcrowding left children
vulnerable to sexual abuse, noting but not interrogating that contemporaries believed
such conditions were conducive to child sexual abuse. D. Ferriter, *Occasions of Sin: Sex
and Society in Modern Ireland* (London: Profile Books, 2009), pp. 8, 49, 53, 76,
139, 183.
[137] Maguire notes that this association between housing and sexual abuse is 'simplistic' as it
'assumes that sexual crimes were little more than crimes of opportunity'. M. J. Maguire,

children were more likely to be sexually abused in poor cramped house-holds than in spacious middle-class homes. There is only evidence that the former were under constant observation by people who *expected* them to be deviant.

Few expressed their sense of rage with the new order in as a militant a fashion as Edmund D. who wrote after being laid-off by Boland's flourmills in Ringsend in Dublin (see Figure 3.1).[138] He was driven 'to voice a grievace *[grievance]* which is afflicting many honest workers that is the use of Electric Power'. In fact, his ire was directed at the way workers were made redundant by employers seeking to use new tech-nology, particularly electricity, to increase profits. In his company twenty-one workers had been 'scrapped'. As he saw it, the Shannon Electric Power scheme[139] had been funded by the public purse and the fruits of this project were now being used against the people: 'my job being confiscated by Electric Power, or the State, or the Firm, (confis-cated is a nice word for robbed) without compensation'.[140] On first reading it might be tempting to dismiss Edmund D.'s six page (A4) letter as an unrealistic rant against progress, but beneath his focus on electricity, is a subtler and more realistic reflection on the responsibility of the state to supply employment and the huge obstacles in modern Ireland to upward social mobility:

I have lived in the slum of Dublin for the best part of my married life, during which time God sent along five children. I was heartbroken because I had not a decent Home to receive them into but I worked hard, struggled + saved + in the end I succeeded in getting a decent House + Building up a Catholic Christian Home. But alas, it is to be ruined by the use of the Social Service against me, so that my former employer may increase his already Huge Profit. I have this House from the Dublin Corporation on the Tenant Purchase Scheme but due to loss of income I cannot pay my weekly stalments ... What does all this mean? Well if I may answer what I see. It means going back to the slums, (after I spending a life's savings trying to get out of them) ... That right of private property shall never be mine, nor the right of any member of my class.

'The Carrigan committee and child sexual abuse in twentieth-century Ireland', *New Hibernia Review*, 11 (Summer, 2006), 79–100, 88.

[138] Edmund D. had written in 1925 to the archbishop requesting assistance to return to his family from Scotland, where he had gone to seek work. At this stage in his struggle he was still in the slums and the priest who wrote to vouch for him and his wife described them as 'a very good couple, practical Catholics, room neat & clean'. Fr Creedon, Presbytery Francis St., Dublin, 30 July 1925. DDA, AB 7 CC, Box 1.

[139] He is referring to the Shannon Hydro-Electric Scheme begun in 1925, which marked the beginning of the electrification of the country and led to the establishment of the Electrical Supply Board (ESB).

[140] Edmund D., X Oak Road, Donnycarney, Co. Dublin, 9 October 1932. DDA, AB 7 CC, Box 3.

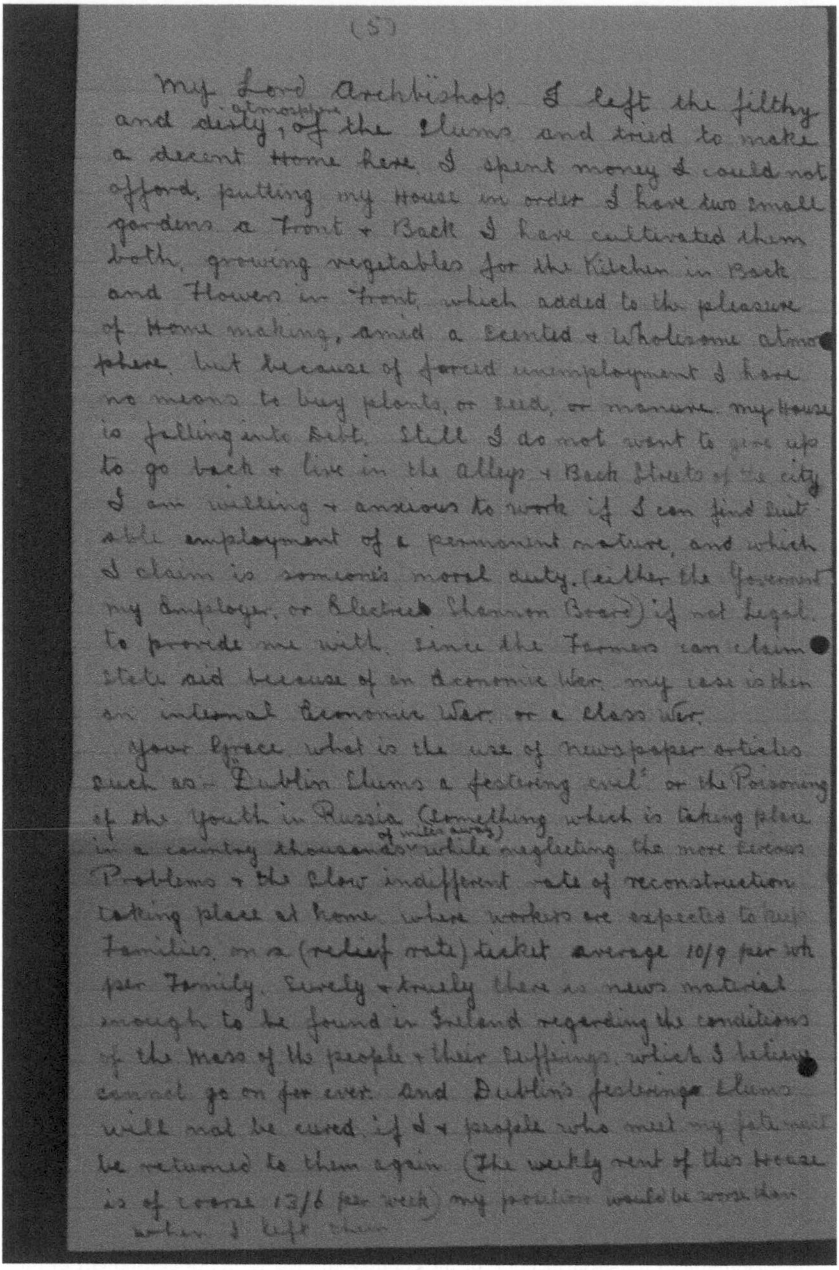

(5)

My Lord Archbishop. I left the filthy and dirty, atmosphere of the Slums and tried to make a decent Home here. I spent money I could not afford, putting my House in order I have two small gardens a Front + Back I have cultivated them both, growing vegetables for the Kitchen in Back and Flowers in front, which added to the pleasure of Home making, amid a Scented + Wholesome atmosphere. but because of forced unemployment I have no means to buy plants, or seed, or manure. my House is falling into Debt. Still I do not want to give up to go back + live in the Alleys + Back Streets of the city I am willing + anxious to work if I can find suitable employment of a permanent nature, and which I claim is someone's moral duty. (either the Government my Employer, or Electrical Shannon Board) if not Legal. to provide me with. since the Farmers can claim State aid because of an Economic War. my case is then an internal Economic War. or a Class War.

Your Grace what is the use of newspaper articles such as – "Dublin Slums a festering evil" or the Poisoning of the Youth in Russia (something which is taking place in a country thousands of miles away) while neglecting the more serious Problems + the slow indifferent rate of reconstruction taking place at home. where workers are expected to keep Families, on a (relief rate) ticket average 10/9 per wk per Family. Surely + truly there is news material enough to be found in Ireland regarding the conditions of the mass of the people + their sufferings. which I believe cannot go on for ever. And Dublin's festering Slums will not be cured. if I + people who meet my fate must be returned to them again. (The weekly rent of this House is of course 13/6 per week) my position would be worse than when I left them

Figure 3.1 A section of the letter written by Edmund D., X Oak Rd., Donnycarney, 9 Oct. 1832.

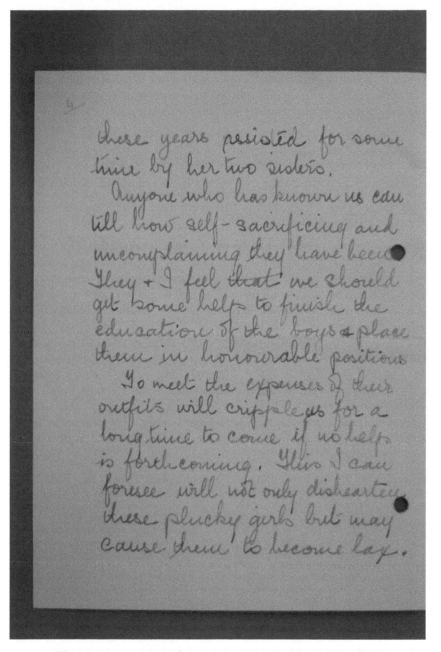

Figure 3.2 A section of the letter written by Marie O'D., X Kilternan, Co. Dublin to the Archbishop of Dublin, 21 Sept., 1938.

He wrote from one of the first Corporation housing schemes built on the north side of Dublin in Donneycarney in 1928, he was more than likely one of the first new occupants and like many rehoused from Dublin's slums was finding it difficult to meet his repayments.[141] After building a picture of a father doing his best to improve his children's lives, and a man proud to fulfill his social role, he held society, the state and 'those who call themselves christian' to account for denying him the right to do his duty.[142]

It is quite clear I am denied the right to provide Food, Clothes, & Shelter for my Wife + Family not to mention Education, if I must be denied the right to earn a living in such a callous manner and by people who call themselves christian & hoist the Flags of Christianity during congress Week but had in mind the Idea of Starving their less fortunate fellow Beings in a week or two after that so that they might increase/ their Profits

He was referring to the lavish festivities that marked the Thirty-First Eucharistic Congress held in Dublin between 21 and 26 June 1932, an event which was very important in allowing the fledgling Irish state to assert its Roman Catholic identity.[143] By calling into question the *bona fides* of those that had hoisted flags on that day, he was implicitly questioning the integrity of this Catholicism.[144] This is doubly significant because the print media had portrayed this event as one of healing that had brought together those from differing political traditions, and the rich and poor, in a display of Catholic unity. He wanted to know why the newspapers were not focusing on the story of Ireland's 'slow indifferent rate of reconstruction . . . where workers are expected to keep Families on a (relief rate) ticket average 10/9 per wk per Family'. Ten years after Irish political independence, for Edmund D., the struggle had born a false dawn for workers' rights:

In conclusion my Lord Archbishop I thought when Ireland was won from England's Grip, it would mean the Land of Ireland given back to the People

---

[141] The Dublin Housing Survey of 1939 revealed that twenty per cent of families in Dublin and twenty-two per cent in Cork survived on incomes of less than 20/- per week. C. O'Connell, *The State and Housing in Ireland: Ideology, Policy and Practice* (New York: Nova Science Publishers, 2007), p. 36.

[142] The idea of not being able to fulfil the natural duties of a father or a mother was also expressed in English pauper letters of the nineteenth century. Gestrich, Hurren and King (eds.), *Poverty and Sickness in Modern Europe*, p. 16.

[143] R. O'Dwyer, *The Eucharistic Congress Dublin 1932* (Dublin: Nonsuch Ireland, c. 2009); *Handbook of the Eucharistic Congress: International Congress* (Dublin, 1932), 31, 117.

[144] He was not alone in expressing the view that unemployment was a crime of social neglect. Benvenisti expressed the view that the failure to 'cure' unemployment was a failure of society's 'collective will'. J. L. Benvenisti, 'Christian morals and the means test', *The Dublin Review*, 46 (1939), 58–70, 65.

of Ireland But my God what a rude awakening for us workers. The Ownership of lucrative property for a few, while the mass of God's creation, struggle in agony in the gutter, still in existence.

He had 'left the filthy and dirty atmosphere of the Slums, and tried to make a decent Home' with a vegetable garden and flowers to add 'to the pleasure of Home making' – thus contrasting the putrid stench of the slums with the 'scented + Wholesome atmosphere' of the workingman's home. Through no fault of his own – through 'forced unemployment' – he was in danger of sliding back into slumdom: 'Still I do not want to give up to [go] back + live in the Alleys + Back Streets of the city I am willing + anxious to work, He argued that it was 'someone's moral duty (either the Government, my employer, or Electric Shannon Board), if not Legal to provide me with, since Farmers can claim state aid because of an Economic War, my case is then an internal Economic war, or a class War'. In referring to the compensation awarded to farmers hard hit by de Valera's economic war with Britain, he implicitly drew parallels with all those who lost their employment due to government policy, but he was also hitting out at the deep class divide in Irish society. To speak of a class war was an anathema in Irish society, which liked to maintain the illusion of a classless society wedded to common national and religious ideals.[145] In fact, charity was often consciously used to dampen any class rivalry that might exist and while inequality was acknowledged it was not unequivocally condemned.[146]

Edmund D.'s letter revealed a deep understanding of the complexities of his society; he was able to raise questions about religious hypocrisy, state responsibility and the difficulty of leaving poverty behind in modern Ireland. However, he still found it necessary to engage to a degree with the very aspects he criticised: he informed the archbishop his wife had been 'a convert', that while the firm he had worked for was 'supposed to be catholic' the 'Key jobs' were 'held by non-catholics + Freemasons.'[147]

---

[145] F. Lane and D. Ó Drisceoil (eds.), *Politics of the Irish Working Class, 1830–1945* (New York: Palgrave Macmillan, 2005), pp. 1–5.

[146] For a clear expression of this see, for example, Rev. J. Kelleher, *A Catholic Nation: Its Destitute, Dependent and Helpless Classes* (n.d. c. 1929), p. 1.

[147] The Freemasons was a male secret society organised around Grand Lodges, while it requires only that members specify a belief in God, in Ireland it was an exclusively Protestant organisation and frequently criticised by Catholics for using its influence to exclude Catholics from certain professions and organisations. As Curtis notes the Jesuit Edward Cahill's *Freemasonry and the Anti-Christian Movement* (Dublin: M. H. Gill, 1929) was an immediate bestseller. Curtis, *A Challenge to Democracy*, pp. 56–57.

In October 1933, Edmund D. wrote again, sadly his position had deteriorated in the year since his initial correspondence. He remained unemployed and he had lost his home; he wrote from a different address.[148] While his first letter had yielded no response, this time he was informed that his letter had been forwarded to the Vincent de Paul, but 'owing to the large increase in population the Conference of that district finds it hard to get round to all the cases sent to them'.[149] He had become a member of the long-term unemployed and he conceptualised his fate as a betrayal at the hands of the state.

Mrs Marie O'D., a mother of seven, seemed not to regard Irish independence in 1922 as representing a break in the realities of power: 'I have always recognised that we owe a duty to both Church and State. Is there no reciprocal duty?' A widow, she was keenly aware of what she had done for her church by raising 'seven souls for God, and seven sturdy workers for Catholicity in Dublin city' and concluded her letter by asking: 'Surely they are worth helping.' While her style was vastly differ-ent to Edmund D.'s, her letter also confronted a growing sense of duty working both ways. Upon her husband's sudden death her three 'self-sacrificing and uncomplaining' daughters had helped her sustain the family. However, she feared that if they were failed in their hour of need, these 'plucky girls' would become 'lax' – a word used often in connection with religious duty. She sought assistance to have her last two boys properly educated. Marie O'D. was dying and fearful of leaving her children exposed. Her priest vouched for her letter and she received £20 pounds. [150]

Conclusion

In the charity letters all those who wrote were aware of the social and cultural codes of behaviour and status, while they often baulked and railed against them, they always wrote within the boundaries of that social system aware of its limitations and benefits. These letters, none-theless, offered the writer a middle ground, an intermediary space between the private and the public spheres, where they could shape the arena of negotiation, represent themselves and make their case to best effect. This act, this process, was often both one of conformance

---

[148] Mr Edmund D., Attracta Road, Cabra, Co. Dublin, 17 October 1933. DDA, AB 7 CC, Box 5.

[149] This is the substance of the note on the top left-hand corner of his letter written by the archbishop's secretary.

[150] Mrs Marie O'D., Kilternan, Co. Dublin, 21 September 1938. DDA, AB 7 CC, Box 7.

and rebellion.[151] The writers were inevitably informed by the pressures of their situation and their understandings of the world they addressed, thus they appropriated the terminology, and often the very spirit and values of the system that judged them. As Martyn Lyons argues 'ordinary writing could challenge orthodoxy as well as reproduce it'.[152] In making a case they had to become adept at seeing themselves through others' eyes, to that end they colluded in the imagining of their situation in order to tap into the prejudices that might assist them: they talked the language of charity in order to receive it. They borrowed words and concepts from newspapers, charity workers, religious discourse and public debate in order to represent themselves – their identity – in the construction of their experience of poverty. However, in the very act of representation they challenged their place in the 'system' by insisting on being heard on their own terms, even if those were terms re-appropriated from that system. With their own hands they insisted on their innocence, their worthiness, their willingness to work and to care for their families if only society, the Catholic Church and state allowed them to do so. If, as King and Stinger have argued, 'servility, gratitude and respect were the basic building blocks of the standard pauper narrative', then it was in the substance of individual appeals that all three of these ingredients were often challenged.[153] Of course everyday resistance 'reflect the conditions and constraints under which they are generated',[154] thus these writers might have feigned conformity, dissembled and manipulated in order to receive what they deemed they needed or deserved.

To appreciate that these writers 'dissembled, strategised and calculated to elicit relief', is not to do them a 'disservice', nor does it cast doubt or undermine their version of poverty, rather it acknowledges that they took the world on its own terms and with very little power, sought to play an active role in their survival.[155] As Scott acknowledges: 'Dissimulation is the characteristic and necessary pose of subordinate classes everywhere most of the time – a fact that makes those rare and threatening moments

---

[151] A. Gestrich and S. A. King, 'Pauper letters and petitions for poor relief in Germany and Great Britain, 1770–1914', *Bulletin: German Historical Institute London*, 35 (November 2013), 12 25, 16.

[152] M. Lyons, *The Writing Culture of Ordinary People in Europe, c. 1860–1920* (Cambridge University Press, 2012), p. 256.

[153] King and Stringer, '"I have once more taken the Leberty to say as you well know"', p. 73.

[154] Scott, *Weapons of the Weak*, p. 242.

[155] This is an anxiety expressed by Jones, although he is clear that this does not undermine the veracity of the poor's account of poverty. Jones, '"I cannot keep my place without being deascent"', p. 41.

when the pose is abandoned all the more remarkable.'[156] In many ways the letters in this collection that threaten religious defection or express deep anger with the church or state represent what Scott has referred to as 'everyday forms of resistance' that 'stop well short of outright collective defiance',[157] but which hint at a relatively widespread narrative of defiance. These acts of defiance could only have had currency and meaning when used between people with a shared worldview, which was undoubtedly the case with these authors and their archbishop. The poor implicitly and explicitly responded to the idea of charity as a form of social control by threatening to play one form of charity against another. However, as Scott argues, the powers-that-be are rarely inclined to make such resistance public hence: 'The nature of the acts themselves and the self-interested muteness of the antagonists thus conspire to create a kind of complicit silence that all but expunges everyday forms of resistance from the historical record.'[158] It is important to include these individual acts of everyday resistance in order to gain a greater understanding of how the poor reshaped their position in society. Their letters were inevitably circumscribed by the realities of begging and by the knowledge of their audience's expectations, but that very fact makes them an intrinsic part of the experience of being poor.

[156] Scott, *Weapons of the Weak*, p. 284.   [157] Ibid., p. xvi.   [158] Ibid., p. 36.

4   Hidden Poverty

'I bear my poverty in silence'

Society's treatment of 'the poor' has always involved complex cultural and moral responses in which compassion competes with resentment, understanding is compromised by suspicion and empathy vies with an instinct to dissociate. In the twentieth-century public debate, official and religious discourse reflected this ambivalence in its desire to preserve the 'historically consecrated distinction between deserving and undeserving', which represented hazy moral categories amenable to interpretation.[1] There was an element of smugness evident in much of this rhetoric largely because those doing the talking were never likely to experience poverty. Thus, when the discussion turned to those who had 'fallen on hard' times, there was a distinct softening of the moral lens and a little less certitude in prescribing a remedy.[2] The fact that poverty could strike outside its customary hunting ground and target the sales man who got sick or the solicitor's widow left with no pension caused considerable discomfort in charitable circles. This reality required a different set of moral criteria and much of the labels given to this poverty underscored a desire to differentiate it. Olwen Hufton noted that in eighteenth-century France this cohort was referred to as 'pauvre honteux' or the honourable poor.[3] This notion of honour explicitly implied a class *and* moral difference by conjuring an intangible sense of quality. This section of the population had an asset the habitually poor did not; they had 'good character', purely by virtue of their class. As Karen Halttunen has

---

[1] Stuart Woolf argued that this distinction was also applied by the welfare state. S. Woolf, *The Poor in Western Europe in the Eighteenth and Nineteenth Centuries* (London and New York: Methuen, 1986), p. 4.

[2] Crossman has argued that during the nineteenth century the Irish Poor Law guardians were more sympathetic to those who had experienced a sudden deterioration in their fortunes. V. Crossman, 'Middle-class attitudes to poverty and welfare in post-famine Ireland' in F. Lane (ed.), *Politics, Society and the Middle Class in Modern Ireland* (Basingstoke: Palgrave MacMillan, 2010), pp. 130–47; pp. 138, 141.

[3] O. Hufton, *The Poor of Eighteenth-Century France, 1750–1789* (Oxford University Press, 1974), p. 214.

argued, good character provided the middle classes with a type of 'moral capital', which in the context of charity gave them considerable leverage.[4]

These people were the 'hidden poor' conceptually and literally: they sought to hide and emphasised this fact (discreetly) in order to identify themselves with this distinct category. Peter Wessel Hansen has observed that the central characteristic of this subgroup was that they 'neither begged nor wanted public poor relief because they were ashamed of their poverty'.[5] They were portrayed as the reluctant poor who struggled in silence until it was no longer possible to maintain the façade of independence, and then help was quietly sought. Of course, this was based on the assumption that those who lived constantly with poverty (the reality or threat of it) were in some way implicated in their own circumstances. There was also a princess and the pea principle at work: the poor – those that bore that identity – were inured to the experience and felt it less; the 'genteel poor' were hurt and wounded by the need to seek assistance. The very fact that they *felt* their poverty proved their moral superiority. They were frequently described as more emotional and sensitive; as Mark Peel has argued, the main difference between 'inferior' and 'superior' people was that the latter 'felt their position'.[6] He found a very similar approach to the increasing phenomenon of middle-class poverty in inter-war Australia, where caseworkers felt great empathy for these 'refined and sensitive people' whose character was undiminished by the realities of poverty.[7] In 1920s and 1930s Ireland, an incredibly similar narrative emerged. The Vincent de Paul noted 'our people who have seen "better days" ... were frequently upset by a visit from the society'.[8] The narrative that surrounded these people often emphasised their innocence and sensitivities: in 1933, in a typical explanation of this type of poverty, the Vincent de Paul explained that these people were 'struck by misfortune':

This is a type which bears its troubles silently and secretly, avoids publicity and is so sensitive about accepting help that extreme care must be exercised by the member who would hope to succeed with it. Such a family is naturally proud of

[4] K. Halttunen, *Confidence Men and Painted Women: A Study of Middle-Class Culture in America, 1830–1870* (New Haven and London: Yale University Press, 1982), p. 48.

[5] P. Wessel Hansen, 'Grief, sickness and emotions in the narratives of the shamefaced poor in late eighteenth-century Copenhagen' in A. Gestrich, E. Hurren and S. King (eds.), *Poverty and Sickness in Modern Europe: Narratives of the Sick Poor, 1780–1938* (London: Continuum, 2012), pp. 35–50, 37.

[6] M. Peel, *Miss Cutler and the Case of the Resurrected Horse: Social Work and the Story of Poverty in America, Australia, and Britain* (The University of Chicago Press, 2012), p. 64.

[7] Ibid., p. 61.

[8] 'Supplement for Irish Conferences, May 1926', *Bulletin of the Society of St. Vincent De Paul*, 91 (May 1926), 16.

previous independence, and its spirit revolts at the idea of even asking friends, not to speak of strangers, for assistance.[9]

This 'type' of poor required a different methodology, one that took account of their finer sensibilities and different life experience: 'The methods which suffice in the case of tenement dwellers will not meet the circumstances of families which hitherto enjoyed the results of steady employment.'[10] It is little wonder that the middle class regarded this group with considerable empathy and anxiety as they induced an unsettling sense of vulnerability. Furthermore, the existence of this group challenged the comfortable conclusions regarding the causes of poverty. It was not so easy to implicate the poor in their own downfall when they came from your social cohort.[11] In 1928 Mr E. R., a civil servant and 'active worker in the Saint Vincent de Paul Society', wrote to the archbishop to request 'a loan' to settle a decree against his parents' farm for £25.[12] He was well versed in the sensibilities of charity, telling the archbishop that he could not provide a priest's reference because such domestic matters were 'sacred and confidential'. He declared himself willing to 'forego any favour His Grace may feel disposed to dispense in this case rather than incur the unpleasantness such disclosures would entail'. He was also a realist and explained his situation 'in confidence' to a priest and was duly sent £25 – a figure significantly above the normal donations of £1 to tenement dwellers.

After World War I the nature of Irish unemployment experienced an alteration similar to that of elsewhere in Europe. The changes wrought by war and international depression resulted in the emergence of a new more pervasive type of poverty.[13] In Germany, for example, unemployment was no longer restricted to unskilled and casual workers of the labouring population but also spread to new groups such as skilled or white-collar workers.[14] Tamara Stazic-Wendt observed a similar store of

---

[9] 'Supplement for Irish Conferences, January 1933', *Bulletin of the Society of St. Vincent De Paul*, 98 (January 1933), 6.

[10] Ibid., pp. 6–7.

[11] Matthias Reiss argues that the emergence of the category 'unemployed' contributed to a shift away from the concept of poverty as a moral failing. M. Reiss, 'The image of the poor and the unemployed: The example of *Punch*, 1841–1939' in A. Gestrich, S. King and L. Raphael (eds.), *Being Poor in Modern Europe: Historical Perspectives 1800–1940* (Switzerland: Peter Lang, 2006), pp. 389–415.

[12] Mr E. R., X Shelbourne Road, Ballsbridge, Dublin, 12 June 1928. DDA, AB 7 CC, Box 2.

[13] J. Garraty, *Unemployment in History: Economic Thought and Public Policy* (New York: Harper & Row, 1978), pp. 103–128.

[14] T. Stazic-Wendt, 'From unemployment to sickness and poverty: The narratives and experiences of the unemployed in Trier and surroundings, 1918–33' in Gestrich, Hurren and King (eds.), *Poverty and Sickness in Modern Europe*, pp. 181–207, 181.

narratives of 'downward mobility' in the letters of those writing for Unemployment Assistance in Trier in Germany between 1918 and 1933.[15] In a world without a safety net, the loss of a spouse, a bad investment, poor business choices or just bad luck, could leave even the well off in need of help. The narrative of middle-class decline sharpened in 1930s Ireland with an increasing concern that this cohort was losing social and economic ground. A writer to the editor of the *Irish Independent* in January 1933 articulated these fears in a way that would become commonplace in future periods of economic recession and destabilisation:

Sir – When will we have champions and a party for the one and only section of the community that suffers in silence, and receives no consideration, relief, or sympathy from any party at present in the domain of politics? I mean the middle class, the professional man and the artisan.[16]

According to this representative of the urban middle classes, the farmer received subsidies and paid no tax, the poor man:

gets free medical relief, free hospital treatment, free midwifery, free schooling for his children, free medical attention for them, free milk and meals. He has his "dole" or outdoor relief if reduced to poverty. He has his cottages at uneconomic rents, to which the middleman contributes without any recompense.[17]

In 1933 the debates surrounding the Johnson Committee's report into Civil Service pay fixated on the idea that these state employees were not paid enough to keep 'up appearances'.[18] As John Porter has observed, for the first time there was a general consensus that civil service salaries should be computed in accordance with 'an index figure based on middle class standards'.[19]

Those who wrote to the archbishop who had known 'better times' made that a central part of their appeal and played on the sense of an honourable difference between them and the habitually poor. In 1924,

---

[15] Ibid., p. 182.

[16] 'The middle class – most numerous party but worst treated', *Irish Independent*, 18 January 1933. Cited by John H. Porter, '"The squeezed middle": The Johnson committee and the Irish middle class under Fianna Fáil, 1932–47' unpublished paper presented at Class and Culture in Twentieth-Century Ireland: Resilience, Resistance, and Transformation Conference, University of Cambridge, April 2015.

[17] 'The middle class – most numerous party but worst treated', *Irish Independent*, 18 January 1933.

[18] 'Memorandum to Ministers – Grave Hardship – Committee's Findings Quoted', *Irish Independent*, 16 August 1933.

[19] Porter, '"The squeezed middle"; Bonus Reduced: Decision of Minister – Johnson Committee's Report', *Irish Independent*, 1 July 1933; 'Middle Class & Wage-Earner', *Irish Press*, 1 July 1933.

Marion G., a solicitor's widow from the wealthy Dublin suburb of Foxrock, wrote to the archbishop: 'I know only the very poor should call on you but we are even worse off after all Your Grace my children are the coming women + men of Ireland – Please God - + when they get along they will help the poor.' She regarded herself as inherently different from 'the poor': her children were the future of Ireland as opposed to 'the poor' who her children, in their proper place, were destined to 'help'. The people of the middle class, like their poorer counterparts, were not free from a reliance on their children, however, they had a sense that their children were entitled to a future that the permanently poor simply could not afford to entertain. In general, they made plans for their children, which involved a great emphasis on education and qualifications. The Saint Vincent de Paul acknowledged the impact of poverty on those people whom 'fate has struck' lamenting it was 'specially tragic in the case of a family in which there are children of a school-going age who have been looking forward to the completion of a normal secondary education'.[20] In a society where secondary education was not free or a statutory right, only those that could pay for it could offer their children this opportunity.[21] However, middle-class parents were often loath to abandon these parental ambitions, as they understood that without a 'good start' their children would not prosper.

For people like Marion G., poverty was portrayed as a disaster that did not accord with their previous life experiences or expectations and that would ruin their future. Therefore, they were at pains to stress the temporary nature of their predicament and the idea that they just needed to get back on their feet. They hid their poverty to protect their social standing and emphasise their shame; they only asked for help when they were faced with choices that were either too unpalatable or imperilled their social position. In 1939 Mark W., a farmer from County Kildare, wrote seeking the sum of £60 to replace a dead mare and explained, 'my only justification in making the request is the fact that it is not for personal gain but in despair of otherwise fulfilling a primary duty'.[22] Like Marion G., Mr W. had already been supported by the archbishop who had funded the education of his two daughters after the farm fell on hard times. Mr W. pointed out: 'I can render best appreciation of that generosity by saying that my two daughters are placed in self supporting

---

[20] 'Supplement for Irish Conferences, January 1933' *Bulletin of the Society of St. Vincent De Paul*, 98 (February 1933), p. 7.

[21] Free second level education did not become available in Ireland until September 1967. See, J. Walsh, *The Politics of Expansion: Irish Education Policy, 1957–1972* (Manchester University Press, 2009), pp. 169–224.

[22] [Mr] M. W., X Castledermot, Co. Kildare, 18 August 1939. DDA, AB 7 CC, Box 7.

positions for two years past.'[23] These people could be invested in – they would repay by their future contributions to society.

To accentuate the uniqueness of their situation, the middle class and middling farmer wrote long, detailed explanations of their situation often rooted in their family history and a particular understanding of their family life. While their stories were necessarily highly personalised, certain common themes emerged, such as an emphasis on discretion and shame and a desire to fulfil one's social and religious duties. In these Irish letters many men described how poverty compromised their masculinity by limiting their role as the breadwinner or caring father. They articulated a very clear idea of patriarchy and the importance of the male breadwinner role. Peel noted that while women could often feel empowered by their ability to make do, men felt unmanned by the same experience.[24] The ways in which the men and women who wrote to the Archbishop of Dublin engaged with the ideas of the appropriate behaviour for husbands, wives, fathers, mothers and children, provide an alternative reading of patriarchal ideology and its negotiation; it may have been imposed from 'on high' but it was also claimed and redefined from below. In these letters gender roles became part of a narrative of inequality and justice denied.

'I feel my position keenly'

A sense of 'feeling one's position' was expressed at some point and in some way in most of the letters written by those unaccustomed to being in need.[25] In 1935, Catherine E. M., the wife of an unemployed accountant who felt 'forced to ask for some assistance', relayed her sense of shame in a formulaic way: 'I feel my position very keenly.'[26] One can almost hear the echoes of the various charity reports: *she is most deserving and feels her position keenly*. Catherine was also discreet in conjuring the shadow of Protestant relatives, '[M]y people are protestant and since I became a Catholic have not been altogether friendly so I fear it would be useless to look to them for any help.' Between feeling her position and

---

[23] Ibid.

[24] M. Peel, *The Lowest Rung: Voices of Australian Poverty* (Cambridge University Press, 2003), p. 125.

[25] Peel noted that the Charity Organisation Society in Australia considered 'feeling one's position' as a central factor in being considered a 'deserving' case for charity. M. Peel, '"Feeling your position": Charity, casework and the dramas of class of Melbourne, 1920–1940', *History Australia*, 2 (2005), 83.1–83.15.

[26] Catherine M., X New Brighton, Seapoint Avenue, Monstown, Co. Dublin, 25 February 1934. DDA, AB 7 CC, Box 5.

sacrificing access to wealthy relatives, she presented a favourable case and apparently without a priest's reference she received £20.

Those in the middle class, who suddenly found themselves unemployed, bereaved or somehow in need, were not versed in the ways of poverty, or accustomed to the contours of struggle, the wiles of begging, and the inconsistencies of charity. Tina McG., who wrote asking for the fare to join her relatives in Canada, had already asked the Mendicity Institution and the Salvation Army to no avail.[27] She made a virtue of her ignorance of the ways of charity:

I have never applied to any Society for help in any form which leaves me quite Ignorant as to where or how to go after a case like mine I bear my poverty in silence no person knows whether I am poor or not[28]

Tina's ignorance was symbolic of her worthiness and that she related this to the fact that she bore her poverty in silence indicated that she intended this as a statement of her character. Christianity in general and Roman Catholicism, in particular, valued those that suffered in silence.

In early twentieth-century Ireland poverty was an identity, it was a character slur; it was not supposed to happen to people of 'good character'. Hence that 'good decent' people were 'brought face to face with destitution'[29] was considered symptomatic of disturbed times, when the natural order of things – and natural justice too – was fundamentally altered and 'good character' was no longer protection from misfortune. As the parish priest of Blackrock, County Dublin, Fr Willie Horan[30] mused, in defence of a previously wealthy widow: 'We are living in times when the worst pinch is felt by those who not alone conceal it but are congratulated on how well they manage.'[31] Fr Horan was writing in 1933, two years before the Widows' and Orphans' Pension was introduced in Ireland, thus the cherished male breadwinner norm left married women very vulnerable upon bereavement. However, widows'

---

[27] One of Dublin's oldest charities, the Mendicity Institution, arrived in the city in 1818; the Salvation Army came to the city in 1888. Both charities offered assistance regardless of religious affiliation. J. V. O'Brien, *A City in Distress, 1899–1916* (Berkeley; London: University of California, 1982), p. 168; A. Woods, *Dublin Outsiders: A History of the Mendicity Institution* (Dublin: A. & A. Farmar, 1998).

[28] Tina McG., X Eastmoreland Place, off Upr Baggot St., Dublin, n.d., *c.* 1933. DDA, AB 7 CC, Box 4.

[29] James F. W., X Clarence Place, Pearse Street, Dublin, 20 February 1934. DDA, AB 7 CC, Box 5.

[30] Fr William Horan, born 1891, ordained 1917 and died 1950. J. A. Gaughan, *The Archbishops, Bishops and Priests who served in the Archdiocese of Dublin* (Dublin: Kingdom Books, 2012), p. 134.

[31] Fr Horan, St John's, Blackrock, Co Dublin, 14 November 1933. DDA, AB 7 CC, Box 5.

vulnerability was caused by the structures of Irish society rather than any disruption to it.[32]

In 1936, sisters Margaret and Katherine C. wrote requesting help to pay their rent, they had been receiving £50 each January since 1931 from the archbishop for this purpose (see Figure 4.1). Margaret and Katherine represented contemporary notions of 'genteel poverty': they were elderly ladies that the world had treated unkindly. According to their priest referee they had had a milliner's shop in Dublin's city centre, which had been 'burnt down during the troubles'.[33] As they explained, they had never 'put one penny astray' – 'It was the Country's troubles that left us as we are.' Their business and investments had faltered in the wake of Irish political independence and their health began to fail. One sister had been under medical supervision for a year and the other had been gravely ill; as they explained, 'worry is killing'. Their lament that 'it is hard on old people to be so badly off, not through our own fault' was one the archbishop heard often and usually responded to generously, particularly, if the writers were 'Ladies' shamed by their decline in fortunes: 'we let no one know our troubles, if we can manage to keep a roof over us we try to fill in the rest by hard striving'.[34] They once again received £50 to keep the roof over their aging heads for another year.

Even women with husbands, qualifications and an extended family, could find themselves ultimately alone and unable to support themselves. In 1935, Mrs Brenda M. K. wrote from a ward in Dublin's St Vincent's hospital seeking assistance. Thirty-three years previously she had been 'the victim of an unfortunate marriage', three years into the marriage a priest found out that it was unconsummated and encouraged her to seek an annulment 'but my Lord I kept too quiet'.[35] Eventually, her case was sent to Rome and after a lot of money she was unsuccessful in securing an annulment. For thirty years she had supported herself as a nurse, but then resigned to care for her father. When her brother died of the flu at twenty-eight years of age, she became the sole person responsible for her mother. Finally, her own health failed and she had to undergo an operation and, due to her inability to work, acquired debts. She was ashamed to beg, but could see no other way out of her difficulties:

---

[32] L. Earner-Byrne, '"Parading their poverty": Widows in twentieth-century Ireland' in B. Faragó and M. Sullivan (eds.), *Facing the Other: Interdisciplinary Studies on Race, Gender and Social Justice in Ireland* (Cambridge Scholars Publishing, 2008), pp. 32–46.

[33] Fr. R. Fleming, The Presbytery, Rathmines, 6 January 1931. DDA, AB 7 CC, Box 3.

[34] Margaret and Katherine C., Eden Park, Sandycove, Co. Dublin, 8 January 1936. DDA, AB 7 CC, Box 6.

[35] Brenda M. K., St Gabriel's Ward, Vincent's Hospital, Co Dublin, 27 February 1925. DDA, AB 7 CC, Box 1.

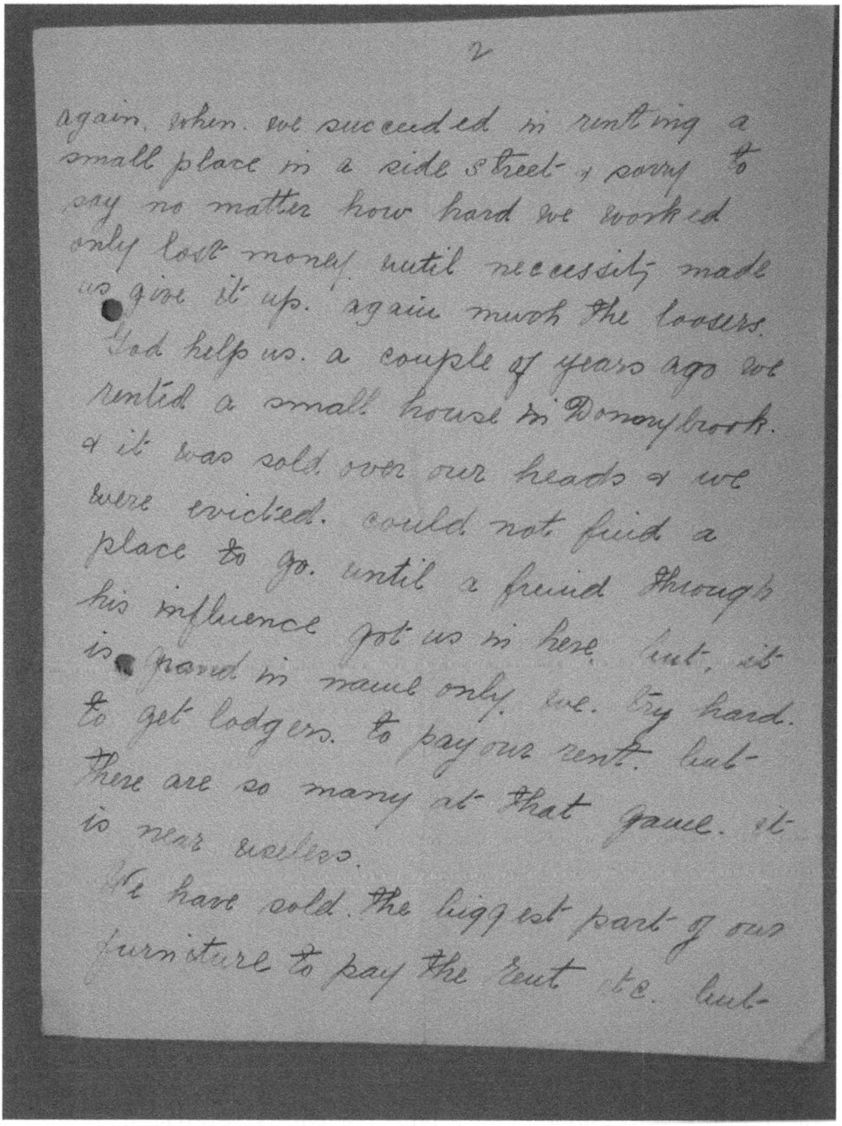

2

again. when we succeded in renting a
small place in a side street & sorry to
say no matter how hard we worked
only lost money until neccessity made
us give it up. again much the loosers.
God help us. a couple of years ago we
rented a small house in Donnybrook.
& it was sold over our heads & we
were evicted. could not find a
place to go. until a friend through
his influence got us in here. but, it
is grand in name only. we. try hard.
to get lodgers. to pay our rent. but
there are so many at that game. it
is near useless.
We have sold the biggest part of our
furniture to pay the rent &c. but

Figure 4.1 A section of one of the letters written by Miss Katherine C., X Eden Park, Sandycove, Co. Dublin to the Archishop of Dublin, 12 Dec. 1930.

Not being able to earn + getting debts worried me a great deal + I'd be ashamed to beg but if my health only gets right I'll be able to work. I *[————————]* as Mother is 76 years + I've a niece whose Mother died + I am 53 not too young I am ashamed to ask you My Lord, if you would be kind enough to help me until I get a little strong + able to work[36]

Brenda's brother had been a vet and she had qualified as a nurse indicating that they had been reared in a comfortable middle-class home. However, a bad marriage, illness and bereavement had reduced all the women in Brenda's family to beggars. She was responsible for her mother, a niece and herself, and although she expressed a sense of shame at having to beg, she was also angry that life had denied her a partner to provide for her, which, to her mind was no more than her due: 'I could have got plenty of good matches + have someone to work for me, + I know my conscience would tell me it was alright.'

'As a man who has seen better days'

In 1934, Mr James F. W. opened the story of his poverty with the motif of decline: 'As a man who has seen better days and had been a member of public boards dispensing charity, I cannot stoop to the appalling degradation of standing in a cue *[queue]* to receive Union Relief.'[37] He was a former civil servant who had been 'compulsorily retired' without a pension four years previously at the age of sixty-five, and had since been 'reduced to a condition of absolute destitution'. Throughout his letter James F. W. avoided any reference to charity, instead he requested 'pecuniary assistance'. He was at pains to establish himself as a man connected to money and used to a certain social standing in society. He managed to do this while also drawing attention to how his family's loyalty to Catholicism had, literally, cost them. His father had left an estate of £16,000 in 1899, but it had been mired in legal challenges – one of them relating to his specific request that £1,000 be given to the Roman Catholic church for masses: 'as the testator was a man of intense religious convictions and a staunch supporter of the Church during his life'. His father's wishes were finally upheld, after twenty-one years of legal wrangling and the loss of £9000 to the estate. The church was paid its share of the estate and 'the testator's children numbering 8, received only a paltry share'.

James F. W. had paid heavily for his father's loyalty to the church and now he had to scatter his family to survive: he had sent two daughters to

---

[36] Ibid.   [37] James F. W., X Clarence Place, Pearse Street, Dublin, 20 February 1934.

England to work; his wife had taken two of the smaller children to France, where she worked as a governess. His eldest son, a grocer's assistant, had kept 'body and soul together' until he lost his job. James F. W. was left 'face to face with destitution in its most striking form'. He pointed out that he needed only temporary assistance as in a year, when he turned seventy, he would be entitled to the Old Age Pension. Keeping the focus on his status and tale of woe, he signed his letter James W. / Trustee of the Late J.W./ Ballinasloe Co Galway'. He received £5, a far cry from the £1,000 his father left for masses and unlikely to see him through to his pension. He had five children between twenty-six and six years of age; his years of primary care fathering lasted longer than most of his western European counterparts.[38] This fact placed a strain, even on those in a comparatively good financial position in life, and while he could rely on the older children to help him, this was precarious in such an unstable economy.

In 1938, Chris D. wrote for a 'little help' that would put him in a position to support his family in 'comparatively good circumstances'. He warned that if he did not receive assistance the 'opportunity will pass' and his family would be 'faced with a future of what I hardly dare to think – seperation from our children, and as I may leave this country, probably seperation from my wife'.[39] He wrote a letter to provide the archbishop with 'the essential parts' of his life story – essential to explaining his demise and his worthiness. This took Chris D. fourteen pages, over two letters, between May and June 1938. In these letters he merged his story with his father's, who had been 'an extensive farmer who bought his farm in 1902 (the home where I was reared) and although an exceptionally good man – who never drank nor spent foolishly – could never seem to get out of debt'. The ebb and flow of his family's fortunes correspond with the historical realities of the time: his father's farm prospered 'for a brief period after the Great War' and plummeted into bankruptcy during the Great Depression and the economic war with Britain between 1932 and 1938. This confirms Cormac Ó Gráda's account of the impact of World War I as a 'relatively prosperous' period for Irish farmers, and Ireland's economic war with Britain as the main reason why Irish agriculture did so badly in the 1930s.[40] As Chris D. explained:

---

[38] Throughout the twentieth-century Irish marital fertility was the highest recorded among developed countries. See, M. E. Daly, 'The Irish family since the Famine: continuity and change', *Irish Journal of Feminist Studies*, 3 (1999), 1–21.

[39] Chris D., Ashgrove, Finglas, Dublin, 12 May 1938. DDA, AB 7 CC, Box 7.

[40] Ó Gráda notes that Irish farmers faced hard times in the 1920s, which is also in keeping with Chris D.'s gloomy picture. C. Ó Gráda, *Ireland: A New Economic History 1780–1939* (Oxford University Press, 1994), pp. 390–393.

From 1932 to 1934 owing to the fall in the price of cattle (from which we derived the largest part of our income) and agricultural produce generally matters became rapidly serious with us having a considerable debt instead of a capital to fall back upon. We simply could not meet the Banks demands for interest together with increased rates etc. and we were faced with the prospect of having to sell our home at a time when the price of land was almost at its lowest ebb or the alternative of having the Bank eventually foreclose and do so.[41]

Prior to this decline in fortunes he had been secondary school educated and, he explained, they 'were not well off but were able to meet' their 'obligations + have the necessities of life'. However, by 1934, in order to forestall disaster, Chris D. secured a temporary position in the civil service with a salary of £5.10.0 per week.[42] Despite all this the bank sent its foreclosure notice in 1935. In a reversal of roles, he took his father in until his death in July 1937.

Chris D.'s narrative impetus was the telling of decline, but his story was carved out of the depth of familial loyalty: he had been a good son to a good father and sought to do the same for his children. He punctuated his letter with references to his father; when he left school he 'worked for my father', when he married in 1924 it was 'with his consent' and his proposed solution to his current predicament was to reclaim 'my fathers home'. He displayed a keen sense of what the idealised roles of various family members represented and he painted his own family as the perfect model for rescue. His wife was a

very good Catholic, + consequently very patient and the best of wives to me + mother to our children. I do not drink or gamble myself + have not smoked since we got into difficulties. A little help towards putting us back + making a start again in our old home would probably be the turning point of our whole lives & that of our children.

His wife was all she should have been to him and his children and he was an ordinary man: he had smoked, but realised what was required of him to secure his family's future, so he had quit smoking in the face of their disaster and had never gambled or consumed alcohol. Through his periods of unemployment, which he documented meticulously, they had 'lived sparingly' and watched their 'small savings' evaporate and their furniture vanish and 'then (as we thought) a last resort' applied for Unemployment Assistance. However, they had been reduced to an

---

[41] Chris D., Ashgrove, Finglas, Dublin, 12 May 1938.

[42] He was educated at Mount Saint Joseph's in Roscrea and Castleknock College. His starting salary in the civil service was comparatively good by contemporary standards, when £4 a week was considered a fair starting point. T. Farmar, *Privileged Lives: A Social History of Middle-Class Ireland, 1882–1989* (Dublin: A & A Farmar, 2010), p. 143.

income of '14/- per week and a food ticket value 5/- from the Conference of St Vincent de Paul'. Despite life's provocations, Chris D. and family 'kept our troubles to ourselves in the hope of I been able to get work of some kind eventually'. In other words, he had hoped to sort the problem himself as the breadwinner. If the archbishop helped him to regain possession of his home the ideal family would be restored:

the children would be in a good home with plenty of food (even if plain) & fresh open air none of which they have here. I would not be compelled to be idle + the oldest children could help considerably – With a cow + pigs + poultry along with the gardens + bee hives.[43]

Chris D., like so many other men, felt stripped of his dignity by poverty and he evoked this sense quite literally in his physical shabbiness: 'Unfortunately I am not even well enough dressed to look for or take up a better class of position.' He had been so emasculated that it was no longer in his power to exact his own rescue:

No other reason would compel me to address this appeal to your Grace but the great need of my wife and little children together with the natural desire to provide for and rear them in a home where they can enjoy the family ties of affection together and learn to help and stand by each other as we would wish to see them in their lives to come true to their religion in the love of God as we are teaching them [44]

This family unit validated not only Chris D.'s existence, but also his Catholicism.

The solution arrived at by the archbishop and the parish priest, Fr Russell – to pay the education of two of his children and have his sons admitted to a Dominican orphanage – hardly represented an ideal solution for Chris D. This effectively separated the family, but he wrote a month later to thank the archbishop for this help as 'it has lightened our burden very considerably and enabled us to provide for the three children now remaining with us'.[45] His plan to salvage his father's farm was gathering pace, and neighbours and friends had rallied round: 'In view of these offers I am much encouraged to think that perhaps with Gods help I may be able to get on my feet again.' However, his 'greatest worry' remained his unemployment, he had had to leave his old flat in Finglas in Dublin, but he had not been willing to succumb to the pit of poverty and degradation that the slums represented: 'On the childrens account we had a great objection to taking apartments in the lower class tenement houses and there seemed to be no other alternative accomodation

---

[43] Chris D., Ashgrove, Finglas, Dublin, 12 May 1938.   [44] Ibid.
[45] Chris D., X, North Great George's St., Dublin, 25 June 1938.

available.' The Vincent de Paul had come to the rescue by paying two weeks' rent on a house in Dublin's city centre.

Chris was not familiar with the welfare system and was dismayed when: 'I was informed at the Labour exchange today that owing to coming inside the city area I will not be entitled to unemployment assistance until I have worked 12 weeks. I did not know this rule existed'. He came from people who usually provided charity: 'My Mothers RIP [Rest in Peace] words have come true to a certain extent she was very charitable and often said I should never need a friend as all her charity was given with that intention.' Chris D. articulated what James F. W. had implied, he should receive charity because his family had given in the past and had credit in the charity bank: 'I also knew of her to help other charities to a large extent which is I am sure one of the reasons that Your Grace and others have come to my assistance now when I am in temporary need.'[46] However, his appeal was doomed – his parish priest recommended that his case be 'closed down'.[47] There is no explanation for this decision, perhaps it was considered that Chris D. had received sufficient charity and/or his plan for his eventual triumph over unemployment – the rescuing of his family farm – was regarded as unrealistic and his case considered no longer of a 'temporary nature'.

'My very manhood seems sapped'

When telling stories in order to explain one's need it was perhaps unremarkable that men engaged in notions of masculinity that abounded culturally and socially. In a society that was organised around the concept of the patriarchal family with its male breadwinner, domestic wife and obedient children, the loss of financial independence was particularly challenging for men's identity. That men characterised their feelings of failure in this regard as failings of masculinity is not surprising. The father who could not provide was a cultural oxymoron. The fear of slipping into the abyss of poverty was often expressed in men's begging letters in terms of their own personal redundancy and their desire to keep it from their families. There is little doubt that begging or needing charity posed a more fundamental challenge to the cultural ideas of manhood than it did to notions of femininity. Women were expected to look beyond themselves for the financial support of their children; they could accommodate the act of begging within an understanding of their

[46] Ibid.
[47] On the corner of Chris D.'s letter of the 25 June 1938 is written 'Father Russell says 'Close down'.

'appropriate role' to protect and provide for children no matter what the personal cost.[48] As David Vincent argues, women gained status as the 'key strategist' in the home, marshalling and managing limited resources to ensure the survival of the familial unit.[49] For men the concept of providing the bread went to the heart of their place in society, and to fail in this regard, to beg, was an anathema to them. This anxiety was compounded by the visceral fear that regaining one's footing, once lost, was incredibly difficult and that their children's futures would be 'blighted' as a result.

In November 1931, Richard B. wrote from County Wexford to the archbishop as a 'proud father of a family', with a detailed story of his – and his family's – decline. While others built their life story over letters, Richard managed to do so in one long letter that brought his reader through his life story as a quest for self-sufficiency. He began, '[I]t is under the most exceptional circumstances that I reluctantly write this letter over 7 ½ years ago I left home for Australia full of ambition, and with two objects in view to do for myself and to get settled in life.' He, like so many young Irish people before and after him, went to the other side of the earth for a life Ireland could not provide – a life where he could be independent and marry:

After some months of casual employment I was successful in obtaining a position in the Government railways of South Australia, at that time, one was considered fortunate in securing what was considered a permanent post. During the first yearI saved enough money to get married, and for four years everything went very satisfactory, gradually getting a nice home together and I was a proud father of a family.[50]

Richard spun an emigrant's tale influenced by international events, government policy and newspaper reports:

At the end of 1929 the effects of depression was noticeable everywhere in Australia, the railways were in a bad way and the Government had started a drastic policy of retrenchment and taxation weekly a batch of men were filling the ranks of the unemployed. First the single up to ten years service were retrenched, then the married men (excepting returned soldiers) according to their service.[51]

---

[48] For an examination of women and charity, see L. Earner-Byrne, "'Should I Take Myself and Family to Another Religion[?]'": Irish Catholic women, protest, and conformity, 1920–1940' in C. S. Brophy and C. Delay (eds.), *Women, Reform, and Resistance in Ireland, 1850–1950* (Basingstoke: Palgrave Macmillan, 2015), pp. 77–100.

[49] D. Vincent, *Poor Citizens: the State and the Poor in Twentieth Century Britain* (London: Longman, 1991), p. 94.

[50] Richard B., Inch P.O., Co. Wexford, 23 November 1931. DDA, AB 7 CC, Box 4.

[51] Ibid.

We can hear the newspaper reports: 'the effects of the depression', the Government's 'drastic policy of retrenchment' and the weekly head count of men 'filling the ranks of the unemployed'. However, Richard deftly kept himself at the centre of these bigger events: 'Knowing too well that my turn must come and that it would be impossible to get further employment, everyday became one of worry and expectation.' He wrote of how 'we witnessed misery and hardship' as the unemployed began to lose their homes, they heard their priest's appeals from the altar for those threatened with eviction, all the time knowing the clock was ticking on their Australian life. His father advised him to return to Ireland where 'influence and friends' would ensure he found a job quickly. However, he was informed by a cable from his sister – a nun in India – that his father had 'died within a few hours of posting my letter. To add further to my misery I received my notice within a few days'. He did not lie down and die, he tried to use 'influence' in Australia by petitioning an Irish member of parliament, but he was advised to leave Australia as nothing would improve for seven years or more.

Richard and his wife lost heavily on the sale of their assets and did not raise enough for them all to travel to Ireland, so he went ahead. However, Ireland was to offer no end to their woes: 'I arrived home in Ireland the end of May last, greatly run down in health, lonely for the little ones I had left behind, and to find many changes, the old home that had bore our name for generations under new management and to miss the welcome of a loving father.' For six months he searched for work while watching his remaining savings 'dwindle away'. Eventually, a sister, who was getting married, allowed him to take over her position in the Post Office, which yielded him a very small salary of '£7.5 a month less £1 rent'. This meant he had no chance of paying for his wife and family to return to Ireland and in the meantime they were residing with his mother-in-law who had 'had her share of ill luck':

So that my family are a heavy burden on her. Every letter I receive from Australia causes me a deep pain and sorrow. It is a bitter realization to know your own flesh and blood are actually in want and not be in a position to help. One needs to be strong of faith not to despair at times. I have never known the taste of drink, having faithfully wore my pioneer badge all the years I was away and as a non-smoker I have prayed daily to the Sacred Heart to help me but so far He has willed otherwise I am resigned to His will.[52]

Richard was a man who was motivated by the intention to help his 'own flesh'; he did not drink or smoke and he came from families 'well known

---

[52] Ibid.

to your Grace'. He had ascertained from the travel agency Messrs Cook & Son that it would cost 'approximately £73 to bring my wife and three little ones home'. He asked that the cheque be made payable directly to the travel agency: the money was not for him, it was for his family. Further emphasising that this was not charity, he promised to repay 'as circumstances permit, through the St. Vincent de Paul Society for the poor, or as Your Grace commands'. He wrote the letter under 'exceptional circumstances', in normal circumstances he did the donating rather than the begging. On the letter sent by Cook & Co. to the archbishop confirming that the transport of a woman and three children from Adelaide to Dublin would cost £73, the archbishop's secretary noted: 'Richard B., Inch P.O. Family brought home from Australia.'

James M^{c}N. was also a father of a young family, he too had 'fallen on hard times', was sure his situation was temporary, had a (convoluted) plan and promised to repay any assistance rendered. However, while James's letters touched on many familiar themes, he built and maintained a relationship with the archbishop over fifteen letters between 1924 and 1930 and he received, in total, £120. Although he deployed similar rhetorical devices to other writers to provide a detailed chronicle of the impact of poverty on male identity, a sense of his personality emerges over his series of correspondence. His letters remain effective in inducing his reader to bat for him. Almost a hundred years later it is impossible not to hope his schemes will work out, despair when they fail and wish you could turn time on its head and right the ending for James McN.

James began his relationship with the archbishop on 25 October 1924: 'My only excuses for daring to ask for your indulgence are 1st the seriousness of my position, 2nd my desire & anxiety to protect, & provide for my wife & young family (5).'[53] Four years previously he had been pensioned out of Dublin Corporation, 'I tried hard to work up a business, lost some money, and now find myself in debt, & severely pressed by my creditors, who have taken drastic action.'[54] James was a man that did not give up. On a pension he had set up his own business, but because of 'unsettled conditions' beyond his control, which had been 'disastrous to many', he was faced with 'breaking up of my home, & loss of household goods, (which means all to my family). My anxiety & hopes, to give my boys a fair untarnished start in life, are likely to be shattered'.[55] James was anxious about his home and position because of what they

---

[53] Mr James M^{c}N., X Bushfield Tce, Donnybrook, Co. Dublin 25 October 1924. DDA, AB 7 CC, Box 1.
[54] Ibid.   [55] Ibid.

meant to his family and to his sons' chances in life: the loss of their home and social standing would handicap them:

My proposal is – that, I assign, mortage *[mortgage]* & give Power of Attorney, to either of the above to receive (a bank, insurance company or private lender), my monthly cheque from the Corporation, an Insurance Policy on my life to be given & assigned to the Lendor.

However, he had not managed to convince anyone of the merits of the scheme. Engaging in the language of the many charitable organisations, he declared: 'As desperate diseases require desperate remedies & being now nearly desperate, owing to the extreme urgency of this matter, I resolved as a last resource to appeal to your Grace.'

James's parish priest wrote to confirm the letter was 'perfectly true' and that he was a 'respectable man + had a large family'. However, the priest provided additional information not (and never) provided by James: he had been pensioned from his job in the corporation's abattoir as a result of illness and he had incurred his debts 'owing to a partner he had, going abroad + leaving the debts with him'.[56] James had possibly omitted his illness because he did not want to appear as a potentially weak bet; perhaps he had not explained his debts for a similar reason, no one liked being conned and it might have raised questions regarding his business acumen. Fr Maloney also explained the fatal obstacle to his plan: 'the Bank people would not advance as they had no security in case Mr McN. died before paying same back'. However, the priest believed 'if he got some temporary relief, he would be alright'. He also made a personal connection between the applicant and the archbishop, again something James had not done, pointing out that his father-in-law had been the archbishop's gardener when he was at Haddington Road.[57] All the ingredients were present for James to receive relief and he was sent £10.

However, illusions of the temporary nature of his situation were quickly shattered, when two weeks later James wrote to thank the archbishop for his cheque and request a further 'loan of £40 or £50'.[58] He explained that his landlord was threatening eviction, which would 'be ruinous' to his family. He cast himself as a man 'straining every effort to get righted' and the stakes were high: if he failed to satisfy his landlord he

---

[56] Fr O'Moloney, The Presbytery, Donnybrook, Co. Dublin, 27 October 1924. DDA, AB 7 CC, Box 1.

[57] The Archbishop had been the parish priest in St Mary's, Haddington Road, Dublin from 1920 to 1921.

[58] Mr J. M^cN., X Bushfield Tce, Donnybrook, Dublin, 13 November 1924. DDA, AB 7 CC, Box 1.

would lose his house in the wealthy suburb of Donnybrook in Dublin[59] and be deprived 'of the chance of restoring my position'.[60] He assured the archbishop that he and his wife would 'sign all necessary document[s] to repay'.

In this letter James had laid out his case well: he was a man, a father, trying to 'right' himself. He had a 'position' and it was within the archbishop's gift to restore him to his rightful place in the world. He was also a man who understood signed documents, who functioned in the world of legally binding contracts. This was not charity, this was an investment *in* 'the deserving'. He was a good investment because he had a plan, but as James had skilfully highlighted, time was not on his side, he 'was in hourly jeopardy' – the sense of drama, of threat, permeated his letters. He also clearly sought empathy: in many of his letters he repeatedly asked, or hoped, that the archbishop could 'picture' his situation. James was successful and was sent £40, but it was barely a month before he wrote again with a further request. He thanked the archbishop for 'saving his house' but now his creditors were 'like birds of prey in their anxiety to devour' him.[61] This appeal James made directly for his children:

I appeal for the sake of my children, whom are too young to know that any change has come in my position, + if possible I intend they should not know especially at this time of year, when of course their young minds are centred in xmas, + they could not understand any trouble.[62]

Protecting his children was part of James's job, this – for him – was the fault line, if he failed to protect his children then he had failed as a father. He designed an I.O.U. which was attached to the letter, underscoring the idea of a loan and of his *bona fides*. He had also sent the archbishop his landlord's receipts and requested that they be returned to him in the stamped addressed envelope he provided. This paperwork not only helped 'to show that it was genuine', but also that James lived in a world where paperwork counted.

However, the archbishop's response was simple and stark. 'Nothing Doing' was written in blue pencil on the top left-hand corner of James's letter. He was undeterred and a week later tried, successfully, to haggle

---

[59] According to the 1911 Census, James McN. married in 1906 and had three children in the first five years of marriage, two of whom were still living by 1911. James was listed as Roman Catholic, the head of the household and a Meat and C. Inspector for Dublin Corporation.

[60] Mr J. M^cN of X Bushfield Tce, Donnybrook, Co. Dublin, 13 November 1924.

[61] Mr J. M^cN of X Bushfield Tce, Donnybrook, Co. Dublin, 10 December 1924. DDA, AB 7 CC, Box 1.

[62] Ibid.

with the archbishop. He acknowledged that the archbishop's response had been a 'great blow + a bitter disappointment', but he would now 'respectfully beg' for a 'loan of about £10, which is half what I asked in my previous letter'.[63] There is no indication why, but James was sent £10 he requested. Considering the apparent finality of the previous note regarding his case, this is surprising and it was rare for the archbishop to reverse his decisions.

James's letters document a sustained attempt, over five years, to save his home and regain his footing in the world of paid employment. This was a fragile and often damaging journey, when illness twice derailed his plans, followed by an accident and eviction. By the end of 1925 the strain of struggling and juggling was apparent in his letters. In December he wrote a long letter that detailed his efforts since the previous March. The beginning indicated that James was aware he was nearing the end of the archbishop's forbearance:

Doubtless you will be surprised, and inclined to throw it in the waste paper basket, having regard to the fact that I am already in your debt, + that about this time last year I was troubling you. I sincerely regret + apologise that my promise to repay you, has not been accomplished, although I assure you through no fault or wish of mine, nor the want of trying.[64]

He was 'sorry to say' that desperation had driven him to the parish's protestant Dean for help in delaying his landlord's demands. James offered an interesting twist on the 'Protestant threat':

I called to the Presbytery + received the greatest rebuff I have got for a long time, when the maid brought me the answer from the Dean, "there is no answer" Why? your Grace may ask, and I answer I do not know, all I can say is that I am very sorry I applied [to] him, it was a protestant gentleman ... I expected very little, but at least thought he would grant me the few month moments interview I asked for, + at least some sympathy. This is rather a poor rendering of Christian Charity, or the teaching of our Lord, to be kind to those in distress.[65]

James's point was rather subtler than a conversion threat; he highlighted that those who truly followed Christ's message would not humiliate a man – a deserving man – in such a fashion.

However I beg to assure your Grace I have no ill will, nor complaint against the Dean, and only that I am in such desperate plight, I feel my position more keenly. You will understand how humiliating it is for a man, to have to appeal, or to

---

[63] Mr J. McN of X Bushfield Tce, Donnybrook, Co. Dublin, 18 December 1924. Ibid.
[64] Mr J, McN of X Bushfield Tce, Donnybrook, Co. Dublin, 16 December 1925.
[65] Ibid.

admit he is down. My very manhood seems sapped + squeezed out of me, + only for my youngsters death would be a relief in one sense perhaps only.[66]

He was a man who felt his 'position keenly' and did not need others to remind him of how he was failing as a man. The whole experience was 'sapping his manhood' to the point where death would be easier than perseverance, except he was a father and death was not an option. While many men hinted at such feelings few were as articulate as James. While he pleaded with the archbishop to accept his apologies for 'this rather jumbled appeal' on the grounds of his 'mental condition', it was his mental condition that he so powerfully conveyed. His next letter came only two weeks later and it palpated with desperation. He begged that the archbishop picture 'for a moment the misery + desolation . . . hanging over my wife + family'. This plea, like all others, was for his children whose chances he could not be responsible for damaging: 'My eldest boy has been promised a nomination for Guinness, this career as well as the other children will be blighted through no fault of theirs.'[67] The world James wrote of was one where debt and poverty tarnished all family members, a world that offered children little chances of escaping the destiny of their parents. If James fell so did his children. The archbishop again relented and sanctioned a further £10 and there would be more benevolence.

James wrote three other letters in 1926: one in June, another in August and the last in November. In the course of these letters he revealed the value of his pension as £199 a year, which represented a very modest middle-class income.[68] With a large family, debts and no secure employment, this sum was not enough to sustain him in the style to which he was accustomed. He had secured a job as an assistant steward but 'met an accident to the head in August', which had set him back. The Landlord, who, in a clear sign of desperation James identified for the first time as 'a Protestant', was again threatening to 'throw' him 'on the roadside' and this 'would be a dreadful calamity' for his 'wife + children'.[69] James was a man 'trying to do [his] best to keep all going', but the writing seemed on the wall with regard to his home. Every year that he had written to the archbishop he counted how long he had lived there – thirteen years, then fourteen years, and finally, fifteen years – as though he knew it was a matter of time before the count stopped.

---

[66] Ibid.
[67] Mr J. M^cN of X Bushfield Tce, Donnybrook, Co. Dublin, 1 January 1925. DDA, AB 7 CC, Box 1.
[68] Mr J. M^cN of X Bushfield Tce, Donnybrook, Co. Dublin, 8 August 1926. DDA, AB 7 CC, Box 2.
[69] Mr J. M^cN., X Bushfield Tce, Donnybrook, Co. Dublin, 27 November 1926. Ibid.

The archbishop did not respond to any of these letters, probably because he too believed the house in Donnybrook was unsustainable, and, definitely, because he was not willing to continue to fund it.

However, James's and the archbishop's relationship was not over. He wrote again in December 1929. It was two years since his last letter and he had a lot to tell the archbishop. His letter came from a new address: the house in Donnybrook had finally been relinquished.

I got a job + things were doing well, until unfortunately I met with an accident, I was incapacitated for a long time, the result being things got very bad, and the home had to be broken up. For nearly two years things have been desperate, knocked about from one place to another.[70]

The fight to keep the family home was one of the main issues the lower-middle class and middle class wrote to the archbishop about precisely because the loss of one's home was symbolic of entering a world where you were 'knocked about'. It was also a public acknowledgement of your loss of status. While James had lost his Donnybrook home, he remained focused on securing another permanent home. This he achieved in March 1929 when the owner of a house in Sandymount 'gave the house in return for the pension'. Finally his pension scheme had paid off and the roof over his head seemed relatively secure. However, his wife had hoped to get boarders to help with the costs, but she had become very ill and had been confined to bed for ten weeks. Then the expectations he had placed on his eldest son were only partly realised:

My eldest son failed in Irish in the Customs, +Exist *[Excise]* Exam, + so failed to get a place. He has been given a small post for the last three weeks, in a slot cigarette machine Co at £1 per week, which is a great God send.[71]

James had a concrete request for the archbishop. He had secured a job working for an English rat and mice extermination company as their Irish agent (see Figure 4.2). This would pay 30/- a week plus commission, but the problem was that he had no appropriate clothing to wear to his training week in London. He explained: 'I am very shabby, as I require a suit, Overcoat, Hat, shoes, + Shirt. I am sure your Grace will agree, that appearance counts for a whole lot, especially with English men.' It was probably a combination of James's acceptance of the loss of his old home, the success of his pension scheme, his son's small wage and James's own prospects that convinced the archbishop to invest another £20 in his cause.

[70] Mr J. M^cN., X Park Avenue, Sandymount, Co. Dublin, 30 December 1928. Ibid.
[71] Ibid.

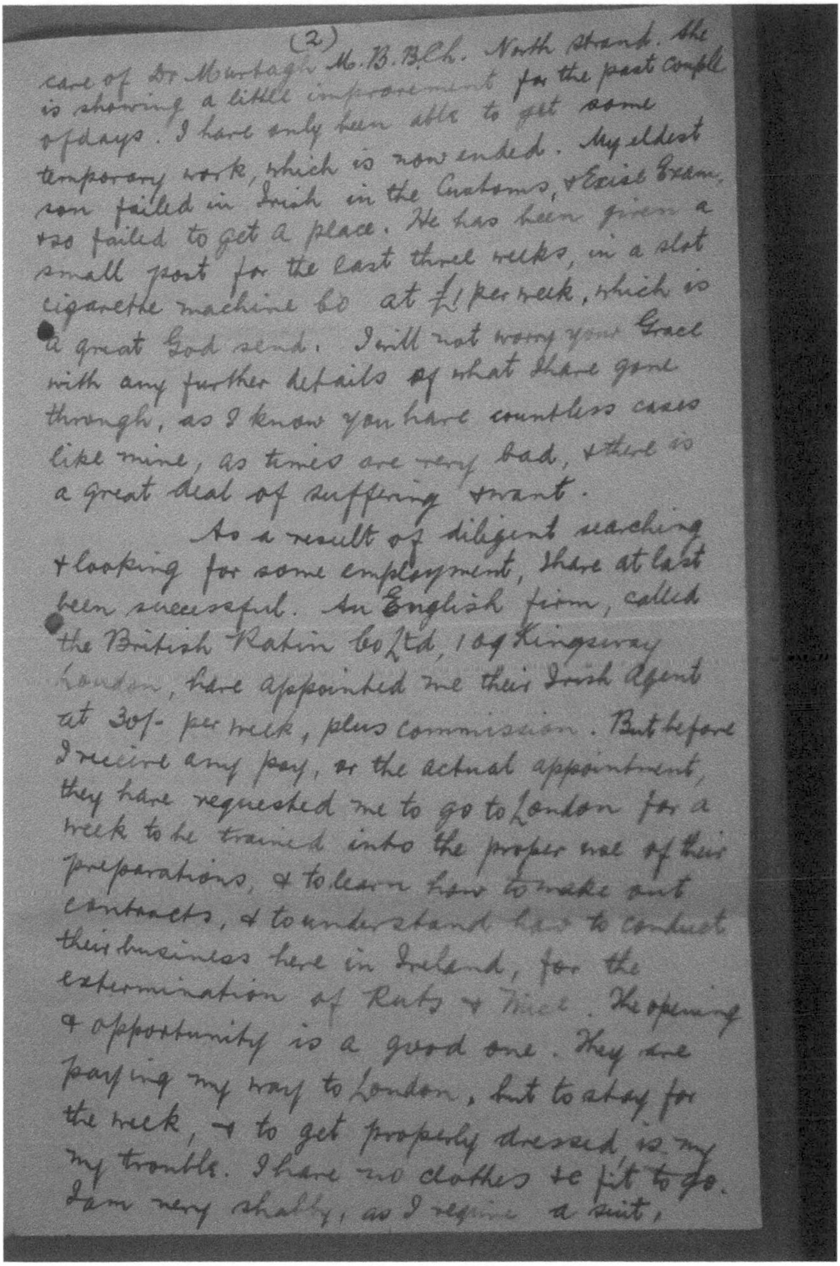

(2)
care of Dr Murtagh M.B.B.Ch. North Strand. She
is showing a little improvement for the past couple
of days. I have only been able to get some
temporary work, which is now ended. My eldest
son failed in Irish in the Customs, & Excise Exam,
& so failed to get a place. He has been given a
small post for the last three weeks, in a slot
cigarette machine Co at £1 per week, which is
a great God send. I will not worry your Grace
with any further details of what I have gone
through, as I know you have countless cases
like mine, as times are very bad, & there is
a great deal of suffering & want.
As a result of diligent searching
& looking for some employment, I have at last
been successful. An English firm, called
the British Ratin Co Ltd, 10 Kingsway
London, have appointed me their Irish Agent
at 30/- per week, plus commission. But before
I receive any pay, or the actual appointment,
they have requested me to go to London for a
week to be trained into the proper use of their
preparations, & to learn how to make out
contracts, & to understand how to conduct
their business here in Ireland, for the
extermination of Rats & Mice. The opening
& opportunity is a good one. They are
paying my way to London, but to stay for
the week, & to get properly dressed, is my
my trouble. I have no clothes &c fit to go.
I am very shabby, as I require a suit,

Figure 4.2 A section of one of the letters written by James McN., X Park Avenue, Sandymount, Co. Dublin to the Archbishop of Dublin, 20 Jan. 1929.

James wrote two weeks later to express gratitude and a sense of restored pride; he was now the 'representative for the firm' in Ireland. He was no longer a supplicant but a business man and took the 'liberty of enclosing a leaflet' of his extermination services, should the archbishop ever require the service. His manhood was restored.[72] A silence of fourteen months followed: 'But Alas! Just as I thought I had things going smoothly & easy, I have received a severe setback.' His rat killing business was going well, but the old mortgage plan had come back to haunt him. Not for the first time James left out crucial details and was vague on exactly how 'a Bombshell was landed' by the rates collector, but a bill of £37 was due by that Saturday or the Bailiffs would arrive. Despite the gaps in James's story he was sent £25, the minimum required to call off the bailiffs.

Four months later James's story took its final twist. He wrote truly defeated:

> Notwithstanding your very great assistance, & my strenuous struggle, things seem to go against me, just as I think we are on the road to success, and were it not for my faith, and the remembrance of your great kindness, I would despair, & lose all heart.[73]

The landlady had deceived him by not transferring the lease and deeds of the house into his name and she had failed to pay anything due on the house. He had another final reminder from the tax collector and he had to embark on legal action to either reclaim his pension or secure the house. The narrative James presented in this final letter was confusing and raised as many questions as it answered, nonetheless, it appears that the archbishop was entertaining assistance and had asked for some documentary evidence. This was evidently not forthcoming as the last note on James's case read: 'No letters forwarded to Abp. Help unlikely.' James's story, as represented in the archbishop's charity cases, ended with this final letter. While his story was unremarkable – many others wrote to save homes, protect children and satisfy creditors – the relationship he managed to forge with the archbishop through his letters was exceptional. It broke most of the rules applied to others and the only reason seems to have been James himself, or at least the 'self' he created in his letters.

---

[72] Mr J. M^cN., X Park Avenue, Sandymount, Co. Dublin 20 January 1929. DDA, AB 7 CC, Box 2.
[73] Mr J. M^cN., X Park Avenue, Sandymount, Co. Dublin, 28 July 1930. Ibid.

'For the four little - Foxrock Orphans'

It was extremely rare for the archbishop to assist those from the Dublin tenements more than once and, when he did so the sums of money were always small. However, when it came to members of the lower middle-class, middle class or indeed the upper-class, he could provide financial assistance several times or over years, particularly, for example, by funding children in private schools. Many of these cases were women, either elderly unmarried women or widows with children. Mrs Marion G. was the most prolific of this type of correspondent: twenty-nine letters survive from her (it is obvious that some are missing from the chain) between 1924 and 1934. Marion and her children received at least £117, almost the same amount as James McN. If one considers that the average civil servant's salary was approximately £179, while a casual labour could earn 6s. a day, it was a considerable sum of money. The rhythm of this charity to Marion G. is worth noting: she received £75 by November 1924 and then nothing (despite nine letters) until 1927 when she received the final £42 in two instalments; although she wrote a further ten letters she received no response after April 1927. She enlisted her eldest daughter who wrote four times between 1924 and 1933. The last letter regarding her case came in 1938 from a Loreto nun who begged one final time on Marion's behalf. This final letter provides another insight into the G. family's perpetual state of crisis and strikes a sad final note in her story. We hear no more about the Foxrock widow after that date.

According to the 1911 Irish census, Marion married a widowed solicitor in his late forties, with two sons from a previous marriage, she never mentioned these boys and it is clear they did not reside with her after their father's death.[74] In late 1919 or early 1920, after only a few years of marriage, Marion's husband died, leaving her with four very young children. Her parish priest explained that she had struggled to 'rear her four little children' and that: 'They are a credit to her. She is worthy of any help you may obtain for her.'[75] Marion had requested help to establish a poultry farm, and her profile as the widow of a

---

[74] Marion's husband is listed in the 1911 Census as a forty-five-year-old widower, solicitor, with two sons aged eight and nine. The boys' mother was from St John's Newfoundland and it appears this is where the boys spent their adulthood: in 1930 the younger son married a woman from St. John's in New York. According to the 1940 American census he and his wife had one daughter.

[75] Fr John Ryan, St Mary's, Foxrock, Co. Dublin, 22 February 1924. DDA, AB 7 CC, Box 1.

solicitor with small children, coupled with the parish priest's reference, secured her £20.

In May 1924, two months later, Marion wrote again, beginning a pattern that continued for the following ten years: making promises, forging plans and lamenting failures. She began: 'I find it very hard to ask you to grant me a final request, but I am driven to it.' Since her previous letter she had begun her poultry business, but it had yet to yield any return, so she hoped to get a tenant. Highlighting her good mothering skills, she pointed out that the parish priest had praised her for how well her children were brought up. She asked for 'a loan' of £20 and promised not to do so again. She was successful.[76] In five months came another, long and complicated, letter, followed by a sequel with more information the following day: there was a new business plan and she explained that she had the support of several high profile people from the legal world, the ex-Lord Chief Justice and Sir Joseph Glynn, a solicitor and president of the Vincent de Paul.[77] The spectre of Protestants also made an appearance, written almost as an after thought on the top left-hand corner of the first page of the letter was the following note: 'A solicitor who knew my husband could have got £100 for us he thought some months ago but the question of my religion arose + prevented it it could only go to a Protestant family.'

This letter contained themes that surface in many similar letters from people who were desperate to maintain their social standing and avoid the label 'poor'. Marion appeared to believe it was important to situate herself in a world of influence and status, to underscore that this was the world she belonged to rather than the one of begging and charity. The tone of her letter was both familiar and deferential; she presumed the archbishop took a personal interest in her and therefore she did not 'want to drag out this letter to worry you'. Marion did not express any fear of irritating the archbishop only a fear of *worrying* him. She also chose her eldest daughter as a focal point, as though she could share her pride and concern about this child with the archbishop:

My eldest girl aged 12 done very well at exams. 1st place all English subjects – silver medal for Catechism, 1st for needlework + good conduct. The nuns are

---

[76] Marion G. X, Foxrock, Co. Dublin, 8 May 1924. Ibid.

[77] Sir Joseph Aloysius Glynn was president of Saint Vincent de Paul between 1917 and 1940. He was an extremely prominent player in the world of charity and philanthropy. For example, he was a member of the Commission on the Relief of the Sick and Destitute Poor, including the Insane Poor, which was established in March 1925 and reported in 1927. See, *Report of the Commission on the Relief of the Sick and Destitute Poor, including the Insane Poor* (Dublin, 1927).

very kind + are waiting payment till I get on I have done all in my power to find a way to make money[78]

The idea of a widow expressing her need through her children was not unusual and crosses the class divide apparent in these letters. However, Marion's presumption of intimacy, the way she attempted to bring the archbishop into her family and make them his to worry about, was something rarely found in the letters of those from the tenements of Dublin. She created a narrative that involved the archbishop in all her ups and downs and that placed it in his gift to save her family from ruin, promising to 'give your Grace an account of my success as you wish it'. She wrote the following day to clarify what the business was she intended to start and how she could assure the archbishop a return on his investment:

When writing yesterday I should have said that the business I was starting I want to buy a second-hand Ford motor car + start on my own I know all about cars +drove my own for years doing all repairs ... I tried every other [way] to make money, but I wont fail in this – At the end of 3 months I shall return money each month to your Grace + if I fail I can sell car + pay you back – I would sign agreement to that effect drawn up by a solicitor God Grant you will help me to start you wont regret it. The children + I are praying hard for this one great chance.
Believe me.[79]

She received £15 in response to this clarification, but she was nearing the end of the archbishop's patience and generosity. By the end of November she was again 'destitute for want of money', she had hoped for £25 from the Solicitor Benevolent Fund, but had received only £5 – there were many solicitors' widows calling on the fund – there was no money to meet the milk and bakery bills and nothing for train fares to school.[80] She was 'nearly distracted – 4 children and no money'. Her poultry farm had brought in no money because the hens had not started to lay. She requested £20 to get her family over Christmas. This sum was the difference between what she had hoped for from the solicitors' fund and what she had actually received; she always made sure the figure she requested had a rationale. In this communication her daughter made the first of several appearances: 'P.S. My little girl is taking letter and anxiously awaits your Grace's reply.' Marion enclosed her daughter's first letter. Written in the deliberate and laboured script of a child, Helen copied her mother's style and echoed her pleas:

---

[78] Marion G. X, Foxrock, Co. Dublin, 14 October 1924. DDA, AB 7 CC, Box 1.
[79] Marion G. X, Foxrock, Co Dublin, n.d. c. 15 October 1924. Ibid.
[80] Marion G. X, Foxrock, Co Dublin, 24 November 1924. Ibid.

My Dear Lord Archbishop,

For the sake of my little sisters and brother, will you grant Mammys last request she will never call on you again, until we pay you back. Will Your Grace please save our home for the last time we shall never worry you again, and always pray for you.

I am, My Dear Lord Archbishop

Your Obedient Child,

Helen <u>G</u>.

Helen, at only twelve years of age, was clearly a full actor in the struggle for her family's survival: she supported her mother's request and reinforced its legitimacy and veracity. She continued to bear that responsibility for at least the following ten years.

When this letter received no response Marion wrote a few days later and called in another influential advocate:

We asked Poor Cardinal Logue to intercede for us in November for he loved children so much – I know you have a Heart of Gold and trust you will help me in this last fight – I shall never never call you again[81]

This reference to 'Poor Cardinal Logue' was particularly interesting as he had died on 19 November 1924.[82] Marion implied that her family's welfare was one of the last things he might have considered, that had he lived – 'for he loved children' – he surely would have helped her, but as he had died no one would ever know. She was implicitly challenging the archbishop to equal the putative benevolence of a dead colleague. For this brief missive she received £20 – again, exactly what she had requested. Marion's letter of gratitude contained the seeds of subsequent appeals: 'P.S. Please ask the Sacred Heart each day to send me some boarders or <u>some</u> way of making money for the education + support of the Children God Grant I won't have to give up our home.'[83] Marion's postscripts often foreshadowed the next letter.

In January 1925 she was granted another request: she wrote in a more upbeat tone than usual, a tone she would muster only a few more times. She began in the mode of keeping a friend apprised:

As "Your Grace" has done so much for myself and children. I would like, and feel it is my duty to let you know how we are getting along. The last generous cheque you sent, with another from a friend, kept us going and fed the Poultry

---

[81] Marion G. X, Foxrock, Co Dublin, n.d. c. 26 November 1924. DDA, AB 7 CC, Box 1.

[82] Cardinal Michael Logue was Cardinal of Armagh between 1893 and 1924. D. Ferriter, 'Logue, Michael' in J. McGuire and J. Quinn et al., Dictionary of Irish Biography, Volume 5 (Cambridge University Press, 2009), pp. 548–550.

[83] Marion G. X, Foxrock, Co Dublin, 28 November 1924. DDA, AB 7 CC, Box 1.

then I had the minors [student boarders] during Xmas. The Poultry did not pay till just now sold 2 doz eggs yesterday for the first time if they continue now shall be able to go on increasing stock by degrees – now your Grace I just want to tell you what I have to do, that is, I am compelled to make, personally, a private collection amongst the judges, barristers + members of the legal profession in order to try + collect at once about £50 or £100.

Clearly, Marion had had to petition many other sources to survive. This was not unusual for widows. Widows of professionals were often assisted by means of an appeal or collections organised by erstwhile colleagues or friends of the deceased husband.[84] While this made them luckier than their impoverished or working-class counterparts, it reveals that widows of any class could be left suddenly very vulnerable. She had sought the advice of friends in the legal profession who had suggested that adding the archbishop's name to her list of benefactors would help encourage others to respond to her 'private collection':

May I? Please say yes. This is the last time I can call on anyone to help us if I get a good lift now I shall be able to turn the corner and if I fail by end of year I must let house for 5 years + take my children to a convent in France where I can get a post as Secretary + Chaffeur. I shall never let my children go down – God alone knows how hard I work + fight/ + he must wish me to keep the home or he would not help me so often.[85]

However unrealistic plans of taking four children to a convent in France and working as a secretary-cum-chauffeur might have been, it was obvious that Marion was unlikely to become independent in the near future. While her poultry farm had begun to show the fragile signs of viability, her family economy remained precarious. Marion relied heavily on the support of the legal profession during the early years of her widowhood, although she seemed aware this could not last: 'This is the last time I can call on anyone to help us.' Of course, this was part of her rhetoric, but it also revealed a knowledge that people would inevitably tire of her requests. She ended this letter with a list of all those who had responded to her initial appeal, most of the names were high profile names among the legal community. The archbishop agreed to have his name added to this impressive list.

[84] Also in this collection is a printed appeal for 'a Dependents' Fund' on behalf of the wife and children of Mr M. C., who had worked in a men's clothing department, and was killed by a 'motor car' on his way to mass. There was also an appeal on behalf of the orphan children of the late Doctor Gerald T. organised by Mr Justice Geoghegan and dated February 1938.
[85] Marion G. X, Foxrock, Co. Dublin, 10 January 1925. DDA, AB 7 CC, Box 1.

She lasted five months before writing again. In May 1925, her opening gambit was bright, breezy and familiar: 'Welcome! A thousand times Welcome home again. I sincerely hope your Grace had a pleasant holiday.' She was once again writing to report on her struggle, however, while she had received a pound from Sir Joseph Downes,[86] all she had was £2-8-4: 'Your Grace I am making a last and Earnest appeal to you for one more gift to help me turn the last corner – as I told you I shall have regular money coming ... at end of June.'[87] Helen was again the child she focused on (the other three are only mentioned once by name in a letter on 24 July 1931) and she skilfully bound Helen's achievements with the archbishop's religious mission:

For the love of The Sacred Heart and in Honour of St. Terese "The Little Flower" (whose name Helen took in confirmation) hear my last call
     Helen is taking part in the play on Monday at the "Sacred Heart Convent" at which I hear your Grace will be present also at the Holy Mass at 11 O'clock. I am sending Helen with the letter perhaps you would see her ... She is a good Holy Child + will tell you all truthfully

Helen remained the child she wished the archbishop to identify with and it appears, from the role that daughter played in rescuing the family later, she chose wisely. Marion ended her letter appealing to the archbishop's role as patriarch, the proud father and protector: 'When I start returning all you have given Your Grace will have reason to be proud of what you have done for the four little – Foxrock Orphans.'[88]

The pattern was firmly established: Marion was making do through a combination of private donations, student boarders, and a very small return from her poultry business, but the corner she claimed to be turning was always the next corner. It is very unlikely that the archbishop was convinced that this would be her 'last appeal', however, he sent her the £20 requested.[89] In her 'thank you' letter came the next request, 'I want ten pounds more to see us over till end of June I shall pay you back the £20 before end of September.'[90] Her request was not granted and the topography of Marion's letters began to display signs of the archbishop's fading patience: a letter from Marion in December 1925 had two thick hard blue lines drawn through it – a sign of irritation perhaps?[91] Although she enclosed a letter from her parish priest confirming her account, the archbishop was unmoved. A letter from her in February 1926 elicited a

---

[86] Sir Joseph Downes was the owner and founder of one of the largest commercial Dublin baking and confectionary businesses Joseph Downes & Son, Ltd.
[87] Marion G., X, Foxrock, Co. Dublin, 22 May 1925. DDA, AB 7 CC, Box 1.   [88] Ibid.
[89] Marion G., X, Foxrock, Co. Dublin, May 1925. Ibid.   [90] Ibid.
[91] Marion G., X, Foxrock, Co. Dublin, 14 December 1925. Ibid.

red pen: in the top-left hand corner the word '<u>No</u>' was written and underlined.[92]

The relationship was beginning to show signs of heightened tension on both sides. Marion's letters were no longer conversational; she had started to 'implore' the archbishop to 'hear' her. In her letter of 19 February 1925 she renewed her promise that in a year she would be independent, but she had two years of rates due and faced losing her home:

My eldest girl shall earn soon + by degrees all shall be returned. At present I have three in bed with measles and I am heart broken over trying to get over this trouble I dread going into the Courts + losing all – This day twelve months you confirmed my girl + granted me a very great request in Honour/ of that day – hear me –[93]

Marion also made reference to her specific lack of support network – outside the legal profession – 'P.S. If I had Father, Mother, Sister or brother – but I <u>have no-one</u>.' Whatever her personal strengths or failings, the odds were stacked against her with no extended family to call on, no pension and no children working – keeping her home was becoming an increasingly unrealistic hope. By March 1926, she made yet another final 'heart broken appeal to you shall never worry you again', informing the archbishop that she had been in court the previous week and had been given twenty one days to pay the amount due on her house or 'they will send in the Bailiffs'. She had received a 'small cheque' from some members of the legal profession, but it was not enough: 'If I could only tell you all I went through you would forgive me for writing so often – Answer the Widow's + orphans prayer once more –.'[94] Whether it was the drama of a court appearance or the continued support of prominent legal people, the archbishop helped her with the £50 debt because she wrote to thank the archbishop for 'saving our home'.[95] However, on this letter the archbishop's secretary noted that 'Letters will not be answered in future.' Marion responded: 'You say you won't read my letters in future – but I can assure 'Your Grace' you may read them as none shall contain any appeal but just to let you know each year how my Children get along.'[96]

Marion G. was not in a position to keep her word, 1927 was punctuated by three letters from her in January, April and June. These letters were short and desperate:

[92] Marion G., X, Foxrock, Co. Dublin, 19 February 1926. Ibid.   [93] Ibid.
[94] Marion G. X, Foxrock, Co. Dublin, 12 March 1926. Ibid.
[95] Marion G. X, Foxrock, Co. Dublin, 18 March 1926. Ibid.   [96] Ibid.

Will Your Grace pardon my disobedience in writing again. I am so miserable –
For the love of "The Sacred Heart" her my <u>last last call</u> –

God will send you thousands in return –

Don't let my things be taken on the Children – I can easily manage all after
this –[97]

This letter yielded £17. The next 'last last Request =' came two
months later. From April 1927 until the end of the correspondence in
1934, the only people writing were Marion and her eldest daughter. Both
mother and daughter wrote two separate letters in February
1930 requesting £50. The roles of mother and daughter were almost
reversed: Marion's handwriting had become sloppy and her letter consisted of only a few lines; Helen's letter was written in a confident script
and was long and detailed containing facts and figures:

Mammy is still fighting away to keep the house going, and finds it an almost
impossible job to make ends meet. She does all the sewing she can get, and earns
a little money in that way. But now, I am afraid we are going to lose our home,
unless your Lordship would be so kind as to save it for us.[98]

Helen adopted her mother's sense of urgency and also managed to
convey how she too was affected by the constant stress of worry:

I had to stay away from class this morning in order to bring this letter, as the
matter is so urgent. I am old enough to understand Mammy's worries and
I cannot concentrate on my work unless Mammy can get this money at once.
Unless we can bring the amount due to Mr Gerald B. at 5 o'c. this evening, the
sheriff will receive orders to evict us.

There is a ring of adult speech in this letter 'I am old enough to understand', she also informed the archbishop that it would be a false economy
for her mother to sell their house as 'she would have to buy a new house,
and that would not be any benefit, as this house only costs £9 a year
ground rent',[99] indicating that many a conversation had been had about
the state of their finances. Helen was baking cakes to keep the roof over
their heads and her mother planned to buy a sewing machine, but failure
seemed imminent.

Helen wrote again a year and half later in July 1931. Although she
was now a workingwoman, her youth was still very much apparent: 'I am
going to ask you a great favour, so <u>please</u> do not be cross with me
when you read this letter.' She was working as a typist in the Hospitals'

[97] Marion G., X, Foxrock, Co. Dublin, 26 January 1927. DDA, AB 7 CC, Box 2.
[98] Helen G., X, Foxrock, Co. Dublin, 17 February 1930. DDA, AB 7 CC, Box 3.
[99] Ibid.

Trust – her salary was barely sufficient to keep them all fed. She earned £2 a week and her sister, who had just started, was on only 30/- a week.[100] As Tony Farmar noted, a good starting salary for a young male apprentice in 1932 was £4 a week.[101] Helen was earning the average wage of a labourer and her sister even less; their salaries reflected the very poor wages young women were paid. Helen painted a picture of a house falling down around its inhabitants. Helen too had a plan: Ireland was bracing itself in anticipation of the Eucharistic Congress to be hosted in the city and the G. family, like many other Dubliners, sought to make some money on the occasion by offering accommodation to the world's Catholic pilgrims. Helen requested '£50 urgently'. In relation to her repayment plan, she stressed 'You can trust me' – was she referring obliquely to the fact that her mother had failed to repay any of the money thus far? Interestingly, Helen expressed a fear of exposure that her mother had never articulated: 'Please do not let anyone else read this letter – I should hate anyone to know how badly we are placed.' Perhaps this fear was the legacy of childhood of straining to 'keep up appearances'.

There was no response. Although Marion wrote six more times, the archbishop maintained his resolve. Helen also tried to re-ignite the correspondence with one final letter in 1933. These final few letters from Marion and Helen were different in tone, the message had become 'starting afresh', and both women requested the large sum of £100 to effect this life change. Charlie, Marion's eldest son, had replaced Helen as the chief focus: 'Charlie is clever like his Poor Daddy but this constant worry over Money Matters is ruining all the Children'[102] Marion's handwriting had deteriorated, the script was large and sprawling and the grammar much less certain. Her letters physically betrayed the increased strain she was under. She also began to threaten – she had relatives in Portsmouth who had offered to give her £250 for a share in her house on condition she allowed Charlie to complete his education in England: 'I could not accept on account of his religion – however, Your Grace if you wont hear me I must try to come to terms with them but this would break all our hearts.'[103] Marion wrote two final letters in 1934, one to the archbishop and one to his secretary. She again faced eviction, however, her letter to the secretary hinted at another reason for the breakdown in relations between her and the archbishop. In this letter

---

[100] Helen G., X, Foxrock, Co. Dublin, 21 July 1931. DDA, AB 7 CC, Box 4.
[101] Farmar, *Privileged Lives*, p. 143.
[102] Marion G., X, Foxrock, Co. Dublin,? February 1931. DDA, AB 7 CC, Box 4.
[103] Marion G., X, Foxrock, Co. Dublin, n.d. *c.* February 1933. DDA, AB 7 CC, Box 3.

she referred to the fact that 'It is now over four years Since I made the one mistake of my life – I know you don't like me but do this for the children – You were very nice to me at one time.'[104] What had happened four years previously? It is possible that there had been some kind of an exchange between the secretary and Marion outside the realm of letter writing. She did refer often to the occasions when she would be at the same event as the archbishop, perhaps there had been an encounter at one of these events. It is simply not possible to know exactly what she meant, however, a letter the archbishop received in September 1938 throws some further light on Marion G.'s struggles.

In September 1938, Sister Mary Imelda of the Loreto Convent Bray wrote to the archbishop about two deserving cases, one of them was a Marion G. of Foxrock. The problem was the same: the family was facing eviction due to non-payment of ground rent and rates, however, the context had changed. According to this nun, when the archbishop had assisted the family it had been 'in a different phase' – 'The Mother at the time was addicted to drink.'[105] Of course, the nun offered no evidence for this claim, but she told it to the archbishop not by way of criticising Marion, but to emphasise that she had overcome this addiction through her religious devotion: 'Some years ago, however, she was cured of that vice by a Novena which she and her children made to Matt Talbot and, I believe the cure is permanent.'[106] The fact that the nun noted that the children had been involved in the 'cure' implies that this was a chosen version of events, one perhaps told by Marion herself. Marion's 'one mistake' may well have been a reference to her drinking. The strain of almost fifteen years on the verge of eviction, possibly with a mother who drank to cope, had driven away Marion's second daughter: 'Three of the children live with her. The eldest girl on a salary of £2-10-1 a week in the Sweeps supports all four. The second girl, unwilling to share their poverty, lives with a friend and gives no help.'[107] Thus Helen had

---

[104] Marion G., X, Foxrock, Co. Dublin, n.d. c. 1934. Ibid.

[105] Sr. Mary Imelda C., Loreto Convent Bray, Co. Wicklow, 16 September c. 1938. DDA, AB 7 CC, Box 6.

[106] Although not formally a saint, Matt Talbot is regarded as a patron of those with addiction problems. Dwyer noted that during the Eucharistic Congress of 1932 'hundreds (if not thousands) visited the grave of the pious Dublin labourer Matt Talbot'. R. O'Dwyer, *The Eucharistic Congress Dublin 1932* (Dublin: Nonsuch Ireland, c. 2009), p. 52.

[107] This is a reference to the Irish Sweep Stakes, which was a major employer of Irish women. Coleman notes this was controversial in 1930s Ireland when male unemployment was the focus of concern. When the issue was raised in the Dáil in 1939 it was claimed that women and girls were often employed for sixteen or seventeen hour days earning up to 30s or £2 a week. See, M. Coleman, *The Irish Sweep: A History*

remained her mother's main support while the other daughter had decided she could not continue to live with her family constantly on the precipice of 'ruin'. Sr Mary Imelda was confident that the family would be 'good Catholic citizens', but the secretary's note was simple '0 for G.' As Marion had managed to hold on to her home until 1938, albeit under the constant shadow of the bailiffs, one can only hope she made it through this final crisis. There is no trace of Marion and her children in the archbishop's archive.

Over the course of Marion G.'s long correspondence with the archbishop her priorities remained the same – saving her house and family – but her style and the 'self' she fashioned developed constantly. Her greatest skill, established at the beginning of her correspondence, was her ability to combine deference and intimacy. The deferential tone stressed that she was a loyal Catholic; the intimate tone assumed that she was Archbishop Byrne's social equal. Marion believed in social standing and the power of 'important people'; the various people she claimed were interested in her case were all 'big' personalities in the world of Catholic Ireland. She had become skilled in eliciting support in this world, nonetheless, her need placed her perpetually on the periphery of that social universe rather than in its bosom and the stress of this eventually told in her letters. The effusive tone of the first few years gave way to an increasingly desperate, less coherent, imploring voice. In this final phase her letters were also less subtle. Although religion had always played a central role in her writing, it had been a positive force of reassurance and proof that she belonged. However, in her final letter she threatened to change religion, rendering it for the first time an expendable part of her life, another thing that poverty could rob. Her early letters, those that still yielded a return, were long and detailed, when her letters were greeted with silence they gradually became shorter and pathetic. Eventually she handed the responsibility of composing poverty to her daughter, who began to provide the detail and coherence. Marion appeared to reach a point of surrender followed by a literary silence.[108]

---

of the Irish Hospital Sweepstake, 1930–1987 (University College Dublin Press, 2009), pp. 36–37.

[108] King and Stringer observed a similar exhaustion of 'literary ingenuity' in the final stages of one of the serial writers they analysed from the collection of nineteenth-century British pauper letters. S. King and A. Stringer, 'I have once more taken the Leberty to say as you well know': The development of rhetoric in the letters of the English, Welsh and Scottish sick and poor 1870s-1830s' in Gestrich, Hurren and King (eds.), Poverty and Sickness in Modern Europe, p. 84.

Conclusion

Those who 'had fallen on hard times' composed long letters often offering detailed chronicles of the 'silent' struggle they had endured before seeking assistance. This was in marked contrast to the long-term impoverished who tended to write shorter bulletins from the front.[109] Poverty is relative. The impoverished wrote letters of immediate and tangible poverty, the middle classes wrote of pending or creeping poverty and of the unpalatable choices they would have to make if they were not assisted. The former resulted in visceral accounts of immediate need, the latter in a detailed chronicling of the fear of social failure. The hidden poor wrote to protect their homes, to continue their children's education or to clear debts. While they went without sufficient food or heat this was often in a bid to 'save' assets or social position because there was an overwhelming conviction, almost universally shared in these letters, that slipping down the social ladder was irreversible and disastrous.

While the impoverished from Dublin's tenements engaged with the rhetoric of 'deserving' and 'undeserving' – the ideology that drove the public and official response to their poverty – the hidden poor employed the discourse that framed the social understanding of their position – the ideas of shame, discretion and misfortune. They wrote of frustrated plans, of dashed expectations, of children's futures. They did not beg, but sought a 'loan' or 'influence'. They did not generally threaten religious defection or complain of injustice, they lamented their misfortune and emphasised how they belonged to the church, how they *were* the church. While the family economy featured prominently in these accounts of need, there was a very different level of expectation and return: these children should be 'protected' from the reality of their parents' misfortune. While they were expected to contribute, they were first guaranteed a future in their own right through secondary education. Their parents called on a world of influence – solicitors and legal documents made regular appearances in their letters. This was the universe to which they belonged; they were the widows of solicitors, the charity givers and nation builders.

---

[109] Van Ginderachter made the same observations of the begging letters written to the Belgian royal family during the nineteenth and early twentieth centuries, as if 'their misery almost spoke for itself'. M. Van Ginderachter, '"If your Majesty would only send me a little money to help buy an elephant": Letters to the Belgian Royal family (1880–1940)' in M. Lyons (ed.), *Ordinary Writings, Personal Narratives: Writing Practices in 19th and early 20th-century Europe* (New York: Peter Lang, 2007), pp. 69–84, 77.

Although on occasion their poverty was symbolic, it was often also very real. This was a world where the financial rug could quite easily be pulled from under a family. Bereavement, an illness or a run of bad luck could dry up even a comfortable family's resources relatively quickly. There was a deep social sympathy for this type of poverty because it touched a cultural nerve, particularly when it involved widows. Most people in the middle classes lived with at least a shadow of the fear that the same fate could befall them or theirs. This was part of the reason that these people received, in general, considerably more generous charitable assistance. A brief glance at the figures mentioned in this chapter compared to chapter three gives some indication of how real that difference was. However, this was also bound up with the notion that charity should not disrupt the *status quo*, on the contrary, it should 'function as a reinforcement of the existing social order'.[110] Thus, people should receive assistance in accordance with their position: a char woman from the tenements would never have received £20 and £50 cheques signed over to Marion G. and James M^cN. As the Vincent de Paul reported about a case involving 'a member of one of the professions': 'The case had to be treated with suitable delicacy. The financial help was of course, much beyond that usually accorded.'[111] This vision of charity's role was in turn bound up with class-based moral assumptions about the worthiness of these applicants. They were less 'suspect' because they were, under normal circumstances, part of the consensus that established the boundaries of legitimate poverty.

[110] Stuart Woolf argued that this view of charity emerged in the fifteenth century and there is little doubt that it still held sway in twentieth-century Ireland. Woolf, *The Poor in Western Europe*, p. 27.
[111] *Bulletin of the Society of St. Vincent De Paul*, 88 (August 1923), 239.

5   The Cost of Poverty
'To live or rather exist'

The fortunate in society earned a living, the poor 'negotiated' one, and their letters to the Archbishop of Dublin were part of, and reflected, that process of negotiation.[1] These letters 'illuminate the lives and strategies' of those whose efforts at survival were rarely recorded or respected.[2] In these letters the poor recorded their survival strategies from reliance on the family economy, charity, statutory relief, pawning, emigration, and familial break up to separation. They also document the cost of being poor and the price paid was high. It cost people their health, their emotional peace and wellbeing and often the comfort of having their family near them. As Olwen Hufton observes, 'vulnerability' was the chief characteristic of the poor because they lived under the constant threat of destitution, hunger, illness and death.[3] Poor people had no sense of financial security or of possession, they could not plan for the future; they could not count on keeping what they owned; they could not securely put down roots. The toll this life exacted is catalogued in letter after letter. These letters do not record passive acceptance or numbed existence; they bear witness to the fact that people were aware of the disadvantages they suffered and the many consequences of poverty. Hundreds of writers made the connection between poverty and physical ill health, mental anguish, and stress. The Irish poor clearly connected their poor diet with their poor health, and most understood the cycle they were trapped in: sick and unable to work, unable to work and sick, ill-clad and unable to work, unable to work and ill-clad. Ironically, the price paid was often the strategy of survival those in poverty employed. Pawning one's bedclothes, sending one's children into care or going to

---

[1] T. Sokoll, 'Negotiating a living: Essex pauper letters from London, 1800–1834', *International Review of Social History*, 45 (2000), 19–46.
[2] T. Hitchcock, P. King and P. Sharpe (eds.), *Chronicling Poverty: The Voices and Strategies of the English Poor, 1640–1840* (London: Palgrave, 1996), p. 1.
[3] O. Hufton, *The Poor of Eighteenth-Century France, 1750 to 1789* (Oxford University Press, 1974), p. 20.

England for work were all decisions made to survive that cost the poor dearly, but they had few alternatives.

'The usual thing has happened, my bed clothes are in the pawn'

Being poor meant living without any sense of possession either of life or goods; everything one owned had to play a role in survival. The pawn-shop allowed everything from wedding rings to boots to become a part of the weekly economy of making ends *almost* meet. The poor listed constantly what they had pawned or sold to keep going. The perpetual reliance on 'the pawn' meant that the poor regarded their belongings (such as they were) as commodities of existence, part of the push and pull of survival. Thomas Lyng began working in the business in the late 1930s at the age of thirteen and was the manager of the Marlborough Street pawnshop (in Dublin's inner city), which was still thriving in the 1990s. He recalled that pawning was central to working-class life in the 1930s and 1940s: 'It was a weekly business – *in* on Monday and *out* on Saturdays. *Absolutely packed* from morning to night, all with women. Very rare to see a man in the place. Pawning all kinds of sheets and bed clothing and old suits, shoes.'[4] The centrality of pawning is reiterated in many of the Irish memoirs of this period: Edith Newman Devlin, who grew up in Dublin in the 1930s, described the pawnshop as the 'economic power-house of the neighbourhood'.[5] Likewise, Elaine Crowley noted the importance of pawning to working-class survival, but she also observed the impact of this process on her mother:

Monday always came and with it my mother's bad humour. Her money was all spent, the rent-man was calling and the week to be got through. Clothes – my father's best suit, overcoat and my camel coloured coat with brown silk arrows highlighting the pleats – were taken from the wardrobe, scrutinized for soiling, creases, missing buttons or any wear and tear; repaired, brushed, sponged and pressed, put into a large brown paper bag and taken to the pawn.[6]

While her mother asserted that 'pawning was no disgrace', Crowley recalled that she used her maiden name when pledging; 'a useless' attempt to hide her shame and embarrassment.[7] For Crowley the clothes

---

[4] K. Kearns, *Dublin's Lost Heroines: Mammies and Grannies in a Vanished City* (Gill & Macmillan: Dublin, 2004), 29.
[5] E. Newman Devlin, *Speaking Volumes: A Dublin Childhood* (Belfast: The Blackstaff, 2000), p. 75.
[6] E. Crowley, *Cowslips and Chainies: A Memoir of Dublin in the 1930s* (Dublin: Lilliput Press, 1996), p. 30.
[7] Ibid.

released from the pawn never felt the same again 'something was gone from them'.[8] Máirín Johnston's memoir highlights that this was not just the strategy of the impoverished or unemployed, many with 'good jobs' in the two main employers of the city (Guinness's Brewery and Jacob's Factory), also needed to pawn:

Nearly everyone in our street went to the pawn, and not just the people in the tenements ... On Monday mornings, Mr Murray's in Ardee Street would be packed with women staggering under the weight of men's suits, shoes, watches, clocks, blankets, sewing machines, children's clothes ornaments and gramophones.[9]

The Irish experience of pawning is similar to that of the British working class; it was a weekly part of the taut working-class budget and largely managed by women, although it might often involve the pawning of a man's 'Sunday suit' or everybody's blankets.[10] In 1942, writing in the wake of a pawnshop strike in Dublin, the Irish republican and socialist, Peadar O'Donnell reflected on how it had 'sent a shiver through a lot of little people', He explained to his middle-class readership: 'The most pawned article of all is the Sunday suit ... The same suit, the same pawnbroker, the same weekly loan – the thing is eternal.'[11] He described how the poor staggered from one source to the next, never quite having enough to relax the relentless cycle of scrimping. In his account the Monday 'pawn pound' may only last until Thursday, when the children's clothes would be surrendered taking them 'out of circulation' until the Unemployment Assistance was paid on Friday and the suit would be released on the Saturday and so on. As Melanie Tebbutt argues, while pawning failed to conform to middle-class ideas of thrift and household management, it was in fact a clear example of organising resources and prioritising needs that required planning and budgeting.[12]

In December 1936, Charles F. wrote from Dublin's Corporation Place as a 'fond father' of two children. His four-page letter summed up how poverty literally stripped people of their belongings. His family was surviving on 16/- Unemployment Assistance, which was exactly the amount he was entitled to as a married man with two dependent

---

[8] Ibid.   [9] M. Johnston, *Around the Banks of Pimlico* (Dublin: Attic Press, 1985), p. 62.
[10] M. Tebbutt, *Making Ends Meet Pawnbroking and Working-Class Credit* (New York: St Martin's Press, 1983), p. 6.
[11] P. O'Donnell, 'People and Pawnshops', *The Bell*, 5 (December 1942), 206–209. This cycle is reiterated in Edith Newman Devlin's childhood memoir of growing up in Dublin in the 1920s and 30s. Newman Devlin, *Speaking Volumes*, p. 75.
[12] Tebbutt, *Making Ends Meet*, p. 17.

children.[13] As Charles explained, 'on this account mostly I am unfortunly unable to buy boots or shoes for myself my wife and children'. He informed the archbishop of the shoe size of his entire family, including himself, pointing out that his 'little lads toes are out on the street'. This he believed had made the child sick:

Quite recently I had a child very ill to some extent this was caused by insufficient clothing. We are practically lying on the boards of our bed just because we have no matterass and I can assure your Grace the usual think has happened, my bed clothes are in the Pawn Office.[14]

For Charles the 'usual thing' was to pawn what you had in order to eat and pay rent. The strategy of pawning clothing and bedding inevitably left people vulnerable to colds, coughs and chills. It also meant they did not have the clothes in which to seek work or go to school. In 1923 Frances L., whose husband was being treated for tuberculosis, wrote to the archbishop 'I am unable to take up any position as I have not clothes to do so with neither can my little girl go to school as she is in a like position (see Figure 5.1).'[15] She was sent £2.

In June 1926 Mr Eamon K. revealed how the chain of pawning could lead to a series of bad luck. He and his four children had been receiving a food ticket of 3/6 from the Vincent de Paul. He was hoping to join his brother in America to find work, however, he had given his wife his 'inside clothing'

to pledge for 2/- to get food and light for the Children and the result was I got a severe cold and fearing it would come serious on me and prevent me when I get my ticket getting to America I stayed in bed on the following Sunday . . . the Gentleman of the St Vincent De Paul came with my Wifes ticket and seen me in bed and when they went back to the society they reported it and consequently they ceased to give any further relief to my children. I was laid up until the following Friday and my 4 Children are all laid up now with the Whooping cough and had no food or fire for the past 4 days only dry bread and a small drop of tea I have no one to help me or my wife and children untill I go to America and I hope and trust in God I will be able to do good for them your Holiness I never miss mass only when I am really sick and I go to my duties every month regular.[16]

---

[13] See schedule of rates of Unemployment Assistance Act, 1933 (46), Attorney General, *Irish Statute Book*. www.irishstatutebook.ie/1933/en/act/pub/0046/print.html#sched1 accessed 10 March 2015.

[14] Mr Charles F., X Corpo Place, Dublin (city), 4 December 1936. DDA, AB 7 CC, Box 6.

[15] Frances L., X Lennox St., Dublin (city), 12 February 1923. DDA, AB 7 CC, Box 1.

[16] Mr. Eamon K., X Elliot Place, Dublin (city), 21 November 1926. DDA, AB 7 CC, Box 2.

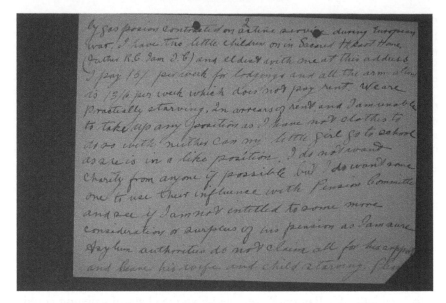

Figure 5.1 A section of the letter written by Frances L., X Lennox St., Dublin to the Archbishop of Dublin, 12 Feb. 1923.

Eamon's letter has the hallmarks of truth – he provided details about his medical examination at the American consul and he named the disease that had struck his family – his letter also revealed the stress of an existence dependent on pawning even one's underclothes. Deciding to stay in bed when ill could have dire consequences in a world where one was constantly monitored and judged. Evidently, Eamon believed that the Vincent de Paul volunteers had regarded his 'taking to the bed' as a sign of laziness and the entire family had paid as a result. Indeed, in 1925 the society noted 'we experience much difficulty in discriminating where families are concerned, the heads of which may be of doubtful character, and whose application would not be entertained but for the children'.[17] The very phraseology used highlights the haphazard nature of such discrimination; a person of 'doubtful character' – this was not certain, it was a 'doubt' – could be cut off as a precaution. In a world determined to weed out the 'malingerer', doubt could be damning for all concerned.

---

[17] 'Supplement for Irish Conferences', *Bulletin of the Society of St. Vincent De Paul*, 90 (November 1925), 15.

The strongest motif that emerges from these letters of need is that of nakedness: poverty stripped literally and figuratively.[18] Letter after letter records the impact of no clothes, insufficient clothes and clothes in the pawn. While the references to nakedness often formed part of a rhetorical strategy as 'ciphers of extreme distress',[19] insufficient clothing was a persistent problem for the poor. There were countless references to the insufficient clothing and bedding of the poor in Irish charitable reports well into the 1950s. Few questioned that clothing, footwear and bedding were real and pressing issues for many working-class families. In 1931, the vice-president of the council of Vincent de Paul railed against the attitude that poverty was inevitable and hence there was 'nothing calling for surprise in the sight of a multitude of poor families suffering depriv- ation of decent housing, suitable clothing and even sufficient food'.[20] The fact that a working-class wage was also often insufficient to cover clothing was a common lament and poor quality or scant clothing is a recurring theme in Irish childhood memoirs. Kearns Blain recalls: 'Da's pay came through the post every two weeks but his wage did not cover the cost of rent, fuel, candlelight, food or new clothing for any of us. Ma wore the same shabby skirt and jumper and broken shoes for years. Her threadbare coat lost all of its warmth.'[21]

Many of the letters featured in this chapter record the impossibility of living on the available government or municipal payments, documenting the need to beg, pawn and borrow to survive while unemployed. In 1935, the president of the Cork council of the Vincent de Paul noted that for a father with three children (and that was a relatively small family) Unemployment Assistance of 16/- was 'inadequate to enable him to give his family proper food, not to speak of clothing and other necessities of life'.[22] In fact, the rate of allowances was considerably smaller for married men living in rural areas where the maximum rate, based on a wife and five or more dependents, was only 12/6 per week. Furthermore, the few married women that qualified were only entitled to 12/- if living in rural

---

[18] Peter Jones noted that clothing stands alongside ill health as one of the strongest motifs in English pauper letters of the late eighteenth and early nineteenth centuries, P. J. Jones, '"I cannot keep my place without being deascent": Pauper letters, parish clothing and pragmatism in the South of England, 1750–1830', *Rural History*, 20 (2009), 31–49, 32.

[19] Ibid., 33.

[20] The Vice-President of the Council read the paper 'The Society and Catholic Action', see, 'Supplement for Irish Conferences', March 1932, *Bulletin of the Society of St. Vincent De Paul*, 97 (April 1932), 9.

[21] A. Kearns Blain, *Stealing Sunlight: Growing up in Irishtown* (Dublin: A & A Farmar, 2000), p. 7.

[22] 'Supplements for Irish Conferences', *Bulletin of the Society of St. Vincent De Paul*, 100 (November 1935), 10.

Ireland and 18/- if living in the county borough or in the borough of Dun Laoghaire in south County Dublin, despite having the same number of dependents.[23] The differential between the rural and urban rates was to take into account the rental markets. However, those that wrote to the archbishop who were in receipt of this payment and living in Dublin tended to be paying rents of between 7/- and 9/- in the 1930s, which represented almost fifty per cent of their welfare payment. The main charities, such as Vincent de Paul and the Sick and Indigent Room-keepers' Society, constantly noted that their resources were being used to supplement inadequate welfare payments and that rent, particularly, though not exclusively, in Dublin, was the main issue of concern. In 1935 the Dublin-based Roomkeepers' Society claimed that 80 per cent of its cases were in receipt of full benefit from government or municipal funds.[24]

In 1943 *The Bell* magazine published a series of articles entitled 'Other People's Incomes' in which they featured Mrs K., a thirty-seven year old mother of six children, whose husband was an unemployed labourer. They lived in Dublin's tenements on '27s. 6d. a week Home Assistance and six food vouchers value 1s. 9 ½ d. each'.[25] Despite all the privations Mrs K. had to endure, the article noted: 'Clothes are Mrs K's greatest worry . . . she has nothing left to sell so she "has to bank on being able to touch the heart of the Vicens-man"'.[26] The Roomkeepers' Society also regularly supplied grants to those in need of clothing either to attend school or seek employment.[27] The poor who wrote to the archbishop may well have indulged in images of nakedness because it helped to emphasise their need, but it was also undoubtedly true that keeping themselves and their children adequately clothed presented a constant challenge in urban and rural Ireland. In June 1923, Mrs Annemaire N., a widow with nine children, wrote from Carlow looking for help to maintain her children in school:

I am humbly placing my case before you to see if you could possibly help me to keep the children to school the 3 eldest are at present preparing for their confirmation I have 4 going to school at present and I could send 2 more if I had a little means to get Clothes etc-[28]

[23] See schedule of rates of Unemployment Assistance Act, 1933 (46), Attorney General, *Irish Statute Book*. www.irishstatutebook.ie/1933/en/act/pub/0046/print.html#sched1 accessed 10 March 2015.

[24] D. Lindsay, *Dublin's Oldest Charity: The Sick and Indigent Roomkeepers' Society, 1790–1990* (Dublin: The Anniversary Press, 1990), pp. 114–116.

[25] Compiled, 'Other People's Incomes - 3', *The Bell*, 7 (October, 1943), 55–62, 58.

[26] Ibid., 61.   [27] Lindsay, *Dublin's Oldest Charity*, p. 117.

[28] Mrs Annemarie N., Myskall , Co. Carlow, 1 June 1923. DDA, AB 7 CC, Box 1.

Annemarie lived on two acres and her husband had worked as a plough-man. She was able to supply references and was sent £1 through her parish priest. Peter Tyrrell, who also grew up in 1920s Ireland near Cappagh, Ahascragh, County Galway, recorded in his haunting memoir that his lack of clothing resulted in his committal to Ireland's industrial school system:

Dad lost his job in the spring and we couldn't go to school, because we had no clothes. I missed the school very much and the lunch which the teacher gave us was very nice indeed. She also gave us a sweet every day. We were always asking Mother to let us go back to school and we were told that very soon we would be getting a parcel of clothes from the States ... The parcel of clothing did arrive, but it was too late. An inspector for child welfare came to inform my parents that we would be all taken and confined to a Catholic home where we should be given a good education and taught a trade, that is all the children under fourteen years.[29]

Over fourteen years later the issue of children's clothing for school still featured as a concern for Ireland's impoverished: in 1935, Mrs B. wrote that her nine 'Children are like little Pagans dont know what school or Chapel is owing to their been barefooted and naked in Clothes, SS Vincent De Paul give me a 4/- order for food but says they have no wardrobe in their Conference.'[30] Johnston recalled that the poor of 1930s Dublin often helped each other, including the lending of clothes to go to Mass or a job interview.[31] In his childhood memoir, Frank O'Connor specifically mentioned his father's refusal to go to Mass when his good clothes were in the pawn: 'I also hated the pawning of the blue suit, because it meant that Father stopped going for walks or to Mass – especially Mass, for he would not have dreamed of worshipping God in anything less dignified than blue serge.'[32] In 1939, Anne C. explained that her family 'often have to stop in bed three days a week to keep warm and my child has to stay away from school'. Her husband had been out of work for more than six months and was in receipt of 16s. 9d. relief from the Labour Exchange 'out of which I have to pay 10/- a week rent leaving six- and six pence to keep myself Husband and little Girl 12 years of age in food for a week'. Like so many other writers, she had sought advice and assistance from the local priest, who had given her 'a bag of coal and some tea and sugar Bread' and told her to 'put my name down for the Society of Vincent De Paul'. She had heard nothing from the Vincent de

[29] D. Whelan (ed.), P. Tyrrell, *Founded on Fear* (Dublin: Irish Academic Press, 2006), p. 5.
[30] Mrs J. B., X Fern's Road, Kimmage, Co. Dublin, 6 December 1935. DDA, AB 7 CC, Box 6.
[31] Johnston, *Around the Banks of Pimlico*, p. 63.
[32] F. O'Connor, *An Only Child* (London: Macmillan, 1961), p. 32.

Paul and exclaimed 'it is terrible that such things are allowed in a Christian country'. She feared that her husband was 'near out of his mind' with the strain of their situation.[33]

In fact, the Vincent de Paul, while better known for supplying small money grants and provisions such as coal, also provided clothing, but it seems this was often harder to obtain. Also, the clothes redeemed from charity vouchers or dockets carried a stigma that was deeply resented and avoided. Angeline Kearns Blain recalled the quality of clothes received from the Vincent de Paul: 'The charity had all the clothes made in the same colour and the same style. The badly made clothing was the colour of horseshite gone green.'[34] In her mother's hands these clothes became exchangeable assets: 'Our mammies, smart as they were, bundled up the uniforms and headed off for the pawnshops to pawn the ugly habits for ready cash...Their parents, in spite of their wants, had too much pride to allow their children to wear the garments of stated and avowed deprivation.'[35] Similarly, Phil O'Keeffe observed of the poor children in her inner-city Dublin neighbourhood of the 1930s, 'the shoes that were given to them by nuns from the various convents disappeared as quickly as they had come, pawned or sold to pay for more essential things'.[36] Clothes were political and refusing to be identified as poor was a passive act of resistance and a deliberate choice to use the meagre resources available in a way the poor thought appropriate and most useful. There were many ways in which the poor could reshape assistance to fit their needs.

The pawn ticket also served as a type of currency when begging – it was like a paper trail of desperation, proof that the need was real. Mrs B., describing herself as 'Catholic mother', regarded the fact that she had pawned all she owned as a sufficient indication that her case was desperate and worthy. She was upset that her empty house was not enough for her parish priest:

Everything that I had in my place of birth sold and pawned to get my Children food we have not abed to lie on only what is infected with bugs and dirt and still one is told by there [their] Catholic Priests there are people worse off than me[37]

Mrs Maeve M., from Little Denmark Street, wrote because she was expecting a baby and all her 'baby colus' and 'bed colus' were in the pawn. She closed her short letter by offering her pawn tickets as her testimony: 'Well father I am sending you the pawn tickets to show you

---

[33] Anne C., X James Street, Dublin (city), 2 January 1939. DDA, AB 7 CC, Box 7.
[34] Kearns Blain, Stealing Sunlight, p. 175.   [35] Ibid., p. 177.
[36] P. O'Keeffe, Down Cobbled Streets (Dingle: Brandon Publishers, 1995), p. 119.
[37] Mrs J. B. X Lr. Kevin St., Dublin (city), 28 March 1932. DDA, AB 7 CC, Box 4.

that i am not telling lies.'[38] Thus even the documentation of pawning was made public, part of what was required to bargain and prove need. The use of pawn tickets as 'proof' was not an unusual part of the charity repartee. In 1933, Timothy B. complained that his priest had refused to supply him with the necessary card for his application to the archbishop: 'he made no effort to find out if my case was genuine or not he did not even give me a chance to show my rent Book or Pawn tickets'.[39]

'The Landlord is pressing me for the rent'

More than food, the hunt for rent dogged the lives of the poor, the roof over their heads loomed constantly in their worries. The Vincent de Paul claimed that the rents the poor were charged were 'outrageously high' and that the 'threat of eviction is a cloud ever present before their eyes'.[40] In Dublin, the Roomkeepers' Society repeatedly debated excluding rent as grounds for assistance, but it was never possible as the issue was so central to the poor.[41] The middle class wrote to the archbishop to save their 'homes'; the working class spoke in terms of a place to live. The emotional and physical security implied by the word 'home' rarely featured in the letters of the impoverished. In 1931 Mrs Eileen D., whose baby had died after birth, wrote on behalf of her five other children. They were surviving on a relief ticket of 17s.6d. for food, but had 'No Rent ... and the Children are in a very bad way they are in their Bare feet and Very little Clothing on them my self and Husband have to go to 7. oc mass on Sunday morning we are in such a way.'[42] While charitable and state agencies could be relied upon for the most basic food rations, clothing and rent were much harder to finance in this haphazard economy of dependence. Liz O'G, a pianist recovering from muscular rheumatism, had been unable to work during her illness and as a consequence her family had 'met with great reverses' and were 'scattered owing through arrears of rent'.[43] In 1927, Mrs O. L. of Phibsboro,

---

[38] Mrs Maeve M., X Little Denmark St., Dublin, (city), 3 March 1937. DDA, AB 7 CC, Box 6.

[39] Mr Timothy B., X Meath St., Dublin (city), n.d. c. 1933. DDA, AB 7 CC, Box 5.

[40] President of the Council of Ireland's address at the Quarterly Meeting, 22 February 1931', Supplement of Irish Conference, April 1931, *Bulletin of the Society of St. Vincent De Paul*, 96 (1931), 4.

[41] Lindsay, *Dublin's Oldest Charity*, pp. 114–116.

[42] Mrs Eileen D., X Foley Street, Dublin (city), 14 November 1931. DDA, AB 7 CC, Box 3.

[43] Liz O'G. , C/o Mrs C., X Pearse St., (Dublin city), 1 July 1929. DDA, AB 7 CC, Box 2. In her first letter Liz explained that while she was only thirty-seven she was the mother of eight. She was a professional pianist and her husband had been a professional violinist

a mother of five children whose husband had been out of work for nine months, felt the strain of the 'Landlord ... pressing' for the rent.[44] Mr Walter M. wrote in 1928, because he could not live on the charity he was receiving from the Vincent de Paul: 'I am also in a very bad plight with my Landlord as I am in arrers of rent and he has told me he will have to take me to court if I cannot meet my arrers soon.'[45]

In all these letters the stress of paying for a room, not a house or a home – just a room in which to sleep and rear children – was repeatedly expressed. The standard of much of this accommodation in urban and rural areas was extremely poor. Peter Tyrrell began his childhood memoir on a rainy summer night when the rain poured in through various holes in the roof:

There was only one other room in the house, where Mother and Dad and my other two brothers slept. There were no windows in the house and the floor was cobble stone because it was intended to be a stable, but Mother once said we moved in when the old house fell down, the gable end of the old dwelling is still standing.[46]

For Tyrrell the hovel that constituted 'home' was central to the drama of his committal to Ireland's industrial school system.[47] He believed that in order to secure release from Letterfrack industrial school, the parish priest would have to visit his home and vouch for the fact that it was suitable for the children.[48] The 1926 census recorded that 22,915 families in the state were living in one-room dwellings even more cramped than Tyrrell's experience.[49]

Despite the standard of accommodation, the threat of eviction prompted many of the appeals written to the archbishop, like Mrs C.'s short letter:

Me and my six children are in a desperate state of distress and were noticed to quit our home. We are to be summoned to court for non payment of rent. This is

but his career had floundered after he spent time in Richmond Asylum. See, Lillian O'G., G.P.O. [General Post Office], College Green, Dublin (city), n.d. c. 1924. DDA, AB 7 CC, Box 1.

[44] Mrs O'L., 6 Phibsboro Ave, North Circular Rd., Dublin, 23 November 1927. DDA, AB 7 CC, Box 2.

[45] Mr Walter M., X Elliot Place, off Corporation St., (Dublin city), 18 February 1928. DDA, AB 7 CC, Box 2.

[46] Whelan (ed.) Tyrrell, *Founded on Fear*, p. 1.

[47] This connection between poor housing, poverty and child committal to the state's 'care' system is confirmed in D. Gwynn Morgan, 'Society and the schools', chapter 3, *Commission to Inquire into Child Abuse* [hereafter *Ryan Report*], (Dublin, 2009), pp. 201–244.

[48] Whelan (ed.) Tyrrell, *Founded on Fear*, p. 39.

[49] *Census of Population, General Report, 1926*, vol. X (Dublin: Stationary Office, 1934) p. 59.

not great fault of myself or my husband. If something is not done for us I will have to seek help from some other Religion.[50]

Even the lowest standard of housing in the thick of Dublin's slums was simply too expensive for the unemployed and impoverished. Mrs Molly K., a widow with four children, received £1 when she wrote from Dublin's Sheriff's street that 'owing to getting into difficulty with the rent we are sharing the floor with other People'.[51] Mrs Rachel K.'s simple letter summed up the central problem for so many people who relied upon charity and relief. Her husband was in London working, due to ill health she had had to return to Ireland, and for several months she had heard and received nothing from him. She explained: 'I get 15/- per week Relief and 3/6 from Saint Vincent De Paul and I find it very hard to manage I have to pay 10/- per week Rent.'[52] Affordable accommodation, particularly in Dublin, was scarce and rent simply claimed too much from a meagre income.[53] Hundreds of writers provided detailed accounts of their income and expenditure revealing that the disparity between income and rent could not have been bridged by even the greatest measure of prudence. While the majority of correspondents were urban and principally Dublin based, there are sufficient letters from people throughout the country to reflect the more general problem of affording a place to live and eke out an existence. In July 1939, Mrs B. H., a widow with three children, wrote from Tipperary: 'My Husband E. H. died Five years ago leaving me in debt, Five years working hard and cant make ends meet, Owing to loss of cattle all my crops melted last year ... The Land Commissioners are sent me six days notice for rent.'[54] Rural widows faced particular problems as their land holding often meant they did not qualify for the widows' pension. Mrs B.'s case struck a cord and she was sent the large sum of £51.11.3 to cover the rent. Similarly, in 1932 Jane R. from County Waterford explained that her sow had died and her fields lay fallow. She could not afford manure and was also in two years arrears of rent amounting to £90: 'if we have to sell the last few cows when they are gone what will become of us [?]'.[55]

---

[50] Mrs C., X Kilfenora Rd., off Stanway Rd., Kimmage, Co. Dublin, n.d. c. 1938. DDA, AB 7 CC, Box 7.

[51] Molly K., X Lr. Sheriff St, Dublin (city), n.d. c. 1926. DDA, AB 7 CC, Box 2.

[52] Mrs Rachel K., X York Street, Dublin (city), 5 April 1938. DDA, AB 7 CC, Box 6.

[53] R. McManus, Dublin, 1910–1940: Shaping the City & Suburbs (Dublin: Four Courts, 2002), pp. 127–128.

[54] Mrs B. H., X Cashel, Co. Tipperary, 29 July 1939. DDA, AB 7 CC, Box 7.

[55] Mrs Jane R., Island of Tarsney, Fenor, Co Waterford, 9 June 1932. DDA, AB 7 CC, Box 3.

'I am In Delicate state of health'

Illness and death helped to swell the ranks of the poor: a family managing to keep its head above water was easily capsized by the sickness of the breadwinner or his/her death. While the poor of 1920s and 1930s, Ireland did not have to deal with the nineteenth-century epidemics of typhus, smallpox or cholera,[56] typhoid and typhus remained a concern, while gastro-enteritis, scarlet fever, measles and tuberculosis continued to reap rich rewards among the poor.[57] Progress was made in the fight against infectious diseases in the 1930s, but this was largely down to medical intervention such as vaccination programmes, rather than radical improvements in the living environments of the poorest citizens. As Mary E. Daly notes, during the early decades of the twentieth century, 'Ireland failed to keep pace with the improvements in life expectancy recorded in other developed countries.' For the period between 1926 and 1935, Ireland had the fifth highest death rate, while for the period between 1945 and 1951, it had the worst in comparison to twenty-two countries in Europe.[58] Infant mortality, which was most susceptible to environmental factors, was double in urban areas where the infectious disease gastro-enteritis claimed many little lives until the late 1940s. Another indication of Irish poverty was the rural/urban dichotomy in mortality rates, and as Daly argues, this differential continued longest in less-developed countries – in Ireland the rural advantage was long lasting. She argues that this adverse mortality in urban areas 'was overwhelmingly a reflection of poverty and environmental circumstances'.[59] Mortality rates could still be mapped by the geography of poverty – the streets of death remained those inhabited by Ireland's poorest citizens in town and country.

Unsurprisingly, ill health was mentioned in the majority of letters written to the archbishop, either in passing or as a central part of an explanation of need and merit. Virginia Crossman notes that by the end of the nineteenth century, there is strong evidence to suggest the poor appreciated the power of illness to secure poor relief. Furthermore, the administrators of the poor relief system reinforced and appreciated the connection between sickness and poverty making

---

[56] J. Prunty, *Dublin Slums 1800–1925: A Study in Urban Geography* (Dublin: Irish Academic Press, 1998), pp. 153–194.

[57] M. E. Daly, 'Death and disease in independent Ireland, *c.* 1920–1970: A research agenda' in C. Cox and M. Luddy (eds.), *Cultures of Care in Irish Medical History, 1750–1970* (Basingstoke: Palgrave Macmillan, 2010), pp. 229–250, pp. 231–234.

[58] Ibid., pp. 230–231   [59] Ibid., pp. 236–237.

'medical certification ... integral to the relief process'.[60] Poor health was both a cause and consequence of poverty and the letters of the poor reveal not just an understanding of that connection but an insistence upon it. This understanding is not unique to Irish poverty letters, but has a strong and relatively long European history that indicates that the impoverished were articulating (sometimes quite strongly) the relationship between ill health, premature death and poverty since at least the eighteenth century.[61] While this narrative explanation of either ill health and/or poverty by the poor must in part be viewed as an attempt to explain unemployment, legitimise need and/or validate moral character; this does not undermine its veracity. In a world that constantly held a question mark over their heads, illness offered a chance to prove one's 'innocence', casting one as victim rather than villain of the social project. Notwithstanding the strategic value of illness, it was quite simply true that ill health caused poverty and that poverty caused ill health, disentangling which came first and why, or how they bled into each other was not the purpose of poverty letters.[62] Rather, the poor sought to have the centrality of illness to their experience of deprivation inscribed in *their* story of poverty. The fact that this rendering of poverty also created a potential moral space in which the poor could increase their bargaining power was principally because it was generally accepted that they were more susceptible to ill health.[63] Society, in general, felt uneasy when poverty opened up the deeper reality of illness and its bedfellow of social inequality, particularly when infant mortality was offered as a barometer of living standards. Contemporaries were aware that those in the lowest socio-economic bracket had a higher death rate at all ages and that infants were most often sacrificed to poverty.[64]

---

[60] V. Crossman, *Poverty and the Poor Law in Ireland, 1850–1914* (Liverpool University Press, 2013), p. 73.

[61] This is a strong theme in essays covering Ireland, England, Wales, Scotland, Germany, Austria, Spain, Denmark, and Sweden. A. Gestrich, E. Hurren and S. King (eds.), *Poverty and Sickness in Modern Europe: Narratives of the Sick Poor, 1780–1938* (London: Continuum, 2012).

[62] A. Tompkins, '"Labouring on a bed of sickness": The material and rhetorical deployment of ill-health in male pauper letters' in Gestrich, Hurren and King (eds.), *Poverty and Sickness in Modern Europe*, pp. 51–68; T. Stazic-Wendt, 'From unemployment to sickness and poverty: The narratives and experiences of the unemployed in Trier and surroundings, 1918–33' in Gestrich, Hurren and King (eds.), *Poverty and Sickness in Modern Europe*, pp. 181–207.

[63] Gestrich, Hurren and King, 'Narratives of poverty and sickness in Europe 1780–1938: Sources, methods and experiences' in Gestrich, Hurren and King (eds.), *Poverty and Sickness in Modern Europe*, pp. 1–33, 4.

[64] *Census of Population, General Report, 1926*, vol. X (Dublin: Stationary Office, 1934), p. 170.

The thousands of letters to the Archbishop of Dublin also testify to the financial cost of ill health, and how frequently the impoverished and those in the lower middle and middle classes could not afford what was necessary to restore either themselves or their loved ones to good health. Approximately thirty per cent of the population qualified for free General Practitioner care through the dispensary system.[65] Many other people, not considered eligible for free treatment, struggled to pay basic medical bills.[66] Dublin and urban dwellers in general had more medical options at their disposal and seemed to find it easier to qualify for free care. Rural dwellers were often further from the free dispensary network and found it hard to qualify if they possessed any land. Based on a sample study of patients in Cork County Home and District Hospital in 1925, Donnacha Seán Lucey concluded that for the long-term patients 'sickness and poverty went hand-in-hand'.[67] Simultaneously, Lucey notes that the 1920s 'reaffirmed attempts to extract payments from patients requiring treatment in local authority hospitals with a policy of rigorous inquiry into the situation of all patients'.[68] This added increased uncertainty for many people, who now had the worry of whether they would qualify for care and, if not, how much they would be pressurised to pay for services.[69] This worry surfaced repeatedly in rural letters to the archbishop, for example, Mary E. B. from County Fermanagh, a widowed-mother suffering from breast cancer for which she needed an operation, explained:

we have a small farm of land & when you have any land you can not get on red line so I have no way of paying I have only one cow since my husband died & do not like to sell him if I could help it so it would cost £15 pounds in hospital.[70]

---

[65] M. E. Daly, 'The curse of the Irish hospitals' sweepstake: a hospital system, not a health system', *Working Papers in History and Policy*, 2 (2012), 1–15, 5. www.historyhub.ie accessed August 2014.

[66] In 1942, the head of the Irish Medical Association noted that fifty per cent of the population was treated through the dispensary system. J. P. Shanley, 'Presidential Address', *Journal of the Medical Association of Éire* [hereafter *JMAÉ*], 11 (September 1942), 1–4, 4.

[67] D. S. Lucey, '"These schemes will win for themselves the confidence of the people": Irish independence, Poor Law Reform and hospital provision', *Medical History*, 58 (January 2014), 44–64, 57.

[68] Rural patients were to be assessed on the valuation of their property and urban patients on their wages, salaries and businesses. Ibid., p. 58.

[69] Lucey notes that the voluntary hospitals were also more focused on payment and were no longer solely operating as charities for the poor. However, by the early 1930s, Irish local authorities had paid for the care of nearly 11,000 poor patients in voluntary hospitals. Ibid., pp. 60–65.

[70] The 'red line' is probably a reference to the 'red ticket' system, whereby people had to apply for free medical treatment i.e. a medical card. Mrs Mary E. B., Fermanagh, c. 1924. DDA, AB 7 CC, Box 1.

The cost of ill health in financial terms was a growing concern for the poor and unemployed internationally during this period. Katrin Marx-Jaskulski's study of unemployment in rural Germany between 1900 and 1930 also points to the pervasiveness of this theme. She argues that 'illness is one of the most important reasons for economic hardship', because of the loss of earnings and the direct and indirect costs of sickness.[71] She highlights, for example, the speed with which a household economy could sink in the wake of illness. German poverty letters document how the poor argued that ill health in the family hampered the breadwinner's ability to seek employment, thus compounding and accelerating the slide into irredeemable poverty.[72] This is also a striking feature of the Irish letters explored here.[73]

Mrs Bronagh D.'s simple missive from Donegal underscored the direct connection between ill health, the inability to work and support legal dependents:

Mrs Bronagh D.
   Gortin Sth
   Castlefin

                                               1–4–24
   Dear Dr Byrne
   I am a Poor Catholic and a ~~must~~ Sufferer from a Sore Leg and has one Child and has no Support I would like to get some Help as I am unable to work I would like in your Kindness you would Send me a little help and May God Reward, you and I will Pray for you always.
   I Remain Dear Dr Byrne
   Sincerley yours
   Mrs Bronagh D.[74]

Almost fourteen years later Nuala B., writing from Listowel in County Kerry, struck a similarly stark and plaintive note while underscoring the vicious cycle of ill health and poverty:

I am writing to you for a little charity as I badly kneed [need] it, as I am only a poor girl in bad health, I am only after coming from a Sanatoruim.

---

[71] K. Marx-Jaskulski, 'Narratives of ill-health in applicant letters from rural Germany, 1900–30' in Gestrich, Hurren and King, (eds.), *Poverty and Sickness in Modern Europe*, pp. 209–223, 220.

[72] Ibid., p. 218.

[73] For a detailed discussion see, L. Earner-Byrne, '"Dear Father my health is broken down": Writing health in Irish charity letters, 1922–1940', *Journal of the Social History of Medicine*, 28 (2015), 894–868.

[74] Mrs Bronagh D., Gortin Sth, Castlefin, (Co. Donegal), 1 April 1924. DDA, AB 7 CC, Box 1.

I am very poor & badly off having nothing to keep me when I lost my health. I am at home now.[75]

Tuberculosis was epidemic in Ireland during this period, and treatment in a sanatorium offered one of the few chances of recovery prior to the 1950s.[76] However, the lack of any aftercare services was a major problem people faced; people like Nuala had little chance of staying well without subsequent support.

Henry G., a father of ten children (aged two months to fifteen years), explicitly linked his wife's declining health with his inability to secure constant employment, which resulted in her becoming malnourished: 'My Missus has fell [fallen] into bad health and unable to be about through lack of nourishment which two Doctors here will certify – all through myself being unable to obtain constant employment.'[77] The mention of two doctors provided authority and support to his claim. It also indicates that he had spoken to his wife's doctors when she was hospitalised and that they had confirmed a reading of her health as one caused by poverty. Similar to the narratives emanating from German unemployed men during this period, Henry offered few specifics regarding his wife's illness.[78] The focus of his appeal was less on the illness than its cause and costs. While he provided a detailed explanation of his budget and the claims made upon it (rent, food, fuel, light and children's clothes), it was his wife's illness that provided the emotional lever in his appeal. It started his letter, punctuated it in the middle – 'Sir I had even to come so low as to have to pawn my clothes to take my missus home from Hospital which leaves me unfit as a christian to attend Mass' – and provided his post script – 'P.S. Sir my Missus has been ordered to the Country for a change of Air but I cant raise the money to send her.'[79] His unemployment had forced him to pawn his clothes in order to do his duty by his wife, but he was still unable to provide her with the means for her recovery: adequate nutrition and fresh air.

In 1925, Dr Brian Crichton lamented the inability of some mothers to breastfeed their infants 'either on account of some failure on their part or as I regret I only too often see due to lack of nutrition or even the verge of

---

[75] Miss Nuala B., X, Listowel, Co. Kerry, 16 February 1939. DDA, AB 7 CC, Box 7.

[76] Ireland's tuberculosis epidemic peaked in 1904 and between 1927 and 1937 Ireland had the slowest percentage decline of mortality from the disease out of twenty European countries surveyed. G. Jones, 'Captain of all These Men of Death': The History of Tuberculosis in Nineteenth- and Twentieth Century Ireland (Amsterdam: Rodopi, 2001).

[77] Henry G., Keogh Square, Inchicore, Dublin, n.d. c. February 1932. DDA, AB 7 CC, Box 3.

[78] Stazic-Wendt, 'From unemployment to sickness and poverty', p. 189.   [79] Ibid.

starvation.'[80] Indicating that little changed throughout the 1920s and 1930s, a study of infant mortality carried out by Dublin Corporation and the Department of Local Government and Public Health 1938, confirmed that 'many expectant mothers were suffering from malnutrition'.[81] While the medical community began to focus on malnutrition from the 1920s onwards, it had been a cause of concern among charity workers and public officials for decades. Charles Cameron, the chief medical officer of Dublin between 1874–1921,[82] noted the monotonous and deficient diet of the average labourer of bread and tea and claimed it contributed to fatal illnesses.[83] In 1938, Dr William Fearon estimated that a weekly income of 30s. was necessary to keep a person, and of this amount 10s. should be spent on food.[84] However, fifty per cent of the population had a weekly income of 20s. or less and spent 8s. or less on food.[85] In the same year, Paula C., whose income fell well short of Fearon's benchmark, complained about the meagre charity she had received of 'Bread and tea and a Baby of one year got a bottle of tea'.[86] While, doctors were probably telling their poor patients that inadequate nutrition was contributing to their ill health, they were also undoubtedly observing the impact of their diet first hand.

Food or the lack of it also looms large in the many childhood memoirs. Kearns Blain mentions the battle for sufficient food constantly, concluding, '[w]hen the choice had to be made between paying off the debt or putting food on the table, mammies went with the grub'.[87] Johnston directly linked her family's bad health with a poor diet, noting that she had been told by the doctor at the factory where she worked in the 1930s, that she needed increased calcium. She recalled: 'The lack of variety in

---

[80] Brian Crichton, 'Infant mortality in Dublin', *Irish Journal of Medical Science*, 4 (1925), 302–305.

[81] M. J. Russell, *Report on the State of Public Health in the City of Dublin for the Year 1938* (Dublin, 1939), p. 67.

[82] See, H. Andrews, 'Cameron, Charles Alexander' in J. McGuire and J. Quinn *et al.*, *Dictionary of Irish Biography*, *Volume*, pp. 271–273; 'Obituary', *Irish Times*, 28 February 1921.

[83] C. A. Cameron, *How the Poor Live* (Dublin, 1904), pp. 10–13.

[84] William R. Fearon worked for the British Food Ministry and the Food Investigation Board (UK) between 1917 and 1919. He returned to Dublin in 1921 to a fellowship in Trinity College Dublin and was employed by the Saint John's Ambulance Brigade to design an ideal diet for mothers in the 1930s. St John's Ambulance Brigade, *St. John's Ambulance Brigade in Ireland: Welfare Department 15 Years of Work, 1920–1935* (Dublin, 1935); Patricia M. Byrne, 'Fearon, William Robert' in J. McGuire and J. Quinn et al., *Dictionary of Irish Biography*, vol. 3, pp. 733–734.

[85] W. R. Fearon, 'The national problem of nutrition', *Studies: An Irish Quarterly Review*, 27 (1938), 12–23.

[86] Paula C., X Talbot St., Dublin (city), *c.* 1937. DDA, AB 7 CC, Box 7.

[87] Kearns Blain, *Stealing Sunlight*, p. 156.

our diet left us vulnerable to all kinds of ailments within and without. In wintertime our fingers, toes and heels swelled up and became red and itchy.'[88] Tyrrell punctuated his narrative with descriptions of good and bad meals, when a meal consisted of more than bread and tea he recorded it in forensic detail. His separation from his parents mixed with his memory of the fine meal he had beforehand:

The goose was boiled with onions, and the soup, which was served in mugs, was delicious. It was by far the best meal we ever had and I can never remember eating so much. After dinner, Dad prayed out loud and thanked God for everything he had sent us. He asked God to be merciful and kind to his children in their new Catholic home.[89]

Each important occasion was recorded through a prism of the food eaten; Easters, Christmases, and letters from home, all became about the food. In fact, the reader is only aware of the years passing by the descriptions of the food consumed at annual events: 'For breakfast on Easter Sunday we have a boiled egg, with tea and an extra slice of bread and marmalade, and margarine. There is roast lamb boiled potatoes and turnip. Supper the same as for any other Sunday plus a slice of cake.'[90] It is clear that food was central to Tyrrell's process of recall and often helped to blunt or accentuate more traumatic experiences.

If one considers premature death as the ultimate manifestation of ill health, then the numerous widows that put pen to paper ranked as the most obvious victims. In February 1936, Mrs Mary B. framed her husband's death in terms of the illness that had caused it:

I hope you will pardon me for writing to you, but I have 6 children. I buried my Husband November 13th from Septic Pheunmonia My Eldest boy is 14 years my youngest girl 13 months I have 25/- relief to live on, and previous to his Death my Husband was out of work, my children are all naked.[91]

This one sentence provides a glimpse of the impact of unemployment and ill health. While Mary did not explicitly connect her husband's septic pneumonia and subsequent death to his unemployment, it is very likely there was a relationship between the two. The descriptions of men walking the streets in search of work, in all weathers, insufficiently clad, are so numerous that one can safely assume Mr B.'s chances of contracting pneumonia were increased as a result of his months of unemployment. It is clear that is how she understood the sequence of events.

---

[88] Johnston, *Around the Banks of Pimlico*, p. 104.
[89] Whelan (ed.) Tyrrell, *Founded on Fear*, p. 8.   [90] Ibid., p. 39.
[91] Mrs Mary B., X Lr Gloucester Place, Dublin (city), 3 February 1936. DDA, AB 7 CC, Box 6.

Mrs Marie P. S, also a widow, wrote in November 1928 about how her little domestic ship had sunk off the rocks of familial ill health:

My sisters all failed in health and had long illnesses & my expenses very heavy so I had to get a morgage [*mortgage*] on my house & since have sold all my silver, glass, antiques, jewellery to pay rates. Now my only surviving sister is an invalid (she taught in Malaga for 20 years) & now I have been for the past ten weeks with Acute Chronic Bronchitis. Doctor Drummond has shown them great kindness & attention without fee or reward expect our deep gratitude – The present times are very bad – the rates & chemists are pressing me far payment[92]

Familial loyalty ran deep and even a widow was expected – in this case willingly – to care for her 'spinster' sisters. Evidently, even those with silver and jewellery to sell and free medical attention, found the cost of medicines unmanageable. Indeed, Marie S. stressed that she belonged to a different class from those habituated to public charity: 'No doubt many are likewise situated but my case merits none but a private charity, & few know of my circumstances & the friends are now dead who could have helped me –.' In all likelihood she would not have qualified for the means-tested dispensary care, leaving her literally reliant on the kindness of others and her own connections and influence. Her religious connections virtually guaranteed her a favourable response: Monsignor Francis J. Wall wrote a note in support of her case,[93] describing her as 'a very respectable and industrious poor creature' and the niece of the former P.P. of St Laurence O'Toole's.[94] She received a generous cheque of £20 from the archbishop's fund.[95]

The mental stress of poverty was rarely considered by contemporaries who wrote *about* the poor. However, those who lived in persistent poverty often articulated and highlighted the mental strain it caused. The letters to the Archbishop of Dublin record the symptoms of profound stress and depression as a result of a sense of impotence and the relentlessness of poverty. While the language tended to be less precise or scientific when describing mental health problems than when writing about physical health, the idea that stress and anxiety were caused by poverty and led to mental illness was clearly and consistently recorded. Although descriptions of complete mental or nervous breakdown were relatively

---

[92] Mrs Marie S., X Pembroke Road, Dublin, 27 November 1928. DDA, AB 7 CC, Box 2.
[93] Francis J. Wall was a member of Archbishop Byrne's council of vicar-generals which met weekly with Byrne's secretaries, Patrick Dunne and Tom O'Donnell, and effectively ran the diocese. T. J. Morrissey, *Edward J. Byrne 1872–1941: The Forgotten Archbishop of Dublin* (Dublin: The Columba Press, 2010), p. 184.
[94] Mgr Francis Wall, St Mary's Haddington Road, Dublin, 11 December 1928. DDA, AB 7 CC, Box 2.
[95] Marie S. wrote to thank the archbishop for his 'generous cheque' on 13 December 1928.

rare, many writers noted the weight of worry. Joanne Bailey has similarly observed that the authors of the nineteenth-century English pauper letters 'saw economic distress as causing emotional distress'.[96] In mid-twentieth-century Ireland, mother of seven Mrs Anna L. lamented that she was 'worried to death trying to make ends meet'.[97] Mrs Marie C. provided a vivid description of ongoing stress: 'I am really distracted and am afraid my brain will snap, as I can not sleep at night, only worry, worry all the time, and trying to be brave and do my duty here.'[98] Women's descriptions of worry were remarkably physical: the brain was burning, snapping, or crushed. In 1931 Molly C. wrote on behalf of herself and her elderly sister as they feared they would lose their home of forty years: 'We are nearly mad with fear of losing our dear old home ... Its a truly terrifying strain, I often fell my heart about to stop with fear – and we are unfit for work.'[99] A mother of nine from the Island Tarsney, County Waterford, warned that she could '...now bear no more' and felt her 'brain burning out with trouble'. She had written twice before and received no reply and she asked 'am I such a mere nothing'?[100]

'I have one daughter my only support'

The importance of the family economy to households in Europe until the early twentieth century has been well documented and a closer examination of how it functioned has become part of the desire to understand how 'people on the margin of subsistence actually did to survive'.[101] If, as David Vincent convincingly argued that, poverty is 'a matter of human relationships which were conducted in a series of contexts from the family outwards',[102] then inevitably the story starts with the family economy. Even the relatively well off often relied on the income of children prior to marriage and dreaded and/or forced the delay of marriage for fear

---

[96] J. Bailey, '"Think wot a mother must feel": parenting in English pauper letters', *Family & Community History*, 13 (2010),12.

[97] Mrs Anna L., Desmond Avenue, Dún Laoghaire, Co. Dublin, 4 March 1922. DDA, AB 7 CC, Box 1.

[98] Mrs Marie C., X Opmantown Rd., Dublin, 7 December 1934. DDA, AB 7 CC, Box 4.

[99] Molly and Mildred C., Clarinda Park East, Kingstown (Dún Laoghaire), Co. Dublin, 15 October 1931. Ibid.

[100] Mrs Jane R., Island Tarsney, Fenor, Co Waterford, 9 June 1932. DDA, AB 7 CC, Box 3.

[101] L. Fontaine and J. Schlumbohm, 'Household Strategies for Survival: An Introduction', *International Review of Social History*, 45 (2000), 1–17.

[102] D. Vincent, *Poor Citizens: the State and the Poor in Twentieth Century Britain* (London: Longman, 1991), p. vii.

of losing that income. Sarah Deutsch has observed that 'the slim phrase "family economy"'[103] hardly does justice to what was a complex and dynamic organism that was capable of accommodating and adapting to a host of challenges that often cut across the interests of individual family members for the sake of the whole. A husband might be dispatched to London for work leaving his wife alone to cope. A mother may part with her children to an orphanage so she can work and older children might have to wait to start their own families in order to contribute to the nuclear family. A child might be required to miss school to earn money or because her clothes were needed for pawning. Older children frequently discontinued their education so they could contribute. The poet and playwright, Patrick Galvin, for example, who grew up in a tenement in 1930s Cork, noted that he left school to earn after his father's unemployment: 'My father was unemployed and the consensus of opinion was that I should look for a job after school. With Mr Goldman's help I applied for a job as a messenger-boy.'[104] Kearns Blain recalled the meaning of her first wage to her family's fragile budget: 'Ma said before I started the job to take two shillings out of my wages to spend on new clothes for myself, the rest of my pay would go for household expenses. The rent for our flat cost nineteen shillings a week, as much as I earned in a week at the factory.'[105] Elaine Crowley, who grew up in 1930s Dublin, was forced to quit school at fourteen years of age, so she could work in a factory and contribute to the family economy.[106] Johnston's mother, who was a widow, was relieved when her son quit school to become a messenger.[107]

As concepts of childhood began to evolve and school attendance regulation required children to stay longer in school, the reliance on at least the income of relatively young children diminished.[108] However, legally, it was only when a child married that a parent's claim on their wages ceased.[109] The reliance on family members was cited so

---

[103] S. Deutsch, *Women and the City: Gender, Space, and Power in Boston, 1870–1940* (Oxford University Press, 2000), p. 31.
[104] P. Galvin, *Song for a Poor Boy: A Cork Childhood* (Dublin: Raven Arts Press, 1990), p. 41. Brady notes the importance of this job for youth employment, J. Brady, *Dublin, 1930–1950: The Emergence of the Modern City* (Dublin: Four Courts Press, 2014), p. 31.
[105] Kearns Blain, *Stealing Sunlight*, p. 211.   [106] Crowley, *Cowslips and Chainies*, p. 150.
[107] Johnston, *Around the Banks of Pimlico*, p. 56.
[108] The 1926 School Attendance Act applied to all children in the Irish Free State and made school attendance until the age of fourteen compulsory. T. Fahey, 'State, family and compulsory schooling in Ireland', *Economic and Social Review*, 23 (July 1992), 375–378.
[109] F. Kennedy, *Cottage to Crèche: Family Change in Ireland* (Dublin: Institute of Public Administration, 2001), p. 125

often in the letters of both the impoverished and the middle classes that it appears almost commonplace. In 1927 Mr John C., an unemployed father of four, presented a relatively typical picture of the family economy *in extremis*. His wife was 'lying very low in Crookstown Sanaturium' with tuberculosis, his eldest daughter was running the home, which left only his daughter's meagre wages from shirt making of 6s.9d. a week. The marriage of a son had represented a severe loss to the family finances: 'I had a Boy who was a good help to us and on account of he getting married we have lost his couple of shillings which was great Benefit in Paying the Rent and Society.'[110] By the 1930s Ireland had one of the lowest marriage rates and one of the highest marital fertility rates in Europe.[111] While historians have considered the impact of the rural economy on marriage patterns in Ireland,[112] these letters provide considerable evidence that marriage in urban Ireland was often regarded as a blow to the family economy. In February 1923, Mrs Elizabeth L. noted how her son's marriage had left her desolate: 'I am asking you for a little of your ever kind assistance, I am a cripple/ through delicate health, and Rhumatism [*Rheumatism*], My Son who was my chief support got married some time ago which leaves me very desolate.'[113]

Even the relatively well off paid a high price for disowning errant children. In the early 1930s a civil servant, Mr H. A. M., from the affluent suburb of Monkstown in south County Dublin, wrote about how he had incurred debts as a result of difficulties with his nine sons. He had been ill for six months with pleurisy and pneumonia. His difficulties were further compounded by the fact that he had thrown one of his sons out of the family home:

It was only quite recently that, acting on the advice of my Parish clergy, I felt bound to put out one of my elder sons who was consorting with a Protestant family and attending their place of worship. By this action I inflicted on myself a serious monetary loss at the very worst time. For this very large family I am the only breadwinner as two of my daughters who are being married this summer keep their small earnings for their weddings. Last year another elder son was

---

[110] Mr J. C., X Foley St, off Talbot St, Dublin (city), 29 August 1927. He wrote previously on 24 July 1927 and Fr Gough wrote on his behalf on the same day. He received £1. DDA, AB 7 CC, Box 2.

[111] M. E. Daly, *The Slow Failure: Population Decline and Independent Ireland, 1920–1973* (University of Wisconsin Press, 2006), p. 4.

[112] See, for example, T. W. Guinnane, *The Vanishing Irish: Households, Migration, and the Rural Economy in Ireland, 1850–1914* (New Jersey: Princeton University Press, 1997), pp. 193–240; A. Cosgrove (ed.), *Marriage in Ireland* (Dublin: College Press, 1985).

[113] Mrs Elizabeth L., X York St., Dublin, 21 February 1923. DDA, AB 7 CC, Box 1.

permanently invalided out of the Navy without pension and is on my hands
since.[114]

Despite a secure and relatively well-paid job, his large family had to
contribute in order for the unit to survive. He was provided with £200
to see him over his difficulties, a huge sum in comparison to most of the
donations meted out by the archbishop.[115]

Mrs May McD.'s letter was a standard description of how an entire
working-class family 'mucked in' to survive. She wrote in May
1924 from the heart of Dublin city requesting financial assistance to
start a business with her son, who had been discharged from the Irish
army. She explained that she had only one daughter bringing in any
money and there were five in the family. She believed she was relatively
lucky to receive £1 a week from her son when he was in the army as,
'there were not many Soliders [soldiers] who gave their Mothers that',
She wished to reward him with a little business.[116] There were certainly
those that wrote of being 'abandoned' by children who refused to help
the wider family. Mrs Mary C. wrote in early 1924 to explain: 'I never
hear from my son who went to America and here I am house keeping for
a man and his children for the sake of a shelter and bit to eat.'[117]
A widow from Cork noted that she had 'only one boy at present earning
(for over a year now) 3 are idle & I have 3 going to school & 2 gone away
I never hear from'.[118]

This reliance on the earnings of children and siblings was also
expected by those assessing the merits of a case. In 1934, a parish priest
dismissed a case for charity on the basis that

their only daughter is employed in a fish shop on Grafton St. Again their only son
carried on a well-known Ladies hair-dressing establishment in O'Connell St.
Although the son is married. Still if they are so badly off, I am sure he would
come to their rescue. He visits them occasionally in his motor car[119]

Mrs Jane F., writing in 1924 from the 'Front Parlour' on Russell Street in
Dublin, explained: 'I have one daughter my only support who is now

---

[114] Mr A. M., X Belgrave Sq., Monkstown, Co. Dublin, n.d. c. April 1934. DDA, AB 7
    CC, Box 4.
[115] The sum £200 is recorded in the top left-hand corner of Mr A. H. M.'s letter.
[116] She received £5 towards her new business and she noted she had received £7 from the
    archbishop's predecessor, Dr Walsh. Mrs May McD., X Wellington Rd., Mountjoy
    Street, Dublin (city), 16 May 1924. DDA, AB 7 CC, Box 1.
[117] Mrs Mary C., X St Joseph's place, off Dorset St. Dublin (city), 12 February 1924. Ibid.
[118] Mrs Karen M., X Convent Road, Doneraile, Co. Cork, n.d. c. 1933. DDA, AB 7 CC,
    Box 4.
[119] Fr Denis Keogh, The Presbytery, 59 Eccles St, Dublin (city), 14 September 1934. Ibid.

dismissed from her job arriving to slackness in trade.'[120] However, when she applied for outdoor relief she had been refused on the grounds that she had a daughter fit for work. Others failed to qualify for relief in Ireland because their husbands had emigrated in search of work. In 1931, Mr Paul M. wrote from London on behalf of his wife and two children, who were in Dublin 'in a condition of semi-starvation'. He needed to return to his wife because she and the children were being denied relief because he was absent: 'The relief people as a matter of fact have threatened to put her case into the hands of the NSPCC trying to make a desertion case out of it.'[121] This confirms Sarah-Anne Buckley's research into the operation of the National Society for the Prevention of Cruelty to Children [hereafter NSPCC] during this period. She argues it increasingly used 'child protection' to punish parents it deemed did not fulfill particular parental norms or constitute conventional domestic units. Furthermore, the society put increasing efforts into tracking down deserting or absent husbands to ensure their financial contribution to the family.[122] It is little wonder that the NSPCC and the 'relief people' – the administrators of Home Assistance – formed an alliance to ensure fathers fulfilled their role as breadwinner.

This family economy, however, had one central hidden player – the working mother – absent from the official record, she played a crucial role in the survival of many working-class families.[123] Pat Thane's observation that, for the British working class, 'the male breadwinner norm was fictional in many cases', holds equally true for Irish working class women as, indeed, does her claim that those who worked at the coalface of charities or social assistance accepted this fact.[124] Marilyn Silverman noted, in her study of Irish working class culture during this period, that women's work, both waged and unwaged, was 'crucial for avoiding poverty and maintaining respectability'.[125] Beverly Stadum succinctly

---

[120] Mrs Jane F., Front Parlour, X Russell St., North Circular Road, Dublin, 11 February 1924. DDA, AB 7 CC, Box 1.

[121] Paul M., Tiler Street, York Road, Kings Cross, London NI, England, 26 June 1931. DDA, AB 7 CC, Box 4.

[122] S. Buckley, *The Cruelty Man: Child Welfare, the NSPCC and the State in Ireland, 1889–1956* (Manchester University Press, 2013), pp. 88–90.

[123] Kennedy, *Cottage to Crèche*, pp. 72–75; S. Deutsch, *Women and the City*, p. 287; C. Breathnach, 'The role of women in the economy of the West of Ireland, 1891–1923', *New Hibernia Review*, 1 (2004), 80–92.

[124] P. Thane, 'Visions of gender in the making of the British welfare state: The case of women in the British Labour party and social policy, 1906–1945' in G. Bock and P. Thane (eds.), *Maternity and Gender Policies: Women and the Rise of the European Welfare State, 1880s–1950s* (London: Routledge, 1990), pp. 93–117, 97.

[125] M. Silverman, *An Irish Working Class: Explorations in Political Economy and Hegemony, 1800–1950* (University of Toronto Press, 2001), p. 296.

put it: 'Poor women lacked the "luxury" of dependency on others.'[126] Edward Gibson's 1862 lament that poor Irish women's options were limited to 'marry – stitch – die – or do worse', remained depressingly pertinent to poor women of 1920s and 1930s Ireland.[127] Galvin recalls how his mother's earnings saved the family: 'When my father was unemployed and my mother scrubbed floors for a living – that was a miracle. Her strength held us. Her gentle hands cradled us in miracles.'[128] The centrality of women's work is recorded in hundreds of the letters written to the archbishop. The poor mother sewed, mended, cleaned, sold fruit and coal, and took in lodgers/boarders and fostered children.[129] She was the one who often arranged work for her children or their placement with relatives or in 'care', if her work meant they could not be properly cared for in the home. She tended to be the family's representative when it came to negotiating additional resources from charities, shopkeepers or facing down the landlord.

While the family economy was vital to the survival of many individuals who clustered together to create these vulnerable units, it had many inherent weaknesses and in some senses left people more vulnerable to the vagaries of life and the injustices of economic forces. The family economy could not protect its members against the exigencies of the life cycle, in fact, the ebb and flow of family life heightened exposure to its dictates.[130] The mother may have been essential to the family, but motherhood in itself increased her chances of poverty and reduced her ability to protect herself.[131] Mrs May H. wrote to the archbishop in 1926 summing up the bind for many poor mothers:

I have got two little children the eldest a little girl is after been very bad with measles but is better thank God and my little boy is bad with them now and owing up to I am been expecting to be a mother soon again I am prevented from getting

---

[126] Stadum, *Poor Women and their Families*, p. xvi.

[127] E. Gibson, 'Employment of women in Ireland', *JSSISI*, 3 (1862), 138–143.

[128] Galvin, *Song for a Poor Boy*, p. 13.

[129] The range of activities undertaken by Irish women differs little from that recorded internationally for poor women. P. Mandler, 'Poverty and charity in the nineteenth century metropolis: an introduction' in P. Mandler (ed.), *The Uses of Charity: The Poor on Relief in the Nineteenth-Century Metropolis* (Philadelphia: University of Pennsylvania Press, 1990), pp. 1–37, pp. 11–12; B. Stadum, *Poor Women and their Families: Hard Working Charity Cases, 1900–1930* (New York: State University of New York, 1992), p. 55.

[130] S. Woolf, *The Poor in Western Europe in the Eighteenth and Nineteenth Centuries* (London and New York: Methuen, 1986), p. 3.

[131] E. Peretz, 'The costs of modern motherhood to low income families in interwar Britain' in V. Fildes, L. Marks and H. Marland (eds.), *Women and Children First: International Maternal and Infant Welfare, 1870–1945* (London and New York: Routledge, 1992), pp. 257–280.

any little work myself as I would like to do because my Husband has always been a very good man to me and the children only he cant get work of any kind'[132]

Young children were expensive, and when they arrived one after another with barely a year's breathing space, there could be up to twelve years before any of them could financially assist the family unit. Motherhood exposed many women to ill health and morbidity, weakening their physical and, on occasion, mental strength. Tyrrell observed that as a result of repeated pregnancies his mother 'became very fat, her hands and joints swelled up. She suffered terribly from rheumatism. Although she was only about thirty-eight, Mother was now an old woman. She cried with pain all the time'.[133] In this harsh world of uncertain employment, insufficient wages, poor diet and insecure accommodation, people aged prematurely and could only rely on their children for a relatively short period. In 1914, David Chart summed up the pitfalls of the family economy for Irish contemporaries:

From the continual financial stress, which turns the laughing girls of the poorer Dublin streets into the weary-eyed women of the tenement houses, no real relief comes until the children begin to grow up and contribute some part of their earnings to the family exchequer ... However, later on, when the boys and girls grow up and marry, the parents, now growing old, are thrown on their own resources and, though they have no one but themselves to clothe and feed, sometimes pass through a period of considerable penury before the Old Age Pension, "God's bounty," as some of the poor call it, descends on them at the age of 70.[134]

In view of Ireland's high celibacy rate, it is hardly surprising that adult siblings often remained together to form non-marital family units. These sibling units were found all over Ireland until at least the 1990s. In June 1938, Miss Maria B. wrote from Limerick to seek assistance for herself and her two siblings:

Since my father's death (1920) it has been a great struggle for me to keep a home for a delicate brother & a sister who has only a small position (serving) & it is only by giving music lessons I am barely able to do so. As the years go on I feel less able to continue.[135]

In many cases throughout the country such family structures endured relatively well until old age and/or ill health threatened the equilibrium

---

[132] Mrs May H., X Hardwicke Place, Dublin (city), 31 May c 1926. DDA, AB 7 CC, Box 1.

[133] Whelan (ed.) Tyrrell, *Founded on Fear*, p. 5.

[134] D. A. Chart, 'Unskilled labour in Dublin: Its housing and living conditions', *JSSISI*, 13 (1914), 160–175, 172.

[135] Miss May B., X Harbour View, Limerick, 6 June 1938. DDA, AB 7 CC, Box 7.

and then the fact that there was no new generation, no children, to help out left the unit very vulnerable.

'...to be near my kiddies'

If families were supposed to rely on each other for financial support, they were also often forced to 'scatter' themselves in times of crisis, in order to survive. Jeremy Boulton, in a study of poor families in eighteenth-century London, argued that the poor adopted a strategy of 'deliberate fragmentation.'[136] In Ireland also it was not uncommon for families to break up, either because of the institutionalisation of children or the emigration of a spouse in search of work. Buckley has traced the increasing use of institutionalisation by the NSPCC in the twentieth century as a solution to various social, economic and moral problems it identified as afflicting impoverished families.[137] Many of the letters to the archbishop record the emotional and practical implications of this strategy; spouses who emigrated in search of work did not always return, others were sorely missed by the remaining family which struggled on alone. Children placed in orphanages or industrial schools often never returned to the family home, instead emigrating upon release. Few can be unaware of how many Irish children were committed to industrial schools during the twentieth century, however, little is known about the dynamics of committal.[138] What were the pressures experienced by families to surrender their children? If there were other options, did they avail of them? How did committal happen outside the courts? The letters written to the archbishop provide many examples of how illegitimate children were sent to orphanages or 'rescue' homes. However, the majority of cases of committal related to legitimate children with living parent/s, who could not afford to keep them for various reasons.[139] This should be no surprise as we know that ninety per cent of Irish children were committed to industrial schools on the grounds of poverty.[140] Nonetheless, to view that process from the perspective of the families themselves reminds us of the human dimension of an unforgiving system.

---

[136] J. Boulton, '"It is Extreme Necessity That Makes Me Do This": Some "Survival Strategies" of pauper households in London's West End during the early eighteenth century', *International Review of Social History*, 45 (2000), 47–69, 48 and 66.

[137] Buckley, *The Cruelty Man*, pp. 70–109.

[138] See, for example, *Ryan Report*, and *Dublin Archdiocesan Commission of Investigation Report* [*Murphy Report*] (Dublin, 2009).

[139] For example, Peter Tyrrell who was taken from his parents because he had missed school due to a lack of appropriate clothing. Tyrrell, *Founded on Fear*, p. 5.

[140] *Commission of Inquiry into the Reformatory and Industrial School System 1934–1936: Report* (Dublin, 1936), p. 10.

Writing sometime between 1926 and 1929 from the North Circular Road in Dublin, Mr James R.'s simple missive is a stark example of how 'normal' it was for poor children to be sent to Catholic orphanages:

> i wish to bring my Case to your attention i am a married man with five children two of them are now in Dominick Street Orphnage and i am out of work i would get work if i hade a Bicycle in the Evening Herald Office, Dear Father i be very thankful to you if you could give me a little Help to get one, and May God Look over you and watch over you; i am sending you a copy of references, His Grace My Lord Archbishops I have the honour to be your Grace Most humble and Obedient Servant, James R.[141]

James R. mentioned the fact that he had chosen two children to send away almost in passing or as proof of his poverty: so deep was the acceptance of this necessity, that retrieving these children was not even central to his plea (although it was obviously implied with a job he could support them). The likelihood of children being sent away was increased considerably on the death or incapacity of a parent, particularly a mother. In September 1938, Mr Anthony F. successfully appealed for funds to help him to return to England to find employment or, at the very least, to avail of the better unemployment benefit there.[142] He had been earning £15 a week working for a British firm based on O'Connell Street in Dublin, but as a result of 'tariffs etc.' (a reference to Ireland's economic war with Britain) the company had pulled out of Ireland. Anthony explained, 'after losing my position my dear wife got ill and died last year'. This bereavement heralded the collapse of his family:

> Most of the money I had managed to save went in Doctors bills etc., and being out of work, I was compelled to give up my house and put my children into schools three of them girls going to Lakelands Sandymount, one to St Patricks, Kilkenny, and one to St Vincents, Glasnevin.[143]

He went to England where he found temporary work, however, he returned to Ireland 'to take up a position in Messrs Clery & Co, for a London firm as a Demonstrator, and in the hope I would find a permanent job to be near my kiddies'. This job was also terminated after a matter

---

[141] James R., X Annamoe Rd, North Circular Road, Dublin, n.d. *c.* 1928. DDA, AB 7 CC, Box 2. He supplied the archbishop with a reference transcribed in his own handwriting from his ex-manager at the Dublin waterworks. In this reference he retained his own personalised use of capitals and quirks of grammar, for example, he had his employer describe him as 'very Decent and Respectable man he is at Present in low circumstances and is worthy of any help that can be given him'.

[142] He noted in his letter that he was in receipt of 10/- relief in Ireland (out of which he paid 7/- a week for a room), but would qualify for 19/- in England.

[143] Mr Anothony F., X Belvedere Road, Drumcondra, Dublin, 6 September 1938. DDA, AB 7 CC, Box 7.

of months and he was 'compelled to exist on 10/- per week' out of which he paid '7/- a week for a room'. He often went without proper food and had abandoned hope of staying near his children. Following investigation, his parish priest supported his story, confirming that he was 'a decent, sober, & good-living man', which secured him £4 to go to England – far from his 'kiddies'.[144] Emigration as a strategy against poverty has been so ubiquitous it has almost been overlooked, in Anthony F.'s case it is barely commented upon. More often than not this strategy was noted in passing and fatalistically accepted. Mrs Kay O'S., for example, lamented that her husband had failed to find work and 'now he is going to England after xmas to work with gods help'.[145] We have already seen that the archbishop's resources were deployed to reunite families separated by failed emigration and that others wrote to him about the impact of emigration upon their families. In 1927, Mrs Agnes S. wrote from Liverpool asking to be rescued from an 'emoril [immoral] husband'; she had no means to fund her return to Ireland.[146] In May 1938 the archbishop was asked by the Dublin Union outdoor relief office to contribute to a fund, along with Vincent de Paul, the Roomkeepers', the Stranger's Friend Society and the British Legion, to help reunite a family by sending a mother and five children to New Zealand, where the father had emigrated.[147] However, many more mothers were effectively widowed by emigration.

Mothers were also placed in a position where surrendering their children to an orphanage was the only option. In February 1923, Mrs Frances L. wrote in desperation: her husband had been a soldier in the Royal Dublin Fusiliers and a patient in Richmond Asylum since the 'European War' (World War I).[148] She had three children, two of whom she had placed in North William Street Orphanage, and she was surviving on 13s.6d. a week from the army, while paying 15s. for lodgings. She was sent £2, but when she wrote again in August it was to inform the archbishop that she had secured a position as a maid in County Louth. However, to take up this position she was sending her last daughter to the orphanage.[149]

[144] Fr Patrick Fahey, 59 Eccles St., Dublin to Fr. Glennon, 7 October 1938. Ibid.

[145] Mrs Kay O'S., x Dean St., Dublin, 30 December 1939. Ibid.

[146] Mrs Agnes S., X Thomas St., Garston, Liverpool, England, 6 December 1927. DDA, AB 7 CC, Box 2.

[147] Fr Kealy, The Presbytery, 24 Killarney St., Dublin, 11 May 1938. DDA, AB 7 CC, Box 7.

[148] Richmond District Lunatic Asylum (Hospital) was opened in 1815 in Grangegorman in North Dublin and has operated continuously as a facility for mental health care.

[149] Mrs Frances L., X Lennox Street, Dublin (city), 6 August 1923. DDA, AB 7 CC, Box 1.

In 1932, a child survivor of this family strategy wrote to the archbishop for help establishing himself in London. David O'N. explained:

I am the youngest in the family and when the crash came to my Father in 1929 Mother could not afford to keep me ... or to pay for my education or anything so I had to be sent to Letterfrack to the Industrial School and I only got out at Christmas when I got out I got a temporary job as a Conductor on the Great Northern Busses ... I left that a month ago when the summer rush was over.[150]

Saint Joseph's industrial school in Letterfrack, Connemara, County Galway, operated between 1885 and 1974 during which period 2,819 boys passed through its doors.[151] It was renowned for its harsh regime. Peter Tyrrell, who was an inmate in the 1920s, recorded the brutal violence inflicted on small children.[152] If David O'N. had just 'got out' of Letterfrack, this means he was only sixteen years of age.[153] He followed the course of so many other ex-industrial school children and emigrated to London in search of work.[154] He was an incredibly vulnerable young adult, totally unaccustomed to the 'outside world'. Although he had acquired skills in Letterfrack ('I played the Euphonium in the Band at Letterfrack and I also know shorthand and Typewriting and some office work and Carpentering'), he did 'not know London at all'. The archbishop sent him £3 for employment agency fees and bus fares. He wrote a month later with news of a job, which he had secured through the Irish community in London, as a general gofer at the Badminton Club at Earls Court for £1 a week. All he needed now was some help to retrieve his 'good suit' and 'only coat' from the pawn. His vulnerability cries out from this letter:

I have suffered so much since coming to London that I will please God never allow myself to get into this dreadful position again. I have learned an awful lot since coming to London and it has done me a lot of good.[155]

---

[150] David O'N., X Westbourne St., Sloane Sq., London, England, 9 September 1932. DDA, AB 7 CC, Box 3.

[151] *Ryan Report*, p. 289.

[152] P. Tyrrell, 'Early Days in Letterfrack: Memories of an Industrial School Boy', *Hibernia*, 28 (July 1964), 8; Whelan (ed.) Tyrrell, *Founded on Fear*. His account was confirmed by the commission of inquiry in 1999, see, *Ryan Report*, pp. 288–394.

[153] It was a notable feature of Irish industrial schools that once a child was committed they were invariably detained until sixteen years of age, irrespective of the age of committal. M. E. Daly, '"The Primary and Natural Educator?": The role of parents in the education of their children in independent Ireland', *Eire-Ireland*, 44 (Spring/Summer, 2009), 194–217, 198.

[154] Whelan noted that emigration was 'integral to the industrial school experience'. Whelan (ed.) Tyrrell, *Founded on Fear*, p. xxvi.

[155] David O'N., X Westbourne St., Sloane Sq., London, England, 16 October 1932. DDA, AB 7 CC, Box 3.

His 'Guardian Angel' continued to watch over him and sent him £2 to settle his account at the pawn. The temporary recourse of sending a child to an industrial school in this case, and in many others, caused the permanent fracturing of this family. David's other siblings were scattered across London, but through poverty were of little practical assistance to each other.[156] David had made a brave and good start at establishing an independent life for himself, but many like him failed in that endeavour and ended up in some other form of institutional care.

The lucky few could count on relatives to temporarily take their children and thus give them a chance of maintaining their family in the long run. In 1922, Mr P. M. wrote about how his health 'failed' after his business collapsed and he had spent four weeks in hospital. However, he was ever since 'idel [idle]' and 'sick and weary walking about in search of employment ... all in vain:'

I would not feel the pinch so badly but when I think on my 3 little children whom I was obliged to let go to the country to my brothers place and he is a man who has already too many children of his own and I fear he will be taking them back to me one of these days. My wife is obliged to go out to business in order that we may exist + keep a roof over our heads. This indeed is a shame for me, yet I can assure your Grace I am quite helpless for want of employment.[157]

He offered himself as a servant to the archbishop. He received a kindly refusal with a cheque for £5.[158] Similarly, Mr A. Byrne wrote 'as a poor Catholic father' of nine children who had had to send three of his children to live with his mother until he found some kind of work.[159] Johnston, who was born in 'the Liberties' in inner city Dublin in 1931, recalls her family's struggle to stay together in the face of unemployment: 'Granny was a godsend during the years of unemployment and without her my mother said that we would have ended up in homes.'[160] By 'homes' she meant orphanages or industrial schools. When her mother turned to the Vincent de Paul 'in desperation', as it was not possible for her to raise her children on the paltry Home Assistance she was awarded, she was horrified by the suggestion that she surrender her children to various orphanages:

---

[156] He commented that his sister (who worked as a 'Lady's help') gave him grocery parcels when she could, but she had little.
[157] Mr P. M., X Summerhill, Dublin (city), 10 March 1922. DDA, AB 7 CC, Box 1.
[158] There is a draft of the Archbishop's response to Mr P. M. offering great sympathy and £5.
[159] Mr A. B., Benburb St., Dublin, 21 September 1938. DDA, AB 7 CC, Box 1.
[160] Johnston, *Around the Banks of Pimlico*, p. 56.

Two men came this time to investigate and gave her two and six, but seeing that her situation was so bad that she was likely to be a constant drain on their resources, they began pressurising her into putting us into Artane Industrial School for boys and Goldenbridge Convent for girls. There we would be assured of a good Christian upbringing as well as food and shelter. My mother couldn't believe her ears so she politely told them not to bother coming again, that she would manage.[161]

Not all mothers were able to reject such painful 'solutions'.

Many of the strategies working-class families employed to ward off destitution resulted in them running the gauntlet of forcible separation from their children. When Johnston's unemployed father had brought his children out busking to raise money, he was 'intercepted by the ISPCC' and questioned in the police station.[162] Frank O'Connor believed his mother, who had been raised in an orphanage, stayed in an abusive marriage because if she left: 'she would have had to take a job as a housekeeper and put me into an orphanage – the one thing in the world that the orphan child could not do.'[163] Kearns Blain described how the 'sanitary lady inspector' was sent to 'spy on the neighbourhood':

She wore a tweed uniform and carried a briefcase. She told Ma and the other women that she had come to inspect the living conditions of every household ... She told Ma and others that if they neglected their children, she had the power of authority from the Irish government to take the children away. The children would be put into a boarding school until they reached the age of sixteen. Her threats mortified Ma and the other mammies.[164]

Thus, according to these memoirs, mothers were 'mortified', horrified, and willing to remain in dangerous domestic situations rather than part with their children. What do these letters reveal about how people *felt* about having to surrender their children to 'care'? Boulton noted that the paupers of eighteenth-century London expressed little emotion about such separation; he wondered if this 'reduced level of family sentiment' could be described as a survival strategy in itself.[165] There seems little doubt that any feelings of loss were tempered by relief – relief that *someone* could care for your child and that you were freed to earn or care for those children left behind. However, many parents did express a desire to remain near their children, others refused to separate from them. There were many reasons why people may not have expressed

---

[161] Ibid.

[162] Buckley notes that child begging was regularly reported the NSPCC as evidence of parental neglect and often resulted in the institutionalisation of the children concerned. Buckley, *The Cruelty Man*, pp. 91–92.

[163] O'Connor, *An Only Child*, p. 36.   [164] Kearns Blain, *Stealing Sunlight*, p. 108.

[165] Boulton, '"It is Extreme Necessity That Makes Me Do This"', 66.

any feelings of regret, pain or longing. Their children were sent to Catholic orphanages or industrial schools and they were writing to the Catholic archbishop; they may have believed separation was best for their children's welfare and that it was a temporary expediency. It is notable that Tyrrell recalled his father asking God 'to be merciful and kind to his children in their new Catholic home', but his memory at the actual point of separation was of his parents' screams.[166] Others expressed their anxiety regarding the loss of their children in a different way – anger: anger at the system, anger at charity and anger at their church. Anger was often easier to express than pain and righteous anger demanded respect and helped to preserve fragile self-esteem.[167]

'She said she was put down as a beggar and it is still playing on her mind'

Ultimately, of course, the most common price of poverty was dignity. The system itself cost people their pride, their sense of self and in many respects it helped to maintain the social inequality that relegated people to the margins. Furthermore, Johnston's memoir testifies to the fact that there was little discernable difference for the poor between the way statutory or charitable resources were dispensed: suspicion permeated both forms of assistance. When Johnston's mother became a widow in 1932 (prior to the widows' pension), she felt treated like a criminal by the local relieving officer:

> The relieving officer, Mr Lawless, came round from the dispensary in Earl Street to investigate our circumstances and to satisfy himself that we were deserving cases. He interrogated my mother as if she had committed a crime by becoming a widow and having all these children that the state would now have to provide for. He gave her a card and told her to call to the dispensary the following Wednesday and collect two and six and warned her that if she gave any false information she would be liable to a hefty fine or imprisonment.[168]

Furthermore, Johnston's mother recoiled against the imperative that the poor must engage in a dramatisation of their need, which required their homes to become a stage set of poverty, displaying no signs of comfort. Of the Vincent de Paul's home visits, she recalled that 'anything in the line of food, clothes or ornaments was to be hidden'. This aspect of performance is why her mother objected so strongly to charity: 'We were

---

[166] Whelan (ed.), Tyrrell, *Founded on Fear*, p. 5.
[167] L. A. Pollock, 'Anger and negotiation of relationships in early modern England', *The Historical Journal*, 47 (2004), 567–590.
[168] Johnston, *Around the Banks of Pimlico*, p. 56.

at all times expected to project the image of total destitution ... Simply being poor wasn't enough, we had to act poor, and that was one of the reasons why my mother wouldn't look for charity.'[169] However, as Johnston's own memoir reveals, this charity encounter with its charade and suspicion was little different from her mother's experience with the relieving officer. There was little difference in the moral philosophy underlying the relief services and charities available to Ireland's poor throughout the 1920s and 1930s and the poor had to routinely engage with the full gamut of provision options in order to survive. It is interesting to note, however, that it did not have to be that way. It was possible to give without taking dignity in return. For example, both Johnston and Phil O'Keeffe note in their memoirs that the Jubilee nurses helped families in a way that did not compromise their self-respect. O'Keeffe wrote, '[T]he Jubilee nurses went about their work in a quiet unobtrusive way, and never troubled the household.'[170] Whereas Johnston observed that '[A]fter a baby's birth, the Jubilee Nurse would come around daily to attend to the mother and child ... There was absolutely nothing they wouldn't do, and so they always got a great welcome from the kids as well as the parents.'[171]

Crowley recalls how in 1930s Dublin, the poor preferred to help each other: 'gracious giving went on all over the city, all over the countr y... It had to be that way. State help was non-existent. A minimum relief system and charity doled out at the discretion of those dispensing it. Cold charity too crushing for anyone with pride. Means and morals tested charity.'[172] Nonetheless, charity *was* an essential player in the 'economy of makeshifts', plugging gaps in other forms of relief while operating on the fundamental principle of not questioning the social system that created poverty.[173] This reality was constantly sketched in the letters of the poor. Some were resigned to it, others worn out by it, and many were angered by it. Some wrote in acceptance of the monitoring, others hurt by the distrust, but all were stung by the humiliation. In the late 1930s, Edmund O'T. wrote primarily to express this sense of humiliation. His family were in receipt of 1s.6d. per week from the Vincent de Paul, whom

---

[169] Ibid., p. 62.

[170] O'Keeffe, *Down Cobbled Streets*, p. 78. Jubilee Nurses were voluntary nurses founded in 1890 who worked in the poorest areas all over Ireland. E. Prendergast and H. Sheridan, *Jubilee Nurse – Voluntary District Nursing in Ireland, 1890–1974* (Dublin: Woolfhound Press, 2012).

[171] Johnston, *Around the Banks of Pimlico*, p. 70.

[172] Crowley, *Cowslips and Chainies*, p. 165.

[173] For an original explanation of the term see, Hufton, *The Poor of Eighteenth-Century France*, pp. 107–127.

he conceded were 'so hard run that they cannot give any more'. However, this meant his family existed on '½ a loaf each day to be divided among the 5 of us'. He believed that to beg was 'to make little' of one's self, something he would not do 'were it not necessary'. He complained that his 'convert wife' was still wounded from her last visit to the archbishop's palace: 'she returned home … not the better of it for a long time. She said she was put down as a beggar and it is still playing on her mind'. However, Edwund O'T. argued that he did not have the luxury of pride: 'We are gone so far that we realy don't care what becomes of us only for the sake of our young children. I am sorry to have to write all this to you but a Broken heart compels me.'[174] Similarly, Liz O'G., the pianist recovering from muscular rheumatism whose family had been farmed out to various relatives, was furious that she had been doubted by the archbishop's secretary:

Your letter received, at which I was greatly surprised I have called on several occasions to the Palace, but have never received any assistance, as stated in your letter. As you told me I should require two priests references, + now I have procured those, you refuse to assist me. I little thought I would ever be necissiated [necessitated] to humiliate myself, to look for assistance from anyone. But this incidence has quite finished me, with the Catholic religion.[175]

She was correct. She had written previously in 1924, but she had not received any funds on that occasion either.[176]

Many who wrote to the archbishop were weary of telling their story of poverty and shopping around for assistance and were not afraid to tell him about the realities of bartering for charity. Mr Michael K., writing from the Legion of Mary's Dublin Hostel for homeless men, the Morning Star, described himself as 'not used to this degrading life of poverty'. He was a farmer's son 'born of decent parents, God-fearing, and respectable'. He had had to pretend to 'join' the Protestants to get assistance from the Salvation Army and admitted that when he failed to beg the price of his bed he felt 'inclined to throw myself into the River'.[177] He was angry that he had been put in a position where he

---

[174] Mr Edmund O'T., X Charlemont Row, Harcourt Road, Dublin (city), n.d. c. 1937. Edmund wrote a total of fifteen letters between 1935 and 1938, his wife wrote two letters and they wrote two letters together. In total they received £19.10.0. See, DDA, AB 7 CC, Box 6 and DDA, AB 7 CC, Box 7.

[175] Liz O'G., c/o Mrs C., X Pearse St., Dublin (city), 3 July 1929. DDA, AB 7 CC, Box 2.

[176] See, Liz O'G., G.P.O. [General Post Office], College Green, Dublin, n.d. c. 1924. DDA, AB 7 CC, Box 1. On this letter it was indicated that she received 'the usual card'.

[177] The Salvation Army came to the Dublin in 1888 and offered assistance regardless of religious affiliation, which made Catholic charities particularly anxious. J. V O'Brien A City in Distress, 1899–1916 (Berkley and Los Angeles: University of California Press, 1982), p. 168.

had to 'deny' his religion and remonstrated that God 'placed me, and all idle men, on earth, not to starve, but to "earn our bread by the sweat of our brow"'.[178] As Peel argues, 'the idea that character or self-reliance was sufficient protection against disaster' was 'an idea that the poor had always questioned'.[179]

Other writers placed their emphasis on the dislike of 'begging', keenly aware how that necessity undermined their social credibility. In 1937 Mrs A. C. of Kilcoole, County Wicklow was resigned to the requirements of poverty and begging. Her husband was 'Idle & there are seven' in the family living on '13/- Releif [relief] and pay Rent out of that'. She found there were no charities in Wicklow:

I have sent to the Convent here for a little help but the Rev Mother Turned the child From the door & said she had nothing. Of course I would not like to send again. The children are hungry & Cold & on account of it Being xmas time I would like to have a bit of Dinner at Least on xmas Day as they get nothing but a bit of Bread & Tea.[180]

She had sent her children begging and was well used to approaching the parish priest herself, but was reluctant to ask for assistance too often. This sense of quickly becoming tiresome was often expressed and captures the bind the poor found themselves in: how to survive when you have nothing without eventually wearing the patience of benefactors. It was simply not within her gift to free her family from begging. She concluded:

I would be ever grateful to your grace if you could possible give me a Little help be it ever so small & sincerely hope I have not offended your grace/ by writing This Begging Letter & am sorry to have to do so but I cannot do anything else I Beg to Enform your Grace that I & my Family are of good Character as the Rev. Father O Riordan Knows me well.[181]

Evidently, Fr O'Riordan vouched for her as she was sent £2 from the archbishop's funds, which would have allowed her limp over Christmas. Within the system there were no longer-term remedies for families like Mrs A. C's. In 1932, Mr J. M. also sensed that after three years of unemployment people were tiring of his need: 'I am realy and truly tired of this useless and wastefull life I am 3 years out of employment which is

---

[178] Michael K., 'Morning Start' Hostel, North Brunswick St., Dublin (city), 27 September 1932. DDA, AB 7 CC, Box 3.
[179] Peel, *Miss Culter*, p. 76.
[180] Mrs A. C., X Sea Rd., Kilcoole, Co. Wicklow, n.d. *c.* December 1937. DDA, AB 7 CC, Box 7.
[181] Ibid.

a lot to long and now that I see that people are getting tired of me been idle so long they will not help me anymore.'[182]

During this period the state's system was changing, slowly and clumsily, from one of 'relief' to 'welfare'. Historians are increasingly questioning how fundamental this shift was either in principle or practice, particularly for those in need. It is revealing that the majority of people who mentioned benefits like Home Assistance and Unemployment Assistance failed to distinguish between these payments, still referring to them all as 'relief' (even after 1929 in Dublin, when the Poor Law finally ceased to operate in its final enclave in the Free State). Furthermore, the introduction of such payments, in particular, Unemployment Assistance did not end the need for the unemployed to petition charitable resources. People struggled with the dictates of the various sources of funding they could tap, most of which were insufficient to protect a family from the sharpest edges of poverty, but nonetheless did not allow recipients to augment the funding. This was just another paradox the poor had to negotiate – they were condemned if idle, but punished if they tried (even through work) to better their circumstances while on benefits or charity. In May 1936, Robert B. from Dublin explained how he had been in 'Reciept of the ablebodied mens assistance', but that had not saved his family from eviction during the winter. Forced to reside with his father-in-law, Robert tried to supplement the insufficient benefit by selling newspapers, but was reported 'to unemployment assistance authoritys so they stopped my relief'. This left his family totally dependent on charity again, thus he 'applyed to St Vincent De Paul Society . . . for a grant of ten shillings (10) three weeks ago and they promised me it Friday Last . . . and they never came'.[183] Similarly, Vincent A. outlined in detail why his 20/- Unemployment Assistance was insufficient: 'I pay 10/- weekly for a furnished room, and 1/- weekly insurance leaving a balance of 12/- to provide for my wife, self and four young children.' Nonetheless, he only qualified for one food ticket of 3/- from the Vincent de Paul, which was not enough to get the nourishment required for his sick daughter. Familiar with the system of suspicion, he supplied a 'medical certificate to show the genuineness of this application'.[184] Writing from the 'Back Parlour' of a house on Greville Street in Dublin, Mrs Margaret J. lamented her own honesty as this had rendered her family ineligible for statutory relief:

---

[182] Mr James M., X O'Brien's Place, Haddington Rd., Ballsbridge, Co Dublin, 15 September 1932. DDA, AB 7 CC, Box 3.
[183] Mr Robert B., X New Lisburn St., Dublin, 11 May 1936. DDA, AB 7 CC, Box 6.
[184] Mr Vincent A., X North Circular Rd., Dublin, 16 February 1936. Ibid.

I appeal through you to the S. Vincent De Paul Ozman House I have put in a number of appeal to them but got no response they pass by the door My Husband got no Reilief [—] owing to me being doing a few days work to help me I was Honest enough to tell them I have 6 small children.[185]

The system encouraged neither honesty nor initiative – it trapped people in poverty and then blamed them for displays of dependence. The irony was not lost on its captives.

In fact, the majority of those who wrote to the archbishop were patching a living together by appealing to various official and unofficial sources, scraping a living by negotiating the 'mixed economy of welfare', often a time consuming and demoralising experience.[186] Mr Peter G. explained to the archbishop that his income of 22/6 per week was insufficient to feed seven: 'I have made seven applacations to the conference of Saint Vincents De Paul but the President has ignored all of them. Ive also made several applacations to the RoomKeepers Scty [society] but they have turned me down I think it is a shame.'[187] The following year, Mrs B., a married mother of two, outlined how she had been refused assistance from the Vincent de Paul Society on the grounds that she was receiving the maximum of 16/- Unemployment Assistance. She had written to the parish priest, but the letter had been ignored, 'now Rev Father as the last rescourse I am writing to you to see if you can send anyone to help me'.[188] This life of 'makeshift' wore people down, it made them run around in circles, it made them angry. In May 1937, Mr Harold M. informed the archbishop that he was new to begging, new to the indignity of it all, and articulated a sense of shock and betrayal:

I respectfully wish to inform "Your Grace" I called upon my parish priest to get a Recommendation to your grace to obtain some help for myself my wife and two Children.
He gave me a Room Keepers Paper and an order for food for 2/6.
I never applied for in my life for assistance to anyone.
The Roomkeepers paper will take 2 or 3 weeks to Investigate.
I owe Rent and the 2/6 order is welcome but it could not help me or my family. I am a respectful Roman Catholic trying to bring up a family as good as I can. I always earned my living and I feel insulted by being offered 2/6 from a Roman Catholic priest.

---

[185] Mrs Margaret J., X Grenville St., Dublin, 17 December 1939. DDA, AB 7 CC, Box 7.
[186] T. M. Adams, 'The mixed economy of welfare European perspectives' in B. Harris and P. Bridgen (eds.), *Charity and Mutual Aid in Europe and North America Since 1800* (New York; London: Routledge, 2007), pp. 43–66.
[187] Mr Peter G., X Bow Lane, James Street, Dublin, 5 November 1935. DDA, AB 7 CC, Box 6. He wrote in April 1932 also see DDA, AB 7 CC, Box 3.
[188] Mrs B., X Lr. Gloucester St., Dublin, c. May 1936. DDA, AB 7 CC, Box 6.

Without any disrespect to my Church or His Grace as its head I and my family have finished with the teachings of my Church from today for my life.[189]

Mrs J. B., from Dublin's inner city, wrote jaded with 'fighting for an honest living for my little hungry family I am Continually turned down by the Catholic sources'. She was raising seven children on a relief ticket which

when 7/- rent and 2/6 Coal is taken from it leaves 17/6 for 9 of us to live on which I need not say most Rev. Fr. Is impossible we are half starved and Sometimes we do be a Couple of days without having a Cup of tea during which time I am Compelled for the sake of the children to apply to [for] help to the Parish only to be told by St Vincent de Paul that I am not entitled to help from them as I am drawing the Relief goes then to other Catholic sources and they want a note from district Priest when one goes to see him he has another Excuse to make although he knows you and your Case well, still he is unable to do any thing for you[190]

It is little wonder, when trapped in the no man's land of charity, people used whatever means they could to extract assistance. Frederick K.'s letter, written in 1938, evokes vividly the sense of impotence and hopelessness such relentless searching induced:

I am writing this letter to tell you of my trouble. I have a wife and 3 Children and I am only living on £1-3-0 per week My wife went to Rev. Father Dunn ... for assistance and he told her to write to OZMOND HOUSE conference of ST FINBAR ST VINCENT-DE-PAUL and they would not help us saying they had no FUNDS but they are givening it to other people in the street. My wife also sent her FORM to the SICK and Rooms Keepers Society and it is in 6 weeks and they never visit us. We also went to the Children Hospital Temple street for Bread and they told her that the Sisters would visit her that was two months ago and they never came. Well Father we are in a very bad way as all of my home is in the Pawn trying to keep my wife and children. My wife in the most HOLY-ROSARY-SODALITY and I myself being to the HOLY-NAME-SODALITY but my wife is thinking of given it all up and Changing her Religion and the Childrens as her Religion will not help her in anyway.[191]

The strategies employed were manifold, but most who wrote to the archbishop had tried several options and failed. He truly was the last port of call.

---

[189] Mr Harold M., X Eccles St. Dublin (city), 14 May 1937. DDA, AB 7 CC, Box 7.
[190] Mrs J. B., X St Kevin's St., Dublin (city), 28 March 1932. DDA, AB 7 CC, Box 4. She received £5.
[191] Mr Frederick K., X Penders Court, Upr Dorest St, Dublin (city), n.d. c. December 1939. DDA, AB 7 CC, Box 7.

Conclusion

From these letters we get a sense of how the experience of poverty was reconstructed by those who lived it, even if the authors felt obliged to shape their telling according to the demands and moral codes of the charity market. There are omissions in the poor's account of poverty that may be explained by the process of negotiation. Very few letters record assistance received from neighbours or friends, and prostitution as a survival strategy is not recorded. The memoirs of the poor stress the reliance on each other; for example, Johnston recalls that '[W]e lived in each other's ears. We depended upon each other for the "lend of the loan" of a cup of sugar, an egg, a few spoons of tea, or a drop of milk.'[192] Similarly, Kearns Blain recalled: 'Women begged and borrowed from each other ... they shared whatever they could from a bit of soap to a pinch of tea to a piece of a candle to a sod of turf.'[193] However, that the poor did not stress this neighbourhood support network when seeking assistance is hardly surprising. Furthermore, we know that charities and state officials were aware of the self-help given within poor communities, in fact, they found it a remarkable phenomenon, but they also recognised that it was never enough to keep the proverbial wolf from the door. Both Johnston and Kearns Blain implicitly reinforce this reality because, while they pay tribute to the generosity of neighbours and family, they also note that all families relied on the pawn and faced the dictates of charity and/or state assistance regularly. Irrespective of these omissions, these letters bear witness to the haphazard existence so many people were forced to cobble together after Irish independence and the toll it took on their lives. Central to the poor's version of poverty was the necessity of pawning to survive, the stress of losing what must be redeemed, the fear and reality of unpaid rent, the necessity of breaking up the family in order to survive, and the implications of ill health and premature death. The letters also represent attempts by the poor to assert their version of poverty and in so doing to assert themselves and their identity in a world so fond of imposing an identity *upon* them. In many of the letters there is a perceptible attempt to establish self-worth by pointing out the ways in which the charity system itself was demeaning and unjust by condemning people to a mere existence rather than a life.

[192] Johnston, *Around the Banks of Pimlico*, p. 63.
[193] Kearns Blain, *Stealing Sunlight*, p. 7.

6   Vetting and Vouching
'It would be a charity to help him'

> [T]he power of the Irish priest has been great ... both because his people have placed unbounded confidence in his advice and guidance, and because he has shown himself as a rule entirely worthy of that confidence.[1]

The process of vetting and vouching is a universal feature of any charity system, whereby potential recipients are investigated, assessed, examined and judged. While in Ireland charities had their own methods, they shared a common aim of assisting the 'genuine' and weeding out 'the undeserving'. To this end Archbishop Byrne informed each applicant: 'If you explain your case to your Parish Priest, or one of the Curates of your parish, he will communicate with me in reference to it.'[2] In effect this placed the parish priest in the position of adjudicator, and in most cases he communicated with the archbishop or his secretary via a letter, leaving to posterity a second view of each case.[3] Christa Hämmerle noted that a similar reference was required of the Austrian poor who petitioned the relief authorities in the early twentieth century and this *Armutszeugnis* (a certificate of poverty) had to be from a doctor or a person of 'higher status'.[4] The relationship between status and charity was also embedded in the process of petitioning the archbishop. The priests that wrote in support or condemnation of the various applicants

---

[1] Rev P. Coffey, *The Church and the Working Classes* (Dublin: CTSI, 1906), p. 44.
[2] An extract from the card sent out to all applicants to the archbishop's fund. See Figure 1.2.
[3] Crossman notes that in nineteenth-century Ireland, clergy of all denominations acted 'as spokesmen of the poor, soliciting aid and organising and distributing relief'. V. Crossman, *Poverty and The Poor Law in Ireland, 1850–1914* (Liverpool University Press, 2013), p. 20; The application forms of Protestant Irish widows to Protestant Orphans' Society had a questionnaire that had to be filled out by the local clergyman. See, for example, File H.24 (5/5/39), NAI, Protestant Orphan Society, 1045/5/5.
[4] C. Hämmerle, 'Requests, complaints, demands. Preliminary thoughts on the petitioning letters of lower-class Austrian women, 1865–1918' in C. Bland and M. Cros (eds.), *Gender and Politics in the Age of Letter Writing, 1750–2000* (Aldershot: Ashgate, 2004), p. 123.

did so on the assumption of their difference and often, their inferiority.[5] Inevitably, these reference letters were shaped by the priests' values, inconsistencies and ambivalence in a similar way to social workers' case files elsewhere.[6]

What emerges from these letters is a rich and complex relationship between the laity, priests and the hierarchy. The priests were the interpreters, the advocates, who often judged and defined the poor. Not only was the priest's interpretation crucial to each individual case, collectively these priests contributed to a broader understanding of poverty and the poor. Their collective assumption, that although poverty was undeniable, virtue was highly contested and as important as need, was one shared more broadly in society – one may be *poor* but not *deserving* of charity. These men of the cloth picked their way, some with compassion, others with disdain, through a world of potential 'touchers', 'inveterate' or 'importunate' beggars and dissemblers. They weighed up the risk of wanton or wasteful charity against threats of defection or Protestant infiltration. This was not just about dispensing charity but also about rewarding deference, perseverance and religious fidelity and punishing impudence, laziness and pride. Many of their assessments were permeated by class prejudice and assumptions, and reveal how often class distinctions were based on ethereal notions of character, morality and truthfulness rather than on economic inequality.[7] This role afforded these largely middle-aged men incredible power,[8] a fact some enjoyed and others feared, but they also had their own susceptibilities and anxieties, which applicants engaged with and sometimes manipulated.[9] As Shurlee Swain observes of female charity workers and their clients in late nineteenth-century Australia, they operated within a relationship

---

[5] Peel argues that the social workers in Australia, America and Britain also 'expected' their clients to be different to themselves. M. Peel, *Miss Cutler and the Case of the Resurrected Horse: Social Work and the Story of Poverty in America, Australia, and Britain* (The University of Chicago Press, 2012), p. 63.

[6] See, for example, B. Stadum, *Poor Women and their Families: Hard Working Charity Cases, 1900–1930* (State University of New York, 1992), p. xx; Peel, *Miss Cutler*, p. 3; L. Gordon, *Heroes of Their Own Lives: The Politics and History of Family Violence* (London: Virago, 1989), p. 14.

[7] Peel notes that class distinctions were forged in these encounters between the investigator and investigated and usually had less to do with economic hardship than with ideas of 'virtue, vice, character, and morality'. Peel, *Miss Cutler*, p. 6.

[8] I have compiled a brief biography of most of the priests cited in this study and the majority was born between the 1870s and 1890s, only a handful were born between 1895 and 1905, i.e. were under the age of thirty-five years when writing these reference letters.

[9] There is much international research to indicate that impact of gender was significant in charitable policy and direction and needs to be factored into any historical analysis of the charity encounter. J. T. Cumbler, 'The politics of charity: gender and class in late 19th Century charity policy', *Journal of Social History*, 14 (1980), 99–111.

'unequal but unstable, in which the boundaries between deserving and underserving were both permeable and shifting.'[10] While the priest and applicant were not equal, they were both active in creating the world of charity.

'A good living man'

The parish priest was undoubtedly kept busy by poverty in Ireland in the first two decades after political independence. Their individual responses were varied – some scribbled a few hasty lines of approval or otherwise, others wrote long letters, on occasion more detailed than the applicant's letter, while others wrote several letters for the one applicant. However, all referees were guided or constricted by contemporary understandings regarding charity and character that shaped the agenda of charity. Hence in 1928, Fr Fitzpatrick of Holy Cross College in Dublin,[11] reduced Peter C.'s rather complicated case to these generic lines:

Dear Pat
    The bearer of this, a fellow named C., is not a bad sort. At least, I know he has made a good start to get work. He has a wife & children. He does not drink.
    If there be anything in the poor box, it would be a charity to help him.
    Yours –
    J. Fitzpatrick.[12]

Peter's petition was predicated on the need to prevent his wife from returning to 'her people', which he had been advised to do by two priests and a member of the NSPCC. He did not explain why this was perceived as necessary, only that he blamed her family for making him quit the National Army and for trying to take her and his child from him. He explained his complicated journey to impoverishment: he had served in the British Army 'Through the European War in France & Mesopotamia', but had deserted to join the Irish Republican Army and then the National Army. Due to his desertion, he was not entitled to war gratuity service pay, pension or assistance from the British Legion. He was subsisting on a weekly food ticket of 3/26 from the Vincent de

---

[10] S. Swain, 'Negotiating poverty: women and charity in nineteenth-century Melbourne', *Women's History Review*, 16 (2007), 99–112, 99.
[11] Fr John Fitzpatrick, born 1891, ordained June 1916 and died 1977. J. A. Gaughan, *The Archbishops, Bishops and Priests who served in the Archdiocese of Dublin between 1900–2011* (Dublin: Kingdom Books, 2012), p. 105.
[12] Fr Fitzpatrick, Holy Cross College, Clonliffe, Dublin, n.d., *c.* 1928. DDA, AB 7 CC, Box 2.

Paul.[13] However, to Fr Fitzpatrick this was a case of 'not a bad sort', who had tried to get work and was a fitting subject for charity – no more and no less.

Other, usually middle-class writers, engendered much longer more involved responses to their plight, where the priests became advocates as opposed to mere certifiers of poverty and character.[14] The case of Fr John Dunlea and Jack A. C. is a revealing example for several reasons. Dunlea's testimonial in this case also contains many of the characteristics scattered throughout the hundreds of priests' letters. While a curate in Monkstown parish in County Dublin he wrote many letters vouching for his parishioners.[15] He had a nose for the 'good-living' – in fact, in his hands it became a hyphenated identity – he had an instinct for 'types', and he went to great lengths for those he felt an affinity with (though he could be equally withering and damning). Although class was not the most important criteria for his advocacy – he seemed to genuinely believe it was his role to help 'solve' people's private difficulties – it was a major factor in his assessment process.

According to Fr Dunlea, Mr Jack A. C. represented a poor bet for charity and yet Dunlea gave him his full and enthusiastic support. Reducing Dunlea's long letter to its essentials serves to highlight how his portrayal of the case radically altered its hue. According to him, Jack had been 'addicted to the "hard-stuff," had mixed with a hard drinking crowd', did not have enough '"punch" in him to make a good business man', and had faced a writ for monies owed to a wholesaler. This debt Dunlea negotiated down to £25 and then paid himself. He did not mention the substantive issue of Jack's letter – that he had stolen £35 from his employer – rather referred to 'this latest disaster' and alluded to the fact that 'he may find himself up on a criminal charge which would be deplorable for himself & for his wife who is a very good type of woman'. In Dunlea's hands Jack's story was characterised as part of an ongoing 'struggle'. The applicant was described as 'rather a fine-looking man and very good-living', who was to be admired for taking the Pioneer Pledge

---

[13] Peter C., X Gardiner St., Dublin (city), 5 March 1928. DDA, AB 7 CC, Box 2.

[14] Walsh has noted that middle-class women's applications for charity were also treated differently to working-class women's appeals by those who ran various Protestant charities for women. O. Walsh, *Anglican Women in Dublin: Philanthropy, Politics and Education in the Early Twentieth Century* (University College Dublin Press, 2005), pp. 108–109. Luddy observed the same for the nineteenth century. M. Luddy, *Women and Philanthropy in Nineteenth-Century Ireland* (Cambridge University Press, 2005), p. 176.

[15] John Michael Dunlea, born 1883, ordained 1908 and died 1947. Gaughan, *The Archbishops, Bishops and Priests*, p. 92.

and maintaining his abstinence from alcohol 'rigidly' for five years, unlike his 'pals': '(they kept it [the pledge] until in their enthusiasm they attended the annual Pioneer meeting in the Theatre Royal, after which they felt "thirsty" and that was the end of that)'.[16] Fr Dunlea was confident he would have been refunded £25 he paid to the suppliers, but the man had lost his job and then his wife became ill. As Fr Dunlea explained, revealing his penchant for philosophising on the role of 'giver', 'I dont regret it. (I always find that, if one does a decent turn for a poor fellow like this, Providence seems to make it up).'[17]

There is little doubt that Jack A.C.'s life had been turned upside down by a series of misfortunes: he had lost his shop in Clontarf (for which he blamed the bank); he had then lost his position as a travelling salesman due to the 'tariff war' (for which he *could* have blamed de Valera!); the bailiff's came to repossess his house and his wife became gravely ill requiring operations for which he had to pay. To this end, he embezzled £35 from his new employer and was then terrified of being discovered.[18] He requested assistance from the archbishop by return of post and received the full £35 to repay his employer and a further £18 in May 1935.[19]

Dunlea's positive spin on Jack A. C.'s struggles must have done much to guarantee such generous assistance. There were hundreds of others who wrote because their lives had been upended by the illness of a loved one, but very few that admitted stealing to resolve the crisis and still fewer who received forgiving consideration. Fr Dunlea's emphasis on 'good-living' and a 'good type' (with a bit of Providence and its reward thrown in) was extremely valuable to this parishioner. The question remains, however, what were those qualities? How did you become a 'good type of woman' or 'good-living'? Clearly, one could have 'erred' several times and still claim these valuable traits, and yet there were many desperately poor people with relatives also made ill, no doubt by the stress and strain of debt, who were still not deemed to be that allusive 'good type'. It is possibly too simple to reduce it to class, but there is no arguing with its centrality in the world of assessing 'character' – a quality that existed beyond *actual* facts or past behaviour, but resided rather in a hazy place between perception and affinity – which allowed a subjective line to be drawn between entitlement

---

[16] Pioneer pledge refers to a promise to abstain from alcohol made by members of the Pioneer Total Abstinence Association of the Sacred Heart, a Roman Catholic organisation of lay people. See, D. Ferriter, *A Nation of Extremes: The Pioneers in Twentieth Century Ireland* (Dublin: Irish Academic Press, 1999).

[17] Fr Dunlea, The Presbytery, Monkstown, Co. Dublin, 25 March 1934. DDA, AB 7 CC, Box 4.

[18] Mr Jack A. C., X Maretimo Rd., Blackrock, Co. Dublin, 22 March 1934. Ibid.

[19] These two sums are noted on the top of Fr Dunlea's letter.

and discrimination.[20] The deeply contradictory nature of this system, reliant as it was on such impressionistic and prejudicial assessments, was alluded to in Fr Dunlea's somewhat conflicted conclusion to his letter:

If you do not think the amount excessive, I think that it is quite a deserving case and it will probably save him from going to the bad again.

I hope you will not have many more applications for this kind of thing from this neighbourhood.[21]

If it were just about second chances – about preventing people from 'going to the bad again' – the neighbourhood would have been immaterial. It is probable that part of the answer resided in the stories of middle-class poverty themselves. Those not used to poverty, not born into it, tended to provide a detailed narrative explanation of their descent. It was as though their poverty had an explanation, had a story that made sense of it; whereas those who were born into poverty laid claims to no such personal explanations for their fate other than fate itself. The generationally poor were explained by the system, their poverty was part of their place and therefore, implicitly, also their identity – hence character could damn them irrespective of their helplessness to change their situation. Middle-class poverty offended the order of things, ran counter to what status and position *should* afford. Although it was relatively common, it needed explaining in order to reinforce – inaccurately, in real terms – its exceptional quality and detach the experience from its victim. A poor middle-class man was not to be contaminated by the experience, because then all of society became likewise undermined. Somewhere in this series of social paradoxes lay the meaning of 'character'.

In 1925 Fr Patrick Dunlea, John Dunlea's brother, wrote a reference for Mrs F. of Mountjoy Place, an incredibly poor neighbourhood. In fact, it was a statement rather than a letter, he evidently felt under no compulsion to explain her poverty other than that it was a true statement of fact and not her fault. Her character was simple to summarise:

Mrs F., X Mountjoy Place, is a deserving case. Through no fault of her own she has been out of work since xmas last.

She is sober, honest, and industrious and goes to the Sacraments regularly.[22]

---

[20] See Crossman for a discussion of Irish 'social hierarchies'. V. Crossman, 'Middle-class attitudes to poverty and welfare in post-famine Ireland' in F. Lane (ed.), *Politics, Society and the Middle Class in Modern Ireland* (Basingstoke: Palgrave Macmillan, 2010), pp. 130–147.

[21] Fr Dunlea, The Presbytery, Monkstown, Co. Dublin, 25 March 1934.

[22] Patrick J. Dunlea, b. 1886, ordained 1910 and died 1965. Gaughan, *The Archbishops, Bishops and Priests*, p. 92; Fr Patrick J. Dunlea's written statement from The Pro-Cathedral, Dublin, 5 August 1925.

She was awarded £1. Obviously little more needed to be said – it was understood. Her case did not arouse suspicions; it was clear-cut to Dunlea that she was a member of the worthy poor: she did not drink, she worked and attended to her religious duties. Admittedly, Patrick Dunlea may also have been by nature more laconic than his brother, but essentially his references were tailored to his neighbourhood's more limited circumstances.

It is interesting to compare two other cases in which the Dunlea brothers were also involved. In 1927, John B., a long-time unemployed postal worker wrote to the archbishop seeking his influence in having him reinstated. He claimed, despite fourteen year's service, 'i was sent away to make room for those Men belonging to National Army who had there time finished in the Army.' While John's letter was cumbersome, he used no full-stops, only commas (although the handwriting was beautiful), it was detailed in terms of his family, his situation and his religious credentials. It was, in short, a relatively standard letter written by some-one who understood what was required of him in terms of 'evidence'. He outlined that he had six young children dependent on him, he provided the names of their Catholic schools and stressed that one was studying for the 'Selesian Brothers.'[23] He explained that he had been out of work for two years (through no fault of his own – he had been unfairly displaced) and despite good 'testimonials' and much effort, he could neither get reinstated nor find new employment. He also included the fact that he was a member of the 'Sodality of the Immaculate Conception.' His immediate problem was the rent; he was in debt to the landlord 'owing to the Idleness for the past 2 years'.[24]

John B. had a solid case and two references. Fr Dunlea testified that John's letter was 'quite true both as regards his family and his reduced and necessitous condition'. He added that his wife, despite being 'in a weak state of health', had earned what she could from 'washing or scrubbing'. Finally, 'he and his wife are thoroughly decent and are very attentive in their religious duties'.[25] Fr Gerard Gough of Lourdes House[26] similarly vouched for John as 'a very deserving case for any help that can be given'.[27] The help given amounted to £1.[28]

---

[23] Roman Catholic religious congregation of brothers and priests known as the Salesians of Don Bosco.

[24] Mr John B., X Fitzgibbon Lane, Mountjoy Square, Dublin (city), n.d. c. March 1927. DDA, AB 7 CC, Box 2.

[25] Fr Dunlea, Pro-Cathedral, Dublin, 3 March 1927. Ibid.

[26] James Gerard Gough, born 1900, ordained June 1923 and died 1958. Gaughan, *The Archbishops, Bishops and Priests*, p. 119.

[27] Written statement by Fr Gough of Lourdes House, 9 Upr. Buckingham St., 3 March 1927. DDA, AB 7 CC, Box 2.

[28] This sum is noted on the top of Fr Gough's written statement.

While in the more salubrious neighbourhood of Monkstown, some five years later, Mr Declan K., a middle-class pensioner, who was clearly new to writing such petitioning letters, provided only the very basic outline of his situation. Without the priest's letter, which filled in most of the crucial blanks in his story, it is hard to see how his appeal would have been entertained. According to him: '[T]hrough a chain of unfortunate circumstances and not through any fault of ours, we find ourselves faced with the loss of our nice home.' He and his wife were doing everything possible to extricate themselves from this situation: his wife was supplementing his 'regular income' with boarders. However, their rent was two quarters in arrears, hence they needed £60 to save their home. He regarded writing to the archbishop as an 'extreme step', only undertaken because 'prayer and personal efforts' had failed. His final plea laid stress on the extra element of 'disaster' in a case of middle class decline: 'We are anxious to keep our home and good reputation and pray that in your benevolence you may see your way to avert disaster which threatens us.'[29]

There was no explanation offered for why, despite a regular income, the rent was in arrears. There was no attempt to expand on the 'chain of unfortunate circumstances' that had caused the derailment of such a domestic unit and no details about that unit. The archbishop had to investigate and sent Declan's letter to the parish and Fr John Dunlea, who responded with a very detailed explanation of the case. He had known them for a long time and they were a 'very respectable, good living pair without children'. Mr K. had a 'good job' in Guinness Brewery, but was at the time of writing, on a pension. He confirmed that through an 'unfortunate coincidence of circumstances' they had got into a 'serious financial tangle'. Mrs K. had required several operations; to recuperate, her doctor had sent her to a 'certain rather expensive Nursing Home', and it appears Mr and Mrs K. 'did not realise what it was going to cost them'. The husband had resorted to a 'money lender' to settle the bill; it was at this juncture that Dunlea (to his surprise) learned of their difficulties and, reluctant to 'see him down for £20', assisted them. However, it had evidently not been enough to restore their financial equilibrium and a year later the husband (unbeknownst to Dunlea, who did not 'know how he came to think of that') had written to the archbishop.[30] Dunlea was obviously a little irritated by Mr K.'s initiative, as he noted in his post-script that '[H]e had told me of his difficulties with the rent, but I did not rise to the occasion as I thought that I had already

[29] Mr Declan K., X Monkstown Rd, Monkstown, Co. Dublin, 8 January 1934. DDA, AB 7 CC, Box 5.
[30] Fr Dunlea, The Presbytery, Monkstown, Co. Dublin, 16 January 1934. Ibid.

"done my bit".' Nonetheless, Dunlea put the case succinctly to the archbishop:

> I think he is a deserving case. The money would not be spent in rioting or drunkness *[drunkenness]*. However, considering his standing with his neighbours and friends, it would be exceedingly painful for his wife & himself if there were a public exposure of their position. This applies particularly to the case of the house rent, because he got the tenancy of the house in preference to some protestants, because he was considered to be a more reliable tenant.[31]

The K.s had a few strikes against them: they had no children, they had been assisted before, and they had been less than forthcoming in laying out their case. However, Dunlea believed the fact that they were 'respectable', did not drink, and had social standing in society – one that had been heightened by their selection over Protestants as tenants for their house in Monkstown (which was quite a Protestant enclave) – outweighed any other concerns. The archbishop was obviously convinced and they were sent the £60 required to keep them in their home.

Essentially, Mr John B. and Mr Declan K. both needed help with their rent and both had wives in 'weak health', who were still doing what they could to contribute financially. According to their referees, they were 'good living' and observant of religious duties. However, here their cases diverged: John had six children and no regular income, whereas Declan had no children and a pension. Declan was less than forthcoming in his letter, while John had offered a very detailed account of his situation. While both received assistance, the difference in the sums involved is remarkable and yet this pattern was repeated over and over again in the archbishop's 'charity cases'. The middle class appeared simply to have a different claim on their church, one that went beyond the number of dependants or the measure of actual need; it was about maintaining the *status quo* and keeping the church's heartland stable.

In February 1924 Harry C., a father of seven from County Roscommon, wrote a simple letter highlighting the banal devastation of rural poverty. His was a bleak landscape of nothingness:

> I beg you will excuse me for troubling your Lordship I have a large weak family without any means, for food or clothing, four boys and three girls, oldest boy 12 years youngest 2 years. I have neither cow or calf, having lost my one and only cow a year since. My wife and children are in great distress, our scanty crops of potatoes are used up since November[32]

---

[31] Ibid.
[32] Mr H.C., Ballaghadereen, Co Roscommon, 25 February 1924. DDA, AB 7 CC, Box 1.

Harry was one of the hordes of underemployed rural labourers and the 'trifle' he earned was not enough to 'keep' his family. On occasion he kept his eldest son home from school to assist in earning enough to feed the family. Mary E. Daly has noted that a laxity in school attendance legislation was largely tolerated because of the realities of rural Ireland and the need for children to help on the land at certain times of the year.[33] Harry had written previously and had received no reply. He apologised for troubling the archbishop again, 'but really I cannot help it our case is so sad, there is nothing so trying on parents as to see their children suffering in great want, it is worse than death'.[34] On the 4 March his parish priest wrote to confirm the severity of his poverty and that he was 'deserving'. He explained:

I have no hesitation in saying, that he is the poorest man in a poor Community. He is a good living man, and our St Vincent de Paul Society has been satisfied that he is a deserving case. The assistance from that Source is very limited.[35]

Although Harry earned the dubious distinction of being the 'poorest man' in a poor community, it was his 'character' as a 'good living man', a man the Vincent de Paul had found to be 'a deserving case', that secured him £5 of charity.[36]

What is clear after examining hundreds of such letters is that poverty alone was no guarantee of charity; in fact, abject poverty was sometimes a liability. Consider, for example, the interesting aside in the rather generic reference supplied for Joseph H. in 1926. Fr Patrick Dargan summed Joseph H. and his circumstances up in a few lines[37]: he had known him for several years, he usually got employment as a fireman, he did not drink, had never been to prison, and had a wife and two or three children. He asserted twice in the letter that he and his family were 'very deserving', although he explained: 'I know the family to be very deserving though wretchedly poor.'[38] The 'though' betrays an often implicit sense that those who were 'wretchedly poor' or 'hopelessly poor' were

---

[33] M. E. Daly, '"The primary and natural educator?": The role of parents in the education of their children in independent Ireland', *Eire-Ireland*, 44 (Spring/Summer, 2009) 194–217.

[34] Mr H.C., Ballaghadereen, Co Roscommon, 25 February 1924. DDA, AB 7 CC, Box 1.

[35] Fr Spelman, The Presbytery, Ballaghaderreen, Co. Roscommon, 4 March 1924. Ibid.

[36] Interestingly, the priest delayed in passing on £5 and Harry C. wrote to the archbishop to enquire on 16 March 1924. When Fr Spelman eventually gave him the money, he wrote to thank the archbishop and decry the priest for his 'negligence'.

[37] Patrick Dargan, born 1892, ordained in 1916 and died in 1957. Gaughan, *The Archbishops, Bishops and Priests*, p. 78.

[38] Patrick Dargan, Holy Cross College, Clonliffe, Dublin, 22 March 1926. DDA, AB 7 CC, Box 1.

somehow suspect, at least, their *bona fides* could not be assumed. These writers had to be cleared of any charge of 'self-inflicted' poverty or the crime of 'hopelessness'; charity could not be wasted in either case.

'An ideal layman'

In 1932 Fr John Neary took time-out from his sick bed to pen a brief resumé of the 'ideal layman' on behalf of his old friend Mr Peter O'N.[39] Peter was a grocer on the North Strand in Dublin, who needed cash quickly in order to continue his business. Neary explained he was:

a daily communicant in W^m St – he is practically a TT (except by D^r's orders) – a member of a couple of Sodalities and he does not gamble. He is straightforward reliable industrious and the essence of loyalty to the church – an ideal layman.[40]

He was sent the large sum of £100 to rescue his business.[41] He was the ideal layman and a good investment, the cash injection could save his business and keep a family from becoming dependent on charity. Neary's summation of an ideal layman is worth considering as it recurs, albeit less explicitly, in many other cases. Essentially, one had to attend religious duties regularly, be hardworking and abstain from alcohol and gambling. These were all qualities that were relatively easy to establish with the exception of 'industriousness'. How could the unemployed prove this all-important trait? It is a term applied with relative generosity to the middle class, while sparingly attributed to the labourer or unskilled worker, particularly when he (or she) was un- or under-employed. The attributes of the ideal Catholic layman were qualities sought by all charities irrespective of denomination in Ireland and beyond. The anxiety over religious observance, the fear of other religions or disloyalty, was not unique to Catholicism.[42]

It was not just in the petitioning letters that religion was expressed as a kind of currency or capital in bidding for assistance, but it was also stressed in the vouching letters from priests and curates. This is hardly surprising as this was a Catholic charity, available unashamedly for practising Catholics, though, it is somewhat remarkable how successful it was as a bargaining chip for all its lack of subtlety. Judging by these

---

[39] John James Neary, born 1877, ordained 1903 and died 1960. Gaughan, *The Archbishops, Bishops and Priests*, p. 204.

[40] Fr Neary, St Agatha's, 595 North Circular Rd., Dublin, n.d. *c.* June 1932. DDA, AB 7 CC, Box 3.

[41] This figure is noted in pencil on the top left-hand corner of Peter O'N.'s letter. Peter O'N., X North Strand, Dublin, 6 June 1932. Ibid.

[42] See Walsh, *Anglican Women in Dublin*, pp. 166–167.

priests' letters, those who stressed their religious observance or raised the spectre of a 'Protestant threat', had assessed their audience astutely: it did elicit support, even when grudgingly given. In fact, when it came to priests making cases on behalf of their parishioners, the idea of Protestants lying-in-wait to either 'steal' Catholic babies or Catholic businesses often loomed larger than in their applicants' missives.

In the case of Mrs Sally O'N. it was Fr Vaughan who invoked the Protestant threat.[43] Although Sally had evidently irritated Vaughan by ignoring his advice regarding opening a shop on Castle Street – which he told her was 'foolish' as other shops there were failing – she possessed other essential qualities that compensated for this display of independence. Vaughan explained she had 'come down badly in the world as the result of her husband's illness', but was 'making a big sacrifice to maintain her girl at [the Mercy Convent School in] Navan'. She led 'an exemplary life – I see her in our Church every day and I believe her to be thouroughly deserving now'. There was a gender as well as a class aspect to Vaughan's reading of Sally's case. Struggling to educate children according to their religion and status was a highly valued endeavour for women, particularly widows, or women whose husband's could not, or did not, contribute. The fact that Sally appeared innocent of her final (and possibly her ultimate) trump card did not diminish her referee's concerns: 'She is surrounded by a bitter Protestant settlement and she does not know it. The other Catholic "shop" next door is about to close down.'[44] She was the ideal laywoman because she was a good Catholic mother threatened by Protestants: this was the case made for her by her parish priest. Her own letter was much more practical, she just wanted a job so she did not have to beg, it did not have to be her own shop. In fact, she would have gladly surrendered it for a secure position in the Sweeps Stakes.[45]

In 1935, Fr Fitzpatrick wrote on behalf of Mr Eoin McC. who was in arrears with his rent and in failing health. While these were the essentials of his case, Fitzpatrick petitioned for assistance as a reward for Eoin's fight to keep his children in the Catholic faith. As Fitzpatrick explained: 'Briefly the facts are: McC., a catholic, riveter in the G.S.R., married a

---

[43] Denis Vaughan, born 1903, ordained 1927 and died 1970. Gaughan, *The Archbishops, Bishops and Priests*, p. 274.

[44] Fr Vaughan, SS Michael & John's, Exchange St., Dublin, 25 November 1937. DDA, AB 7 CC, Box 7.

[45] Mrs Sally O'N., X Castle Stores, Castle St., Dublin, 23 November 1937. Ibid. Coleman observes that the Sweeps, a major employer of women, had a reputation for awarding jobs via patronage. Sally's request would appear to have been an informed one. M. Coleman, *The Irish Sweep: A History of the Irish Hospital Sweepstake, 1930–1987* (University College Dublin Press, 2009), pp. 36–37.

Protestant. A long a bitter fight for the faith of the five children ended with her death two years ago.'[46] Eoin's marriage was reduced to a battle against Protestantism, which had only been resolved when God intervened and took the life of his wife. Since then, apart from the eldest daughter, the various children were scattered among Catholic orphanages and Fitzpatrick believed Eoin deserved help because: 'He has made a splendid effort now for two years & deserves to be assisted.' He was sent £5.

'[H]e is one of the most notorious touchers in my district'

A 'toucher' is a term swallowed up by time and changes in attitude, or at least shifts in sensitivities. It literally meant someone who would 'touch' or 'tap' anyone for money. Rationally, one would suppose that people who were labelled 'touchers' were not actually in need, but instead opportunists who would rather beg than forage for themselves. However, the use of the term in the letters in Archbishop Byrne's archives reveal that the term was often applied to those who were accepted to be in great need. For example, the parish priest of York in England, wrote in July 1924 on behalf of Mrs D. describing her as 'a respectable woman, but a wonderful beggar. She is not well off'.[47] Mrs D.'s poverty was accepted, her respectability was assured and yet she was somehow in the wrong for being a 'wonderful beggar'. There was obviously something in the very art of supplication that could be criticised, even when it was accepted that begging was necessary. The difficulty then is in understanding what this term implied about these people, if it did not question their poverty or need.

Fr Tim Condon, the parish priest at the Pro-Cathedral on Marlborough Street in Dublin city,[48] served a very poor community and had perfected the skill of detecting 'touchers'. In August 1935, he put forward the case of an elderly widow, Mrs O'R., the mother of a deceased priest, who was resident in St Monica's, a care home for elderly ladies run by the Sisters of Charity.[49] She was in need of a weekly allowance for her 'own private needs'. Condon had investigated and had been informed that the nuns had received £100 to maintain her, but as she had no money of her own, the nuns gave her '1/- each Friday for pocket money'. Condon's tone was

---

[46] Fr Fitzpatrick, The Presbytery, Fairview, Dublin, 8 March 1935. DDA, AB 7 CC, Box 4.

[47] J. Chadwick, St Wilfred's Rectory, York, England, 21 July 1924. DDA, AB 7 CC, Box 1.

[48] Timothy Condon, born 1897, ordained 1921 and died 1962. Gaughan, *The Archbishops, Bishops and Priests*, p. 121.

[49] Mrs O'R. did not write herself, she had asked Fr Condon to plead her case.

supportive, if patronising; he believed that 'a few extra shillings in the week for a time' would satisfy her. While Mrs O'R.'s situation was pitiable, she was a woman reduced to meagre pocket money with no independence or autonomy, she was far from the worst of such cases. However, Condon summed up her greatest claim on the archbishop:

She refused to take any money from me personally. Poor Mrs O'R. is a sad case She is blind and in addition desolate. She is not in any sense "a toucher". She is a perfect lady and a model of virtue.[50]

She received £2. What made Mrs O'R. a 'model of virtue' and definitely not a 'toucher?' Was it merely her erstwhile social position? Was it simply a question of class? It is interesting that Condon placed the term 'toucher' in inverted commas. Although he had a penchant for inverted commas generally, here it seemed to signify not just a caricature but also an understood code. Indeed, he appears to have understood, even if benignly, poverty and its *personae dramatis* in terms of caricatures. Four years later he wrote regarding a very poor parishioner, whom he recommended without reservation: Mrs Marie C. was 'a decent pious "creature" – who never touched and who accepted help with reluctance and always with gratitude.' Again the use of inverted commas around the word 'creature' underscored this as a word that signified something other than its literal meaning; she was a *type* of poor person Condon presumed the recipient of his letter would instantly recognise. Apart from being pious and inferior – a pious *creature* – she was also reluctant and grateful and had known suffering: 'Her poor Sister sanctified herself on a bed of terrible suffering and died in the Lord. R.I.P.'[51] These were all accepted attributes that protected one from an accusation of 'touching' or abusing the system of charity established for just this type of 'creature'.

There was a dilemma for the poor in the balancing act of seeking assistance: how did one avoid being perceived as a 'toucher' when your poverty was relentless and the charity system, upon which you relied, was predicated on short-term relief and an acceptance of the social system that created the poverty cycle in the first place? Mr Arthur T. of Dominick Street in Dublin city failed in this endeavour because of his persistence – rather than his persistent need – which made him a marked man. A narrative developed about Arthur that was shared by the priests of his diocese: he was a 'real "toucher"'. He wrote to the archbishop in

[50] Fr Condon, The Presbytery, 82 Marlborough St., Dublin, 5 August 1935. DDA, AB 7 CC, Box 6.
[51] Fr Condon, The Presbytery, 82 Marlborough St., Dublin, 30 May 1939. DDA, AB 7 CC, Box 7.

September and November 1932 as an unemployed tailor seeking assistance to get a sewing machine to start a business – this was quite a common
request. He signed off hoping he was 'worthy of a help'.[52] Fr Condon's
response contained all the paradoxes Arthur and his like faced. Although
Condon testified to the fact that Arthur was well known to him, he got his
name wrong.[53] While he dismissed him as a 'notorious toucher', he
'admitted' he was in 'bad circumstances', but he had dropped him when
his begging became too regular:

Anthony T. is very well known to me – he is one of the most notorious touchers in
my district. The more he gets the more he wants and he never seems to make an
effort to better his condition himself.
     I must admit that he is in bad circumstances I would not go so far however as to
say (as the meditation in Clonliffe had it) that "his case in an especial one".
     I have personally helped him times without number. When I discovered that he
regarded my donations as part of the week's programme I had to drop him.
     There are the facts of his case.[54]

How could Arthur defend himself against this logic? How did damning a
person as a parasite with no will for 'bettering his condition' represent
facts? If Arthur's situation had not improved in a market riddled with
unemployment how was he to survive without begging? Finally, did it not
make sense, when in 'bad circumstances', to return to the well that gave?
Was Arthur's response to his situation not a rational one? Whether or not
Arthur could have done more to improve his circumstances, Condon in
no way offered a case based on evidence of dereliction; his case was
founded on prejudice and an instinctive dislike of Arthur's lack of shame
and his persistence. There was something about the *way* Arthur begged
that repelled Condon. It could have been as simple as a tone of voice, a
lack of deference, or something deeper, something hard to prove or
justify, something that the title 'toucher' flagged and silenced.
     In August 1936 Arthur wrote again. He now had two children and was
struggling to keep up the payments on his sewing machine. Arthur by
contrast dealt in facts: he provided a detailed account of his income and
outgoings and supplied the 'book of machine', which presumably
detailed his instalments for the sewing machine.[55] Arthur's 'genuine'

---

[52] Mr Arthur T. X Lr Dominick St, Dublin (city), 2 November 1932. DDA, AB 7 CC,
Box 3.
[53] The confusion probably arose as according to the 1911 census Arthur's father's name
was Anthony.
[54] Fr Condon, The Presbytery, 82 Marlborough St., Dublin, 29 September 1932. DDA,
AB 7 CC, Box 3.
[55] His machine book is not in the collection, so was probably returned to him.

inability to secure employment had obviously satisfied those in official-dom as he was in receipt of relief:

I am in receit *[receipt]* of Sixteen Shillings relief in which I pay rent of 4/- and 1/- Society. I also pay 3/- per week for a sewing machine that I have out on the weekly system, and the value of the machine is £15.0.0. I have five pounds paid off it and it is a great burden to us paying for it each week when I am doing no work. I have made an application to St Vincent De Paul for material and did not get any reply.[56]

This left him with 7s a week to feed a family of four, and if he ceased paying for the machine, he would lose what he had invested thus far. He used pawning to limp from one week to the next: 'Some time ago I even had to pleadge my tailors Sissors to pay towards machine.'[57] He wanted the archbishop to give 'a few lines to St Vincent De Paul' in time for his parish's next conference meeting.

On this occasion it was Fr Frank Kenny who muddied the waters for Arthur T. with a deadly first sentence: 'A. T. is a real "toucher"', who was 'after each of us in turn'.[58] The priests in the parish had discussed Arthur, they had compared how they had all been approached by him, and had agreed he was a 'toucher'. Kenny also wrapped the word 'toucher' in inverted commas giving it the assig-nation of something that is understood, that had a shared meaning for those versed in the language of charity. Kenny complained that he had redeemed items from the pawn for Arthur, but he was 'back in a short time with a fresh wad of pawn-tickets'. However, Kenny must have been aware the pawn was not a one-off-affair, it was part of a repertoire of survival, and its inherent value was its constancy. Kenny's letter is a master class in prejudicing a case based on suspicion:

I went to his place in Dominick St. and while it is poor, it is no worse than very many others … it was Tim Condon who got him the machine and I think paid for most of it. The St V. de. P. have also helped him: I am quite sure you heard him mentioned as been *[being]* fairly worthless: of course I do not wish to prejudice you, and indeed the children are to be pitied, but it is really very hard to know what he does with the money.[59]

---

[56] Mr Arthur T., X Lr Dominick St., Dublin (city), 25 August 1936. DDA, AB 7 CC, Box 6.

[57] Ibid.

[58] Francis Joseph Kenny, born 1905, ordained 1929 and died 1981. Gaughan, *The Archbishops, Bishops and Priests*, p. 149.

[59] Fr Kenny, The Presbytery, Pro-Cathedral, 83 Marlborough Street, Dublin (city), 28 August 1936. DDA, AB 7 CC, Box 6.

Essentially, he could not argue Arthur was *not* poor, only that he was not exceptionally so. Hearsay did the rest: Arthur T. was 'mentioned about' as 'fairly worthless'. However, Kenny had a heart (he pitied children), so he did not wish to 'prejudice' Arthur's case – and thus his children's welfare – but he had to express his puzzlement at where the money went and by implication where any further donations might go. If Arthur had been aware of the case made against him, it is likely he would have shown Kenny his payment book for his machine and pointed out that Condon never mentioned anything about this machine in a letter he wrote in which he admitted 'dropping' Arthur. He would also have given Kenny a detailed account of income and expenditure, as he had given the archbishop. However, it is unlikely any of these 'facts' would have made a difference; the *impression* that Arthur was 'worthless' was firmly established. Impressions masqueraded as facts, investigation rested on assumptions and Arthur, poor as he was, was not deemed innocent or of any intrinsic value.

It required a fairly insubstantial case to condemn someone as 'a plausable scoundrel' who 'haunted' priests for money,[60] or to allege someone used charities as 'easy subsidies' because they had 'Begging in the blood.'[61] Of course, these kinds of offensive and lazy character assassinations, made in the assured comfort of being on the right side of life, belied the damage such a system inflicted on those so casually disregarded. However, most of the persistently poor had little way of avoiding becoming tiresome and were therefore subject to the labels of irritation. Mrs E. H., a widow with three children, who nursed her elderly father, was a classic case. She wrote asking the archbishop to intervene to help her secure assistance from the Vincent de Paul Society.[62] Her parish priest explained that she was 'well known to me and to the Vincent de Paul Society and other charitable institutions for the past eight or ten years' and they were 'growing tired of her as she is very persistent'. Mrs H. was lucky in her priest who tried to get the Vincent de Paul people to reopen her case and offered her his valuable compassion: 'My personal view is that she deserves a little help at the moment.'[63]

---

[60] J. O'Connell, 25 Killarney St. Dublin (city), 1 April 1933. DDA, AB 7 CC, Box 5.
[61] J. Redmond, The Presbytery, 85 Iona Road, Glasnevin Dublin, 20 April 1939. DDA, AB 7 CC, Box 7. John Redmond, born 1889, ordained 1917 and died 1969. Gaughan, *The Archbishops, Bishops and Priests*, p. 248.
[62] Mrs Edith H., X, Lr Dorset St, Dublin (city), 17 February 1929. DDA, AB 7 CC, Box 2.
[63] D. Ó Ceallacháin, 59 Eccles Street, Dublin (city), 22 February 1929. Ibid.

'She is an exceptionally good woman + mother'

In a world charged with assessing 'appropriate behaviour' it is little wonder that gender played a role in both dictating what was fitting behaviour and how each case should be dealt with. This exercise was given heightened significance because the people doing the assessing in this particular charity encounter were all celibate men. A celibate man can have had little personal understanding of parenthood or the strain poverty imposed on marriage and domestic harmony. Yet the role of the local curate or parish priest was hugely important in 'resolving' many of these private problems and this reality was reflected in the position held by priests in many organisations working with the poor. For example, between 1933 and 1955, the presidents and vice-presidents of the NSPCC were all priests.[64] Cara Delay noted how often women in post-famine Ireland went to their priests to seek assistance with complex moral and sexual problems from rape to extra-marital affairs.[65] It was often the priest who was called when a daughter became pregnant 'out of wedlock' or when incest was suspected. It was regularly the priest that negotiated resolutions in broken homes or helped a wife flee an abusive marriage. However, just as Sarah-Anne Buckley has observed regarding the role of the NSPCC and domestic violence, there was no attempt to address the issue in any substantial manner.[66] Many of the gender assumptions that emerge in this collection (both on the part of applicants and clerics) reflected cultural and social expectations about men and women. However, any response to the social problems unearthed in these letters also had to be viewed and dealt with within the strict code of Catholic morality. In many respects the moral culture of Catholicism was similar to that of Victorianism and thus what one would have encountered also in the various Protestant churches. However, the period between 1920 and 1940 witnessed several important changes in what was acceptable to other religious groupings with regard to the control of fertility and the break-up of marriages. Catholicism brooked no such softening of its moral lines – officially, moral compromise remained an anathema – morality was an absolute science. The Irish Free State period (1922–1937) represented a period when Catholic morality was explicitly or implicitly embedded in legislation resulting in

---

[64] S. Buckley, *The Cruelty Man: Child Welfare, the NSPCC and the State in Ireland, 1889–1956* (Manchester University Press, 2013), p. 82.

[65] C. Delay, 'Confidantes or competitors? Women, priests, and conflict in post-famine Ireland', *Eire-Ireland*, 40 (Spring/Summer 2005), 107–25.

[66] Buckley, *The Cruelty Man*, p. 82.

increased censorship, a legal ban on divorce and contraception.[67] In many respects this is well trodden ground for Irish historians, but we know little about how people dealt with the impact of unlimited fertility or what happened when a marriage was violent or how people solved moral quandaries on a day-to-day basis and what role the Catholic Church played therein.

The feature that is most striking in the general response of the clergy to families 'in trouble' was the willingness to 'take the mother's side'. Resilience in women was recognised and often supported by priests, though this rarely translated into an expressed desire to change a system that condemned so many of them to surviving as they did. In 1926, Fr Waters's assessment of Mrs G., who had been abandoned by her husband, in many respects sums up this attitude: 'Mrs G. keeps the flag flying and is at present at the nadir of her fortunes, and thus a good chance that she will be greatly + permanently benefitted by this charity.'[68] Similarly, in a few lines Fr Thomas J. McGrath reduced the case of Mrs S. to its essentials:[69]

Mrs S. of College Place in this parish is a married woman, a convert, with seven young children whom I consider is deserving of relief. Her husband is on strike at present and she is in great need. She has been approached by members of her former religion but she will have nothing to do with them.[70]

Women who could prove they stood fast in the face of adversity – or in the face of Protestants – were virtually guaranteed some form of assistance. Although it was often meagre (Mrs S. received a £1) and was thus not likely to change their immediate future, in some cases it had the potential to do so. In 1939, Fr Seán Byrne helped Mrs H. of Crumlin get off the moneylender's books,[71] because he 'thought, [she] had made an honest effort to reduce her arrears of rent, & had got herself into the

[67] M. Finnane, 'The Carrigan committee of 1930–31 and the "moral condition of the Saorstát"', *Irish Historical* Studies, 32 (November 2001), 519–536; S. McAvoy, 'The regulation of sexuality in the Irish Free state' in E. Malcolm and G. Jones (eds.), *Medicine, Disease and the State in Ireland, 1650–1940* (Cork University Press, 1999), pp. 253–266; M. Curtis, *A Challenge to Democracy: Militant Catholicism in Modern Ireland* (Dublin: The History Press Ireland, 2010), pp. 78–102.

[68] Fr Waters, 15 Idrone Terrace, Blackrock, Co. Dublin, 18 December 1926. DDA, AB 7 CC, Box 2. This refers to a letter written by Mrs Angela G., X Belgrave Sq., Monkstown, Co. Dublin, 1 December 1926. However, Mrs G. must have generated a negative report from another source as there is a 'No' written on the top of her letter.

[69] Thomas J. McGrath, born 1884, ordained 1910 and died 1949. Gaughan, *The Archbishops, Bishops and Priests*, pp. 173–174.

[70] Thomas J. McGrath, St. Agatha's, Nth. William St. Dublin (city), 21 July 1937. DDA, AB 7 CC, Box 6. Mrs S. was granted a £1.

[71] Seán Byrne, born 1909, ordained 1933 and died 1978. Gaughan, *The Archbishops, Bishops and Priests*, p. 43.

"Jewmans" books in so doing'.[72] Thus he 'considered it better not to let her get herself further involved.'[73]

Other forms of assistance were even longer term in their potential impact. In 1932, Fr Flavin secured £25 for Mrs C. to allow her to train as a maternity nurse.[74] Mrs C. was the mother of seven children (eight years to six months) and married to 'Paul C. (traveller) out of work for over 2 years – not reliable.'[75] Flavin argued that if Mrs C. was funded to the tune of £3 a week to feed her children and train herself, she would be almost guaranteed work thereafter because there was an opening for a maternity nurse in the district.[76] Similarly, in 1924, Mrs May McD., a widowed mother from inner city Dublin, who according to her parish priest was 'an exceptionally good woman + mother', was funded to set up a new business with her unemployed son.[77]

Women on their own, either through bereavements or *de facto* separation, were very likely to receive the advocacy of their parish priest, particularly when they were deemed to have fought for their children. In 1929, Mrs Angela O'B. wrote to save her ailing business: she was a widow who, like so many other widows, was struggling to run a boarding house.[78] Fr Ryan described her as a 'very respectable and industrious widow'.[79] He established that it was ill health and a slackening in boarders that had resulted in her trouble and 'took it for granted ... that she is telling the truth'. He recommended her 'as a very worthy woman. She has done well for her family which is very much to her

---

[72] 'Jewman' was a common term used for moneylenders. All the following sources confirm both the frequent use of this term and that it was women who engaged such resources. K. Kearns, *Dublin's Lost Heroines: Mammies and Grannies in a Vanished City* (Dublin: Gill & Macmillan, 2004), p. 28; A. Kearns Blain, *Stealing Sunlight: Growing up in Irishtown* (Dublin: A & A Farmar, 2000), 178; E. Crowley, *Cowslips and Chainies: A Memoir of Dublin in the 1930s* (Dublin: Lilliput Press, 1996), p. 38.

[73] Fr Seán Byrne, Presbytery, 9 St Agnes Rd., Crumlin, Dublin, 30 March 1939. DDA, AB 7 CC, Box 7.

[74] John Cashel Flavin, born 1890, ordained 1915 and died May 1940. Gaughan, *The Archbishops, Bishops and Priests*, p. 108.

[75] Fr Flavin, The Presbytery, Dundrum, Co. Dublin, 1 March 1932. DDA, AB 7 CC, Box 4.

[76] The sum of £3 was a reasonable figure, for example, this was the sum J. Maguire had estimated a working man needed to earn in 1925 in order to be able to afford rent in Dublin. See, J. Maguire, 'The housing problem in Ireland and Great Britain and the essentials of its solution', *JSSISI*, 14 (1925), 47–60, 49.

[77] Fr Doherty, 59 Eccles St., Dublin (city), 26 May 1924. DDA, AB 7 CC, Box 1. She received £5. Fr James Doherty, born 1890, ordained 1907 and died 1945. Gaughan, *The Archbishops, Bishops and Priests*, p. 84.

[78] Mrs Angela O'B., A. House, X Lower Mount Street, Dublin (city), 22 April 1929. DDA, AB 7 CC, Box 2.

[79] Fr Ryan, St Andrew's, Westland Row, Dublin (city), 25 April 1929. DDA, AB 7 CC, Box 2.

credit'.[80] He had met her the previous week and she had given no 'hint' that she was in trouble, nonetheless, the £15 cheque received halted her landlord's legal action and, according to her parish priest, 'changed completely poor Mrs O'B.'s outlook on life. It was like the sunshine breaking up and getting through a big black cloud. She was very grateful, even to tears'.[81]

Parish priests were often called in to assist deserted wives and in these cases part of the job was assessing the wife's responsibility for her situation. In 1936, Fr P. B.[82] of Dún Laoghaire parish advocated on behalf of Mrs S. 'a "grass widow"'.[83] He explained that after an interview with her and her sister he had established the following:

Her husband, who left her years ago, is a drunkard. He drank through a big farm and left Mrs S. quite penniless. She does not know where he is at the moment; she has no hope that he will ever reform and help her. She is youngish well dressed and well got up – but of course, I am not a judge of external appearance.[84]

His observations are telling because of course 'external appearance' was absolutely crucial: Mrs S., in the absence of a home to display (she was taking refuge with her sister), had only her own appearance to represent her 'respectability'. The priest took the time to detail those appearances in a letter that was actually about gaining funding for the continued education of her three eldest children. It cannot have harmed Mrs S.'s case that her parish priest reported: 'As far as I can make out the case is a very deserving one. Apparently some Protestant connections of Mrs S. tried to get hold of the children, and made rosy promises, but Mrs S. stood fast.'[85]

If mothers were often reduced to the barebones of virtue and self-sacrifice, then their male counterparts were often dismissed as the simplistic opposite. In 1931, Fr Manning took a few lines to encapsulate Mrs G. and her husband: 'She is a very decent respectable woman, but is unfortunately married to a useless, careless husband.'[86]

---

[80] Thomas F. Ryan, born 1878, ordained 1903 and died 1963. Gaughan, *The Archbishops, Bishops and Priests*, p. 256.

[81] Fr Ryan, 28 April 1929. Ibid.

[82] This was most likely Patrick Joseph Bergin, born 1912, ordained 1936 and died 1969. Gaughan, *The Archbishops, Bishops and Priests*, p. 30.

[83] A term used to describe women who were *de facto* widows due to desertion or the disappearance of their spouse.

[84] Fr P. B., 7 Eblana Avenue, Dún Laoghaire, Co. Dublin, 20 March *c.* 1937. DDA, AB 7 CC, Box 6.

[85] Ibid.

[86] T. Manning, St Peter's Church, Phibsboro, Dublin, 22 December 1931. DDA, AB 7 CC, Box 4.

Many other men were presented as inept or incompetent and therefore of very little use to their wives. In 1932, Fr A. J. Camac wrote a compassionate plea for Mrs W. and her eight children, who were dependent on an out-of-work writer reduced to the occasional loyalty payment. Although the father had held 'quite lucrative positions in his time', the priest believed that 'owing ... to a certain want of balance has failed to retain any of them'.[87] Throughout the letter Mr W.'s fragility and flightiness were presented as the main reason for the family's distress: 'W. himself is rather of the actor-like & Micawber type "always waiting for something to turn up," thinking in thousands & yet sometimes hungry to the verge of starvation.' It was 'for the sake of the mother & children, the local conference of the S V de P is keenly interested in the case'.[88] Even if the portrayal of this man was condescending, it was considerably more benign than many other less educated men received.[89]

D., a bricklayer (referred to only by his surname without the prefix of 'Mr' by the priest to underscore the lack of respect afforded him), was presented in sharp contrast to his delicate wife. He was the sort of man who 'wanted to make "whoopee" 'while his pregnant wife and four children starved'.[90] Though he earned £4.4.0 a week, his wife only received £2.0.0 and with that amount she had to provide for him and four children. According to Fr Condon, D. was the antithesis of deserving:

By no stretch of my imagination could I consider him deserving. He is very negligent about his duties and seems in no way inclined to become fervent. He beats up his wife now and then. With these particulars to hand you will be able to judge for yourself as to do justice to his appeal. The wife however is a good woman and very deserving ... As she is about to become a mother and as her prospects of a fair deal from D. are not bright you may feel inclined to befriend herself.[91]

Befriending women stretched to when they had, in adverse circum-stances, temporarily 'fallen', but were believed to be essentially good.

---

[87] A. F. Camac, St Peter & Pauls, Baldoyle, Dublin, 13 April 1932. Anthony Francis Camac, born 1899, ordained 1923 and died 1977. Gaughan, *The Archbishops, Bishops and Priests*, pp. 46–47.

[88] T. Manning, St Peter's Church, Phibsboro, Dublin, 22 December 1931.

[89] It was indicated on Walter W.'s letter that he received £5. Mr W., X. Baldoyle, Dublin, 11 April 1932. DDA, AB 7 CC, Box 3.

[90] Fr Condon, The Presbytery, Pro-Cathedral, 82 Marlborough Street, Dublin, n.d. *c.* January 1938. DDA, AB 7 CC, Box 6.

[91] Ibid.

In December 1922, Mrs M. McM. wrote following the death of her daughter because she was 'absouslty [absolutely] without money'[92] or anybody to help her. Fr Flanagan looked into the case:

I have ascertained that after a long period of abstinence there was a breakdown recently due to the death of a daughter. Applicant is financially at zero – is now ill and confined to bed. The only assets, as far as I can discover, are the house and the furniture thereof. It is a pitiable case.[93]

Mrs McM. had made no mention of her drinking, but as Fr Flanagan raised it not to condemn her, but to heighten how pitiable the case was, there is little reason to think it untrue. There was also an understanding that on occasion, people – even 'deserving' people – had to censor their lives in order to make a good case for charity. In 1929 Fr Moriarty,[94] while pointing out that Mrs R. had failed to admit that her husband's unemployment was as a result of his drinking, still recommended her for charity:

There is a slight 'suppressio veri' in her not referring to the fact that it was more through intemperance than anything else that her husband – in the past at all events was unable to procure employment. Still she herself is a very deserving woman and she has done her best and succeeded in looking after her children + provided them with an admirable education + I think you may safely recommend her to his Grace's charity.[95]

'...the woman herself is very worldly.'

Many of the observations that Delay made about Irish Catholic women and their clergy in post-famine Ireland remain pertinent to the 1920s and 1930s. She noted, for example, that 'by writing to priests, bishops, and even the pope, women demonstrated their belief in their right to respect and support from their clergy'.[96] However, this relationship was complex and often entailed bitter struggles between priests and women for status in their communities. As Delay observed, women and their priests were both 'intimates and adversaries'.[97] Priests may have often

---

[92] Mrs M. McA., [9] Mountjoy Square, North Dublin (city), December 1922. DDA, AB 7 CC, Box 1.
[93] Fr John Flanagan, The Presbytery, The Pro-Cathedral, Dublin (city), 4 December 1922.
[94] Andrew J. Moriarty, born 1879, ordained 1902 and died 1952. Gaughan, *The Archbishops, Bishops and Priests*, p. 194.
[95] Fr A. Moriarty, The Presbytery, 595 North Circular Road, Dublin, 3 December 1923. DDA, AB 7 CC, Box 1.
[96] Delay, 'Confidantes or competitors? Women, priests, and conflict in post-famine Ireland', 116.
[97] Ibid., 111.

acted as confidantes and advocates, but they could also exercise their significant social and moral power to tame women and ensure that they toed the social line. While resilience in women was admired 'wilfulness' was not. Women had to demonstrate the right measure of caring and compliance. If they failed to achieve this balance they could – irrespective of their children – be left in the cold. The response to the case of Mrs Elaine G. in 1927 is an interesting one: the parish priest had obviously been too cowardly to tell her to her face that he deemed her too 'wilful' to receive charity, but did not hesitate to do so behind her back:[98]

Not to appear heartless, I put my name to a paper from Mrs G. Viking Rd. She is in distress but is self-willed in regard to two children she has. I don't wish to interfere with your freedom in the matter.[99]

The priest presumed that 'self-willed in regard' to her two children was self-explanatory. It is likely that she had refused to take advice regarding her children's education or training. She had almost certainly failed to show the sort of deference her priest expected from a Catholic mother. She had not bargained astutely in relation to those children, as other mothers managed to use that streak of 'self-will' to exact some kind of power in a desperate situation. In 1924, Fr Farrell wrote about the B. family, which comprised six children and a widow.[100] He explained that the deceased husband had been a Protestant and had become a 'Catholic of a kind.' The proverbial Protestant relatives, Farrell claimed, had prevented the man from dying in a Catholic home and now 'sought' the children. Furthermore, he explained, the mother was not of 'the same social standing as her deceased husband was ... a weak Catholic'.[101] In the priest's view the Catholic front was weak on two levels: the mother was not wealthy like her husband's people and she was 'weak' in her faith i.e. susceptible to being bought. The mother was clearly playing hardball:

Though 2 children are in the Sacred Heart Home and 2 are in Lakelands Industrial School (not committed) she had made arrangements to take them out, to allow them to be put into Protestant Schools on doing which, she would be helped financially.[102]

---

[98] Joseph Young, born 1889, ordained 1915 and died 1959.
[99] Fr Young, The Presbytery, 117 North Circular Road, Dublin, 19 December 1927. DDA, AB 7 CC, Box 2.
[100] Thomas J. Farrell, born 1880, ordained 1907 and died 1940. Gaughan, *The Archbishops, Bishops and Priests*, p. 99.
[101] Fr Farrell, The Presbytery, Pro-Cathedral, 82 Marlborough St., Dublin, 24 January 1924. DDA, AB 7 CC, Box 1.
[102] Ibid.

By threatening to place her children in Protestant schools, she was using the only card she had left to play, if she wished to become financially independent and reunite what was left of her family. The priest, believing that she was 'down and out' and 'temptation is therefore very great', requested and received £30 to help her resuscitate her husband's manu-facturing business.

In 1934, Mrs Ellen M. G. wrote to the archbishop for assistance stating that she had had to send her children to Protestant schools, because she could not afford a 'Catholic education.' She was a convert and argued that if she had remained a Protestant, like her brother, she would not have been so reduced in circumstances.[103] Her priest was scathing in his response pointing out that the husband was in 'constant employment', he explained:

the woman herself is very worldly. She goes to the pictures on an average of six times a week, the seventh evening being devoted to cards she has not been to the sacraments for at least three years.

The four children despite the remonstrances of the priest of the district are attending a Protestant school.[104]

Thus, Mrs Ellen M. G. was characterised as having no regard for any of the established norms of her adopted religion or her society: as a mother she devoted her life to pleasure and trivia and as a Catholic she sent her children to Protestant schools. The priest offered an anecdote to testify to her lack of deference, claiming she boasted about her friends in the archbishop's palace: 'She said to Fr Murphy "Do you know who is a great friend of mine?" He said "No". And she replied "Old Dunne of Donnybrook".'[105]

'I arranged to have her sent to Pelletstown'

The role of the priest in Irish society has been controversial both in the past and in the writing of history.[106] This is possibly because of the priest's ubiquitous presence in Irish society and his enormous power to influence social behaviour and resolve local and private problems.[107] Marilyn Silverman argues that in the mid-1920s 'local Catholic

---

[103] Mrs Ellen M. G., X Ranelagh Road, Co. Dublin, 4 April 1934. DDA, AB 7 CC, Box 4.
[104] Fr Fleming, The Presbytery, Rathmines, Co. Dublin, 28 April 1934. Ibid.
[105] This was a reference to Archbishop Byrne's secretary, Patrick Dunne.
[106] T. Inglis, *Moral Monopoly: the Rise and Fall of the Catholic Church in Modern Ireland* (University College Dublin Press, 1998).
[107] Delay, 'Confidantes or competitors? Women, priests, and conflict in post-famine Ireland', 107–25.

clergymen began to move into the political spaces created by the events of the previous fifteen years', because they 'now had the time, energy, and inclination to address, in a more formal and deliberate way, the morals, interests, and politics of working people'.[108] The priest controlled access, not just to many possible remedies to any given situation, but also to the response of the community. If someone was to be ostracised, boycotted or shunned, the priest was in an incredibly powerful position to encourage, discourage or even instigate this process.[109] He was capable of immense compassion, good advice and cruel condemnation, but in whichever mode he chose to operate, he had a power few of his parishioners could ignore. As Phil O'Keeffe recalls in her memoir: 'Doctors, nurses and priests were a different people. They stood on pedestals, and we were the ones looking up to them.'[110] In his childhood memoir, the Cork author Christy Kenneally recalled that all the local women flocked to one particular priest for confession because, as his aunt explained, 'if you told dat man you were after murderin' your husband, he'd say, sure you didn't mean it darlin'.[111] In Peter Tyrrell's memoir the priest had been pivotal to his committal to the industrial school in Letterfrack in 1924 at the age of eight. He also understood that the priest held the key to his release: he believed that if the parish priest deemed the parents and home fit for his return then he could be freed. However, for him this entailed playing by the priest's rules: 'The essential thing is that the parents attend mass and contribute generously to the priest when he calls.'[112] As the social historian Kevin Kearns claimed: 'So much depended on the local parish priest. He put a personal face on the Church ... To many mothers, he *was* the Church.'[113] In his social history of Dublin, the priest was presented as the one that sent battered wives back to abusive husbands and led the charge to drive pregnant country girls from their home or, alternatively, as a family counsellor, community activist, political and legal advocate.[114]

The priests' letters in this collection provide incredibly varied examples of the exercise of this power. In general they confirm the central

---

[108] M. Silverman, *An Irish Working Class: Explorations in Political Economy and Hegemony, 1800–1950* (University of Toronto Press, 2001), p. 278, pp. 307–308.

[109] Ibid., p. 288; Delay, 'Confidantes or competitors? Women, priests, and conflict in post-famine Ireland', 120.

[110] P. O'Keeffe, *Down Cobbled Streets* (Dingle: Brandon Publishers, 1995), p. 103.

[111] C. Kenneally, *Maura's Boy* (Cork: Mercier Press, 1996), p. 119.

[112] D. Whelan (ed.), P. Tyrrell, *Founded on Fear* (Dublin: Irish Academic Press, 2006), p. 89.

[113] K. Kearns, *Dublin's Lost Heroines: Mammies and Grannies in a Vanished City* (Dublin: Gill & Macmillan, 2004), p. 161.

[114] Ibid., pp. 87, 111, 157, 161, 163.

role of the priest in the lives of ordinary Catholics and the degree to which the priest was involved in problem solving. However, this was a much more complex process of brokerage and negotiation than the unequal balance of the relationship might suggest. In 1935, Mrs Eleanor O'B. wrote to the archbishop seeking assistance to pay the maintenance of her baby daughter in a care home. She had married a medical student in secret without the consent of his parents. When she had a baby daughter she was obliged to place her in the care of the Catholic rescue home the Saint Patrick's Guild founded and run by Miss Josephine Cruice.[115] She played her strongest hand when writing to Archbishop Byrne explaining:

A lady named Miss Smiley offered me £50, and clothes for myself if I would let her have baby, the arrangement would mean that my baby would be brought up as a protestant, that I want to avoid at all costs, though at times it seems that letting any baby go where she would have a home would be best after all[116]

Miss Ellen Smyley ran the Protestant Smyley Homes for children, and her name had become synonymous with proselytism to the Catholic hierarchy. This case throws up a few interesting issues regarding the moral landscape of early twentieth-century Ireland. Eleanor was a married woman, her child was not 'illegitimate', however all those involved in the case, the priest, Miss Cruice, the archbishop and Eleanor colluded in keeping her marriage a secret because it would damage her husband's career and standing. This conspiracy of silence effectively denied her child a family home and relegated her to institutional care. Fr Condon of Marlborough Street was deeply angered by Eleanor's tactics and critical of her marriage:

Three years ago I predicted for her the consequences of her folly in getting married secretly and warned her of all the difficulties she might have to face as a result. Her husband – still a student – has never acknowledged her as his wife to his friends – He has not been able either to give her any support. It will probably be a long time before he can bring to light the hidden things of darkness and give this unfortunate girl and her child – their rightful place.[117]

It was to Eleanor he 'spoke very strongly' regarding 'her disgraceful and uncalled for threat – of having to hand over her child failing assistance from Drumcondra [the archbishop's address]'. He forced her to admit that her threat was only a ploy 'to extract money to meet Cruice's demands'.

---

[115] See Chapter 3, note 88.
[116] Mrs Eleanor O'B., X Belvedere Place, Dublin, 4 June 1935. DDA, AB 7 CC, Box 4.
[117] Fr Condon, The Presbytery, Pro-Cathedral, 82 Marlborough St., Dublin, 21 June 1935. Ibid.

However, he reserved his harshest criticism for Cruice describing her as a 'hard master', who extracted a handsome fee of 10/- per week for boarding Eleanor's child. Foster mothers only received 7/6 per week 'so Miss Cruice made 2/6 on the deal'. It was clear in Condon's opinion Cruice was motivated by more than mere religious zeal: 'I had a few stand up fights with Miss Cruice during my term of office for trying to push on cases to me where no money was available. "Nothing for nothing" should be the motto of St Patrick's Guild.'[118] Cruice's guild had a bad history. In 1924 it had come to the attention of the Dublin Board of Health for placing a child in a home where two children had previously died. The following year seven children, who had been placed out to nurse by the guild, ended up in the Dublin Union (workhouse) and the authority accused the society of 'dumping' these infants.[119] Furthermore, Cruice's extortionist fees and resolute insistence on payment had been brought to Archbishop's Byrne's attention in 1924 in relation to another case.[120] When Eleanor had become ill she was no longer able to work to pay for her child and Cruice threatened to make the 'baby homeless'.

While Condon was clear about his objections to Cruice's operation, he did not feel it necessary to explain why he considered Eleanor as 'one so undeserving'.[121] In reality, both women were operating in a market created by Condon's willingness to keep things in 'darkness', thus affording such exploitation of the vulnerable and desperate. It is likely that Eleanor was not of the same social standing of her 'medical student' husband, but it remains remarkable that this aspect of class (if that is what the subtext to this moral tale was) trumped Mr O'B.'s moral responsibility for his wife and child. However, all of those concerned implicitly accepted that Mr O'B. could not be disturbed from his 'friends' or his study to rescue his wife and daughter from Cruice's clutches. While Eleanor did not receive anything like £50 she requested, nor did she get any assistance in establishing her position as a wife, she did have her immediate debts cleared. She exacted something from the discriminatory and hypocritical moral universe because she played it at its own game. However, she and her daughter were still the ultimate losers.

---

[118] Ibid.

[119] M. J. Maguire, *Precarious Childhood in Post-Independence Ireland* (Manchester University Press, 2007), pp. 78, 92.

[120] L. Earner-Byrne, 'The rape of Miss Mary M: A microhistory of sexual violence and moral redemption in 1920s Ireland', *Journal of the History of Sexuality*, 24 (January, 2015), 75–98.

[121] Fr T. Condon, The Presbytery, Pro-Cathedral, 82 Marlborough St., Dublin, 3 July 1935. DDA, AB 7 CC, Box 4.

In 1937 Mrs B., the mother of fourteen children, the youngest twelve months old, wrote concerning her eldest unmarried daughter who had had two children. The series of correspondence relating to her case offers a rare glimpse of the social dynamics involved in the committal of 'illegitimate' children and unmarried mothers to institutional care. Mrs B. explained that her daughter had had a daughter in 1933, at which point she had

placed the case in Hands of Rev. Fr Dunlea c. c. failing to get the Boy to marry her she was only 16 years old. I acted on the advice of Fr Dunlea I took the Baby a Brough it up as one of my own she now goes to Rutland st school. I let her Mother go out to work.[122]

However, her daughter 'picket up with another Boy and he would not marry her because she had the Child. She is after having Baby Boy for this young man'. The mother then recorded all the attempts she had made to resolve the situation according to the dictates of her society

I am after doing everything to get them married its no use. I went to our Parish Priest Rev. Lucey cc. I went to his Parents. I placed him in the Hands of Inspector Johns Molesworth Street. He brough him to Court and for the Lack of Witness to prove she was seen in His Company which the young woman who was to come Died and the case was put out of the court.[123]

Mrs B. portrayed herself as trapped between the demands of eleven children, the love she felt for her eldest daughter (and presumably her children) and the wrath of her husband as well as his failing health. She claimed that her husband had 'casted her [his daughter] out of her Home' and had only recently relented and allowed her to return. She was at pains to depict her daughter as 'not Bad only Foolish', a good Catholic 'Remember she stills go to her Duty Every First Friday. Early Mass every Sunday.' However, she was 'Depressed lately' as she 'has not any friend in the world to give her a cup of Tea only myself. and if I turn her out with her children (God) knows what would be her End.' She repeated several times that her daughter was willing to work to support her children, but could not get childcare and Maria B. was too burdened with her own children to take on that role. She wrote asking 'Your Highness' to 'save her poor soul from further sin'.[124]

The parish priest had a very different reading of the situation: he had entered the B. family drama as Emily was about to have her second child and so 'arranged to have her sent to Pelletstown' a mother and baby

---

[122] Mrs Maria B., X Tolka Road, Ballybough, Dublin, 21 July 1937. DDA, AB 7 CC, Box 6.
[123] Ibid.   [124] Ibid.

home.[125] However, according to him the father refused to agree to this and thus the baby was sent to a friend.[126] Rev Lucey exercised himself in locating the baby to ensure it was baptised.[127] The baby was returned to the family when the mother failed to make maintenance payments. Lucey claimed it was the mother who did not 'want the girl and her children', but the father did. He also recorded that, against his advice, the family had pursued the 'supposed father of the second baby' in court. This was a reference to the affiliation orders procedure, introduced in 1930 to enable women to sue the putative father for the maintenance of their child.[128] While the priest's interpretation of the family dynamics appears at odds with Mrs B.'s, it is possible to reconcile them if one reads between the lines of both letters. It is likely Mrs B. was honest that it had been the second baby that had posed the real problem for her, she had been willing to follow Fr Dunlea's advice and absorb Emily's first child into her large brood, but the second child was the last straw. She simply felt unable to cope and fearful for the direction her daughter's life was taking. The father, by contrast, appeared more challenged by his daughter's first pregnancy, refocusing his wrath on the father of the second child. It is possible his weakening health made him less inclined to punish his daughter. The truth lies in the intimacy of family relations. Rev Lucey's reading was necessarily at one remove and not influenced by emotion or fear, but by the overriding concern to keep things quiet, to resolve the situation by making it disappear: by institutionalising the mother and her children. His advice not to pursue the father in court was probably driven by a horror of such public methods – pursuing an affiliation law suit hardly accorded with the shame a woman was supposed to feel in such circumstances. He also fundamentally doubted Emily's character, the 'supposed father' remark indicated he did not believe her. The fact that, according to contemporary parlance, Emily was a 'repeat offender' (i.e. had had more than one infant outside marriage), meant it would have been particularly difficult for her to gain

---

[125] Pelletstown (or St. Patrick's Home) on the Navan Rd., Dublin, run by the Sisters of Charity of Saint Vincent de Paul (later known as the Daughters of Charity) and closed in 1985. It had (like most of the other mother and baby homes) an appalling infant mortality rate, for example, in 1939 it had a death rate of 23 per cent. L. Earner-Byrne, *Mother and Child: Maternity and Child Welfare in Dublin, 1922–1960* (Manchester University Press, 2007), p. 199.

[126] Rev Lucey, St. Agatha's, 595 N.C.R., Dublin, 28 July 1937. DDA, AB 7 CC, Box 6.

[127] Daniel J. Lucey, born 1895, ordained 1919 and died 1966. Gaughan, *The Archbishops, Bishops and Priests*, p. 161.

[128] Illegitimate Children (Affiliation Orders) Act, 1930. L. Earner-Byrne, 'Reinforcing the family: The role of gender, morality and sexuality in Irish welfare policy, 1922–1944', *The History of the Family*, 13 (2008), 360–369.

a compassionate hearing.[129] Only after every other avenue tried by the family had failed was it willing to accept the priest's idea of a solution:

> I saw the various members of the family to-day and all have agreed to her going to High Park including herself. The parents are very anxious that her two children should be put into the Sacred Heart Home Drumcondra.[130]

St. Mary's Refuge, High Park, Drumcondra, County Dublin, was a Magdalene asylum for unmarried mothers and the Sacred Heart Home was a Catholic orphanage from which the children would have gone directly into the industrial school at High Park.[131] It is likely that the children were not released until they were sixteen years of age, and Emily stood every chance of spending the rest of her life working in the laundry at High Park.[132]

In January 1926 Fr Costello of Ashford, County Wicklow, was asked to investigate a case of incest in his parish.[133] He had initially been unaware of the case of 'incestuous concubinage' and had been visiting the father and daughter in question as 'man and wife for nearly twelve months'.[134] Clearly the community did not inform the priest of the situation, revealing a certain amount of collective resistance, or at least non-co-operation with the priest's role. He had been concerned with getting the children to school, but when he discovered the facts he did all he could 'to induce them to separate'. He had managed to get the

---

[129] The terms 'repeat offenders', 'habitual offenders' and 'fallen women' litter charitable and official writings on the subject revealing the social conviction that these women had broken moral and cultural codes and committed moral crimes. In 1930, the Department of Local Government and Public Health sought to remove 'repeat offenders' from county homes and transfer them to Magdalene asylums. *Annual Report of the Department of Local Government and Public Health, 1928–9* (Dublin, 1930), p. 112.

[130] Rev Lucey, St. Agatha's, 595 N.C.R., Dublin, 28 July 1937.

[131] St Mary's Refuge operated by the Sisters of Our Lady of Charity between 1856 and 1991. When Emily entered it held 215 other women. M. McAleese, *Report of the Inter-Departmental Committee to establish the facts of the State involvement with the Magdalen Laundries* (Dublin, Department of Justice and Equality, 2013), pp. 21–22, p. 296.

[132] While the McAleese report claimed that the average stay in High Park was just under five years, this has been strongly contested by the Justice for Magdalenes Research [JFMR] project, which points out that the McAleese report only provided information relating to 42 per cent of residents in all Magdalene asylums, furthermore using the electoral registers for the 1953–1954 period, it contends that the average stay at High Park for 63.4 per cent of women who appear on the register was eight years. Furthermore, it found that the names of 50 per cent of the women registered to vote in 1954–1955 were found on the gravestones of the institutions. McAleese, *Report of the Inter-Departmental*, p. 170; C. McGettrick, 'Deaths, Institutionalisation & Duration of Stay, 19 February 2015', pp. 14–16 and 57–60.
    www.magdalenelaundries.com/JFMR_Critique_190215.pdf accessed 14 May 2015.

[133] John M. Costello, born 1880, ordained 1905 and died 1964. Gaughan, *The Archbishops, Bishops and Priests*, p. 67.

[134] Costello, Ashford, County Wicklow, 9 January 1926. DDA, AB 7 CC, Box 1.

daughter and her children admitted into the county home in Rathdrum, but she had returned to her father within a week. The priest's campaign had involved pressurising the daughter by 'impressing on her especially, the fate that awaited her in eternity if she continued her sinful life'. Costello displayed absolutely no understanding of child sexual abuse and appeared to hold Mr H.'s daughter equally responsible for the incestuous relationship. He finally succeeded 'in conjunction with the local police, in having three of the children sent to an industrial school and hope tomorrow to bring the mother to High Park and her infant (aged 7 months) to the Sacred Heart Home'. Many victims of abuse were dealt with in this way.[135] It seemed easier for Irish society to incarcerate them rather than the perpetrators.[136] Of course, this 'in-house' resolution prevented the scandal of a court case, but it also allowed society avoid dealing with the needs of its most vulnerable members.

There was often a class element to the handling of these cases and certainly elements of class prejudice influenced the 'solutions' proffered. In 1926, Fr Jim McSweeney sought, and received, recuperation of £40 that he had spent on three cases from his district involving unmarried mothers.[137] One case involved a girl with a 'bad family record' and a 'bad record' of her own, who as a result was refused help by the Holles St. Ladies' Association.[138] To 'save her & the child' – presumably from the Protestant alternatives – he had spent £15. The other case involved 'a young girl of a good family in trouble with a medical student'. The priest had 'sent the girl to Belfast' and arranged for the child to be boarded out. He explained 'we cannot hurry marriage till student is qualified + it would spoil his career if we forced the pace now'. Again a priest was pivotal in keeping things quiet, so that they could be resolved according to the class sensibilities of the time. The fact that this was achieved at a huge cost to the women and children involved was rarely noted or

---

[135] Buckley has noted that Irish cases of incest continued to be heard in camera after 1922, while in Northern Ireland and Britain this practice ceased. Furthermore, in Ireland incest continued to be classified as a misdemeanour with a maximum sentence of seven years. The average sentence for the crime fell by five years to two years' imprisonment between 1922 and 1950. S. Buckley, 'Family and power: incest in Ireland, 1880–1950' in A. McElligott, L. Chambers, C. Breathnach and C. Lawless (eds.), *Power in History. From Medieval Ireland to the Post-Modern World* (Dublin: Irish Academic Press, 2011), pp. 185–206, 186, 190, 197.

[136] J. Bourke, *Rape: A History from 1860 to the Present* (London: Virago, 2007), p. 119–146; E. O'Sullivan, '"…otherwise delicate subject": child sexual abuse in early twentieth-century Ireland' in P. O'Mahony (ed.) *Criminal Justice in Ireland* (Dublin: Institute of Public Administration, 2002), pp. 176–201, 198.

[137] Fr Jim McSweeney, Westland Row, Dublin, 29 Dec. c.1926. DDA, AB 7 CC, Box 2.

[138] Holles St. Ladies' Association was a charitable group attached to the National Maternity Hospital on Holles Street and thus frequently referred to as Holles Street.

considered. McSweeney signed off explaining: 'I might mention that my district is the poorest + therefore most troublesome in the parish.' He was clearly implying that poorer areas were more susceptible to moral problems, which was somewhat ironic in view of the second problem he outlined. However, this conviction was widely shared by contemporaries and was rooted in a deep-seated prejudice that the poor were inherently of inferior character. The fact that those with money could solve their problems in other ways was rarely considered when passing this judgement, although it was clearly known.

'These are the facts of his case'

While so much rested on the priest's view of a case, many of their references were uncertain and ambiguous. They may have adopted the language of 'facts', but in reality much of their opinion seemed formed by impression, perception or gossip. Peel makes a very similar observation about the techniques employed by caseworkers during the same period in America, observing that 'impressions were often deceptive, but they continued to serve as the foundations for judgements that could mean the difference between relief and no relief'.[139] Hence he argues that 'performing poverty' was so important to secure assistance, people had to 'appear' or 'act' poor and failure to do so could result in a negative recommendation. These Irish priests' letters also reveal inherent contradictions, in a single letter a priest could turn from 'a fact' to 'a sense' in a matter of lines with the objects of scrutiny being alternatively condemned and forgiven in the one letter. Fr Thomas Power's letter,[140] concerning Mr B. of Richmond Hill, vacillated between support, uncertainty and dismissive (unjustified) criticism. He began benignly by stating that

[t]he man is not a bad sort and would make a decent effort to support himself, if given a chance. He doesn't drink nor can I find evidence that he ever did so. Of course my evidence is not too reliable because I am a stranger to the district and hence am unable to check up on statements.[141]

However, he proceeded to doubt Mr B.'s explanations for the failure of his shoe business (stiff competition that undercut him), arguing that 'an efficient man in that line need not fear competition' and concluding with a completely unfounded presumption that 'he was lazy and feckless like

---

[139] Peel, *Miss Cutler*, p. 230.
[140] Thomas Power, born 1892, ordained 1918 and died 1967. Gaughan, *The Archbishops, Bishops and Priests*, p. 243.
[141] Fr Power, The Presbytery, Rathmines, Co. Dublin, 16 March 1934. DDA, AB 7 CC, Box 4.

so many others'. Thus within the two pages of his letter he had moved from admitting his evidence was not reliable, to a gut instinct that the man in question was 'not a bad sort', to writing him off as 'lazy and feckless'. If the recipient of his letter was not perplexed at this point, Power then explained that all he wanted to do was 'be honest' and let his reader 'know all the facts because it is very easy to be generous with other people's money'. However, cautionary notes on excessive generosity aside, Power believed that £5 (the sum Mr B. himself had requested) would 'be money thrown away', thus the archbishop should give nothing less than £10. Remarkably, such a confused and confusing reference yielded the £10 for 'our cobbler', as Power condescendingly put it.

Charity was an inexact science. The quest for the sincere and the genuine was no simple matter, particularly as those very concepts were ill defined and in the eye of the beholder. The majority of priests assumed they were engaged in a truth-detecting exercise, establishing whether people were as poor as they claimed, if they really had no other options but charity or if they were unemployed or in debt through no 'fault' of their own. Fr Brophy of Naas, County Kildare explained, regarding Mrs Marie S. and her family, 'I know she and her family are poor, but I cannot say yet whether their poverty is due to negligence on their part.'[142] In what ways could Marie S. and her family be negligent? The meaning was implied by Brophy's concern that there was 'work for all willing' in the new water works in the area. If he established that Marie S.'s husband was unwilling to work then the case of negligence would be clinched. However, as the Vincent de Paul had helped them previously, he was fairly confident that 'neither husband nor the wife are importunate beggars'.[143] Still he requested time to investigate.

Brophy's investigation amounted to a fishing expedition in the local community of informants. He opened his letter to the archbishop's secretary on 25 January 1938 with the damning, if ambiguous, lament that upon further inquiries he feared 'it will be hard to lift them out of poverty and misery'. In terms of the philosophy of charity, this state of affairs was as potentially harmful as not being 'genuine' or 'deserving'. Charity people often argued that there was little point in assisting those that could not eventually assist themselves, these people were surrendered to the poor relief system. He explained that the President of the Vincent de Paul had confirmed that he had helped the family with food and a grocery ticket

---

[142] Laurence Brophy, born 1907, ordained 1931 and died 1971. Gaughan, *The Archbishops, Bishops and Priests*, p. 38.

[143] Fr Brophy, St Conleth's Presbytery, Newbridge, Co. Kildare, 22 January 1938. DDA, AB 7 CC, Box 7.

during the previous Christmas and secured a 'gift' of 10/- for them from the Army Benevolent Fund. Mr S. had called again upon the society the previous week and received £1, at this meeting he was 'in rags'. The President confirmed that he was 'not an importunate beggar' and provided him with bedclothes. However, Brophy's interpretation of this report reaffirms the idea of continuous need as a black mark against someone. He commented that if that account was not 'bad enough', he had received an even 'worse account from a person I regard as reliable'. Brophy relayed this informant's information as a statement in direct quotation:

This person made the following statement:– I made inquiries about the S. family. I was told they were badly off, but at the same time that he was too lazy to work. And even if he did take up a job any place his wife was there standing over him all day and advising the employer not to work him too hard. This has happened again and again with the result that no one would be bothered with them.

They have clothes and go to Naas regularly but do not go to Mass. This morning they were up when their neighbours were passing to Mass but they did not go, and when these people were returning from Mass they had a gramophone playing at a great rate. The wee girl had new boots on to-day and was well rigged out otherwise, but in spite of all this they say they are often hungry. Naturally when he is no good to work they must be handicapped trying to live on 12/6 a week. I was told also it was in the Free State army he was for short time. I suppose he was too lazy to drill there.

They were splendid for going to Mass till recently.

Mrs R. I know gives them milk daily, but apart from all this it is said they are often hungry.[144]

He apologised for 'the foregoing long quotation', but had felt it was necessary as it expressed 'the state of things very fully'. In many ways Brophy was correct, although the statement is thoroughly confusing and contradictory, it did in fact express many of the paradoxical judgements that the 'poor' were subjected to. It also revealed the difficulty in divining the signals that the external manifestation of anyone's life might give to one intent on looking for proof of worthiness. This informant had asked around and received the sort of patchwork picture of a family's life that such investigations are bound to throw up, particularly when the motivations of those informing can be as multifaceted and complex as the apparent behaviour of this family. Thus the picture that emerged is one tugged and pulled by different impulses, the spiteful and righteous, the generous and forgiving, the curious and jealous, and the earnest and confused – all the voices of a community ring through the long quotation. The only voices absent are those of the S. family, who appear like actors

[144] Fr Brophy, St Conleth's Presbytery, Newbridge, Co. Kildare, 25 January 1938. Ibid.

on a stage, analysed by a public that drift in and out of various acts of the drama of the S. family's life, knowing little about what happens backstage. The S. family was portrayed alternatively, and even simultaneously, as 'badly off' and 'too lazy to work'. This was Mr S.'s fault for being even 'too lazy to drill' and his wife's for being overprotective. They had clothes but appeared about in rags; they went to Naas town (i.e. out in public), but not to Mass, but they were 'splendid for going to Mass till recently'. They went hungry often, but they danced as their neighbours prayed, a kind neighbour (Mrs R.) provided them with milk (i.e. *believed* they were deserving) but still 'it is *said* they are often hungry'.

Brophy confessed that he no longer knew 'what to advise'. Before receiving this information he had been willing to try to use 'influence' to secure Mr S. a job, but now, 'if he is such a poor workman he would hardly be retained'. Thus, based on a picture drawn of a family by a community with all its motivations and value judgements, the S. family was left to other sources of charity or to luck. The results of Brophy's inquiries reflected the inconsistencies and conflicts upon which charity itself was based. There was compassion mixed with suspicion, concern undermined by ridicule and, ultimately little more to separate the 'deserving' from the 'undeserving' than hearsay and impression. All of this was underpinned by a fundamental distrust of those dependent on the goodwill of others.

In many of the reference letters there was an undertone of derision, as though there was something mildly theatrical about poverty and its protagonists – and that was often how people themselves were portrayed, as bit parts in a game of give and take. The fact that those in need were battling with often huge and sometimes insurmountable obstacles and were trapped in a drama they only partly controlled, was easily lost or glossed over in these narratives of reductionism. This could often be rather benign and not militate against understanding, like Fr Condon's portrayal of Mr and Mrs O'D. who had to 'subsist on 10/- per week':

O'D. himself is man of learning and professes to have a wide knowledge of the Classics. In the course of my visitation I found him one evening immersed in Cicero . . . His wife is a lunatic of an agreeable type. Her principal eccentricity is a warm admiration for De Valera. She can be heard any day going along the streets loudly acclaiming him as "the king of Ireland" She is widely known for her frequent public professions of admiration and devotion for His Excellency. I mention this fact realising as I do that with a loyal and law-abiding man like yourself it is likely to win your sympathy in her appeal.
In all seriousness I can give her a sincere recommendation.[145]

---

[145] Fr Condon, The Presbytery, 82 Marlborough St., Dublin, 27 July 1933. He did secure them £2. DDA, AB 7 CC, Box 5.

However, it could also lead to the callous dismissal of people enduring truly hard lives, like a 'brokenhearted mother' from Crumlin, who wrote in July 1938 explaining her sense of isolation and betrayal upon leaving her inner city life for the promised land of the Dublin suburbs. Mrs H. was the mother of ten children and her eldest son, who was twenty-three, suffered from paralysis since birth. She was evidently proud (and knew she was judged in this regard) about how she cared for him, noting 'we get great praise from the Doctors and he has no bed sores T God [thank God]'. Her husband was unable to work due to heart trouble and remained at home as her son's 'nurse' and she thanked God that he did not drink or smoke. Her youngest child was three months old and she lived 'a miserable existence;' she had £1–4 a week plus 10/- a week for 'the cripple boy', out of this she had to pay 7/10 rent, 1/2 light and she owed on her rent. She felt aggrieved that 'the[y] made [her] come out here to live' thus tearing her away from the support network of the city:

When I was in westland row parish Father Rafter kept my little boy in everything he wanted but since I came out here to live it is terrilble it is a big change the roomkeepers wished helped us twice a year the[y] do not come out to crumlin we are lost so Dear Father if you could do anything for me We will always pray for you[146]

Mrs H. was habituated to charity's scrutiny and accepting of its demands. She included in her letter her 'relief cards' so the archbishop would 'know the case is genune'.[147]

Fr Howe of Crumlin did not question any of the essential facts of Mrs H.'s 'miserable life' merely the spirit of the woman herself.[148] He acknowledged that he had called monthly to her husband who was a 'permanent invalid' and that they had a 'deformed child'. However, he declared: 'I have never been sure of these folk being genuine yet I have nothing against them. They seem to parade the monstrosity a little too much.'[149] The family had recently been 'rested' as a case by the Vincent de Paul, he surmised this was probably for the classic charity dilemma, 'they were not accomplishing anything, nor ever able to satisfy the party'. So, the H. family could not be 'saved', their poverty was entrenched and with ten children, an invalided husband and a son requiring fulltime care, Mrs H. was accused of parading these facts too much. While Howe admitted he had 'very little definite', that did not prevent him from

---

[146] Mrs H., X Clonard Road, Crumlin, Dublin, July 1938. DDA, AB 7 CC, Box 7.
[147] Ibid.
[148] John J. Howe, born 1908, ordained 1931 and died 1983. Gaughan, *The Archbishops, Bishops and Priests*, p. 134.
[149] Fr Howe, 9 St Agnes Road, Crumlin, Dublin, 20 July 1938. DDA, AB 7 CC, Box 7.

painting a scene that reduced this family to caricatures in a community he appeared to fundamentally mistrust: 'I did find them having a "swell" tea one night when they were complaining of hunger – Bacon, eggs, sausages etc. They were apologetic about the feast. Still that is very little to go on – in Crumlin.'[150] Crumlin, a settlement made up of those relocated from the poverty of inner city Dublin, was the site of deception, little was as it appeared, and even when it appeared incontrovertible there was something vaguely distasteful about it to this priest. In such a short missive he had utterly disregarded the heartache of caring for such a severely disabled adult child. The exhausting life of raising ten children without a breadwinner was all part of a picture of 'monstrosity' and Mrs H. a person who *might* be using the realities of her life to extract help. The passing of time does little to diminish the horror of this world vision. It begs the question: how could Mrs H. have played her hand in such a way that would not have caused offence?

Needless to say, empathy and charity are not automatic bedfellows, but what is surprising is the degree to which charity could smother empathy. When people were set the task of weeding out the appropriate cases for charity, compassion could be easily sidelined by caution, misunderstanding or raw prejudice. The priests were, in real terms, little qualified to understand the lives they encountered in their parish, particularly the lives of complex, large and impoverished families. In easy sentences people and their toil could be, literally, written off because the priests could not *imagine* these lives, and because they carried to each case their own unique life experiences, coloured by a host of values and beliefs.[151]

In March 1933, Sharon F. wrote asking for help to defray the costs of her mother's death.[152] Her letter, on behalf of herself and two sisters, elicited an apparently agreed clerical version of their lives, which had little to do with the real women and everything to do with *ideas* about their behaviour. Fr Taylor explained that there was a 'long story' behind this case,[153] but he was not going to elaborate, suffice to say:

I often advised the mother to send them away to service – their ages range from 17 to 23 approx. They were no more inclined for this than she and I am afraid they will be drifters.

---

[150] Ibid.
[151] It should be noted that only a handful of the priests featured in this collection were born in Dublin, although there is little evidence of a rural–urban dimension to the encounter between these priests and their largely urban parishioners.
[152] Sharon M. F., Knockanarrigan, Dunlavin, Co. Wicklow, 25 March 1933. DDA, AB 7 CC, Box 5.
[153] Michael F. Taylor, born 1868, ordained 1900 and died 1972. Gaughan, *The Archbishops, Bishops and Priests*, p. 271.

The eldest was away in a good situation in England but the foolish mother called her home when she got ill about two months ago.[154]

So Taylor gave advice, which, despite his denouncement of them as 'drifters', they followed: one daughter was in a job in England. However, he did not approve of the fact that her dying mother had wished to have her daughter near her and castigated the deceased woman as 'foolish'. There was, evidently, little room for sentiment or filial affection when one was unable to afford it. Taylor admitted that he had not actually seen the family 'within that period' and referred the archbishop's secretary to the parish priest Fr Leahy.[155] Leahy did little to disrupt the narrative web Taylor had begun to weave, but he gave the historian more of an idea *why* this family had so displeased these clerical overseers. Leahy began by setting the ground cautiously – any money granted would never be repaid and would lead to subsequent requests – but he did not hesitate for longer than a paragraph before establishing the real grounds for refusal: 'To my mind these girls are either too lazy or too grand to work.'[156] In his *mind* these girls had notions about themselves, something in their (and their deceased mother's) behaviour had offended Leahy's sensibilities and caused him to believe they held themselves in high regard. These were fatal flaws in women, particularly in women who needed sympathy and charity. However, Leahy merely confirmed that Taylor's advice had been followed, two of the daughters had been working, one as a maid in a hospital and another as a maid in Kildare town. This was hardly substantial evidence for the prosecution wishing to convict them of illusions of grandeur, but there was a sting in the tale – whispers of inappropriate behaviour: 'The second [daughter] was complained of to the P. P. by her mistress for keeping late hours at night.' Leahy was confident (as bachelor men might be) that the 'the responsibility rests with the Mother, who fail[ed] to train them in any way'. Yet, he proceeded to offer up more evidence that did little to condemn them and everything to recommend them for compassion:

The Father died about 5½ years ago, the brother 1½ & the Mother about 3 weeks ago.

The girls live about 4½ miles from here with an uncle who has the old age pension. There is a probability that the house – a labourers cottage – may be taken from them by the Board of Health.[157]

---

[154] Fr Taylor, Dunlavin, Co. Wicklow, 30 March 1933. Ibid.
[155] James W. Leahy, born 1899, ordained 1925 and died 1970. Gaughan, *The Archbishops, Bishops and Priests*, p. 157.
[156] Fr Leahy, The Presbytery, Donard, Co. Wicklow, 7 April 1933. DDA, AB 7 CC, Box 5.
[157] Ibid.

They were bereaved not once but three times in the previous six years, they lived with an uncle on the pension (any implication this made them rich was preposterous), which in all likelihood made them carers rather than dependents, and they faced losing their home, presumably because it was unfit for habitation. However, the basis of Leahy's ire was not factual; these women did not have the right attitude, their demeanour negated their need. As Leahy explained, 'some reliable men' told him that they did have relatives who were willing to take them, 'but they prefer to remain as they are and be independent'. Anonymous men claimed unnamed relatives could take these women and *make* them as they *should be* – dependent, but they wished to remain 'as they were' –*independent*. These women were not judged on their poverty, or their recent bereavement; they were judged on their characters, which were not deemed appropriately humble, feminine or dependent. A simple and devastating 'No' was written on the top of Leahy's letter – the archbishop had been convinced they were not 'deserving'.

Conclusion

The relationship between the Catholic Church and 'its poor' was often torn between distrust and compassion. While there was always a tendency to reduce the complexity of human endeavour to 'types', hence people became 'touchers', 'intemperate beggars', 'feckless', or 'ideal laymen' and 'good mothers'. Many priests were addled and harried hunting for the 'genuine case', when, irrespective of the narrative of 'blame' and 'fault', all around them was desperate need. Thus they vetted and vouched and, in so doing, helped to create the discriminating culture of charity that ruled the lives of so many and that ultimately trapped giver and receiver in a myopic vision of the world that precluded imagining one based on equality. At the same time, despite the ambivalence when it came to Christian charity and the misunderstandings based on gender assumptions and mean-spiritedness, there were also many cases of compassion, forgiveness and empathy. For example, Fr Doherty's compassionate plea and reflection on the wider realities of social suffering, when he wrote on behalf of a widowed mother of four: '. . . I only wish I could help . . . but there are so many similar cases in my poor District.'[158] Or Fr Moriarty, who understood that people must censor their lives to

---

[158] Fr James Doherty, 59 Eccles St., Dublin, May 1924. DDA, AB 7 CC, Box 1.

make a 'deserving case', and still recommended Mrs O'R. despite her 'suppressio veri' regarding her husband's drinking.[159]

Priests frequently became actively involved in forging 'solutions' to family problems, be it breaking up an incestuous relationship, placing 'illegitimate' children in orphanages or, helping the victims of domestic abuse to secure employment and a modicum of independence from savage violence. It is obvious from these letters that the priests were often ill qualified to face the challenges that poverty, marriage and numerous children presented to many of their parishioners. Nonetheless, they were regularly the central figure in negotiating a solution, and their suscepti-bilities, personalities and worldview were crucial in deciding what kind of advice or assistance these parishioners received. There is little doubt that deep class convictions played a role in the way the poor were considered and helped, but there were also many other factors at play, some obvious, such as the role of faith and Catholicism, others less so, like prejudice, sexism and fear.

---

[159] Fr Moriarty, The Presbytery, 595 North Circular Road, Dublin, 3 December 1923. Ibid.

Conclusion
'Peopling the Past'

At various points along the route people were kneeling in prayer, while some overcome with grief, burst into tears as the horse-drawn hearse approached.[1]

On the morning of 9 February 1940 Archbishop Byrne died. His body was moved from his residence to the Holy Cross Church in Drumcondra, where it lay for two days to allow thousands of mourners to pay their respects. As the archbishop's body was removed to the Pro-Cathedral for the funeral, the bells of the city's churches tolled, house blinds were drawn and shops were closed.[2] In the bitter easterly winds that blew that day, people from all over Ireland lined the route to the Pro-Cathedral. Some wore mourning badges of the Papal colours, with a black crepe cross, some merely bowed their heads, others knelt and prayed, while others wept. Some of the people featured in this book were probably among those crowds. Thomas Morrissey has observed that, while history has largely neglected the archbishop since that day, 'he would have been happy with such anonymity as a further link with the poor, who leave no mark in history's pages'.[3] Morrissey has reminded us of the 'forgotten archbishop' and this book has sought to allow the poor with whom he was so associated to leave their mark on the page of history too.

The ink was barely dry on the pages of Irish political independence when the poor of Ireland began to write to the archbishop and by the time of his death over 4,000 letters had been sent to him. In some senses those who wrote to the archbishop were an intermediary generation, still referring to the Home Assistance payment as 'poor relief' or 'outdoor

---

[1] 'There were many touching scenes', *Evening Herald*, 12 February 1940. Cited in T. J. Morrissey, *Edward J. Byrne 1872–1941: The Forgotten Archbishop of Dublin* (Dublin: The Columba Press, 2010).

[2] 'Removal of Archbishop's Remains: Route Thronged By Mourners', *Irish Times*, 13 February 1940.

[3] Morrissey, *Edward J. Byrne 1872–1941*, p. 275.

relief' and negotiating charity to survive, while beginning to adapt to the Unemployment Allowance of 1934 and the Widows' and Orphans' Pension of 1935. Life cycle poverty was mitigated to some degree by these welfare measures, but these payments were often so small that they simply became just another part of the 'economy of makeshifts'. The experience of poverty in Ireland during this period was characterised by 'stasis and continuity'.[4] The slums of the nineteenth century survived largely intact until well after the 1940s. Thus the aspirations of political independence did little to house people any better than the dispassion of colonial rule had done. The profile of the poor remained largely unchanged: the people found in this book are the children and grand-children of Jacinta Prunty's nineteenth-century subjects, still surviving by the drama and drudgery of the 'mixed economy of welfare', begging, borrowing and saving to survive.[5] Women continued to dominate the poverty narrative and experience; they are over-represented in this collection accounting for 1,747 letters compared to 1,365 written by men. While both sexes presented themselves as 'thwarted providers',[6] it was women that ran the 'economy of expediency'.[7]

The idea that the structures of society and the economy might play a role in poverty gained increasing traction in the late 1920s and early 1930s. However, this did not preclude contemporaries from distinguishing between categories of poor people and thus allowing certain sections of society to be blamed for their poverty while others were exonerated.[8] Those who had seen 'better days' experienced a more empathetic charity encounter, while the generational poor continued to live or die by perception and still had to prove themselves 'deserving'. Proving that you would

---

[4] Pimpare makes this point in relation to the history of poverty in America. S. Pimpare, 'Towards a new welfare history', *The Journal of Policy History*, 19 (2007), 234–252, 239.

[5] Prunty noted that on the south side of Dublin, the Liberties and the Townsend Street docklands areas were the poorest, while on the northern side of the city Beresford Street, Mecklenburgh Street (later Tyrone Street and Waterford Street) and the North Strand, and the Sheriff Street docklands predominated. In 1920s and 1930s Church Street, Bolton Street, Dorset Street and Gloucester Street continued to be the addresses of the poor. Gardiner Street and Dominick Street, 'colonised by the poor' by the end of nineteenth century, continued to be their domain throughout the twentieth century. J. Prunty, *Dublin Slums, 1800–1925: A Study in Urban Geography* (Dublin: Irish Academic Press), p. 338.

[6] Bailey made this observation of English nineteenth-century pauper letters. J. Bailey, '"Think wot a mother must feel": parenting in English pauper letters', *Family & Community History*, 13 (2010), 5–19, 5.

[7] E. Ross, 'Hungry children: housewives and London charity, 1870–1918' in P. Mandler (ed.), *The Uses of Charity: The Poor on Relief in the Nineteenth-Century Metropolis* (Philadelphia: University of Pennsylvania Press, 1990), pp. 161–196, 163.

[8] For a good example of this duality see, 'Pagan view of Poverty: The social system', *Irish Independent*, 21 July 1931.

not become a constant burden remained as essential to any successful appeal as it had been in the eighteenth and nineteenth centuries. Thus strong intellectual currents from the nineteenth century continued to exert an influence even while the gradual erosion of the *laissez faire* economics persisted, meaning competing, apparently contradictory impulses, pervaded any discussion of poverty and hence any policy initiatives. The history of Irish poverty is no tale of progression. In fact, had the Irish poor continued to live under British rule, they may have fared better with the emergence of an earlier and more comprehensive welfare state. That is not to present an ideal view of the experience of poverty in Britain, but the widows' pension arrived a decade sooner there and was not restricted to widows with children.[9] The Beveridge revolution of the 1940s was much more far-reaching than its pale Irish equivalent and, of course, there was nothing to rival the National Health Service [NHS], which was launched in Britain and Northern Ireland in 1948.[10]

There is significant evidence that greater numbers of people were no longer able to make ends meet during the tough 1930s with all charities witnessing a substantial increase in demand. Many organisations fretted about the risk of poverty spreading to the middle classes whose upward trajectory seemed, for the first time since the mid-nineteenth century, to be compromised or at least could no longer be taken for granted.[11] Small farmers and rural labourers fared particularly badly during the 1930s in the face of the international depression and an economic war with Britain. Although only a quarter of the letters in this collection were from outside Dublin, the struggles and tactics of the rural authors featured here were not all that dissimilar to their urban counterparts. However, the network of charity in rural areas was weaker, and many rural people articulated a sense that it was more difficult to reveal their need in small rural communities where great store was placed on self-sufficiency and reputation. Furthermore, there is evidence that means tested welfare

---

[9] For a sanguine view of the history of poverty in Britain see, D. Vincent, *Poor Citizens: the State and the Poor in Twentieth Century Britain* (London: Longman, 1991) and I. Gazeley, *Poverty in Britain, 1900–1965* (Basingstoke: Palgrave Macmillan, 2003).

[10] For the impact of the NHS in Northern Ireland see, P. Martin, 'Social policy and social change since 1914' in L. Kennedy and P. Ollerenshaw (eds.), *Ulster Since 1600: Politics, Economy, and Society* (Oxford University Press, 2012), pp. 308–324; For the situation prior to the NHS see, P. Martin, 'Enduring the pauper taint: Medical benefit in welfare reform in Northern Ireland' in V. Crossman and P. Gray (eds.), *Poverty and Welfare in Ireland 1838–1948* (Dublin: Irish Academic Press, 2011), pp. 223–236.

[11] J. H. Porter, '"The squeezed middle": The Johnson committee and the Irish middle class under Fianna Fáil, 1932–47' unpublished paper presented at Class and Culture in Twentieth-Century Ireland: Resilience, Resistance, and Transformation Conference, University of Cambridge, April 2015.

discriminated more heavily against those with a small bit of land versus property-less urban dwellers. It was harder for rural people to qualify for certain benefits and many lamented how they were refused free medical dispensary care because of their landholdings. While local welfare land-scapes undoubtedly varied, we have yet to establish to what degree the culture of begging and receiving differed. It is likely this was a much more consistent experience, but only further detailed research will clarify the regional variations. The only claim this book can make is that collectively these letters give a good sense of the national culture of poverty and charity; however, the local texture is predominately one of urban poverty.

While many other forms of income were probably more important than charity, these charity letters offer an insight into how all resources were strategically aligned in the cosmos of the poor. Every letter sent either from Dublin's poverty pit or the fields of County Roscommon documents what the price of survival was to each individual correspond-ent and their families. This allows for the creation of a history with the individual at its core and provides a better understanding of the general experience of poverty. In exploring these strategies this book has also attempted to gauge the toll they exacted from the poor. It provides a sense of the fears, anxieties and feelings of love that bound families together, but also the impact of visceral need that literally strained these units at the seams. The ultimate price of poverty was dependence; it was inevitable that the poor must rely on other family members, neighbours, charities, the pawn, moneylenders, faith and religion, family breakup, emigration and the state. As David Vincent's insightful study of poverty in Britain establishes, 'in essence poverty was not a condition but a practice',[12] thus the poor relied upon 'intricate webs of dependencies'[13] that took great skill to manage and maintain. These letters record a significant repertoire of techniques and resources called upon to survive. A record had to be kept, because it was also proof of ingenuity, resilience and worthiness. It was itself part of what had to be *seen to be done* to elicit any further help and to avoid being condemned as idle or culpable. When the poor documented where they had sought help, what small jobs and big sacrifices they had undertaken, they left to history a paper trail of their elaborate survival mechanisms, but this record also formed another part of their negotiation strategies – a record of survival itself was a strategy. Thus these letters reflect and were part of the experience of poverty.

Historical reconstruction is highly complex and despite the holy grail of objectivity, it is ultimately subjective; each historian establishes their

---

[12] Vincent, *Poor Citizens*, p. vii.   [13] Pimpare, 'Towards a new welfare history', 239.

own unique 'affinity and distance between history and source'.[14] This historian draws a distinction between truth and fact: what the letter writer wished to express and how and why they expressed it is of central importance for a social and cultural understanding of poverty. Not all letters were factually accurate, and undoubtedly exaggeration, distortion and lies played a role in the negotiation process. In fact, these tactics in themselves tell us much. The poor employed words, frayed at the edges by over use, but nonetheless pressed into service again and again to evoke a world of indignities, injustice and manipulation in which they played a role. Furthermore, as the detailed analysis in this book reveals, the poor dealt in no less concrete factual terms than the priests who assessed their case and character. The latter could be informed by instinctive compassion, discriminatory assumption or inexperience, any of which could override or disregard 'fact'.[15] How the poor rhetoricised their understandings of the moral and social perceptions of poverty, responsibility and entitlement, is not just important in its own right, but also because, as Peel so eloquently put it: 'words help the powerless hold the powerful to account'.[16] We must take those words seriously and listen to what was being said, even if it constituted in part 'ritual conformity'[17] or 'orchestrated performances' in the 'drama of charity',[18] because beneath these rhetorical ploys, and often alongside them, very real things were being said about poverty.

Thomas Adams argues that the provision of welfare – and one could include charity – involves 'a complex amalgam of justifications and motives that inspires the behaviour of providers and recipients and gives legitimacy to their transactions'.[19] The words of the poor, the way they articulated requests, the reaction of the priests, the *modus operandi* of Ireland's charity market, not only mirrored many of the features of statutory relief, it also reflected society itself. Virginia Crossman made a similar observation for the nineteenth-century Irish poor law system,

---

[14] L. Thatcher Ulrich, *A Midwife's Tale: The Life of Martha Ballard, Based on Her Diary, 1785–1812* (New York: Vintage Books, 1991), p. 34; I. Clendinnen, 'Fellow sufferers: history and imagination', *Australian Humanities Review*, 1997–98. (Electronic journal).

[15] Crossman makes a similar observation regarding poor law inspectors and priests in the nineteenth century. V. Crossman, *Poverty and The Poor Law in Ireland, 1850–1914* (Liverpool University Press, 2013), p. 18.

[16] M. Peel, *Miss Cutler and the Case of the Resurrected Horse: Social Work and the Story of Poverty in America, Australia, and Britain* (The University of Chicago Press, 2012), p. 15.

[17] P. Mandler, 'Poverty and charity in the nineteenth century metropolis' in Mandler (ed.), *The Uses of Charity*, pp. 1–37, 1.

[18] Ross, 'Hungry children: housewives and London charity', p. 187.

[19] T. M. Adams, 'The mixed economy of welfare European perspectives' in B. Harris and P. Bridgen (eds.), *Charity and Mutual Aid in Europe and North America Since 1800* (New York and London: Routledge, 2007), pp. 43–66, 43.

arguing that if it was harsh, it nonetheless represented 'popular notions of entitlement and eligibility'.[20] Furthermore, she noted that the way people framed their applications for poor relief in the nineteenth century indicated that they were aware of 'prevailing attitudes to eligibility'.[21] Similarly, the charity letters of the early twentieth century reveal an awareness of the sensibilities of the system and a sense of *entitlement* to charity and relief. Through their persistence, negotiation and anger, they were articulating a sense that society bore some responsibility for their impoverished existence, although they were not yet articulating a *right* to a basic standard of living. In these letters anger often functioned as a way of establishing entitlement and insisting upon innocence and respect, whereas threats of apostasy represented an attempt to wield some power in an inherently manipulative charity market. Indeed, these threats and their success raise important questions about the balance and nature of power relations in the charity encounter and in the relationship between the Catholic Church and its flock.

The paradox at the heart of the letter exchange was that it was based on a common bond, a sense of humanity and spirituality, but it often highlighted the distance between these impoverished lay writers and their religious 'superiors'. In the undulating rhythm of the spoken word, etched on the pages of these letters is the fraught world between passivity and agency, compassion and suspicion, need and entitlement, inclusion and alienation that the poor had to negotiate on a daily basis. At the very least the struggle for survival that the poor engaged in throughout this period, and arguably are still engaged in, warrants attention and acknowledgment, if not respect – something that is still not commonplace. Their letters are the artefacts of that struggle.

Mary Fissell has observed that while 'the grand accomplishment of social history was to put ordinary people into history', it has been less successful in capturing 'the meanings men and women made' of life and their place in it.[22] The poor are so often the objects of the story of poverty, seen perpetually through others' eyes, condemned to relentlessly tell stories of their lives in exchange for help. As a result they become adept at seeing themselves through the eyes of others and often collude in the imagining of their situation in order to tap into the very prejudices that confine them. However, their words have the potential to unlock for history not merely their perspective, but also their knowledge. It is timely to listen to the words of the poor, and perhaps historical distance will

---

[20] Crossman, *Poverty and the Poor Law in Ireland*, p. 226.   [21] Ibid., p. 87.
[22] M. E. Fissell, *Vernacular Bodies: The Politics of Reproduction in Early Modern England* (Oxford University Press, 2004), p. 9.

make it easier to actually hear what they are telling us about poverty and its vulnerability and inherent injustice. This is the story of the experience of poverty during the first two decades of political independence, its anatomy, its flavour, its words, its colour, and its people.

If it does anything, this book 'peoples the past'.[23]

---

[23] R. Lawton, 'Peopling the past', *Transactions of the Institute of British Geographers*, 12 (1987), 259–283, 263. Cited in Prunty, *Dublin Slums, 1800–1925*, p. 239.

Bibliography

Primary Sources

Pamphlets and Official Reports

V. Brady, *The Future of Dublin – Practical Slum Reform* (Dublin, 1917).
Bulletin Saint Vincent de Paul, 1918–1940.
R. M. Butler, 'Dublin: Past and Present', *Dublin Civic Week Official Handbook* (Dublin: Civic Week Council, 1927).
C. A. Cameron, *Municipal Public Health Administration* (Dublin, 1914).
  How the Poor Live (Dublin, 1904).
Census of Population 1926, General Reports.
D.A. Chart, *The Story of Dublin* (Dublin, 1913).
P. Dunne, *Waiting the Verdict: Pension or Pauperism: Necessitous Widows and Orphans in the Free State* (Dublin, n.d. c. 1930).
T. N. Burke, *Evils of Drunkenness* (Dublin: Catholic Truth Society, 1918).
E. Cahill, *Freemasonry and the Anti-Christian Movement* (Dublin: M. H. Gill, 1929).
G. K. Chesterton, *Christendom in Dublin* (London, 1932).
Citizens' Housing Council, *Interim Report on Slum Clearance in Dublin 1937* (Dublin: Cahill & Co., 1937).
Citizens' Housing Council, *Report on Slum Clearance – 1938* (Dublin: Cahill & Co., 1938).
E. Coey Bigger, *Welfare of Mothers and Children, Ireland*, Vol. 4 (Carnegie UK Trust, 1917).
P. Coffey, *The Christian Family and the Higher Ideal* (Dublin: Catholic Truth Society of Ireland, 1931).
  The Church and the Working Class (Dublin: Catholic Truth Society of Ireland, 1906).
Committee on the Relief of Unemployment, 1927: Final Report (Dublin, 1928).
Commission on the Relief of the Sick and Destitute Poor, *Report of Commission on the Relief of the Sick and Destitute Poor including the Insane Poor* (Dublin, 1927).
Commission of Inquiry into Health Insurance and Medical Services, *Committee of Inquiry into Health Insurance and Medical Services, Final Report* (Dublin, 1927).
Commission to Inquire into Child Abuse [Ryan Report] (Dublin, 2009).

Committee of Inquiry into Widows' and Orphans' Pensions, *Committee of Inquiry into Widows' and Orphans' Pensions, Reports* (Dublin, 1933).

P. Cowan *Report on Dublin Housing* (Dublin: Cahill and Co., 1918).

The Difficulties of the Housing Problem and Some Attempts to Solve it (Dublin, n.d. *c.* 1916).

A. Crofts, *Property and Poverty* (Dublin, 1938).

Dáil Éireann, *Official Reports of the Debates of Dáil Éireann*, 1919–1940.

Report of Inquiry into the Housing of the Working Classes of the City of Dublin (Dublin, 1943).

Department of Local Government and Public Health, *Annual Reports of the Department of Local Government and Public Health*, 1922–1940.

Department of Local Government and Public Health, *Report of the Conference between the Department of Local Government and Public Health and Representatives of Local Public Health and Public Assistance Authorities, 1930*, (Dublin, 1930).

L. Gordon Smith and F. Cruise O'Brien, *Starvation in Dublin* (Dublin, 1917).

Handbook of the Eucharistic Congress: International Congress (Dublin, 1932).

J. Kelleher, *A Catholic Nation: Its Destitute, Dependent and Helpless Classes* (Dublin: Catholic Truth Society of Ireland, n.d. *c.* 1929).

J. B. Hughes, *Poverty in Dublin* (Dublin, 1914).

Irish Catholic Directory, 1922–1940.

Irish Catholic Directory, *The Evils of Proselytism* (1925).

John Keating, *Souperism* (Dublin: Catholic Truth Society of Ireland, 1914).

G. C. Lewis, *Observations on the Habits of the Labouring Classes in Ireland* (Dublin: Miliken and Sons, 1936).

A. M. MacSweeney, *Poverty in Cork* (Dublin, 1917).

L. McKenna, *James Connolly* (Dublin: Catholic Truth Society of Ireland, 1920).

M. McAleese, *Report of the Inter-Departmental Committee to Establish the Facts of the State Involvement with the Magdalen Laundries* (Dublin: Dept. of Justice and Equality, 2013).

J. R. O'Connell, *The Problem of the Dublin Slums* (Dublin, 1913).

Pastoral Address issued by the Archbishops and Bishops of Ireland to their Flocks on the Occasion of the Plenary Synod held in Maynooth 1927 (Dublin: Browne and Nolan, 1927).

Report of the Departmental Committee Appointed by the Local Government Board of Ireland to Inquire into the Housing Conditions of Working Classes in the City of Dublin (London, 1913).

Report of Inquiry into the Housing of the Working Classes in Dublin, 1939–43 (Dublin: Government Publications Office, 1943).

Report on the Commission of Inquiry into the Reformatory and Industrial School System (Dublin: Stationery Office, 1936).

M. Spring Rice, *Working-Class Wives: Their Health and Conditions* (London: Virago, 1981 [1939]).

W. H. Thompson, *War and the Food of the Dublin Labourer* (Dublin, 1915).

G. D. Williams, *Dublin Charities: Being a Handbook of Dublin Philanthropic Organisations and Charities* (Dublin, 1902).

Archival Sources

> Dublin Diocesan Archives, Archbishop Byrne's Papers.
> National Archives of Ireland, Department of An Taoiseach S series;
>   Department of Local Government and Public Health.
> University College Dublin Archives, Fitzgerald Papers.

Newspapers, Journals and Periodicals

> *Dublin Historical Record.*
> *Dublin Statistical Society.*
> *Geographical Review.*
> *Hibernia.*
> *Irish Ecclesiastical Record.*
> *Irish Independent.*
> *Irish Press.*
> *Irish Times.*
> *Irish Rosary.*
> *Journal of the Statistical and Social Inquiry Society of Ireland.*
> *New Hibernia Review.*
> *The Bell.*
> *The Catholic Bulletin.*
> *The Dublin Journal of Medical Science.*
> *The Dublin Review.*
> *The Irish Journal of Medical Science.*
> *The Irish Monthly.*
> *Irish Theological Quarterly.*
> *The Journal of the Irish Free State Medical Union.*
> *Saothar.*
> *Statistical Society of Ireland Journal.*
> *Studies: An Irish Quarterly Review.*

Secondary Sources

Books, Chapters and Articles

E. K. Abel, 'Valuing care: turn-of-the-century conflicts between charity workers
    and women clients', *Journal of Women's History*, 10 (1998), 32–52.
L. Abrams, *Oral History Theory* (London and New York: Routledge, 2010).
T. M. Adams, 'The mixed economy of welfare European perspectives' in B.
    Harris and P. Bridgen (eds.), *Charity and Mutual Aid in Europe and North
    America Since 1800* (New York and London: Routledge, 2007), pp. 43–66.
H. D. Akenson, 'Keeping separate: boundary maintenance systems' in D.
    Harman Akenson (ed.), *Small Differences: Irish Catholics and Irish Protestants,
    1815–1922* (Montreal: McGill Queen's University, 1988), pp. 108–126.
C. S. Andrews, *Man of No Property: An Autobiography* (Dublin: Mercier, 1982).

J. Bailey, '"Think wot a mother must feel": parenting in English pauper letters', *Family & Community History*, 13 (2010), 5–19.

S. Bhattacharya, 'History from below', *Social Scientist*, 11 (April 1983), 3–20.

A. Bielenberg, *Ireland and the Industrial Revolution: The Impact of the Industrial Revolution on Irish Industry, 1801–1922* (London and New York: Routledge, 2009).

D. Birdwell-Pheasant, 'The early twentieth-century Irish stem family: a case study from Co. Kerry' in M. Silverman and P. H. Gulliver (eds.), *Approaching the Past: Historical Anthropology through Irish Case Studies*, (New York: Columbia University Press, 1992), pp. 205–235.

C. Bland and M. Cros (eds.), *Gender and Politics in the Age of Letter Writing, 1750–2000*, (Aldershot: Ashgate, 2004).

G. Bock and P. Thane (eds.), *Maternity and Gender Policies: Women and the Rise of the European Welfare State, 1880s–1950s* (London: Routledge, 1990).

J. Boulton, '"It is extreme necessity that makes me do this": some "survival strategies" of pauper households in London's West End during the early eighteenth century', *International Review of Social History*, 45 (2000), 47–69.

P. Bourdieu, *In Other Words: Essays towards a Reflexive Sociology* (Oxford: Polity, 1990).

J. Bourke, *Rape: A History from 1860 to the Present* (London: Virago, 2007).

B. Boydell, 'Impressions of Dublin – 1934', *Dublin Historical Record*, 37 (1984), 88–103.

P. Bracken, *Light of Other Days* (Cork: The Mercier Press, 1992).

J. Brady, *Dublin, 1930–1950: The Emergence of the Modern City* (Dublin: Four Courts Press, 2014).

I. Brandes, '"Odious, degrading and foreign" institutions? Analysing Irish workhouses in the nineteenth and twentieth centuries' in A. Gestrich, S. King and L. Raphael (eds.), *Being Poor in Modern Europe: Historical Perspectives 1800–1940* (Switzerland: Peter Lang, 2006), pp. 199–227.

C. Breathnach, 'Lady Dudley's district nursing scheme and the congested districts board, 1903–1923' in M. H. Preston and M. Ó hÓgartaigh (eds.), *Gender and Medicine in Ireland, 1700–1950* (New York: Syracuse University Press, 2012), pp. 138–153.

'Medicalizing the female reproductive cycle in rural Ireland, 1926–56', *Historical Research*, 85 (2012), 674–690.

C. Breathnach (ed.), *Framing the West: Images of Rural Ireland, 1891–1920* (Dublin, 2007).

'Smallholder housing and people's health, 1890–1915' in Breathnach (ed.), *Framing the West*, pp. 175–192.

The Congested Districts Board of Ireland, 1891–1923 (Dublin: Four Courts Press, 2005).

'The role of women in the economy of the West of Ireland, 1891–1923' *New Hibernia Review*, 1 (2004), 80–92.

E. Bhreathnach, J. MacMahon and J. McCafferty (eds.), *The Irish Franciscans 1534–1990* (Dublin: Four Courts Press, 2009).

R. Breen and C. Williams (eds.), *Understanding Contemporary Ireland: State, Class and Development in the Republic of Ireland* (London: The Macmillan Press, 1990).

C. S. Brophy and C. Delay (eds.), *Women, Reform, and Resistance in Ireland, 1850–1950* (Basingstoke: Palgrave Macmillan, 2015).

A. Brown (ed.), *Masters, Midwives and Ladies-in-waiting, the Rotunda Hospital 1745–1995* (Dublin: Farmar & Farmar, 1995).

S. J. Brown and D. W. Miller (eds.), *Piety and Power in Ireland, 1760–1960* (Belfast: Institute of Irish Studies, 2000).

S. Buckley, 'Found in a "dying" condition': nurse-children in Ireland, 1872–1952' in E. Farrell (ed.), *'She Said She was in the Family Way': Pregnancy and Infancy in Modern Ireland* (London: Institute of Historical Research, 2012), pp. 145–152.

The Cruelty Man: Child Welfare, the NSPCC and the State in Ireland, 1889–1956 (Manchester University Press, 2013).

'The NSPCC in Ireland, 1889–1939 – a case study', *Saothar*, 33 (2008), 59–70.

H. Burke, *The People and the Poor Law in Nineteenth Century Ireland* (West Sussex: Argus Press, 1987).

P. Burke and R. Porter (eds.), *The Social History of Language* (Cambridge: Cambridge University Press, 1987).

S. Carey, *Social Security in Ireland, 1939–1952: The Limits of Solidarity* (Dublin: Irish Academic Press, 2007).

L. Clarkson, 'The modernization of the Irish diet, 1740–1920' in J. Davis (ed.), *Rural Change in Ireland* (Belfast: Institute of Irish Studies, 1999), pp. 32–45.

C. Clear, *Social Change and Everyday Life in Ireland, 1850–1922* (Manchester University Press, 2007).

'Women in de Valera's Ireland, 1932–48: a reappraisal' in G. Doherty and D. Keogh (eds.), *De Valera's Irelands* (Cork: Mercier Press, 2003), pp. 104–114.

'"A living saint if ever there was one": work, austerity and authority in the lives of Irish women of the house, 1921–1961' in J. Hill and C. Lennon (eds.), *Luxury and Austerity* (University College Dublin Press, 1999), pp. 212–229.

I. Clendinnen, 'Fellow sufferers: history and imagination', *Australian Humanities Review*, 1997–98. (www.australianhumanitiesreview.org/archive/Issue-Sept-1996/clendinnen.html) Accessed 2 July 2016. (Electronic journal).

A. Coakley, 'Mothers and poverty' in P. Kennedy (ed.), *Motherhood in Ireland: Creation and Context* (Cork: Mercier Press, 2003), pp. 207–217.

M. R. Cohen, *The Voice of the Poor in the Middle Ages: An Anthology of Documents from the Cairo Geniza (Jews, Christian, and Muslim from the Ancient to the Modern World)* (New Jersey: Princeton University Press, 2005).

M. Cohen and N. Curtain (eds.), *Reclaiming Gender: Transgressing Identities in Modern Ireland* (New York: St Martin's Press, 1999).

M. Coleman, *The Irish Sweep: A History of the Irish Hospital Sweepstake, 1930–1987* (University College Dublin Press, 2009).

L. Colley, *Captives: Britain, Empire and the World 1600–1850* (London: Jonathan Cape, 2002).

P. Conlan, 'The secular Franciscans' in Bhreathnach, MacMahon and McCafferty (eds.), *The Irish Franciscans 1534–1990*, pp. 260–70.

S. Connolly, '"The moving statute and the turtle dove": Approaches to the history of Irish religion', *Irish Economic and Social History*, 51 (2004), 1–22.

264   Bibliography

P. Conroy, 'Motherhood interrupted: Adoption in Ireland' in P. Kennedy (ed.),
    Motherhood in Ireland: Creation and Context (Cork: Mercier Press, 2003),
    pp. 181–93.
O. Coogan, *Politics and War in Meath 1913–1923* (Dublin: Folens, 1983).
A. Cosgrove (ed.), *Marriage in Ireland* (Dublin: College Press, 1985).
M. Cousins, '"Sickness", gender, and National Health Insurance in Ireland,
    1920s–1940s' in M. H. Preston and M. Ó hÓgartaigh (eds.), *Gender and
    Medicine in Ireland, 1700–1950* (New York: Syracuse University Press,
    2012), pp. 169–188.
    Poor Relief in Ireland 1851–1914 (Bern: Peter Lang, 2011).
    The Birth of Social Welfare in Ireland, 1922–1952 (Dublin: Four Courts Press,
    2003).
C. Cox, *Negotiating Insanity in Southeast Ireland 1830–1900* (Manchester
    University Press, 2013).
C. Cox and M. Luddy (ed.), *Cultures of Care in Irish Medical History, 1750–1970*
    (Basingstoke UK: Palgrave Macmillan, 2010).
S. A. Crane, 'Writing the individual back into collective memory', *American
    Historical Review*, 102 (1997), 1372–1385.
M. Crawford, 'Dearth, diet and disease in Ireland, 1850: a case study of
    nutritional deficiency', *Medical History*, 28 (1984), 151–161.
D. Crew, 'The ambiguities of modernity: welfare and the German State from
    Wilhelm to Hitler' in J. Eley (ed.), *Society, Culture, and the State in Germany,
    1870–1930* (Michigan, 1996), pp. 319–344.
M. Cronin, *Country, Class, or Craft?: The Politicisation of Nineteenth Century Cork*
    (Cork: Cork University Press, 1994).
V. Crossman, *Poverty and the Poor Law in Ireland, 1850–1914* (Liverpool:
    Liverpool University Press, 2013).
    '"Attending to the wants of poverty": Paul Cullen, the relief of poverty and the
    development of social welfare in Ireland' in D. Keogh and A. McDonnell
    (eds.), *Cardinal Paul Cullen and his World* (Dublin: Four Courts Press,
    2012), pp. 146–165.
    and P. Gray (eds.), *Poverty and Welfare in Ireland 1838–1948* (Dublin: Irish
    Academic Press, 2011).
    'Middle-class attitudes to poverty and welfare in post-famine Ireland' in F.
    Lane (ed.), *Politics, Society and the Middle Class in Modern Ireland* (New York:
    Palgrave MacMillan, 2010), pp. 130–147.
    '"Facts notorious to the whole country": The political battle over Irish Poor
    Law reform in the 1860s', *Transactions of the Royal Historical Society*, 20
    (December 2010), 157–169.
    Politics, Pauperism and Power in Late Nineteenth-Century Ireland (Manchester
    University Press, 2006).
    The Poor Law in Ireland, 1838–1948 (Dundalk: Dundalgan Press,
    2006).
E. Crowley, *Cowslips and Chainies: A Memoir of Dublin in the 1930s* (Dublin: The
    Lilliput Press, 1996).
L. Cullen, *The Emergence of Modern Ireland, 1600–1900* (London: Batsford,
    1981).

M. Cullen (ed.), *Girls Don't Do Honours: Irish Women in Education in the Nineteenth and Twentieth Centuries* (Dublin: Women's Education Bureau, 1987).

J. T. Cumbler, 'The politics of charity: gender and class in late 19th Century charity policy', *Journal of Social History*, 14 (1980), 99–111.

A. Curthoys and A. McGrath (eds.), *Writing Histories: Imagination and Narration* (Melbourne: Monash Publications in History, 2000).

B. Curtis, 'Magdalen asylums and moral regulation in Ireland' in A. Potts and T. A. O'Donoghue, (eds.), *Schools as Dangerous Places: A Historical Perspective* (New York: Cambria Press, 2007), pp. 119–43.

M. Curtis, *A Challenge to Democracy: Militant Catholicism in Modern Ireland* (Dublin: The History Press Ireland, 2010).

M. E. Daly, 'Death and disease in independent Ireland, c. 1920–1970: A research agenda' in Cox and Luddy (ed.), *Cultures of Care in Irish Medical History*, pp. 229–250.

'"The primary and natural educator?": The role of parents in the education of their children in independent Ireland', *Eire-Ireland*, 44 (Spring/Summer, 2009), 194–217.

Slow Failure: Population Decline and Independent Ireland (Wisconsin University Press, 2006).

'Marriage, fertility and women's lives in the twentieth-century Ireland', *Women's History Review*, 15 (2006), 571–585.

'The Irish family since the Famine: continuity and change', *The Irish Journal of Feminist Studies*, 3 (1999), 1–21.

The Buffer State: The Historical Roots of the Department of the Environment (Dublin: Institute of Public Administration, 1997).

Women and Work in Ireland (Dundalk: Dundalgan Press, 1997).

'Women in the Irish Free State, 1922–39: The interaction between economics and history,' *Journal of Women's History* (Winter/Spring, 1995), 89–116.

'Working-class housing in Scottish and Irish cities on the eve of World War I' in S. F. Connelly, R. A. Houston and R. F. Morris (eds.), *Conflict, Identity and Economic Development, Ireland and Scotland, 1600–1939* (Preston: John Donald, 1995), pp. 217–27.

'Housing conditions and the genesis of housing reform in Dublin 1880–1920' in M. J. Bannon (ed.), *The Emergence of Irish Planning 1880–1920* (Dublin: Turoe Press, 1985), pp. 77–130.

Dublin – The Deposed Capital, 1860–1914 (Cork: Cork University Press, 1984).

J. Daybell, 'Scripting a female voice: women's epistolary rhetoric in sixteenth-century letters of petition', *Women's Writing*, 13 (2006), 3–22.

C. Delay, 'Confidantes or competitors? women, priests, and conflict in post-famine Ireland', *Éire-Ireland*, 40 (Spring/Summer 2005), 107–125.

G. Dening, 'Performing on the Beaches of the mind: an essay', *History and Theory*, 41 (February 2002), 1–24.

'Writing: praxis and performance' in Curthoys and McGrath (eds.), *Writing Histories*, pp. 45–53.

S. Deutsch, *Women and the City: Gender, Space, and Power in Boston, 1870–1940* (New York: Oxford University Press, 2000).

D. Dickson, *Dublin: The Making of a Capital City* (London: Profile Books, 2014).

A. Digby and J. Stewart, (eds.), *Gender, Health and Welfare* (London and New York: Routledge, 1996).

'Poverty, health, and the politics of gender in Britain, 1870–1948' in Digby and Stewart, (eds.), *Gender, Health and Welfare*, pp. 67–90.

T. Ditz, 'Formative ventures: eighteenth-century commercial letters and the articulation of experience' in R. Earle (ed.), *Epistolary Selves: Letters and Letter-writers, 1600–1945* (Aldershot: Ashgate, 1999), pp. 59–78.

R. Dunphy, *The Making of Fianna Fáil: Power in Ireland, 1923–1948* (Oxford University Press, 1995).

R. Dyson, 'Who were the poor of Oxford of the late eighteenth and early nineteenth centuries?' in Gestrich, King and Raphael (eds.), *Being Poor in Modern Europe*, pp. 43–68.

R. Earle (ed.), *Epistolary Selves: Letters and Letter-Writers, 1600–1945* (Aldershot: Ashgate, 1999).

'Introduction: letters, writers and the historian', in Earle (ed.), *Epistolary Selves*, pp. 1–12.

L. Earner-Byrne, 'The rape of Miss Mary M.: A mircrohistory of sexual violence and moral redemption in 1920s Ireland', *Journal of the History of Sexuality*, 24 (January, 2015), 75–98.

'"Dear Father my health is broken down": Writing health in Irish charity letters, 1922–1940', *Journal of the Social History of Medicine*, 28 (2015), 894–868.

'"Should I Take Myself and Family to Another Religion [?]": Irish Catholic women, protest, and conformity, 1920–1940' in Brophy and Delay (eds.), *Women, Reform, and Resistance in Ireland, 1850–1950*.

'Reinforcing the family: The role of gender, morality and sexuality in Irish welfare policy, 1922–1944,' *The History of the Family*, 13 (2008), 360–369.

'"Parading their poverty": 'Widows in twentieth-century Ireland' in B. Faragó and M. Sullivan (eds.), *Facing the Other: Interdisciplinary Studies on Race, Gender and Social Justice in Ireland* (Cambridge: Cambridge Scholars Publishing, 2008), pp. 32–46.

Mother and Child: Maternity and Child Welfare in Dublin, 1922–60 (Manchester University Press, 2007, 2013).

'Moral repatriation': The response to Irish unmarried mothers in Britain, 1920s–1960s' in P. Duffy (ed.), *To and from Ireland: Planned Migration Schemes c. 1600–2000* (Dublin: Geography Publications, 2004), pp. 155–174.

T. Fahey, 'State, family and compulsory schooling in Ireland', *Economic and Social Review*, 23 (July 1992), 375–78.

B. Fahy, *Freedom of Angels: Surviving Goldenbridge Orphanage* (Dublin: O'Brien Press, 1999).

T. Farmar, *Privileged Lives: A Social History of Middle-Class Ireland, 1882–1989* (Dublin: A. & A. Farmar, 2010).

E. Farrell, *'A Most Diabolical Deed': Infanticide and Irish Society, 1850–1900* (Manchester University Press, 2013).

(ed.), *'She Said She was in the Family Way': Pregnancy and Infancy in Modern Ireland* (London: Institute of Historical Research, 2012).

M. Farry, *The Aftermath of Revolution: Sligo 1921–23* (University College Dublin Press, 2000).

D. Ferriter, 'The stupid propaganda of the calamity mongers'?: The middle class and Irish politics, 1945–97' in F. Lane (ed.), *Politics, Society and the Middle Class in Modern Ireland* (New York: Palgrave Macmillan, 2010), pp. 271–287.

Occasions of Sin: Sex and Society in Modern Ireland (London: Profile Books, 2009).

The Transformation of Ireland 1900–2000 (London: Profile Books, 2004).

A Nation of Extremes: The Pioneers in Twentieth Century Ireland (Dublin: Irish Academic Press, 1999).

A. Findlater, *Findlaters –The Story of a Dublin Merchant Family 1774–2001* (Dublin: A & A Farmar, 2000).

M. E. Fissell, *Vernacular Bodies: The Politics of Reproduction in Early Modern England* (Oxford University Press, 2004).

Patients, Power, and the Poor in Eighteenth-Century Bristol (Cambridge University Press, 1991).

D. Fitzpatrick (ed.), *Terror in Ireland, 1916–1923* (Dublin: Lilliput Press, 2012).

Oceans of Consolation: Personal Accounts of Irish Migration to Australia (New York: Cornell University Press, 1994).

'Marriage in post-famine Ireland' in A. Cosgrove (ed.), *Marriage in Ireland* (Dublin: College Press, 1985), pp. 116–131.

'Class, family and rural unrest in nineteenth century Ireland', *Irish Studies*, 2 (1982), 37–75.

M. Flynn, *Nothing to Say: A Novel* (Dublin: Ward River Press, 1983).

L. Fontaine and J. Schlumbohm, 'Household strategies for survival: an introduction', *International Review of Social History*, 45 (2000), 1–17.

B. French, 'Gendered speech and engendering citizenship in the Irish Free State: ordinary women and County Clare District Courts, 1932–34' in Brophy and Delay (eds.), *Women, Reform, and Resistance in Ireland, 1850–1950*, pp. 139–162.

M. Fulbrook and U. Rublack, 'In relation: The "social self" and ego-documents', *German History*, 28 (2010), 263–272.

P. Galvin, *Song for a Poor Boy: A Cork Childhood* (Dublin: Raven Arts Press, 1990).

J. Garraty, *Unemployment in History: Economic Thought and Public Policy* (New York: Harper & Row, 1978).

T. Garvin, *Preventing the Future: Why was Ireland so Poor for so Long?* (Dublin: Gill & Macmillan, 2004).

A. J. Gaughan, *The Archbishops, Bishops and Priests who served in the Archdiocese of Dublin between 1900–2011*, (Dublin: Kingdom Books, 2012).

I. Gazeley, *Poverty in Britain, 1900–1965* (Basingstoke UK: Palgrave Macmillan, 2003).

C. Geertz, *The Interpretation of Cultures: Selected Essays* (London: Fontana Press, [1973], 1993).

D. Gerber, 'The immigrant letter between positivism and populism: American historians' uses of personal correspondence' in Earle (ed.), *Epistolary Selves*, pp. 37–55.

A. Gestrich, 'Solidarity and care: a research area of the GHIL', *Bulletin: German Historical Institute London*, 35 (November 2013), 4–11.

and S. King, 'Pauper letters and petitions for poor relief in Germany and Great Britain, 1770–1914', *Bulletin: German Historical Institute London*, 35 (November 2013), 2–25.

E. Hurren and S. King (eds.), *Poverty and Sickness in Modern Europe: Narratives of the Sick Poor, 1780–1938* (London: Continuum, 2012).

Hurren and King, 'Narratives of poverty and sickness in Europe 1780–1938: Sources, methods and experiences' in Gestrich, Hurren and King (eds.), *Poverty and Sickness in Modern Europe*, pp. 1–33.

King and Raphael (eds.), *Being Poor in Modern Europe*.

V. M. Gialanella (ed.), *Gender and Power in Irish History* (Dublin: Irish Academic Press, 2009).

L. D. Ginzberg, *Women and the Work of Benevolence: Morality, Politics and Class in the Nineteenth-Century United States* (New Haven, CT: Yale University Press, 1993).

L. Gordon, *Hero of their Own Lives: The Politics and History of Family Violence* (London: Virago, 1989).

P. Gray, 'Irish social thought and the relief of poverty, 1847–1880', *Transactions of the Royal Historical Society*, 20 (2010), 141–156.

B. S. Gregory, 'Is small beautiful? Microhistory and the history of everyday life', *History and Theory*, 38 (February 1999), 100–110.

T. W. Guinnane, *The Vanishing Irish: Households, Migration, and the Rural Economy in Ireland, 1850–1914* (New Jersey: Princeton University Press, 1997).

'The Poor Law and the pension in Ireland', *Journal of Interdisciplinary History*, 24 (1993), 271–291.

K. Halttunen, *Confidence Men and Painted Women: A Study of Middle-Class Culture in America, 1830–1870* (New Haven and London: Yale University Press, 1982).

C. Hämmerle, 'Requests, complaints, demands. Preliminary thoughts on the petitioning letters of lower-class Austrian women, 1865–1918' in Bland and Cros (eds.), *Gender and Politics in the Age of Letter Writing*, pp. 115–134.

W. Hansen, 'Grief, sickness and emotions in the narratives of the shamefaced poor in late eighteenth-century Copenhagen' in Gestrich, Hurren and King (eds.), *Poverty and Sickness in Modern Europe*, pp. 35–50.

A. D. Harman, 'Keeping separate: boundary maintenance systems' in D. Harman Akenson, *Small Differences: Irish Catholics and Irish Protestants, 1815–1922* (Montreal: McGill Queen's University, 1988), pp. 108–126.

D. H. Harman, *Small Differences: Irish Catholics and Irish Protestants, 1815–1922* (Montreal: McGill Queen's University, 1988).

B. Harris and P. Briden, 'Introduction: The "mixed economy of welfare" and the historiography of welfare provision' in Harris and Bridgen (eds.), *Charity and Mutual Aid in Europe and North America*, pp. 1–18.

R. Harris, 'Negotiating patriarchy: Irish women and the landlord' in Cohen and Curtain (eds.), *Reclaiming Gender*, pp. 207–226.

M. Hartigan, 'The religious life of the Catholic laity in Dublin, 1920–1940' in
    J. Kelly and D. Keogh (eds.), *History of the Catholic Diocese of Dublin* (Dublin:
    Four Courts, 2000), pp. 331–48.
L. Harte, (ed.), *Modern Irish Autobiography: Self, Nation and Society* (Basingstoke
    UK: Palgrave Macmillan, 2007).
J. P. Haughton, 'The social geography of Dublin,' *Geographical Review*, 39
    (1949), 257–77.
D. Heinisch, 'Petitions of the Council of the Free Imperial City of Frankfurt am
    Main', *Bulletin: German Historical Institute London*, 35 (November 2013),
    26–42.
H. Hendrick, *Approaches to the History of the Western Family 1500–1914*
    (Cambridge University Press, 1995).
G. Himmerlfarb, *Poverty and Compassion: The Moral Imagination of the Late
    Victorians* (New York: Alfred Knopf, 1991).
T. Hitchcock, P. King and P. Sharpe (eds.), *Chronicling Poverty: The Voices and
    Strategies of the English Poor, 1640–1840* (Basingstoke, UK: Macmillan,
    1997).
T. Hitchcock, 'A new history from below', *History Workshop Journal*, 57 (2004),
    294–298.
L. Hollen Lees, *The Solidarities of Strangers: The English Poor Laws and the People
    1700–1948* (Cambridge University Press, 1998).
K. Holmes, *Between the Leaves: Stories of Australian Women, Writing and Gardens*
    (Crawley: The University of Western Australia, 2011).
C. Holohan, 'Conceptualising and responding to poverty in the Republic of
    Ireland in the 1960s: a case study of Dublin, *Social History*, 41 (January
    2016), 34–53.
J. Horne, (ed.), *Our War: Ireland and the Great War* (Dublin: Royal Irish
    Academy, 2009).
R. A. Houston, *Peasant Petitions: Social Relations & Economic Life on Landed
    Estates, 1600–1850* (Basingstoke: Palgrave MacMillan, 2014).
G. L. Hudson, 'Arguing Disability: Ex-servicemen's own stories in early modern
    England, 1590–1790' in R. Bivins and J. V. Pickstone (eds.), *Medicine,
    Madness and Social History: Essays in Honour of Roy Porter* (Basingstoke
    UK: Palgrave Macmillan, 2007), pp. 105–117.
K. Hudson, *Pawnbroking: An Aspect of British Social History* (London: The Bodley
    Head Press, 1982).
O. Hufton, *The Poor of Eighteenth-Century France* (Oxford University Press,
    1974).
C. Hug, *The Politics of Sexual Morality in Ireland* (London: Macmillan Press,
    1999).
E. Hurren, 'The business of anatomy and being poor: Why have we failed
    to learn the medical and poverty lessons of the past?' in Gestrich, King and
    Raphael (eds.), *Being Poor in Modern Europe*, pp. 135–155.
M. Johnston, *Around the Banks of Pimlico* (Dublin: Attic Press, 1986).
G. Jones, 'Women and Tuberculosis in Ireland' in M. H. Preston and
    M. Ó hÓgartaigh (eds.), *Gender and Medicine in Ireland, 1700–1950* (New
    York: Syracuse University Press, 2012), pp. 33–48.

'*Captain of all These Men of Death*': *The History of Tuberculosis in Nineteenth- and Twentieth Century Ireland* (Amsterdam: Rodopi, 2001).

P. Jones, '"I cannot keep my place without being deascent": Pauper letters, parish clothing and pragmatism in the South of England, 1750–1830', *Rural History*, 20 (2009), 31–49.

T. E. Jordan, 'The quality of life in Victorian Ireland, 1831–1901', *New Hibernia Review*, 4 (2000), 103–121.

S. Kahl, 'The religious roots of modern poverty policy: Catholic, Lutheran, and Reformed Protestant traditions compared', *European Journal of Sociology*, 46 (2005), 91–126.

M. Kanya-Forstner, 'Defining womanhood: Irish women and the Catholic Church in Victorian Liverpool', *Immigrants & Minorities*, 18 (1999), 178–184.

M. B. Katz, 'The history of an impudent poor woman in New York city from 1918 to 1923' in P. Mandler (ed.), *The Uses of Charity: The Poor on Relief in the Nineteenth-Century Metropolis* (Philadelphia: University of Pennsylvania Press, 1989), pp. 227–246.

A. Kearns Blain, *Stealing Sunlight* (Dublin: A & A Farmar Publishers, 2000).

K. Kearns, *Dublin's Lost Heroines: Mammies and Grannies in a Vanished City* (Dublin: Gill & Macmillan, 2004).

Dublin Tenement Life: An Oral History (Dublin: Gill & Macmillan, Dublin, 1994).

A. Kelly, 'Catholic Action and the development of the Irish welfare state in the 1930s and 1940s', *Archivium Hibernicum*, 53 (1999), 107–17.

Kelly and Keogh (eds.), *History of the Catholic Diocese of Dublin*.

L. Kelly, 'Rickets and Irish children: Dr Ella Webb and the early work of the Children's Sunshine Home, 1925–1946' in A. MacLellan and A. Mauger (eds.), *Growing Pains: Childhood Illness in Ireland, 1750–1950* (Dublin: Irish Academic Press: 2013), pp. 141–158.

S. Kelly, 'And so to bed': Bone and joint tuberculosis in children in Ireland, 1920–1950' in MacLellan and Mauger (eds.), *Growing Pains: Childhood Illness in Ireland, 1750–1950*, pp. 175–194.

C. Kenneally, *Maura's Boy: A Cork Childhood* (Cork: Mercier Press, 1996).

J. Kenneally, 'Sexism, the church and Irish women', *Éire-Ireland*, 21 (Fall 1986), 3–16.

F. Kennedy, *Frank Duff: A Life Story* (London: Continuum, 2011).

Cottage to Crèche: Family Change in Ireland (Dublin: Institute of Public Administration, 2001).

Three Storeys Up: Tale of Dublin Tenement Life (Dublin: Marino Books, 1997).

K. A. Kennedy (ed.), *From Famine to Feast: Economic and Social Change in Ireland 1847–1997* (Dublin: Institute of Public Administration, 1998).

P. Kennedy (ed.), *Motherhood in Ireland: Creation and Context* (Cork: Mercier Press, 2003).

A. Kessler-Harris, 'Gender ideology in historical reconstruction: a case study from the 1930s', *Gender and History*, 1 (1989), 31–49.

A. J. Kidd, 'Charity organization and the unemployed in Manchester, c. 1870–1914', *Social History*, 9 (1984), 45–66.

E. Kiely and M. Leane, *Irish Women at Work 1930–1960: An Oral History* (Dublin: Irish Academic Press, 2012).

S. Kilfeather, *Dublin: A Cultural History* (Oxford University Press, 2005).

S. King and A. Stringer, 'I have once more taken the Leberty to say as you well know': The development of rhetoric in the letters of the English, Welsh and Scottish sick and poor 1780s–1830s' in Gestrich, Hurren, and King (eds.), *Poverty and Sickness*, pp. 69–91.

S. King and A. Stringer, 'Negotiating the law of Poor Relief in England, 1800–1840', *History*, 96 (2011), 410–35.

'Welfare regimes and welfare regions in Britain and Europe, *c.* 1750–1860', *Journal of Modern European History*, 9 (2011), 44–67.

'Friendship, kinship, and belonging in the letters of urban paupers 1800–1840', *Historical Social Research*, 33 (2008), 249–77.

'Regional patterns in the experiences and treatment of the sickpoor, 1800–1840: rights, obligations and duties in the rhetoric of paupers', *Family & Community History*, 10 (2007), 61–75.

'Pauper letters as a source', *Family & Community History*, 10 (2007), 167–70.

Women, Welfare and Local Politics, 1880–1920: "We Might be Trusted" (Brighton, UK: Sussex Academic Press, 2006).

D. La Capra, *Writing History, Writing Trauma* (Baltimore: John Hopkins University Press, 2001).

M. Laffan, *Judging W. T. Cosgrave: The Foundation of the Irish State* (Dublin: Royal Irish Academicy, 2014).

F. Lane (ed.), *Politics, Society and the Middle Class in Modern Ireland* (New York: Palgrave Macmillan, 2010).

and D. Ó Drisceoil (eds.), *Politics of the Irish Working Class, 1830–1945* (New York: Palgrave Macmillan, 2005).

'"The doctor scolds me": The diaries and correspondence of patients in eighteenth century England' in R. Porter (ed.), *Patients and Practitioners. Lay Perceptions of Medicine in Pre-Industrial Society* (Cambridge University Press, 1985), pp. 205–48.

R. Lawton, 'Peopling the past,' *Transactions of the Institute of British Geographers*, 12 (1987), 259–283.

J. J. Lee, *Ireland, 1912–1985: Politics and Society* (Cambridge University Press, 1989).

D. M. Leeson, *The Black and Tans: British Police and Auxiliaries in the Irish War of Independence* (Oxford University Press, 2011).

J. Leonard, 'Survivors' in Horne (ed.), *Our War*, pp. 209–223.

M. Levine-Clark, '"Embarrassed circumstances": gender, poverty and insanity in the West Riding of England in early Victorian Years' in J. Andrews and A. Digby (eds.), *Sex and Seclusion, Class and Custody: Perspectives on Gender and Class in the History of British and Irish Psychiatry* (New York: Rodopi, 2004), pp. 123–48.

J. Lewis, 'Gender, the family and women's agency in the building of "welfare states": the British case', *Social History*, 19 (1994), 37–55.

D. Lindsay, *Dublin's Oldest Charity: The Sick and Indigent Roomkeepers Society, 1790–1990* (Dublin: The Anniversary Press, 1990).

V. Long and H. Marland, 'From danger and motherhood to health and beauty: health advice for the factory girl in early twentieth-century Britain', *Twentieth Century British History*, 20 (2009), 454–81

D. S. Lucey, '"These schemes will win for themselves the confidence of the people": Irish independence, Poor Law Reform and hospital provision', *Medical History*, 58 (January 2014), 44–64.

M. Luddy, *Prostitution and Irish Society, 1800–1940* (Cambridge University Press, 2007).

Women and Philanthropy in Nineteenth-Century Ireland (Cambridge University Press, 2005).

'Religion, philanthropy and the state in late eighteenth- and early nineteenth-century Ireland' in H. Cunningham and J. Innes (eds.), *Charity, Philanthropy and Reform* (Basingstoke, 1998), pp. 148–67.

A. Lüdtke, 'Introduction: What is the history of everyday life and who are its practitioners?' in A. Lüdtke (ed.), *The History of Everyday Life: Reconstructing Historical Experiences and Ways of Life* translated by William Templer (New Jersey: Princeton University Press, 1995), pp. 3–40.

M. Lyons, *The Writing Culture of Ordinary People in Europe, c. 1860–1920* (Cambridge University Press, 2012).

'"Ordinary writings" or how the "illiterate" speak to historians' in M. Lyons (ed.), *Ordinary Writings, Personal Narratives: Writing Practices in 19ᵗʰ and early 20ᵗʰ-century Europe* (New York: Peter Lang, 2007), pp. 13–32.

M. Lysaght, 'A north city childhood in the early century', *Dublin Historical Record*, 38 (1985), 74–87.

A. MacLellan and A. Mauger (eds.), *Growing Pains: Childhood Illness in Ireland, 1750–1950* (Dublin: Irish Academic Press: 2013).

R. MacManus, *Dublin, 1910–1940: Shaping the City and Suburbs* (Dublin: Four Courts, 2002).

J. Macnicol, *The Movement for Family Allowances, 1918–1945: A Study of Social Policy Development* (London: Heinemann, 1980).

M. J. Maguire, *Precarious Childhood in Post-Independence Ireland* (Manchester University Press, 2007).

'The Carrigan committee and child sexual abuse in twentieth-century Ireland', *New Hibernia Review*, 11 (Summer, 2006), 79–100.

P. Mandler (ed.), *The Uses of Charity: The Poor on Relief in the Nineteenth-Century Metropolis* (Philadelphia: University of Pennsylvania Press, 1990).

'Poverty and charity in the nineteenth century metropolis: an introduction' in Mandler (ed.), *The Uses of Charity*, pp. 1–37.

P. Martin, 'Social policy and social change since 1914' in L. Kennedy and P. Ollerenshaw (eds.), *Ulster Since 1600: Politics, Economy, and Society* (Oxford University Press, 2012), pp. 308–324.

P. Martin, 'Enduring the pauper taint: Medical benefit in welfare reform in Northern Ireland' in Crossman and Gray (eds.), *Poverty and Welfare in Ireland*, pp. 223–236

K. Marx-Jaskulski, 'Narratives of ill-health in applicant letters from rural Germany, 1900–30' in Gestrich, Hurren and King (eds.), *Poverty and Sickness in Modern Europe*, pp. 209–223

S. McAvoy, '"Perpetual nightmare": Women, fertility control, the Irish state, and the 1935 ban on contraceptives' in Preston and Ó hÓgartaigh (eds.), *Gender and Medicine in Ireland*, pp. 189–202.

'Sexual crime and Irish women's campaign for a Criminal Law Amendment Act, 1912–35' in M. Gialanella Valiulis (ed.), *Gender and Power in Irish History* (Dublin, 2009), pp. 84–99.

'The regulation of sexuality in the Irish Free state' in E. Malcolm and G. Jones (eds), *Medicine, Disease and the State in Ireland, 1650–1940* (Cork: Cork University Press, 1999), pp. 253–266.

K. Milne, *Protestant Aid 1836–1986: A History of the Association for the Relief of Distressed Protestants* (Dublin: Protestant Aid, 1989).

M. Moffitt, *Soupers and Jumpers: The Protestant Missions in Connemara 1848–1937* (Dublin: The History Press, 2008).

A. Morgan and B. Purdie (eds.), *Ireland: Divided Nation, Divided Class* (London: Links, 1980).

D. G. Morgan, 'Society and the schools', *Commission to Inquire into Child Abuse* [Ryan Report], (Dublin: Official Publications, 2009), pp. 201–244.

T. J. Morrissey, *Edward J. Byrne 1872–1941: The Forgotten Archbishop of Dublin* (Dublin: Columba Books, 2010).

J. Murphy, 'Suffering, vice and justice: religious imaginaries and welfare agencies in postwar Melbourne', *Journal of Religious History*, 31 (2007), 287–304.

M. Murphy, 'Revolution and terror in Kildare, 1919–1923' in Fitzpatrick (ed.), *Terror in Ireland*, pp. 194–205.

U. Newell, *The West Must Wait: County Galway and the Irish Free State, 1922–32* (Manchester University Press, 2015).

E. Newman Devlin, *Speaking Volumes: A Dublin Childhood* (Belfast: Blackstaff Press, 2000).

J. V. O'Brien, *"Dear, Dirty Dublin": A City in Distress, 1899–1916* (Berkeley: University of California Press, 1982).

S. Ó Cinnéide, 'The development of the Home Assistance service', *Administration*, 17 (1969), 284–308.

N. Ó Ciosáin, 'Boccoughs and God's Poor: Deserving and undeserving poor in Irish popular culture', in T. Foley and S. Ryder (eds.), *Ideology and Ireland in the Nineteenth Century* (Dublin: Four Courts Press, 1998), pp. 93–99.

C. O'Connell, *The State and Housing in Ireland: Ideology, Policy and Practice* (New York: Nova Science Publishers, 2007).

A. O'Connor, 'Representations of unmarried mothers in Irish Folklore' in M. Cinta Ramblado-Minero and A. Pérez-Vides (eds.), *Single motherhood in twentieth-century Ireland: Cultural, historical, and social essays* (New York: The Edwin Mellon Press, 2006), pp. 49–58.

F. O'Connor, *An Only Child* (London: Macmillan, 1961).

J. O'Connor, *The Workhouses of Ireland: The Fate of Ireland's Poor* (Dublin: Anvil Books, 1995).

L. O'Connor, *Can Lily O'Shea Come out to Play?* (Dingle: Brandon Books, 2000).

S. O'Connor, *Growing Up So High: A Liberties Boyhood* (Dublin: Hachette Books Ireland, 2013).

D. Ó Corráin, *Rendering to God and Caesar: The Irish Churches and the Two States in Ireland, 1949–73* (Manchester University Press, 2007).

P. O'Dea (ed.), *A Class of Our Own* (Dublin: New Island Books, 1994).

I. O'Donnell, 'Lethal violence in Ireland, 1841–2003: famine, celibacy, and parental pacification', *British Journal of Criminology*, 45 (September 2005), 671–95.

P. O'Donnell, *Adrigoole* (London: Jonathan Cape, 1929).

A. O'Dowd, 'Well wear and soon tear: clothes we once wore' in C. Breathnach (ed.), *Framing the West: Images of Rural Ireland 1891–1920* (Dublin: Irish Academic Press, 2007), pp. 232–252.

R. O'Dwyer, *The Eucharistic Congress Dublin 1932* (Dublin: Nonsuch Ireland, c. 2009).

M. Ó hÓgartaigh, *Kathleen Lynn: Patriot Doctor* (Dublin: Irish Academic Press, 2005).

C. Ó Gráda, 'Infant and child mortality in Dublin a century ago' in Preston and Ó hÓgartaigh (eds.), *Gender and Medicine in Ireland*, pp. 49–68.

'"The greatest blessing of all": The Old Age Pension in Ireland', *Past and Present*, 175 (2002), 124–161.

'The rise in living standards' in Kennedy (ed.), *From Famine to Feast*, pp. 12–22.

Ireland: A New Economic History 1780–1939 (Oxford: Clarendon Press, 1994).

P. O'Keeffe, *Down Cobbled Streets* (Dingle: Brandon Publishers, 1995).

E. Peretz, 'The costs of modern motherhood to low income families in interwar Britain' in V. Fildes, L. Marks and H. Marland (eds.), *Women and Children First: International Maternal and Infant Welfare, 1870–1945* (New York: Routledge, 1992), pp. 257–80.

M. Peel, *Miss Cutler and the Case of the Resurrected Horse: Social Work and the Story of Poverty in America, Australia, and Britain* (The University of Chicago Press, 2012).

'Charity, casework and the dramas of class in Melbourne, 1920–1940: "Feeling your position"', *History Australia*, 2 (2005), 83.1–83.15.

The Lowest Rung: Voices of Australian Poverty (Cambridge University Press, 2003).

S. Pimpare, 'Toward a new welfare history', *The Journal of Policy History*, 19 (2007), 234–252.

L. Pollock, 'Anger and the negotiation of relationships in early modern England', *Historical Journal*, 47 (2004), 567–590.

R. Porter, *Patients and Practitioners: Lay Perceptions of Medicine in Pre-Industrial Society* (Cambridge University Press, 1985).

F. W. Powell, *The Politics of Irish Social Policy, 1600–1990* (Lampeter: Edwin Mellen Press, 1992).

E. Prendergast and H. Sheridan, *Jubilee Nurse – Voluntary District Nursing in Ireland, 1890–1974* (Dublin: Woolfhound Press, 2012).

M. H. Preston and M. Ó hÓgartaigh (eds.), *Gender and Medicine in Ireland, 1700–1950* (New York: Syracuse University Press, 2012).
Charitable Words: Women, Philanthropy, and the Language of Charity in Nineteenth-Century Dublin (London: Praeger, 2004).

D. Price, *The Flame and the Candle: War in Mayo 1919–1924* (Cork: Collins, 2012).

J. Prunty, *Dublin Slums 1800–1925: A Study in Urban Geography* (Dublin: Irish Academic Press, 1998).

N. Puirséil, *The Irish Labour Party, 1922–1973* (University College Dublin Press, 2007).

C. Ramblado-Minero and A. Pérez-Vides (eds.), *Single Motherhood in Twentieth-Century Ireland: Cultural, Historical, and Social Essays* (New York: The Edwin Mellon Press, 2006).

C. Rattigan, *'What else could I do?': Single mothers and infanticide, Ireland 1900–1950* (Dublin: Irish Academic Press, 2012).
'"Dark spots" in Irish Society: Unmarried mothers and infanticide in Ireland from 1926–1938' in Ramblado-Minero and Pérez-Vides (eds.), *Single Motherhood in Twentieth-century Ireland*, pp. 83–122.

S. Rains, *Commodity Culture and Social Class in Dublin, 1850–1916* (Dublin: Irish Academic Press, 2010).

J. Redmond, 'In the family way and away from the family: examining the evidence in Irish unmarried mothers in Britain, 1920s–40s' in Farrell (ed.), *'She Said She was in the Family Way'*, pp. 163–185.
'"Sinful singleness"? Exploring the discourses on Irish single women's emigration to England, 1922–1948', *Women's History Review*, 17 (2008), 455–476.

C. Reidy, 'Poverty, alcohol, and the women of the state inebriate reformatory in Ireland, 1900–1918' in Brophy and Delay (eds.), *Women, Reform, and Resistance in Ireland, 1850–1950*, pp. 119–138.

J. Robins, *Custom House People* (Dublin: The Institute of Public Administration, 1993).

E. Ross, 'Hungry children: housewives and London charity, 1870–1918' in Mandler, *The Uses of Charity*, pp. 161–196.

E. Ross, *Slum Travellers: Ladies and London Poverty, 1860–1920* (Berkeley: University of California Press, 2007).

W. Ruberg, 'The letter as medicine: studying health and illness in Dutch daily correspondence, 1770–1850', *Social History of Medicine*, 23 (2010), 492–508.

L. Ryan, 'Irish Newspaper representation of women, migration and pregnancy outside marriage in the 1930s' in Ramblado-Minero and Pérez-Vides (eds), *Single Motherhood in Twentieth-Century Ireland*, pp. 103–122.

J. C. Scott, *Weapons of the Weak: Everyday Forms of Peasant Resistance* (New Haven, CT: Yale University Press, 1985).

A. Sczesny, 'Poverty research from below: letters and petitions by the poor', *Bulletin: German Historical Institute London*, 35 (November 2013), 57–72.

M. Sevegrand, *L'Amour en Toute Lettres: Questions à l'Abbé Viollet sur la Sexualité (1924–1943)* (Paris: Albin Michel Histoire, 1996).

M. Silverman, *An Irish Working Class: Explorations in Political Economy and Hegemony, 1800–1950* (Toronto: University of Toronto Press, 2001).

J. M. Smith, *Ireland's Magdalen Laundries and the Nation's Architecture of Containment* (Manchester University Press, 2007).

'The politics of sexual knowledge: the origins of Ireland's containment culture and the Carrigan report (1931)', *Journal of the History of Sexuality*, 13 (2004), 208–33.

T. Sokoll, *Essex Pauper Letters 1731–1837* (Oxford University Press, 2006).

'Writing for relief: rhetoric in English pauper letters, 1800–1834' in Gestrich, King and Raphael (eds.), *Being Poor in Modern Europe*, pp. 91–111.

'Negotiating a living: Essex pauper letters from London, 1800–1834' in J. Schlumbolm and L. Fontaine (eds.), *International Review of Social History*, 45 (2000), 19–46.

'Old age in poverty. The record of Essex pauper letters, 1780–1834' in T. Hitchcock, P. King and P. Sharpe (eds.), *Chronicling Poverty: The Voices and Strategies of the English Poor, 1640–1840* (London: Palgrave, 1997), pp. 127–54.

B. Stadum, *Poor Women and their Families: Hard Working Charity Cases, 1900–1930* (Albany: State University of New York Press, 1992).

L. Stanley, 'The epistolarium: on theorizing letters and correspondences', *Auto/Biography*, 12 (2004), 201–235.

T. Stazic-Wendt, 'From unemployment to sickness and poverty: The narratives and experiences of the unemployed in Trier and surroundings, 1918–33' in Gestrich, Hurren and King (eds), *Poverty and Sickness in Modern Europe*, pp. 181–207.

C. Steedman, *Labours Lost: Domestic Service and the Making of Modern England* (Cambridge University Press, 2009).

Dust (Manchester University Press, 2001).

Landscape for a Good Woman (Brunswick, NJ: Rutgers University Press, 1987).

A. Suzuki, 'Lunacy and labouring men: narratives of male vulnerability in mid-Victorian London' in Bivins and Pickstone (eds.), *Medicine, Madness and Social History*, pp. 118–128.

S. Swain, 'Negotiating poverty: women and charity in nineteenth-century Melbourne', *Women's History Review*, 16 (2007), 99–112.

J. S. Taylor, 'Voices in the crowd: the Kirby Lonsdale township letters, 1809–36' in Hitchcock, King and Sharpe (eds.), *Chronicling Poverty*, pp. 109–26.

M. Tebbutt, *Making Ends Meet Pawnbroking and Working-Class Credit* (New York: St Martin's Press, 1983).

P. Thane, 'Visions of gender in the making of the British welfare state: The case of women in the British Labour party and social policy, 1906–1945' in Bock and Thane (eds.), *Maternity and Gender Policies*, pp. 93–117.

D. Thompson (ed.), *The Essential E. P. Thompson* (New York: New Press, 2000).

E. P. Thompson, *The Poverty Theory and Other Essays*. (Merlin Press: London, 1978)

The Making of the English Working Class, (New York: Vintage, 1966).

A. Thomson, *Moving Stories: An Intimate History of Four Women Across Two Countries* (Manchester University Press, 2011).

A. Tompkins, '"Labouring on a bed of sickness": The material and rhetorical deployment of ill-health in male pauper letters' in Gestrich, Hurren and King (eds.), *Poverty and Sickness in Modern Europe*, pp. 51–68.

P. Touher, *Fear of the Collar: Artane Industrial School* (Dublin: O'Brien, 1991).

P. Townsend (ed.), *The Concept of Poverty* (London, 1970).

P. Tyrrell, 'Early days in Letterfrack: Memories of an industrial school boy', *Hibernia*, 28 (July 1964), 8

L. T. Ulrich, *A Midwife's Tale: The Life of Martha Ballard, Based on Her Diary, 1785–1812* (New York: Vintage Books, 1991).

M. Van Ginderachter, '"If your Majesty would only send me a little money to help buy an elephant": Letters to the Belgian Royal family (1880–1940)' in M. Lyons (eds.), *Ordinary Writings, Personal Narratives: Writing Practices in 19th and early 20th-century Europe* (New York: Peter Lang, 2007), pp. 69–84.

M. Van Leeuwen, 'Historical welfare economics in the nineteenth century: mutual aid and private insurance for burial, sickness, old age, widowhood, and unemployment in the Netherlands' in Harris and Bridgen (eds.), *Charity and Mutual Aid in Europe and North America*, pp. 89–130.

W. E. Vaughan (ed.), *A New History of Ireland VI: Ireland Under the Union, 1870–1921* (Oxford University Press, 1989).

D. Vincent, *The Rise of Mass Literacy: Reading and Writing in Modern Europe* (Cambridge: Polity Press, 2000).

Poor Citizens: the State and the Poor in Twentieth Century Britain (London: Longman, 1991).

Literacy and Popular Culture: England 1750–1914 (Cambridge University Press, 1989).

B. M. Walsh, 'Marriage in Ireland in the twentieth century' in Cosgrove (ed.), *Marriage in Ireland*, pp. 132–150.

J. Walsh, *The Politics of Expansion: Irish Education Policy, 1957–1972* (Manchester University Press, 2009).

O. Walsh, *Anglican Women in Dublin: Philanthropy, Politics and Education in the Early Twentieth Century* (University College Dublin Press, 2005).

D. Weinbren, 'Supporting self-help: charity, mutuality, and reciprocity in nineteenth-century Britain,' Harris and Bridgen (eds.), *Charity and Mutual Aid in Europe and North America*, pp. 67–88.

J. Weiss, 'Origins of the French welfare state: poor relief in the Third Republic, 1871–1914', *French Historical Studies*, 13 (1983–4), 47–77.

J. Welshman, *Underclass: A History of the Excluded, 1880–2000* (London: Hambledon Continuum, 2006).

D. Whelan (ed.) P. Tyrrell, *Founded on Fear* (Dublin: Irish Academic Press, 2006).

I. Whelan, 'The stigma of Souperism' in C. Póirtéir (ed.), *The Great Irish Famine: The Thomas Davis Lecture Series* (Cork: Mercier Press, 1995), pp. 135–154.

S. E. Whyman, *The Pen and the People: English Letter Writers, 1660–1800* (Oxford University Press, 2009).

D. Wierling, 'The history of everyday life and gender relations: on historical and historiographical relationships' in Lüdtke (ed.), *The History of Everyday Life*, pp. 149–168.

S. Williams, *Poverty, Gender and Life-Cycle under the English Poor Law 1760–1834* (Woodbridge: Boydell Press, 2011).

A. Wingenter, 'Voices of Sacrifice: Letters to Mussolini and ordinary writing under Fascism' in Lyons (ed.), *Ordinary Writings, Personal Narratives*, pp. 155–172.

A. Woods, *Dublin Outsiders. A History of the Mendicity Institution 1818–1998* (Dublin: A. & A. Farmar, 1998).

S. Woolf, *The Poor in Western Europe in the Eighteenth and Nineteenth Centuries* (London and New York: Methuen, 1986).

A. Woollacott, 'From moral to professional authority: secularism, social work and middle-class women's self-construction in World War I Britain', *Journal of Women's History*, 10 (1998), 85–111.

P. Yeates, *A City in Civil War: Dublin 1921–1924* (Dublin: Gill and Macmillan, 2015).

A City in Turmoil: Dublin 1919–1921 (Dublin: Gill and Macmillan, 2012).

T. Zeldin, 'Personal history and the history of the emotions', *Journal of Social History*, 15 (1982), 339–347.

Theses

A. Foley, *'No sex Please, we're Catholic': The influence of the Catholic church on declining marriage rates in Ireland between the Famine and the First World War*, (University College Dublin M. Litt. Thesis, 1999).

C. T. Gallagher, *'Charity, poverty and change: the Society of Saint Vincent de Paul in Dublin, 1939–54* (University College Dublin MA Thesis, 1988).

C. Lincoln, *'Working class housing in Dublin, 1914–1930*,' (University College Dublin, MA Thesis, 1979).

R. Roulston, *'The Church of Ireland and the Irish state: institution, community and state relations, 1950–1972* (University College Dublin, PhD thesis, 2011).

Index

Lightning Source UK Ltd.
Milton Keynes UK
UKHW022200260719
346914UK00020B/554/P